W9-BXB-029

Geniuses of the American Musical Theatre

 Also by Herbert H. Keyser

Women Under the Knife: A Gynecologist's Report on Hazardous Medicine 1984
Prescription for Disaster: Health Care in America 1993
Two Drifters Off to See the World 2002
A Chautauquan Searches Paris for the Best Tarte au Citron 2005

Geniuses of the American Musical Theatre

THE COMPOSERS AND LYRICISTS

HERBERT H. KEYSER

APPLAUSE
THEATRE & CINEMA BOOKS

An Imprint of Hal Leonard Corporation
New York

Published in 2009 by Applause Theatre and Cinema Books
An Imprint of Hal Leonard Corporation
7777 West Bluemound Road
Milwaukee, WI 53213

Trade Book Division Editorial Offices
19 West 21st Street, New York, NY 10010

Printed in the United States of America

Book design by Damien Castaneda

Library of Congress Cataloging-in-Publication Data

Keyser, Herbert H.
Geniuses of the American musical theatre : the composers & lyricists / Herbert H. Keyser.
p. cm.
Includes bibliographical references.
ISBN 978-1-4234-6275-0 (hardcover)
1. Composers—United States—Biography. 2. Lyricists—United States—Biography. 3. Musicals—United States—History and criticism. I. Title.
ML385.K485 2009
782.1'4092273—dc22
[B]
2008042689

www.applausepub.com

To Barbara,

who for the past three decades has lovingly shared with me the beautiful music of these geniuses . . . and made my life so much more special!

Contents

Foreword

FANS OF THE AMERICAN MUSICAL THEATRE COME in all shapes and sizes. We share an unbridled passion for a specific world of entertainment that has given us, and the world, countless hours of pleasure. Yes, we will discuss and argue and compare notes deep into any evening, knowing that we will never really be able to convince our fellow enthusiasts that our opinion is the right opinion. (There is an old theatre adage that goes: "You are entitled to your opinion. You're *wrong*, but you're entitled to . . .") But that's part of what makes us so passionate about the musical theatre. We love it, we will discuss it at the drop of a hat, and we will defend it at any cost.

Herbert Keyser's stories of many of the great composers and lyricists of the musical come from his own personal passions. It is fascinating to discover that he came to the musical on his own, as both his parents were deaf. There is an odd connection to be made here: for anyone who saw the extraordinary production of BIG RIVER that Deaf West produced a few years ago, including a run on Broadway honored with a Tony, you saw how the visual world of the deaf, and the lyrical world of the musical, made for happy partners. I had a unique experience early in my career when I worked for the National Theatre of the Deaf, as, of all things, its musical director. We did an American opera—Gertrude Stein and Virgil Thomson's FOUR SAINTS IN THREE ACTS—but the notion was the same as BIG RIVER: to use all the tools available to create something unique and theatrical for audiences both hearing and deaf. Music possesses a structure that must be respected. Sign language is visual and poetic, but it has its own music. Put together, and applied to the discipline of a musical, there exists the ability of creating an evening of theatre at a unique level of artistry.

Keyser's love of the American musical has led him to focus on biographies of many of the great composers and lyricists. As he says in his introduction, while the stories of many of these ladies and gentlemen appear in bits and pieces in other books, a collection of short and focused essays on these artists alone is something that probably hasn't been done before. And the result makes you realize the extraordinary accomplishments of what sure looks like a golden age. I have often felt that many of these writers became better than they might have been because the world in which they were operating was filled with contemporaries who were their equals or better. Keyser calls them "geniuses," and while the artists themselves might object to that moniker, Keyser makes a good case for his use of his chosen word. Looking at the entirety of the history of the American musical theatre through these essays, they are indeed geniuses.

When all is said and done, we can't ever get enough of hearing about these creative people. Their stories are as interesting—and as varied—as the shows they wrote. Each one came from a distinctly different background, but they, like Keyser, gravitated to the same world. They may have thought they were just doing their jobs, but when we look at the body of work of the creative artists in this book, the rest of us can only marvel, pull out another CD, hook up our ipods—or just go off and see another production of a musical. That's what I know Herbert Keyser is doing right now, and what I will do as soon as I finish this foreword.

Ted Chapin

Preface

IT WAS IN THE YEAR 1950. I WAS A SENIOR IN HIGH school. I don't remember feeling any threat of being drafted, although the Korean problem had already started. I had been quite a good student in the years leading up to that time. Although my family was extremely poor, I fully expected I would be going to college on a scholarship. A lot was expected of me. My older brother had been the only other person in my family to move on to higher education. My parents and grandparents, with whom I lived, all agreed that I was the one to become a physician. In the future my parents wanted to be saying "my son the doctor."

I was the only one not relishing the idea.

It wasn't that I was so certain of some other occupation that would make me gloriously happy. In fact, in the stupidity of my youth, I didn't have the faintest idea of where I was headed.

What I can recall most clearly was a simple idea that came into my head. When I would turn on the television set and watch what were mostly local television shows, I was certain I could do as well as the performers I saw.

I found the address for a company credited at the end of a number of shows—Donn Bennett Productions—and went to the television studio and offices. When asked by the receptionist what I was there for, I told her that I was looking for employment, performing on their shows.

"What can you do?" she asked.

"I sing. I dance. I act."

The total extent of my singing, dancing, and acting was accomplished in the privacy of my room. I was completely untrained. In other words, I lied. However, it got me in for an audition, where I was asked to read. When I was done I heard the following response:

"Thank you. We'll call you if we can use you."

Though I previously stated that I was completely untrained, there was a caveat to that. The explanation for that lies in knowing the history of my parents. These two absolutely spectacular individuals were both born deaf. I developed a speech pattern of slow, careful enunciation, so that they could read my lips. As a result, I became a Philadelphian without a Philadelphia accent. That was something the production company was interested in.

Shortly after my audition I received a call back from Donn Bennett Productions.

"Would you be interested in doing commercials?"

Thus began my life in show business. At the production studio over time I was added to a group of singers, and then a group of dancers, and eventually given speaking roles in local sitcoms.

Over that year and the next four in college, I organized a theatrical group that put on productions in the Philadelphia area during the school year. I was committed to somehow making myself into a performer. I filled my troupe with proven talent. The performers were young, up and coming, and getting started in their careers. I found a teenage dancer who was marvelous. His name was Mickey Calin and ultimately he became the second male lead in the original cast of WEST SIDE STORY. From there he went on to a very successful film career under the name Michael Callan.

I was able to connect with a female vocalist who was only about fifteen years old. Her name was Sandy Galitz, but she was using the name Sandy Gale. However, since Sunny Gale was famous at the time, she eventually changed her name to Sandy Stewart. She had a wonderful career including *The Perry Como Show*. She ultimately married composer Moose Charlap and still performs today, sometimes with her son, Bill.

One of the dancers in the troupe was a teenager who competed as Miss Pennsylvania in the Miss America pageant. I believe that she finished third, but it is difficult to be certain after more than fifty years.

I was not in a class with these wonderful young performers, but the association with them kept my dream going.

I spent my summers working in the mountains at a resort. I apprenticed backstage with lighting and scenery, and got small singing and dancing roles, even getting my own gig once a week, heading up the guest talent show. But I made certain that I got a chance to sing.

My family was in despair. Their great hope was going down the drain in a profession they perceived as worthless.

It is difficult to fully understand how much pain they were going through. My mother never heard a single sound in her entire life. She loved me dearly and came to see every performance of mine that she could. Afterward she would tell me, "You have to get out of show business, because you are a terrible singer." Now that is true love!

And then a terrible thing happened to me.

I was accepted to medical school. My life in show business came to a close. I believe that neither my family nor any of the people who saw me perform were particularly concerned about the end of that career.

I have spent the past fifty years very happily ensconced in the world of medicine. During all that time I never lost my profound love of music and the theatre. Even while studying medicine I was part of the school choir.

Those five years in show business did give me enough of a taste to encourage me to write and utilize what I had learned to become a speaker. I used whatever talent I had within my profession and lectured on America's health care system.

My wife and I, during all those years, were constant theatergoers. As my children grew up, they knew they would hear their father singing at the kitchen sink, or elsewhere in the house, all the songs he had learned from show after show.

After fifty years away from actually performing an idea occurred to me. I decided to investigate the lives of all the great composers and lyricists who had given me so much pleasure. I wanted to tell the stories of their lives, while singing their music to audiences who would find these lives to be as intriguing to them as they were to me. I began the research four years ago, and started doing performances one year later.

The stories were so enthralling, so poignant, at times tragic and at other times so inspirational, that I decided to combine them in a book. Searching through literature I found that although there was a great mass of full-length books about these geniuses, no single volume told all their stories in a shortened version. And so this anthology found its origin in a dream I had more than fifty years ago, and finally became a reality.

I omitted some truly great composers and lyricists, not because I thought less of their talent; there was just insufficient biographical data to allow me to fully tell their life stories. Included in that group would certainly be Lynn Ahrens an Stephen Flaherty (RAGTIME), Jerry Bock and Sheldon Harnick (FIDDLER ON THE ROOF, FIORELLO!, SHE LOVES ME), Richard Adler and Jerry Ross (THE PAJAMA GAME, DAMN YANKEES), Cy Coleman (LITTLE ME, BARNUM, SWEET CHARITY, CITY OF ANGELS, THE WILL ROGERS FOLLIES), Stephen Schwartz (GODSPELL, PIPPIN, WICKED), Claude-Michel Schonberg and Alain Boubil (LES MISERABLES, MISS SAIGON), Vernon Duke, Marvin Hamlisch, Mel Brooks, Maury Yeston, Carolyn Leigh, Bob Merrill, Richard Whiting and a host of others, including the new young composers and lyricists just in the early stages of their careers. I apologize to all of them for leaving them out.

Though I sincerely hope that all who read this book will find these stories enchanting, no one can possibly derive more pleasure than I did, during the past four years of delving into the lives of these icons, these Geniuses of the American Musical Theatre.

Herbert H. Keyser

Acknowledgments

THOUGH THE RESEARCH ON THIS BOOK BEGAN almost four years ago, its true life as a published document began about one year ago.

My residence during the summer for more than a decade has been the Chautauqua Institution in western New York State. A cultural center for more than 125 years, one of its claims to fame is that George Gershwin wrote a significant portion of his *Concerto in F* in a practice shack there, generally used by the music students studying each summer.

In an effort to refurbish those shacks, a fund-raising effort was started in which each contributor of twenty-five thousand dollars could have his or her name permanently listed on one of the shacks. The only exception was the shack that had been the site of Gershwin's accomplishment. The asking price to be associated with that shack was seventy-five thousand dollars.

Unrelated to that campaign, the Institution had asked me to perform the story of the life and music of George Gershwin at a separate event. In the audience was a long time Chautauquan, Bob Fletcher. Many years ago Bob had started a company known as Fletcher Music, which achieved significant national status, primarily in the sale of organs. He was now retired. Fletcher, a major philanthropist, decided he wanted to make the contribution to the Institution and name the Gershwin shack in honor of one of his daughters. He approached me to ask if I could repeat my performance of Gershwin privately for the members of the board of his philanthropic foundation, to serve as a reason why he wanted to make that contribution. I did and the contribution was made. Today when people ask me what is the largest amount of money I have ever been paid to perform a life story of one of these Geniuses, I casually say, "Seventy-five thousand dollars."

Bob, who is generous to a fault and a dear friend, inquired about who was going to publish this work of mine. When I told him that I had not yet sought a publisher, he took it into his own hands to try to be of assistance. I cannot fully express how grateful I am for what he then helped me accomplish.

Through his long association in the field of music, he introduced me to Keith Mardak, the CEO of Hal Leonard Corporation, who has been warm and generous in his efforts to get this book rolling in his huge company. I cannot thank him sufficiently for his interest in my work.

Keith passed me on to the next level in the person of John Cerullo, the group publisher for Hal Leonard. I did get to meet John, and he patiently and gently walked me through the process he wanted to follow. Though this was to be my fifth book, every organization operates a little differently, and it was wonderful to feel his encouragement and support.

John passed me on to Marybeth Keating, the project editor for *Geniuses* who has been a constant for me ever since. Her kind reassurance through this long process has sustained me.

Before she ever received my manuscript, I sought out every possible assistance I could muster up. My first approach was to the most talented and accomplished writer to whom I had real access, my son, Chris Keyser, who had long since established himself as a writer and producer in Hollywood. In the midst of his own very hectic schedule, he sloshed through the hundreds and hundreds of pages I sent to him. The responses were detailed and sometimes painful, but always delivered with a soft touch in order not to totally demoralize his father. "Do you really want to put this in?" "You need to make a better transition." "I think you need to rewrite this paragraph." That, of course, was unrelated to all the changes in grammar or punctuation.

From there it went to my wife, Barbara, who also went through the entire manuscript. Somewhere, in between the time that I read and re-read and Chris read all through these pages, the gremlins got their hands into it. Barbara found hundreds of errors in spelling, punctuation, and the occasional "Do you really think that he could have gotten married a hundred years before he was born?"

Chris and Barbara put a phenomenal number of hours into this work, and I am eternally grateful for all that they did.

By the time that Marybeth got my manuscript, there couldn't possibly be anything further that needed to be changed. Of course, when she handed it over to Gary Sunshine, the copy editor, you might have thought that no one had ever reviewed the manuscript. His diligent work and challenging author's queries have added so much to my manuscript. I thank him sincerely for all that he did.

Beyond that there were others whose contributions have been so important, including the interior and cover designer, Damien Castaneda. Of course, none of that would have been accomplished without the oversight of Marybeth, who was also responsible for all the work involved in obtaining the photographs.

I also want to thank my longtime friend and entertainment lawyer, Daniel Sklar, who handled the legal end of the agreement.

Although all of these wonderful people were the backbone that enabled me to get this document into print, and without whom it would have been impossible, there are two other groups of people who cannot be forgotten. They truly made this book come to life.

First I want to thank all the phenomenally brilliant people in alphabetical order from Arlen to Youmans. The absolutely astounding work that they created and the amazing lives that they led are what is at the heart of this book. I can never express how much joy they have provided to me personally and to our society as a whole. I absolutely love their music. Beyond that, having the opportunity for the past four years to learn so much about their lives has been a glorious gift to me.

Finally, I never would have been able to put together this anthology were it not for the effort over a number of decades from so many wonderful writers who researched each one of these lives in detail and recorded them for posterity. As has been written about others in the past, I stand on their shoulders.

Geniuses of the American Musical Theatre

Harold Arlen, c. 1960s.
(Photofest.)

HAROLD ARLEN

HYMAN ARLUCK WAS BORN ON FEBRUARY 15, 1905. HIS family had moved from eastern Europe around 1885 to Louisville, Kentucky. His father, Samuel Arluck, became a cantor in Louisville. He was so good that a group of people from Buffalo, New York, encouraged him to travel 500 miles to apply for a position there as a cantor. Very impressed, the board of the congregation hired him immediately, but told him that he must have a wife. He left assuring them that he would return with one. He traveled home by way of Cincinnati. Living there was Celia Orlin, whom he had met on a previous visit as a traveling cantor. After persuading her family, they were married in the Orlin family home on April 15, 1904. They traveled immediately to Buffalo, and in less than one year Celia gave birth to twins. The first died within a day and the second, Hyman Arluck, weighing four pounds, survived. In 1912, a second son, Julius, was born. By then Hyman was singing in his father's choir. When Hyman was nine, the family purchased a piano, because Celia believed Hyman was talented. She wanted him to become a music teacher.

By the time he was in high school, to his parents' dismay, Hyman was more interested in ragtime and jazz than the classical music he had been studying. His father actually wanted him to be a doctor or a lawyer.

But his mother was content just to see him become a teacher. Hyman was not a particularly good student, however, and he cut many classes.

Arluck organized a group called the Snappy Trio to play at local clubs. But Prohibition forced the clubs to close down. The group grew to four members, and they called themselves the Se-Mor Jazz Band. His father was extremely unhappy with the developments and tried all sorts of methods to end his son's musical career, which only resulted in Arluck running away from home. He and a friend took jobs in the galley of a boat traveling on Lake Erie from Buffalo to Detroit. They got sick on board and jumped ship. They hitched a ride on a train to Cleveland, where Arluck ended up at a relative's home and was sent back to his family.

In 1923, at age eighteen, Arluck put together the Southbound Shufflers, arranging and writing their music. But he became disenchanted with them and moved to a more prosperous group, The Yankee Six. It grew to eleven and changed its name to the Buffalodians.

Variety reported in 1925 that there were 60,000 jazz bands working. The Buffalodians decided to try for New York where one of the most successful orchestras was Paul Whiteman's. Novelty ballroom dancing was the big craze, with the Charleston and the Black Bottom leading the way. There, Arluck established what would become a lifelong friendship with actor-dancer Ray Bolger. When he was twenty-one and Bolger was twenty-two, they moved into an apartment together.

When in 1926 the Buffalodians played the Palace in Times Square, Arlen did all the arranging. He was meeting other musicians as well and befriended the African-American bandleader Fletcher Henderson. Henderson hired him to do some arranging for his band. Arluck would go to Harlem to hear Ellington and Armstrong. He also studied the music of Berlin, Kern, and Gershwin.

Composer Harold Arlen, 1943. (Photofest.)

Arluck "loved performing" more than writing. He believed that his exposure to Jewish cantorial music and African-American gospel music were the basis for what he was writing as the new jazz.

In 1926, Arluck had a falling out with the bandleader of the Buffalodians and quit. Arnold Johnson's band, which was quite successful, hired Arluck to be their pianist and male vocalist. That really pleased him because the band was being heard on the radio and his parents could hear him in Buffalo. Arluck "fell in love" with the band's female vocalist, Frances Williams.

Toward the end of 1928 he realized that some people he contacted in the business had difficulty with his name. He decided that "Arlen" would have an easier sound than Arluck.

Meanwhile he kept trying to get a role in a Broadway show. He auditioned for the notoriously mean Shubert brothers. He sang ten songs while being ignored by Jake Shubert, who was shuffling papers all the while. Arlen stopped and Shubert asked what was wrong. He responded, "I ran out of throat," and walked out.

The reputation of the Shubert brothers was well known in the theatrical community. E. Y. "Yip" Harburg, the extremely socially-conscious lyricist, said that this particular time in history had been so helpful in providing him with material about which to write. It was the time of Mussolini, Hitler, Stalin, and the Shuberts.

Finally, Vincent Youmans hired Arlen for a part in a show titled LOUISIANA LOU, the name of which was ultimately changed to GREAT DAY. But Youmans was a highly neurotic alcoholic, and an extremely difficult person. He hated writing down his music, so he hired Arlen to be a musical secretary, as well as a performer. Arlen quit the show while it was in production midway through 1929, possibly out of boredom. "It was a lucky accident," he later said. The show opened two weeks before the Wall Street crash and closed after thirty-six performances.

But among his other duties he was the rehearsal pianist for the dancers. He would have long waits in between playing and would fumble around on the keyboard. When asked what he was playing, he would say, "Nothing." One day Harry Warren, a new young composer, heard the music that Arlen was playing and liked it. Warren suggested that Arlen show it to the lyricist Ted Koehler. The song became Arlen's first professional hit, "Get Happy."

In 1930, the song was incorporated into a Broadway show, Ruth Selwyn's NINE-FIFTEEN REVUE starring the new popular singer Ruth Etting. Most of the music for that

Ruth Etting, composer Harold Arlen, songwriter Ted Koehler, and Max Winslow on the set of LET'S FALL IN LOVE, 1933. (Photofest.)

show was written by Kay Swift, who later became George Gershwin's lover. The show only lasted for seven performances. But "Get Happy" was the big hit and got a job for Arlen and Koehler writing for the EARL CARROLL'S VANITIES.

The early days of the Depression had arrived , but everything in the lives of Arlen and Koehler was going well. It was the tail-end of the era of speakeasies and gangsters. Owney Madden, who had murdered five people before he was seventeen, controlled Manhattan. He was the boss of illegal alcohol distribution, the protection rackets, and legitimate businesses like the Cotton Club. Bands such as Ellington's and Cab Calloway's were regulars. The in-house songwriters for the Cotton Club shows were Dorothy Fields and Jimmy McHugh. Dan Healy, who had performed in Berlin's YIP, YIP, YAPHANK and the ZIEGFELD FOLLIES, became disenchanted with performing. Ultimately, he became head of production for the Cotton Club.

Healy liked Arlen and Koehler's music and hired them to replace Fields and McHugh. Black musicians preferred the work of Gershwin, Hoagy Carmichael, and Arlen to all other white composers. But their favorite was Arlen. More than any he felt the music of Harlem and showed no trace of bigotry. Arlen became friends with the black musicians, but the situation was quite different for them. He could eat at the Club. They couldn't. He could use the restrooms. They had to use restrooms for "colored" only. He could bring friends. They couldn't.

Life was really good for Arlen. Working with Koehler was so easy that he would not find out how difficult collaborators could be until much later in his career.

In 1930, Arlen became eligible for membership in ASCAP (the American Society of Composers, Authors and Publishers) in the company of Kern, Berlin, Gershwin, Porter and Rodgers, though he had not yet written a single Broadway show. But it wasn't a good time to be on Broadway. In 1930, almost all of the Broadway musicals failed. And in 1935, only ten were produced, dozens fewer than the years before the Crash. Arlen and Koehler, on the other hand, were doing much better financially than the Broadway composers, just from their success at the Cotton Club.

In 1931, Arlen persuaded Koehler to take a walk on a cold day in Manhattan. They walked for two miles as Arlen increased the pace, humming a tune. As the story goes, Koehler began putting words to it and by the time they returned they had almost completed, "I Love a Parade." It became a hit in the 1931 Cotton Club show RHYTHMANIA along with "Between the Devil and the Deep Blue Sea."

He and Koehler wrote "I Gotta Right to Sing the Blues" in 1932 for Earl Carroll's Vanities. And, on a roll, he composed, "I've Got the World on a String" for the new Cotton Club show.

They soon faced a problem. They had written a scat

Broadway and Hollywood collaborators Harold Arlen and E. Y. "Yip." Harburg at rehearsal for BLOOMER GIRL, 1944. (Photofest.)

song for Cab Calloway, which included his famous refrain "Hi-De-Ho" when suddenly Calloway quit. Ellington would be brought in to replace him, but Ellington was no singer. So they latched on to Ethel Waters, who worked on Broadway and in Harlem, but whose career was fading. They wrote a very special song for her, which she introduced on Sunday, April 6, 1933. That song was "Stormy Weather."

Prohibition was officially ended by the Roosevelt administration in March of 1933 and so was the era of the speakeasy. Their final Cotton Club show was in 1934 and contained what has become a favorite for jazz vocalists, "Ill Wind." While doing the Cotton Club shows the two men occasionally took other assignments. In 1932, Arlen wrote "Satan's L'il Lamb" with Yip Harburg and Johnny Mercer.

In 1934, Harburg and Ira Gershwin asked Arlen to write the score for a new musical. Arlen was torn. He had always worked with Koehler, who had guided him through his career. But Koehler said he would be a fool to turn them down. It did not adversely affect their relationship, and they would work again together.

Arlen was constantly busy. He agreed to play dual piano with Roger Edens as accompaniment for Ethel Merman at the Palace. He was even allowed to sing some of his own hits. If George Gershwin was the finest pianist of these great Broadway composers, Harold Arlen, Johnny Mercer, and Cole Porter were the best performers.

Dating a lot, Arlen made the gossip columns with the actress Frances Williams, but nothing between them was serious. She was more interested in her career than romance. Then, Earl Carroll put Anya Taranda, a young Russian model, in his Vanities. She would become advertising's "Breck Girl." Anya was the one to whom Harold was attracted.

Arlen got two other offers that he accepted in 1934. He did a twelve-week run of performing in New York and followed by touring. Shortly after, he and Ted Koehler agreed to go to Hollywood to write a movie, when most movie musicals were failing. Theirs failed as well, but Arlen didn't mind because he wanted to return to New York and Anya.

On his return he wrote the COTTON CLUB PARADE in 1934, and a new show with Ira Gershwin and Harburg. Gershwin was very disciplined and Harburg was frenetic, but the three of them worked well together writing LIFE BEGINS AT 8:40. It starred Bert Lahr and Ray Bolger and was a big success.

Among the things Arlen loved during the writing was that occasionally they would cross the street and visit George Gershwin while he was working on PORGY AND BESS. They would play their new songs for one another. Arlen was one of the first to hear "Summertime."

One day Arlen played a complicated melody for Gershwin that he was working on. Gershwin said it was lovely, but too difficult and couldn't be sung. Kern heard it as well and agreed. Another year would pass until Yip Harburg wrote the lyrics to the wonderful "Last Night When We Were Young."

Because LIFE BEGINS AT 8:40 was a hit, Arlen was called back to Hollywood. He and Anya were headed west, to the displeasure of his father, because Anya was Russian Orthodox, not Jewish. Arlen was hired to write a movie musical with Lew Brown, formerly of the songwriting team of DeSylva, Brown, and Henderson. It starred Eddie Cantor and was called STRIKE ME PINK. That movie and three others written with Harburg all did poorly. Arlen did not like the way Hollywood worked. The composer had absolutely no say in how the process moved ahead, as opposed to the composer's significant role on Broadway. Busby Berkeley, who was directing the films, liked Harry Warren better. So he replaced Arlen's songs with those from Warren. Even Warren wasn't happy with that.

Harold and Anya settled into Hollywood, buying a home in Beverly Hills, next to the Rombergs, across the street from the Cantors. They also spent a great deal of time with the Gershwins. All his friends put pressure on Arlen and Anya to marry. In 1936, accompanied by his brother and a friend, Arlen and Anya went to upstate New York, and against his parents wishes, married.

Arlen and the Gershwins were so close that one day George rushed over to Harold's house to play the new song he had written for Fred Astaire, "They Can't Take That Away from Me."

On July 4, 1937, George Gershwin moved out of his own home, where he was living with Ira and Leonore Gershwin. Ira's wife Leonore was repelled by George's falling down, dropping silverware and dishes, and drooling. She attributed it all to his "neurotic" behavior, and was constantly chastising him about it. Refusing to tolerate her attacks any longer, Gershwin moved into Harburg's house, because Harburg and Arlen were leaving together for New York City. When Arlen saw Gershwin there, he said that Gershwin should be in a hospital, not in a private home.

While in New York, Arlen and Harburg wrote HOORAY FOR WHAT. It was fraught with problems, firings, and changes, and yet it was a success. Its best song was "Down with Love."

One week later, in New York City, they were shocked to hear on the radio of George Gershwin's death. Of all other composers Arlen's favorite was Gershwin.

In 1937, MGM paid Sam Goldwyn seventy-five thousand dollars for the rights to THE WIZARD OF OZ. The word was out that they had selected Jerome Kern and Ira Gershwin to write the score. But suddenly a contract was signed with Arlen and Harburg for twenty-five thousand dollars, a very small amount. It was a "work-for-hire" for the studio; they'd have to content themselves with royalties from the commercial success of the songs, rather than from the film itself. Some say Kern turned it down. Others say he was surprised when it was offered to Arlen and Harburg. Others say Arthur Freed, the assistant producer, always wanted Arlen.

Life in Hollywood was free and easy. The people in the movie industry wandered in and out of each others' homes. One day Arlen decided to pop in on a new neighbor and found William Powell and Carole Lombard making love on the living room rug. Supposedly, Powell looked up at Arlen and said, "So you wrote 'Stormy Weather'?"

The filming of THE WIZARD OF OZ was a disaster, with constant struggles, firings, and quitting. The problems were unbelievable. The munchkins were described as drunks, soliciting sex and carrying weapons. Margaret Hamilton got so severely burned in the filming she was out for six weeks. Garland left for a week with a cold, costing one hundred and fifty thousand dollars.

After being frustrated in the attempt to find the right music, Arlen and Harburg finally came up with "Over the Rainbow," only to discover that the MGM executives wanted it cut after an in-house screening. They were devastated. Freed supported them and demanded a meeting with Louis B. Mayer. Freed said, "'Rainbow' stays or I go." Freed prevailed. After two previews shown without it, it was seen in the third and the audience loved it. "Over the Rainbow" stayed on the Hit Parade for fourteen weeks. GONE WITH THE WIND won the Academy Award for Best Picture but "Over the Rainbow" got Best Song.

When the war broke out in Europe, the filming of movies shrunk and there was little work. In 1941, Arlen and Koehler wrote one of their great ballads, "When the Sun Comes Out."

Meredith Willson, later of THE MUSIC MAN fame, commissioned Arlen to be one of a series of composers to write patriotic songs for a radio broadcast. Arlen worked diligently to produce "American Minuet." Quite an elegant work, it has never been heard other than on that broadcast. Nothing else was happening for Arlen other than a constant social life of golf and gin rummy with his music buddies, until 1941, when he began to work with a young singer-composer lyricist, Johnny Mercer. They had met at parties in the late thirties.

Movies were becoming more interested in jazz and blues. Warner Brothers signed Arlen and Mercer to do a movie called HOT NOCTURNE. They began with a ballad, the very lovely "This Time the Dream's on Me." But they needed a blues song and Arlen locked himself in his study with a copy of W. C. Handy's *A Treasury of the Blues*. He told Anya not to disturb him for any reason and did not emerge for a day and a half. At that point, he went immediately to Mercer where he played what he had written several times and left. He returned not completely happy with the lyrics Mercer had written, though he liked some parts. They worked on it together for another week.

While they were working on the score for the movie, a close friend and a very prominent composer, Richard Whiting, died suddenly of a heart attack in his forties. Every Saturday night show people and musicians came to the Whiting home to be with the family. Mickey Rooney, Judy Garland, Martha Raye, and Mel Torme were there one Saturday when Arlen and Mercer came rushing in. They went straight to the piano to play the song they had just completed. Martha Raye, dumbfounded by the beauty of the song, for once could not speak. Judy Garland and the sixteen-year-old Margaret Whiting wanted to see who could learn the song first. Arlen and Mercer had written the classic, "Blues in the Night."

The name of the picture was changed to BLUES IN THE NIGHT. The song was on the Hit Parade for thirteen weeks, while the most famous performers scrambled to record it.

Patriotic movies were the rage and the two of them wrote STAR SPANGLED RHYTHM, which included "Hit the Road to Dreamland" and the big smash, "That Old Black Magic." Margaret Whiting was only eighteen when she recorded the song and it became the biggest hit of her long career.

Arlen and Mercer went on to write a number of patriotic films with popular songs like "My Shining Hour" and "Ac-cent-tchu-ate the Positive," and "One for My Baby (and One More for the Road)," one of the all-time greatest torch songs. It would be recorded by Sinatra, Tony Bennett, Bobby Short and others.

But things were not at all great at home. While Arlen worked and played with his friends, Anya, excluded from the clique of wives, stayed at home brooding. It was very similar to the problems faced by Jerome Kern's foreign-born wife. In 1943, with Anya's brother, a problematic young man, sleeping in their spare room, a fire awakened them. No one was injured but much important memorabilia was lost. The rumor was that a vindictive Anya was an arsonist, but it was much more likely that her inebriated brother accidentally started it with a cigarette.

The end of the war brought the end of the Arlen-Mercer collaboration and Arlen went back to Harburg.

They had written one movie in 1943, CABIN IN THE SKY, as Arlen returned to creating music rooted in African-American culture. For it he wrote, "Happiness Is Jes' a Thing Called Joe," sung by Ethel Waters.

In 1944, Arlen wrote his most successful Broadway show, BLOOMER GIRL. It dealt with the Civil War. Agnes de Mille was selected as the choreographer. In it she programmed a ten-minute ballet about the death of Civil War soldiers. Harburg hated it and insisted it be withdrawn. A major battle ensued with Arlen supporting de Mille. But Harburg prevailed and as a compromise the producer allowed it to be done once, at the first preview. The audience reaction was so overwhelmingly positive that it was re-inserted. The show became a hit, running for two years and 654 performances.

Broadway beckoned again as he wrote an all-black show with Johnny Mercer in 1946, ST. LOUIS WOMAN. Originally it was supposed to star Lena Horne. But she quit and the show had an unsuccessful three-month run. It did have one of the great Arlen classics, "Come Rain or Come Shine."

When Arlen's brother Jerry was drafted into the Army, their father called him to help. Harold pulled strings and got Jerry into the Air Force band to play in the touring WINGED VICTORY, which kept him out of harm's way.

After the war Arlen's father came to him and said, "Chaim, do something for your younger brother." He helped him again by getting him the role of conductor of the touring company for BLOOMER GIRL. But there were so many complaints about Jerry that he was fired. Arlen's father blamed him for not coming to Jerry's defense.

It was a difficult time. TV was expanding and there was little work for Arlen. An attempt was made to create a new radio show where Arlen would play and sing mostly his own music. But there was no network interest.

By the early 1950s, The House Un-American Activities Committee (HUAC) was hitting its stride. Although Arlen, a Republican, was not touched, he was greatly affected. His frequent collaborator Yip Harburg was a strong leftist and was blacklisted. At the same time Anya was becoming more and more of a problem. She rarely left her bed while Arlen was out playing golf and drinking too much.

In 1948, an idea came up for a musical called CASBAH, but all the lyricists Arlen had worked with were retired or busy. So the suggestion was made that he write with Leo Robin, who was already quite successful in the movies, having written the lyrics for "Hallelujah," "Beyond the Bluc Horizon," "June in January," "Sometimes I'm Happy," and "Thanks for the Memory" for Bob Hope. The movie was

NBC's *Dupont Show of the Week*, "Happy with the Blues" episode, September 24, 1961. Shown from left: Harold Arlen, Peggy Lee, and Vic Damone. (Photofest.)

unsuccessful, but for it they wrote, "Hooray For Love."

Soon the work dried up again. To make matters worse Arlen's parents and brother moved to California, which only made the situation more difficult with Anya. She became more erratic and Arlen couldn't work. Finally Anya's doctors suggested she be hospitalized as a protection for herself. Jerry took her to the hospital, but a few days later Harold signed her out. Right after that, Harold, distraught, disappeared. The family searched for him for three days. He had gotten drunk and disappeared to Hawaii, where he got even more drunk, ultimately being admitted to a hospital there.

In 1951, he completed a movie musical with an old friend, Dorothy Fields. The movie, THE FARMER TAKES A WIFE, failed.

Arlen got two of his friends, Harry Warren and Buddy Morris, to join with him and take all three wives on a European jaunt. It was like a second honeymoon, but the luster wore off soon after their return. Though Harold was fine as he began working with Moss Hart and Ira Gershwin to make a movie with Judy Garland, A STAR IS BORN, Anya got worse again. Following an episode in which she slapped Celia Arluck, Harold's mother, in the face, a psychiatrist put her back in a sanatorium in Malibu. She would "remain there for the next six years."

As usual there were constant problems with Garland while filming, but Arlen and Gershwin moved ahead and wrote the beautiful "The Man That Got Away." When Garland was to record the song there were terrible fights. She wanted it in a higher key. Hugh Martin, her vocal coach and a devotee of Arlen, said that it ruined the song. While this was happening, Arlen's father suddenly died, and Harold was caught up in the struggle about the music, his father's death, his mother's bereavement, and Anya's hospitalization.

Though Arlen was in a terrible mental state he began working with Ira Gershwin for the score of THE COUNTRY GIRL, starring Grace Kelly. A STAR IS BORN got six Academy Award nominations. Judy Garland had given birth the night before the ceremony and a special TV hook-up was arranged in her hospital room to televise her anticipated acceptance of the Best Actress statue. But when the awards were announced Grace Kelly won for THE COUNTRY GIRL and best song went to "Three Coins in the Fountain." A STAR IS BORN lost in every category in 1954.

In 1950, Truman Capote had won the O. Henry Award for his short story "House of Flowers." Though Capote was a rank amateur when it came to writing lyrics, Arlen agreed to work with him on a Broadway musical adaptation of the story. Harold decided to leave Malibu and moved to New York with his mother and brother Jerry, who was selected to be the show's conductor. While working Arlen developed severe abdominal pain, and was admitted to the hospital and operated upon. He was found to have a severely ulcerated liver that was bleeding. There was no treatment except transfusions. He developed stomach and esophageal bleeding, which was treated with pressure balloons and transfusions. He was expected to die. Marlene Dietrich and Lisa Kirk visited his bedside constantly. Many had predicted that, ultimately, Arlen would marry Kirk. But Arlen miraculously recovered and Kirk vanished from his life. Pearl Bailey played the lead in HOUSE OF FLOWERS and there were battles from the beginning. Before long choreographer George Balanchine quit, and the director Peter Brook was replaced. The reviews were very mixed when it opened at the end of 1954 and it closed in five months.

Arlen needed to work to keep his mind off Anya. He rarely spoke of her even to friends. After a while his name began to appear in gossip columns, as he was seen out at events with women. Because he was still married, his mother chastised him for the way the press constantly linked him to his friend Marlene Dietrich. He was also mentioned with Margaret Truman, Gloria Vanderbilt Lumet, and Marilyn Monroe.

Arlen and Ira Gershwin were creating music quite different from their contemporaries. They were using forms, like key changes in the middle of a melody, which made their music atypical for the time, gaining them a reputation as the most creative and accomplished musicians of their era. A young producer, Bobbie Breen, understood this and wanted them to write an opera based on ST. LOUIS WOMAN. Breen was producing PORGY AND BESS in Moscow and persuaded Gershwin and Arlen to come there. He also asked Truman Capote to come and write about the trip. The arrangements were a fiasco with lost passports and visas and Arlen stranded in Stockholm on the way. Arlen finally arrived at the Moscow theatre disheveled, unshaven, and exhausted. He fell asleep during the performance only to have Capote, seated behind him, hitting him on the back as Breen, from the stage, called on honored guests in the audience—including Arlen—to stand and be acknowledged. The entire trip became a disaster when Capote, hired to promote the event, wrote a devastating column saying he hated PORGY AND BESS, with all those "depressed people." Only Arlen escaped his wrath in the column.

Meanwhile Arlen and Harburg began work on a new show, PIGEON ISLAND. It started with Harry Belafonte in the lead, but he became ill and needed surgery. They turned to Lena Horne. The show was not good, especially Harburg's book, so the producer David Merrick turned it into more of a showcase for Horne and changed the name to JAMAICA. Arlen got sick again during the production. But the show ended up running for more than a year and a half, based on Horne's performance alone.

Arlen kept working on the BLUES OPERA taken from ST. LOUIS WOMAN. In November 1957, the conductor Andre Kostelanetz played a Blues Opera Suite from that score.

A year later in 1958 Celia Arluck died.

Arlen soon persuaded a reluctant Johnny Mercer to write a musical based on SARATOGA TRUNK. It opened in December 1959, was panned and closed immediately. At the end of the writing Arlen was sick again and Mercer wrote the last three songs alone. It would turn out to be Arlen's last new show on Broadway. But it was a good time for him in another way. Anya was released from the hospital and they bought a home in Beverly Hills near Ira Gershwin and Harry Warren.

In 1959, the completed BLUES OPERA was to be produced and shown in multiple European cities. Quincy Jones was brought in to arrange it in a modern jazz version, with the title changed to FREE AND EASY. Arlen, hearing Jones's arrangement, said, "To enjoy it you've got to be on the weed." It closed in Paris and never re-opened. The music from that and ST. LOUIS WOMAN was said to be some of Arlen's greatest, but it has never been revived on Broadway.

In interviews in later years, when asked to name his favorite of all the songs he had ever written, Arlen chose one that is not widely known, "Last Night When We Were Young." It was the song that George Gershwin and Jerome Kern had told Arlen was too difficult for any lyrics to be written. He wrote it with lyrics by Harburg in 1935 with Harburg for a radio broadcast.

There was little work for Arlen until an offer came from Hollywood in 1961 to write the music for an animated film called GAY PURR-EE with Harburg. It was the last piece they would write together. It was quite good but received little attention. Anya was once again getting worse and now she was experiencing strange contortions of her facial muscles.

In 1963, Arlen was approached by CBS to do a retrospective of his work with Walter Cronkite. On that show Andre Previn said Arlen was not a songwriter. He was a composer. Others wrote songs with repeats that could be removed and shortened if necessary. But it was not true for Arlen's work. No matter how long it was, you could not take one bar out. There was no filler.

In the sixties, Arlen met Martin Charnin and they wrote several songs together for no particular production. Finally in 1965 it was reported they would write a show for Jason Robards. Saint Subber, who had experienced failures with HOUSE OF FLOWERS, OUT OF THIS WORLD and others, was promoting it. It would be about postwar Japan, titled SOFTLY. But they never achieved a satisfactory book and the project died.

Arlen and Capote wrote several new songs for an Off-Broadway revival of HOUSE OF FLOWERS. It opened in January 1967 and closed in March.

By the summer of 1969 Anya was much worse and tests revealed she had a malignant brain tumor. She was operated upon in August but could not get out of bed until December; she died in March of the following year. Arlen was terribly depressed. Eventually, after attempts were made to reach him, his brother and sister-in-law found him overdosed. He gradually improved.

By 1971, he was persuaded to write again. At New York City's experimental Café La Mama, he met a young lyricist, Leonard Melfi, who was thirty-five years his junior. They were a strange pair in that Melfi was in dress and lifestyle a true Village hippie. They wrote a musical play for TV called CLIPPETY CLOP AND CLEMENTINE. It was a comedy about a horse-and-carriage driver, and was to star Sammy Davis, Jr. It was completed in 1972, but no one would buy it.

Years passed, and it wasn't until 1981 that the Goodspeed Opera House did a revival of BLOOMER GIRL, for which Arlen and Harburg wrote one additional song. By then Arlen was housebound. He was still in a state of depression over the loss of Anya and his walk had become a shuffle. Doctors determined he was suffering from Parkinson's disease, but at the suggestion of his brother the diagnosis was kept from Arlen. He stayed at home and watched TV alone most of the time. Arlen turned down all invitations and resigned from the ASCAP board. His major activity was calling Irving Berlin every day. In 1976, Mercer died of a brain tumor and in 1981 Harburg died of a heart attack, followed almost immediately by the death of Harry Warren. Just before Warren's death Arlen went to the theatre for the last time to see Warren's big hit 42ND STREET.

Harold Arlen's depression intensified with the death of Ira Gershwin in 1983. He was unable to go to the funeral.

Numerous award ceremonies were held in his name but he could not attend any except for the Johnny Mercer award he received in 1982. Arlen left the celebration after a very short interval.

In 1985, he was operated on for prostate cancer and was confined to a wheelchair. That same year, his sister-in-law found his long lost Oscar for "Over the Rainbow," which pleased him no end.

On April 23, 1986, after having a lunch of matzoh ball soup, Arlen went to bed and peacefully passed away. His estate was left to his nephew, Jerry's son Sam.

In his long career Arlen wrote more than five hundred songs, eleven Broadway shows, five Cotton Club shows, and twenty-four motion pictures. He was truly one of the greatest geniuses of American musical theatre.

MAJOR WORKS

SHOWS:

EARL CARROLL'S VANITIES **(1930)**
BROWN SUGAR **(1931)**
YOU SAID IT **(1931)**
RHYTHMANIA **(1931)**
EARL CARROLL'S VANITIES **(1932)**
SATAN'S LI'L LAMB **(1932)**
COTTON CLUB PARADE **(1932)**
COTTON CLUB PARADE **(1933)**
COTTON CLUB PARADE **(1934)**
LIFE BEGINS AT 8:40 **(1934)**
HOORAY FOR WHAT! **(1937)**
BLOOMER GIRL **(1944)**
ST. LOUIS WOMAN **(1946)**
HOUSE OF FLOWERS **(1954)**
JAMAICA **(1957)**
SARATOGA **(1959)**
FREE AND EASY **(1959)**
ARLEN WROTE THE SCORE FOR TWENTY-SIX FULL-LENGTH FILMS FROM 1936 TO 1973.

COMPOSITIONS:

ARLEN WROTE MORE THAN 550 SONGS.

Irving Berlin, 1950.
(Photofest.)

IRVING BERLIN

WHEN ASKED, "WHAT PART DID IRVING BERLIN PLAY in American music?" Jerome Kern, considered by many to be the greatest American composer, answered, "Irving Berlin does not have a place in American music. He *is* American music." Deciding who would be the most important of these geniuses has been an almost impossible task. However, it is absolutely clear that Irving Berlin was one of the most complicated artists and the most difficult to understand.

In the fall of 1893, the *SS Rhynland*, a Belgian passenger ship, landed in New York. The vast majority of the passengers were Russian Jews.

Among them were forty-six-year-old Moses Baline, a cantor, and his family: his wife Lena and six children, ages nineteen, sixteen, eleven, eight, six, and the baby, five-year-old Israel, who was born in Mohilev, twenty-five miles east of Minsk, in White Russia.

The Balines became tenement dwellers on the Lower East Side of Manhattan. They even had to take in a lodger to survive. Nine of them lived in three rooms on the third floor on Cherry Street, one of the most dangerous streets in that neighborhood. But children don't see themselves as living in poverty. To quote Berlin, "There was always bread, butter, and hot tea." To make a living, Moses became a kosher poultry inspector. Lena became a midwife. All the children worked; Israel delivered newspapers. Eight years later in 1901 Moses died of inhalation pneumonia, probably from paint fume exposure. Just shy of fourteen, Israel, or Izzy, as he was then known, dropped out of school to help support the family. He soon decided he was not pulling his weight and left home to live a Dickensian life on the streets of lower Manhattan. Izzy slept in flophouses every night, like an orphan. He had no education and his only skill was what his father had taught him as a cantor, singing. He was a small boy with a raspy voice, making rounds of bars singing for tips from the local clientele. Prostitution, gambling, drinking, and opium smoking were the local enterprises.

In 1902, Izzy got hired for his first job as a chorus boy in a show, but was dropped before it ever was produced. It was a time when struggling singers were hired to go into saloons and plug songs for publishers. They were called "boomers" or "buskers" and got paid five dollars a week. Izzy became a busker and as he went from saloon to saloon he learned all he could about how to play from the local piano players. At seventeen, he was hired by Mike Salter, known as "Nigger Mike," a Russian Jew with an olive complexion, to work in the Pelham Café as a singing waiter.

Mike wanted Izzy to write songs as well, so Baline wrote his first lyrics, "Marie from Sunny Italy." He knew nothing about writing music, so that fell to the piano player. The song was not that good, but a publisher actually bought it for seventy-five cents. Izzy received thirty-seven cents. The credit on the sheet music read "lyrics by I. Berlin."

As time passed Izzy decided he wanted to write his own music. He would sing the melody to the piano player, who wrote it down. That way the song would be entirely his creation.

Berlin had moved into an apartment with Max Winslow. Winslow worked for a publisher, and introduced Izzy to a young composer Edgar Leslie. Together they wrote a song that yielded them each two hundred dollars in royalties. That was followed by a second song, which sold 3000 copies. The publishing house offered Izzy a permanent job writing lyrics for twenty-five dollars a week plus royalties. The sheet music business was at its height and the publishing houses flourished.

At the publishing house the music for his early songs was composed by his employer, Ted Snyder. Berlin was only twenty-one years old, but in his first year he published two dozen songs including his first hit, "My Wife's Gone to the Country (Hurrah! Hurrah!)." It sold 300,000 copies.

Berlin wanted to sing, not primarily compose, so he auditioned for the biggest name on Broadway, the Shubert Brothers. When they rejected him, he realized his strength was in writing. As a result he tried, with some success, to sell his music to established performers. Fanny Brice bought his "Sadie Salome, Please Come Home" and performed it in the ZIEGFELD FOLLIES. Berlin was beginning to gain a name, a reputation, and the beginning of financial success.

He decided that he needed to go to the center of musical theatre, London, and learn more from them. There he was not known as Izzy Baline, but as an American composer, Irving Berlin. It was a decision that would have a major effect on his career. In England he was exposed to the transposing piano. He had been limited to writing everything on the black keys in the key of F-sharp. The new piano would help him with harmonies and fill in notes. Now there would be no question. These would be his lyrics and his music.

It was the beginning of the era of syncopation and ragtime and Berlin's contribution would be "Alexander's Ragtime Band."

Producer Jesse Lasker put the song in his new show, but it made no impression and was dropped. Berlin threw it into his trunk file where he accumulated unused material.

Unfazed, he wrote four songs for the FOLLIES OF 1911. With his new popularity, a second producer tried "Alexander's Ragtime Band." This time the public loved it. Though the show was poor and closed, the song caught on, and performers around the country sang it. By year's end it had sold one million copies of sheet music. At age twenty-three, Berlin earned thirty thousand dollars just from that one song.

A crazy rumor started and quickly died that he had a little African-American boy hidden away who wrote for him. The story hurt him deeply. But despite that bad publicity he was now being called the Ragtime King.

His success was topped off by an invitation to the Friars' Club. Berlin's acceptance speech was a song he had written the night before. It was so special they made it a part of their annual show, THE FRIARS' FROLIC OF 1911. Berlin was now on Broadway with his name in lights. Irving's sixteen-minute performance completely won over the audience. He looked like a kid onstage, small, dark, and frail. Old Lower East Side friends came but he ignored them as he had no intention of looking back.

Success brought lots of money. As a result he bought a house for his mother in the "country," today known as the Bronx. She lived there until she died in 1922. For himself, he bought a bachelor suite two blocks north of Central Park on 112th Street. With his newfound success he became a part owner of the publishing house where he had started working.

But Berlin knew that ragtime was losing its power and he needed to find something new.

As was common then, young singers came to his office hoping to buy a new song to perform. One day two women came in and got into an argument over a song. After Berlin broke it up he sold the song to one of them, but asked the other, Dorothy Goetz, on a date. Soon Berlin was in love and to him that meant marriage. Within weeks he proposed. They were married in February 1912. To avoid the cold weather, they honeymooned in Cuba. On their return Dorothy became ill and died within a few months, either of typhoid fever or pneumonia. Married only five months, Berlin was extremely depressed and went into seclusion. He could not work at all until he wrote "When I Lost You," a simple, bittersweet song, totally different from anything he had previously written.

Berlin, not immodest, believed he knew why he became one of the greatest of the American theatre composers. He understood so clearly how to combine the feeling of the music with the lyrics. He said there was a story even within the rhythm, the key, and the chords. He believed that was his advantage, writing both music and lyrics himself. Because he was untrained, rumors existed for years that he wrote none of his songs. The rumors were nonsense. He always had talented musical secretaries, who would transcribe from his singing or playing what he had written. But he composed everything himself.

His own piano playing was considered poor. Johnny Green, who became one of our greatest orchestrators, was his secretary for a brief time. Once Green respectfully asked Berlin if he would consider using a different chord that Green thought worked better. "Let me hear yours," Berlin said.

"And mine."

"And yours again."

"And mine."

And on and on. Then pausing, Berlin exclaimed, "Use mine!"

He tried to break out of his depression by returning to Europe. Berlin performed there, and came back to life. He decided to move away from ragtime, and on his return to the States, he was asked to write a new show for Irene and Vernon Castle, who had created a new dance craze. The show was called WATCH YOUR STEP. It was Berlin's first effort at writing an entire score. He had hoped for a musical with a solid story, but this was just a revue.

The show was a rousing hit, so the producer, the famous Charles Dillingham, encouraged Berlin to write another for the Castles, STOP, LOOK AND LISTEN. It was a smaller success, but contained one of Berlin's favorite songs, "I Love a Piano."

The beginning of World War I cast a pall over Broadway in 1915 and 1916 and Berlin's style became passe. Jazz was coming into vogue with new innovations. On Broadway Jerome Kern was now the major composer. Berlin was only twenty-eight but it was said that he had passed the torch to Kern.

In 1918, Berlin, always extremely patriotic, proudly became an American citizen. He was surprised to be drafted at age thirty and reported to Camp Upton in Yaphank, Long Island. Accustomed to working into the wee hours of the morning and sleeping until late noon, he was a misfit soldier. Once he got into trouble for having his valet clean his room and polish his shoes while he was on drill. One day the camp commander, who knew very well who Berlin was, told him they wanted to build a new community house for the base and needed to raise thirty-five thousand dollars. He asked Berlin to write a show the soldiers could perform on the base. Berlin suggested he could go one better. He would write a show the soldiers could do on Broadway. It was YIP, YIP, YAPHANK and he arranged for it to be seen at the Century Theatre. It was a phenomenal hit.

Berlin's mother Lena was there for opening night. At show's end, the standing-room crowd shouted for Irving. Finally a small, meek looking soldier appeared. Before the idea of the show had even arisen Berlin had written a number as a lark for the soldiers. Around the base it had been picked up as a kind of theme song. The soldiers sang it for their own pleasure. Now it became the finale of the show as Irving came out on the stage in his uniform and sang, "Oh, How I Hate to Get Up in the Morning."

There were encores. The troupe lifted him on their shoulders, carrying him around. On the way home in a limousine, his mother naively asked Berlin,"How ever did you escape?" After he asked what she meant, she responded, "When the gangsters captured you on the stage, I thought you would never get away."

The show ran to packed houses not for one performance, but for thirty-two. It raised eighty-three thousand dollars. At the last performance, in a touching scene, the cast of servicemen marched down the aisle, out the front doors, down Broadway, to the dock and boarded a ship to serve in Europe. Although the war ended two months later, no community house was ever built. And no one ever knew where the money went.

By 1919, Berlin was writing again for the FOLLIES, even though he disliked Flo Ziegfeld immensely. Berlin had strong moral values. He resented Ziegfeld's blatant promiscuous behavior. Though married to Billie Burke, Ziegfeld kept a seventeen-year-old showgirl, Olive, as a mistress. He dropped her for her girlfriend, Anna, so Olive found a new lover in Jack Pickford, Mary Pickford's brother. Olive married Pickford and Jack took out an insurance policy on her life just before they went on a ship to Europe. She was found dead in her cabin during the cruise. Jack claimed Olive didn't know he had syphilis and took his pills, accidentally. He was never charged.

Meanwhile, Ziegfeld dropped Anna and she committed suicide. She said, in her note, that Ziegfeld didn't love her anymore and beside that her best girlfriend Olive was dead. It was a tawdry world. Unlike some of the other great composers, Berlin was never unfaithful in his marriages.

Berlin's hit song in the 1919 FOLLIES was "A Pretty Girl Is Like a Melody." One can just imagine the set of the FOLLIES, with its giant staircase coming out of nowhere. One by one, a stream of gorgeous showgirls glided down the stairs in exquisite gowns, serenaded by a chorus singing, "A Pretty Girl Is Like a Melody."

Berlin wanted to be more independent, and joined with Sam Harris to build the Music Box Theatre. He had

Composer and lyricist Irving Berlin in rehearsal for THIS IS THE ARMY, 1942. (Photofest.)

become so famous that Harris wanted to call it the Irving Berlin Music Box, but Berlin refused. Here, the annual Music Box Revue began.

The big hit song of THE MUSIC BOX REVUE OF 1921 was "Say It with Music."

Berlin was already a well-established Broadway celebrity when in 1919 Alexander Woollcott established the Round Table at the Algonquin Hotel. This was a regular meeting of some of the greatest literary and artistic minds, including people like George S. Kaufman, Robert Benchley, Dorothy Parker, Franklin P. Adams, Marc Connelly, and Anita Loos. They were brilliant, but they were also possessed of a wit that could border on the vicious. (They were, in fact, informally known as "The Vicious Circle.") One story told how Kaufman, standing next to Connelly, rubbed Connelly's totally bald head and said, "That feels like my wife's rear end." Connelly rubbed his own head and, without pause, retorted, "You're right."

Woollcott loved Berlin, and brought him into their circle. The group produced their own amateur show one season. They rented a Broadway theatre and showed it for one night. At one of these performances Robert Benchley did a monologue as a confused office treasurer giving a report. The show was terrible, but Benchley was wonderful. So Berlin persuaded him to do it in the THE MUSIC BOX REVUE OF 1923.

Berlin, a brilliant entrepreneur, knew how to cultivate friendships with all the most important people in the media. He probably would have been a great politician. Though Berlin was only in his early thirties, Woollcott, who called him Izzy as a sign of how close they were, wrote a biography of him.

Like all artists, great composers frequently wrote songs that reflected their own lives. Berlin had been widowed for a number of years when in 1921 he wrote "All by Myself." The next year, his mother, the only member of his family to whom he was still close, died. Irving was seen as being generally depressed when in 1924 he wrote the haunting, "All Alone."

In February of that year, he went one night to a famous speakeasy, Jimmy Kelly's, where as a boy he had worked as a singing waiter. There he met Ellin Mackay. She was a regular patron of the Music Box Theatre, smitten by the person who was seen as show business's most eligible bachelor. In her own right she was the most eligible debutante. Twenty-one and beautiful, the daughter of a multimillionaire, she had grown up with her father, Clarence Mackay, and two sisters at Harbor Hill, Long Island, in a house designed by Stanford White. At the turn of the century its cost was an astronomical six million dollars. Her mother deserted the family when Ellin was very young, moving to England to marry a doctor who had once operated on Clarence.

Clarence's father, John, had come to America as a penniless Irish immigrant at eleven. His father died when John was very young, very much like Berlin's. In his teens John became an itinerant miner in Virginia City, where, as in Berlin's Lower East Side, murders were common. At thirty he switched to building shafts as a contractor. Soon he discovered the phenomenally profitable mine, the Kentuck.

As the years went by John's wife moved to Paris,

although they remained married. John, meanwhile, was becoming even more wealthy, through his involvement in the new telegraph business, laying cables across the ocean. John's eldest son Willie was killed in a horseback riding accident, and thus, upon John's death, the management of the family fortune fell to Clarence. He was an incompetent businessman who devoted his life to sports. Clarence was Catholic, rigid, snobbish and a virulent anti-Semite.

On hearing of his daughter Ellin's new love, Irving Berlin, he spent a fortune to ensure that she not marry "that Tin Pan Alley tunesmith." He hired private detectives to try to find dirt on Berlin. Clarence stated they would get married "over his dead body." To break up the relationship, Clarence took Ellin on a trip to Europe asking her to reconsider the marriage. She stayed for almost a year. Berlin became deeply dejected. While she was away, he wrote "Remember" and the beautiful, "What'll I Do?"

Berlin suffered professionally in 1925. He was thrown into a backstage battle with George S. Kaufman and the stars of a new show, the Marx Brothers. Kaufman had little patience for romantic songs and the Marx Brothers hammed it up so much, THE COCOANUTS didn't seem to need any music at all. While it was a smash hit and was eventually the basis for the Marx Brothers' first film, it didn't provide any hits for Berlin.

Finally, frustrated by the actions of Clarence Mackay, on New Year's Eve 1925 Irving told Ellin he was going to Europe in two days, with or without her. She agreed to get married on Monday, January 4. To be inconspicuous they went to City Hall by subway. It was the first time in her entire life that Ellin had ever ridden on the New York City subway. She was twenty-two and he was thirty-seven. She repeatedly tried reaching her father after the ceremony, but Clarence would not respond and she grew distraught. Hounded by paparazzi, they went on a two-month honeymoon to Europe.

Ellin was also rejected by her Social Register friends, who suggested that "those people should marry their own kind." Ellin was actually disowned by her father. One story said Clarence threatened Berlin that Ellin would get nothing from his estate. Berlin responded that he would give Ellin two million dollars on the day they married. On January 8, Woollcott held a farewell party for their honeymoon trip to Europe and they left on the ninth. Ellin, a journalist, wrote broadsides against high society for *Vogue*.

The press was filled with ridiculous rumors including the story that Berlin would convert to Catholicism and they would be remarried at the Vatican. Another was that Berlin had written "Always" for his new bride. The truth about "Always" is quite a funny story. One of Berlin's musical secretaries was Arthur Johnston, a ladies' man. Long before Irving met Ellin, one of Johnston's girlfriends asked Berlin to write a song about her. He wrote "I'll Be Loving You, Mona." By the time it was done, so was Mona. As a result Berlin put it into his trunk of unused songs. In 1925, he remembered it, took it out, and changed the word "Mona" to "always." (He tried to use it in THE COCOANUTS, but Kaufman rejected it.) Thus, the only true part of the rumor about its origin is that he gave it to Ellin as a gift, with all the copyrights.

Ellin became pregnant while in Europe. At the same time Rodgers and Hart were writing two musicals. By mistake they had promised a show to two different producers. One was called PEGGY-ANN and the other BETSY. PEGGY-ANN was great and BETSY looked like a dud. It starred Belle Baker, a close friend of Berlin. A few days after Ellin had the baby, Baker called Berlin to say the show was a stinker without one good song for her. It was opening the following day. Her plaintive cry was, "Please write me something tonight!" He said he had a half-finished song in his trunk which he had thought would be good for her, but hadn't ever completed it.

"Please come over here. We'll feed you. Half-finished by you is better than what I've got now, which is nothing," responded Baker.

He had completed the first eight bars but couldn't figure out a bridge. By six in the morning it was done. And he presented her with "Blue Skies."

Rodgers and Hart were in the audience for the opening, unaware that Ziegfeld had added the song. There were twenty-four encores for "Blue Skies." When Belle forgot the lyrics, Berlin actually stood up in the audience and sang with her. The show failed, but the song was a huge hit. Rodgers and Hart, furious, did not speak to Berlin or Baker for years.

The years 1926 through 1928 were unproductive for Berlin, with 1928 being particularly terrible. Ellin lost the only family member with whom she still had a close relationship, her grandmother. At the end of the year, she delivered her second child, Irving Berlin Jr. At twenty-five days of age he died of what we now call SIDS (Sudden Infant Death Syndrome). Because he died on Christmas day, anti-Semitism reared its head. Her Catholic friends said it was God's punishment for marrying a Jew. The tragedy did result in her father's reappearance in her life. He sent condolences.

Still in a slump, Berlin tried his hand at an original film musical, , REACHING FOR THE MOON, in 1930. Unfortunately, Berlin did not have the same authority on movie set as he did in a Broadway rehearsal hall; almost all of the score was cut from the final release, leaving two songs to become popular hits on their own: "Say It Isn't So" and the memorable "How Deep Is the Ocean."

With the onset of the Depression, composers and publishing houses began selling their work to movie companies. But Berlin sold nothing. He retained the rights to all his music.

In 1929, Ellin's mother, Kitty, developed diabetes, became blind, and was abandoned by the doctor with whom she had run off to England. He had an affair with a nurse forty years his junior. Kitty died in 1930 but not before converting to Clarence's religion, Catholicism. It was at Kitty's funeral that Ellin saw her father only for the second time since she got married.

A kind of reconciliation occurred between Clarence and the Berlins. Clarence had been the largest single stock market loser in America. He lost Harbor House and all of his holdings. Still, Berlin, though he was having his own economic setbacks due to the Depression and no new successes, gave Clarence one million dollars to help him survive. But it was said to the very end Clarence still despised his son-in-law.

The country had lost faith in its politicians. As a result the Gershwins had the first hit on Broadway in years, OF THEE I SING, a political satire. It ran for a year in Berlin's Music Box. It offered Berlin the incentive to try once again. His insecurity had built up with one failure after another during the Depression. For the first time he would try what the Gershwins had done, a political satire with the brilliant young writer Moss Hart. It was called FACE THE MUSIC. It was 1932 and Berlin was back, but still losing money. He needed a big hit and came up with the idea of a revue constructed like a newspaper. In 1933 he went with Moss Hart to Bermuda to put together AS THOUSANDS CHEER. He wrote the best score of his career, one that included "Supper Time" about a lynching down south, "Heat Wave," and a song he had partially written sixteen years earlier, "Easter Parade."

In 1934, Berlin made the cover of *Time* magazine and NBC ran a five-part series based on his work, over the course of five consecutive Sunday evenings. Reaching a new peak, he was a celebrity. Actually, he was a national icon. His financial situation changed markedly with the huge success of AS THOUSANDS CHEER.

Around that time Mynna Grant, a substitute telephone operator, gradually worked her way up in his organization. Irving was constantly forgetful, and Mynna made certain everything that had to be done was accomplished. Berlin's business partner in his publishing house was Saul Bornstein.

AS THOUSANDS CHEER was to be his last Broadway effort for seven years. The film studio, RKO, only a dozen years old, was in bankruptcy by the early 1930s. Berlin liked the idea of working in a small, friendly, and struggling environment and he really liked Fred Astaire, who was their principal star.

An interesting story about Astaire was that his original screen test had the following evaluation: "Can't act. Slightly bald. Enormous ears. Bad chin line. Also dances." In 1935, Berlin wrote the music for a new movie with Fred Astaire and Ginger Rogers, TOP HAT, including "Top Hat, White Tie and Tails" and the fabulous, "Cheek to Cheek." It was said that he wrote it in one day. (Berlin wrote "Let Yourself Go" for FOLLOW THE FLEET almost as rapidly.) It was his first success in Hollywood. Irving Berlin had created that debonair persona that is associated with Astaire.

During the filming of TOP HAT Berlin's strange relationship with his siblings became apparent. His youngest sister committed suicide. Ill with physical and mental problems, and living in poverty with her husband, she had been subsidized very modestly by her brother Irving. He tearfully attended the funeral and quickly returned to work. Biographers said he had the ability to put personal tragedy aside. No one denies his musical genius, but this and other responses to his siblings' problems later in his life indicate some quirk in his personality. Possibly his behavior was due to his difficult childhood and whatever role his siblings might have played in his relegation to a street life as a very young teenager.

In 1936, Hollywood honored him with a black-tie event to celebrate twenty-five years of composing. The event was full of celebrities. Twenty-five composers sang one song from each of the twenty-five years. Jerome Kern was the emcee and bands led by Ted Lewis and Johnny Green played. In six months Berlin followed up with another Astaire-Rogers movie, FOLLOW THE FLEET, which featured his hit song "Let's Face the Music and Dance."

Irving and Ellin had a wonderful and very active social life. The Berlins were very close friends of George Gershwin, who was reaching his peak with PORGY AND BESS in 1935. On June 20, 1937, the Berlins had dinner with George Gershwin. The pain in Gershwin's head grew so severe that he had to be helped from the table. Forty-eight hours later he was in Cedars of Lebanon Hospital and on July 11, Gershwin died at the age of thirty-eight.

Shortly thereafter, Ellin gave birth to her third daughter and last child. Meanwhile in Berlin's professional life, Darryl F. Zanuck at 20th Century Fox had stolen Berlin from RKO, trying to outdo the Astaire-Rogers movies. Together, they would create ALEXANDER'S RAGTIME BAND, ON THE AVENUE, and SECOND FIDDLE. Of the three, only ALEXANDER'S RAGTIME BAND was a financial success. But, like the other two, it garnered poor reviews. Berlin returned to RKO for one last Astaire-Rogers movie, CAREFREE. Its best song was "Change Partners."

The Berlins went vacationing to London and there they saw the signs of imminent war. Irving returned home and wanted to write something patriotic. He asked Mynna to find a song he had written and rejected for YIP, YIP, YAPHANK twenty-one years earlier. He had thrown it into his trunk. It was not easy to find, because it had no title. Ted Collins was looking for a patriotic song for his singer Kate Smith. It was, of course, "God Bless America."

Introduced on November 11, 1938, "God Bless America" immediately took off like wildfire. The proceeds over the years, hundreds of thousands of dollars, all went to the Boy Scouts and the Girl Scouts. "God Bless America" and "Always" were the only two songs to which Berlin ever relinquished his rights. The day after the former was introduced, Ellin's father Clarence Mackay died.

Once World War II began, Berlin went back to Hollywood for a big hit with Bing Crosby, HOLIDAY INN.

Composer Irving Berlin and Nanette Fabray rehearsing for MR. PRESIDENT, 1962. (Photofest.)

(Photo courtesy of The Rodgers and Hammerstein Organization. All rights reserved.)

It contained "Be Careful It's My Heart" and Berlin's greatest hit, "White Christmas." The song had a strong pull for U.S. soldiers. In the first ten years it sold three million copies of sheet music, and fourteen million records.

Ever the patriot, Berlin contacted General George Marshall and said he would like to re-create YIP, YIP, YAPHANK. Marshall agreed. Berlin contacted a young producer, Bob Lissauer, and asked him to enlist in the service and work on this new adventure, to be titled THIS IS THE ARMY. He signed up Ezra Stone, famous for playing Henry Aldrich in the radio comedy *The Aldrich Family*, to be the director. Berlin wanted 300 men in the service to rehearse at Camp Upton, write it in a month, and perform it for several weeks. As difficult as it must have been to accomplish in the environment of that time, the group was racially integrated. Berlin was at the height of his career. He also began showing signs of being very difficult. Things didn't move smoothly. Production took two months with Berlin and Stone clashing frequently. One day Berlin walked in on a rehearsal and realized Stone had added a few words to one of his songs. Berlin ripped up the music and said, "It will always be words and music by Irving Berlin! And nobody else."

The show opened on July 4, 1942, at the Broadway Theatre. At the finale, Berlin appeared in his World War I uniform and plaintively sang, "Oh How I Hate to Get Up in the Morning." It also featured "This Is the Army Mr. Jones" and the very sad, "I Left My Heart at the Stage Door Canteen."

A huge success, it was extended to September 26. The show moved from Washington, D.C., to Philadelphia and St. Louis. There the final battle occurred between Stone and Berlin. Berlin said there were too many Jews and too many of Stone's friends in the show and they had to be cut. No one could believe these words came from the cantor's son. There actually were more Italians than Jews in the show. But Berlin would not budge, and the cuts were made.

Subsequently, the show was made into a movie. It raised almost ten million dollars for Army Emergency Relief.

The decision was made to do a foreign tour, but Stone was dropped from the staff. In October 1943, they left for Europe. The following February, Eisenhower proposed that it be seen by soldiers on all fronts. By June it had been seen up and down Italy. In July 1944, Berlin finally returned home, exhausted. The show, during August, went on without Berlin to Egypt. In September and October it was performed in Iran. Berlin rejoined them on December 30 in New Guinea. They had traveled the Pacific on inferior ships, with bad food, and in danger. The audiences were huge, as large as 15,000. The last performance was in Maui on October 22.

It had been seen by 2.5 million soldiers and civilians. At the age of fifty-seven Berlin returned to Washington to receive a medal from President Harry S. Truman. He had achieved what his goal had always been: respect.

By this time Rodgers and Hammerstein had become the most powerful composing team on Broadway. In 1945, as producers, they asked Jerome Kern to write the score for ANNIE GET YOUR GUN.

Kern came to New York, collapsed on the street from a stroke, and died on November 11. Berlin agreed to replace him. He wanted to call the show IRVING BERLIN'S ANNIE OAKLEY. Rodgers and Hammerstein were just as tough negotiators.

They said "No, it's our idea, our play."

Berlin acquiesced and went to Atlantic City where in a week he wrote "Doin' What Comes Natur'lly" and "You

Can't Get a Man with a Gun" for Ethel Merman. Following that, he wrote "There's No Business Like Show Business" and "They Say It's Wonderful."

At one run-through during rehearsals, Berlin, hypersensitive, thought he saw a lack of interest by Rodgers and Hammerstein as they rehearsed "There's No Business Like Show Business." At the next rehearsal it was gone.

Rodgers complained, "I'm crazy about it. Put it back."

Berlin gave his explanation for why it had been removed, and Rodgers insisted again that the song be placed back into the score. Berlin petulantly said he didn't know if he could find it. But it was restored.

On another occasion, Joshua Logan, the show's director, wanted an additional song. He said he needed a duet between the leads. When he got home there was a call from Berlin, who sang him a song he had written in fifteen minutes.

"How did you do that?" Logan asked.

"I had to. Rehearsals start on Monday."

The song was "Anything You Can Do." In addition to all the previous songs, the show also had "The Girl That I Marry" and "I Got the Sun in the Morning."

Everyone agreed it was one of the greatest scores ever written. Even so it started off badly out of town. It had poor orchestrations that had to be redone by Robert Russell Bennett. The roof of the theatre collapsed, delaying the opening for several weeks. A rumor was started that the roof story was made up because of problems with the show.

Viewers were disappointed it was not more like the recent Rodgers and Hammerstein hits OKLAHOMA! and CAROUSEL. But it ran for more than three years on Broadway and in 1950 was made into a movie.

Around this time Berlin's right-hand woman, Mynna, examining documents in the safe, discovered that Berlin's partner, Bornstein, was stealing from him. Berlin forced Bornstein out of the partnership. Strangely, Berlin also fired Mynna shortly after that, although she had been with him for so many years. The reason given was that she complained about work being requested of her by Ellin. Irving Berlin's behavior had become much more erratic. He was now a severe insomniac and addicted to Nembutal, a sleeping pill.

In 1948, he wrote EASTER PARADE starring Fred Astaire and Judy Garland. The featured song in the film was "A Couple of Swells." The movie was hugely successful and it earned $6.8 million.

Berlin had reached sixty. He was frequently agitated and constantly worried about his business dealings, with no good cause. He became very cheap, feeling everyone was taking advantage of him, even Ellin. Meanwhile, Ellin was writing very successfully in her own right, having published two novels. She wrote about religious intolerance and when Anne Morrow Lindbergh and her famous husband, Charles, spoke out favorably about their visit to Nazi Germany, Ellin confronted her head-on, saying she was a "willing dupe of the Nazis."

Meanwhile, Berlin was encouraged to write a show, MISS LIBERTY, with the playwright Robert E. Sherwood. At the same time the production for the movie ANNIE GET YOUR GUN was not going well. Garland, chosen for the lead, was troubled with drugs and both she and Busby Berkeley were fired. Betty Hutton was hired to fill her role. MISS LIBERTY received universally poor reviews and lasted only nine months, and that only because of advanced sales. But Betty Hutton did a great job salvaging a bad year. The movie ANNIE GET YOUR GUN was a big moneymaker.

In 1950, Berlin had another big success on Broadway, CALL ME MADAM, suggested by the life of the socialite ambassador Perle Mesta. The most significant hit of the show was written late in production, the charming duet "You're Just in Love."

But Berlin's personality was deteriorating. When another sister developed cancer and was dying, her son, Irving Berlin Kahn, came to see him. He asked, as her brother, if Irving could help with the medical bills.

Berlin's response was, "She's your mother. When you use up all your money, I'll help out. And don't call yourself Irving Berlin Kahn. Just use the initial."

His last Hollywood venture, the movie THERE'S NO BUSINESS LIKE SHOW BUSINESS, was a failure. Still Berlin was making more money from royalties than any other songwriter. His ASCAP payments for 1954, 1955 and 1956 were all over one hundred thousand dollars each year.

He slipped into five years of a major period of depression, malnutrition, and addiction to Nembutal. Berlin's temper became unbearable, especially toward his daughters. He lived in solitude on the upper floor of his Beekman house, usually eating alone. For a while he suffered from shingles, a painful nerve disorder, and only went out at night. But he had a coterie of people he called at all hours, including Harold Arlen, Harry Ruby from Camp Upton, and the writers Ed Jablonski and Stanley Green.

In 1961, at age seventy-three, one last opportunity appeared. He was approached by Lindsay and Crouse to write a musical called MR. PRESIDENT. He believed he could make a grand comeback. The show starred Nanette Fabray. The out-of-town previews were terrible without one lasting song. But Lindsay, Crouse, and Berlin had all become extremely difficult and refused to change anything.

The world he had known was vanishing. Hammerstein had died in 1960, and Cole Porter would die in 1964.

When Berlin was seventy-five, Arthur Freed persuaded him to work on a musical biography of his life, to be titled SAY IT WITH MUSIC. After six years of constant battles with the studio and repeated changes of script writers, filming was finally set to commence in 1969.

With the expectation of the film SAY IT WITH MUSIC being released and a tribute the *Ed Sullivan Show*

Irving Berlin, c. 1914. (Photofest.)

had put together for Berlin's eightieth birthday, he believed that his career was on the ascendancy. But the filming of SAY IT WITH MUSIC never did start and the project was cancelled. Berlin withdrew again into seclusion before 1970 as he had from 1957 to 62.

Around that time Alec Wilder and James Maher wrote the definitive anthology of music, *American Popular Song: The Great Innovators*. The material on Berlin was very positive. Even so, when Berlin read it he angrily rang them up. Berlin actually called them names and threatened them. By then, in the industry, Berlin had become associated with abusive phone calls.

Berlin received constant requests to use his music, which he regularly declined. George Abbott wanted to do a big show featuring Berlin's work and was turned down.

At age eighty-four, Berlin refused to attend a reunion of the survivors of THIS IS THE ARMY.

When his last sibling, Gussie, died in 1978, Berlin became the sole survivor of his family. He rarely spoke with anyone, even his wife. But those who did have the opportunity to speak with him said he was not in any way senile.

Berlin was especially heartbroken when his dearest friend, Harold Arlen, to whom he spoke on a daily basis, died in 1986. Their conversations were no longer about music. They would ask how each slept the night before. Once when Arlen asked, Berlin responded, "I slept well, but I dreamt that I didn't." He was also terribly saddened by the loss of another friend, Fred Astaire, the following year.

In the latter years of his life access was granted to only a few, primarily Ellin, with whom he would eat at 5 p.m. She dressed for dinner every night. He saw no other

MAJOR WORKS

SHOWS:

WATCH YOUR STEP **(1914)**
STOP! LOOK! LISTEN! **(1915)**
THE CENTURY GIRL **(1916)**
YIP, YIP, YAPHANK **(1918)**
ZIEGFELD FOLLIES **(1919)**
MUSIC BOX REVUE **(1921)**
MUSIC BOX REVUE **(1922)**
MUSIC BOX REVUE **(1923)**
MUSIC BOX REVUE **(1924)**
THE COCOANUTS **(1925)**
FACE THE MUSIC **(1932)**
AS THOUSANDS CHEER **(1933)**
LOUISIANA PURCHASE **(1940)**
THIS IS THE ARMY **(1942)**
ANNIE GET YOUR GUN **(1946)**
MISS LIBERTY **(1949)**
CALL ME MADAM **(1950)**
MR. PRESIDENT **(1962)**

COMPOSITIONS:

BERLIN WROTE MUSIC AND LYRICS FOR OVER 1,500 PIECES.

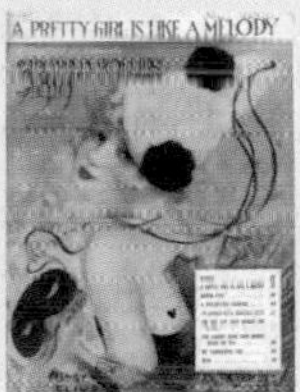

family members or grandchildren, all of whom were mostly driven away by his hostility. For his hundredth birthday ASCAP had created a giant celebration, but he refused to attend. ASCAP even wanted to show it to him in his apartment on closed circuit television. But he refused. Three months later, in 1988, at age eighty-five, Ellin died from a series of strokes. She left him over ten million dollars.

Once asked how she felt about marrying out of her class, Ellin said, "You're right. I married up."

Irving did not attend the funeral. In September 1989 he died quietly at home. The bulk of his estate was left to his three daughters with strict, very restrictive instructions concerning the use of his music. A huge number of songs had become top ten hits and a very large group reached number one.

He wrote the music and lyrics for 1,500 songs. He wrote our foremost popular songs about Christmas, Easter, and patriotism, and the song that is considered the anthem of all show business, "There's No Business Like Show Business."

Leonard Bernstein.
(Photofest.)

LEONARD BERNSTEIN

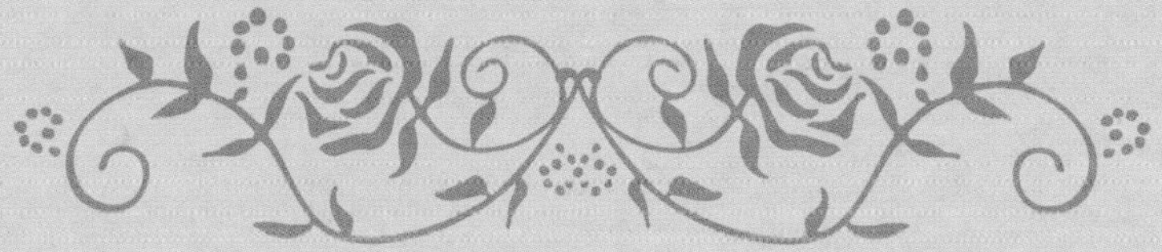

SAMUEL BERNSTEIN WAS BORN IN 1892 IN THE UKRAINE. His father was a rabbi who spent all his time studying and praying. He paid little attention to his family or the world around him. His mother, on the other hand, worked hard on the farm, while raising the family. As the story was told, his father was so religious that one day when Samuel's yarmulke (skullcap) fell off, his father gave him a severe beating.

One of the problems that Samuel faced in his youth was a common form of anti-Semitic persecution in tsarist Russia. Young Jews were kept in the army as draftees for many years. Like many others, sixteen-year-old Samuel deserted, and with money from relatives who had already emigrated to the United States, made his way out of eastern Europe in 1908. When he arrived at Ellis Island, his name was changed from Shmuel Josef to Samuel Joseph Bernstein.

When he arrived in the United States he worked twelve hours daily, six days a week for five dollars. He lived on the Lower East Side of New York, while he studied English at night. He attempted to get a job with the post office, but failed the spelling test.

His uncle Harry offered him a job in his barbershop, which would ultimately lead Sam into his lifetime career. He went from the barbershop to a job as a stock boy for a wholesaler. It was likely that Sam would have become successful in whatever direction fortune had led him. An aggressive and tough businessman, Sam eventually became the head of the largest beauty supply company in New England.

In 1917, Sam married Jennie Resnick. Sam was not particularly handsome, whereas Jennie was quite beautiful. In later years their children would write that they didn't believe that their parents loved each other. Jennie married to escape from the terrible life she was living as an impoverished young girl. Sam was on the rebound from an affair with a gentile whom he was forbidden to marry.

Their marriage was not good. Jennie left him after one year, came back, then left again two years later. Sam spent his time studying the Torah and operating his business. Jennie liked parties and going to the movies. Their interests seemed incompatible and they constantly fought.

In August 1918, Jennie gave birth to Louis. He was always called Leonard and his name was later legally changed to that. Shirley Anne was born in 1923, and their last child, Burton, was born in 1932. By then Sam was extremely successful running the Samuel Bernstein Hair Company.

Leonard grew up in Roxbury, Massachusetts. As a youth he was known for his amazing memory and at age nine began taking piano lessons. He was bright enough to be accepted into the prestigious Boston Latin School for grades seven through twelve. One of his classmates was Teddy White, who, as Theodore H. White, became a famous author. Even then Bernstein began thinking of music as a career. However, his father felt quite differently. Sam wanted Leonard to take over the business he had created. In later years when Sam was asked why he had resisted Leonard's efforts to study music, his wonderful response was, "How did I know he was going to become Leonard Bernstein?"

Following Lenny's wonderful bar mitzvah speech, Sam gave his son a new piano and a vacation on a cruise ship through the Panama Canal. Once on board, Lenny captivated the passengers by playing the piano all evening long.

At age fourteen he began studying with Helen Coates, who became a lifelong friend.

Bernstein's sister Shirley remembered that, as a child, she never went to bed without hearing her brother playing. His parents never gave him a curfew as to when he had to stop and go to sleep. At times Shirley would play with him, but not at his level. When she made a mistake, she said, he would hit her. Shirley absolutely adored him and felt he was more like a parent than Sam and Jennie. As the years went by her personal life was significantly affected by their relationship, because she compared every suitor to him, with all the others falling short.

Religion remained a significant factor in the family's life. Sam was very strict about sexuality. As a young woman Shirley always had to have her arms covered. Though his company sold cosmetics, privately he called the women who used his products "two-dollar whores." Whenever he saw lipstick on Shirley, he would wipe it off.

Sam's personal biases would cause him to miss out on a tremendous business opportunity. A young man, Charles Revson, came to ask Sam to invest in a new company making nail polish. It disgusted Sam so much that he threw him out of the office. Revson went on to create the giant Revlon Corporation.

Meanwhile, Lenny was growing up and successfully entering piano competitions. The personality he developed was not very pleasant. He became calculating and manipulative in his personal relationships. After graduating from the Boston Latin School he was admitted to Harvard and began seeking out influential people to mentor him. Leonard's first efforts were directed toward Jose Iturbi, the pianist and conductor, without success. After that failed, he turned his attention to Arthur Fiedler, to no avail.

In order to be able to obtain more piano lessons he earned money playing jazz piano. Sam was unwilling to subsidize this endeavor and did everything in his power to ensure that Lenny would go directly into his father's business rather than spend his life involved with music.

Bernstein's personality was captivating. He had a large circle of friends and seemed always to be on an emotional high. He seemed to feel that he was destined to be famous. His first girlfriend was Beatrice Gordon, whose aunt had a cottage near the Bernstein summerhouse in Sharon. She was only one of the many young women who constantly surrounded him.

He also dated Mildred Spiegel, who was two years older than Lenny. He could be found wandering around her house, lifting pot covers to see what was cooking for dinner and giving her mother giant bear hugs. Mildred claimed no one ever had the same effect on her as this wondrous young man.

In his effort to find a mentor Lenny had now turned his attention to Sergei Koussevitsky. He took Mildred to see Koussevitsky conduct the Boston Symphony Orchestra in the least expensive balcony seats, all that he could afford. At the end of the concert everyone was on their feet, loudly applauding. Mildred turned to see Lenny still seated and unresponsive. When she asked, "Why aren't you standing?" he responded, "I'm so jealous!"

The incident provides some insight into the extremely self-centered personality at the core of Leonard Bernstein.

How he became a Harvard student is of interest. He had told close friends he was going to attend the Curtis Institute in Philadelphia to study music. He said he had already had an interview and was certain he was accepted. No one can be certain whether that was true. If it was, there is the possibility his decision was overruled by his father. He later said his broad education at Harvard was the best thing for him. Obviously, at the time he thought differently. Nevertheless, while at Harvard, Bernstein spent most of his

Leonard Bernstein, c. 1960s.
(Photofest.)

time involved in music. Though he expended little effort on his other subjects, he did very well. He was generally recognized by the students around him as brilliant. There is absolute agreement among those who knew him that he was charming, outgoing, and gregarious, and that he possessed his father's penchant for speaking as an absolutely authoritative figure, even when he was wrong.

His piano technique improved remarkably, and his performances were receiving excellent reviews.

By 1937, he had become extremely enamored of the works of Aaron Copland. One night when he went to a theatre on Broadway, he found himself seated next to a strange looking man with glasses positioned low on his hook nose. It was Aaron Copland. By the end of the evening Bernstein had been invited to a party at Copland's apartment. They became intimate friends.

Copland found Lenny quite beautiful. Though Bernstein was only five feet eight inches tall, he seemed larger than life to those around him. He was the center of attention wherever he appeared and was absolutely committed to becoming "famous." He continually needed reassurance from Copland that he would achieve this goal.

Bernstein liked to think of himself in terms of Gershwin. As he developed, similiarties emerged. Critics would react harshly to their classical compositions and never adequately appreciate their genius for writing popular music. Both had great ambition and a constant desire to learn more.

When Gershwin died in the summer of 1937, Bernstein was working at a summer camp as a counselor, Camp Onota. Lenny had been assigned to play the piano as background for the Sunday lunch with the parents. So saddened by the news, he asked to be excused. The camp director insisted he play. So Lenny played a Gershwin prelude to a hushed crowd. It was at Camp Onota that he first met lyricist and writer Adolph Green, who would become a lifelong friend.

In attempting to identify when Bernstein's interest in conducting began, both Beatrice Gordon and Mildred Spiegel confirmed that he applied to be the assistant conductor of the Harvard Symphony. Possibly it started after he met Dimitri Mitropoulos.

Mitropoulos had become a star in Athens when he conducted, without a score or baton, while playing the piano. Koussevitsky had seen him and invited him to guest-conduct in Boston. Mitropoulos was twenty years older than Bernstein.

Bernstein had heard that Mitropoulos would be at a tea in his honor at Harvard. Lenny would later say that his mother made the wrong turn when driving him back to Harvard and he accidentally found himself in front of the house where the party was held. Others related that he had intentionally planned to crash the party. Bernstein was infatuated with Mitropoulos when they first met. He played the piano there and was invited by Mitropoulos to come see him at the Boston Symphony rehearsal. Friends stated that they then had an affair. When Mitropoulos left Boston he gave Lenny his picture and told him, "Do not sleep in too soft a bed." In 1938, they spent a week together in Minneapolis.

Bernstein graduated cum laude from Harvard in 1939. His father wanted him to enter the business, but it was agreed that he could spend the summer in New York City. He rented an apartment with Adolph Green, who was performing at the Village Vanguard with his comedy group, The Revuers. Bernstein looked for work unsuccessfully while trying to compose at night. He sought a fellowship at Juilliard for the fall, but that fell through.

Lenny decided his best opportunity would come through utilizing his "friendship" with Mitropoulos. He had not heard from him, however, since their liaison in Minneapolis. Mitropoulos encouraged him to go to Curtis to study conducting, promising to help him later gain the position of assistant conductor of the Minneapolis Symphony. So Lenny auditioned for Fritz Reiner at Curtis. Although Bernstein did not think it went well, Reiner must have seen something in him, and he was accepted into the program.

At Curtis he studied piano as well as conducting and became very close to another pianist, Annette Elkanova. They frequently practiced together and became emotionally involved. Elkanova said that Lenny had asked her to marry him. One of the descriptions she later gave of them was that they "smoked like fiends." Bernstein had been a heavy smoker since he started at the age of fourteen.

His time at Curtis was punctuated by some difficulty in getting along with other students. He had come later to Curtis than the others, having already graduated from Harvard. Younger students did not fully appreciate his genius and questioned the extent of his photographic memory. When in classes for sight-reading, they thought he was lying about never seeing the pieces before, when in fact he hadn't. They also claimed his behavior was that of one who thought he was a "bigshot."

During that time he had another girlfriend, Shirley Gabis. She said he was "incredibly vibrant." His personality was seductive. But soon she realized that he never allowed his true self to be revealed.

Bernstein cultivated relationships based on what they might provide for him. As an example, Mitropoulos had promised there would be a position for him in Minneapolis. As a result, Lenny planned to leave Curtis after one year. But, in April 1940, Mitropoulos sent a telegram saying there would be no job. Bernstein was devastated and told a friend that he had foresaken heterosexual behavior in expectation of that promise. And, in another letter to a friend he seemed heartbroken when he no longer received responses from Mitropoulos, realizing that "the thing" was over.

In March 1940, Bernstein heard that Koussevitsky, who became Bernstein's idol, was opening a music school at Tanglewood, the new summer home of the Boston

Symphony. He applied, auditioned, and was accepted. Tanglewood, a 200-acre estate, was gorgeous.

Koussevitsky was a phenomenon, a tough taskmaster, and an inspiration to the conducting students. Apocryphally, once at a rehearsal a musician kept making the same mistake and Koussevitsky shouted, "Ged (sic) out! You're fired!" As he left the musician shouted back to him, "Nuts to you!" to which Koussevitsky replied, "It's too late to apologize."

Three hundred students arrived in July. They had spectacular teachers like Koussevitsky, Copland, Hindemith, and Piatigorsky. Tuition was one hundred dollars, plus twelve to fifteen dollars per week for lodging.

Koussevitsky led the normal large classes for conducting. He also had an advanced class of just five students, including Bernstein. As a result, Lenny got the opportunity to conduct the student orchestra and made a great impression on everyone. He was magnetic and the center of attention. Koussevitsky became like a second father to him and was soon calling him "Lenny" and then "Lenyushka."

Koussevitsky wanted Bernstein to come to Boston to study with him that fall. Bernstein's mind was jumping ahead. He had made another conquest and he was certain Koussevitsky would name him his assistant conductor. He would drop out of Curtis. However, he wanted to be certain not to offend Reiner when he told him that. He wrote Reiner a letter telling him of his great successes at Tanglewood and attributed it all to what he had learned from Reiner.

Reiner was furious when he learned that Bernstein did not intend to return. He contacted Koussevitsky and told him the Bernstein scholarship was for two years and he was expected to complete his term. Immediately, Koussevitsky sent Bernstein as telegram telling him to go back to Curtis. Once again, Lenny was devastated, feeling he had lost both of them as advocates. Bernstein returned to Curtis, but letters to his friends and former teacher Helen Coates indicated his "mood of despair." He was frequently "ill" and taking to his bed.

He spent the year mostly waiting to return in the summer to Tanglewood. He received a conducting diploma from Curtis, but unlike his friend Annette Elkanova, he did not receive one for piano studies.

Once again Lenny came close to marriage. This time it was to Kiki Speyer, the daughter of the Boston Symphony English horn player, Louis Speyer. She was extremely beautiful and worked at Tanglewood. They were always together. They had definitely decided to marry, even to the point of selecting names for future children. Kiki said there was heavy necking and petting, but never intercourse, "because when I was a girl you did not have sexual intercourse before marriage."

Kiki characterized him as being "difficult to be with." He seemed to want to make her feel inadequate. But he could get away with it because his personality was so overwhelming. She said he was "secretive" and never completely honest. Kiki thought that most people did not completely understand this negative aspect to his personality. She said when they went out, even when they started as a couple, they would be joined by more of Lenny's friends. He would ignore her as he was the center of all attention. If she didn't stay close by to him, he would vanish and apologize the next day for his behavior.

Kiki had opinions about Lenny's family dynamics. She did not like Sam Bernstein, but thought Lenny's mother Jenny was wonderful. She saw Lenny's sister Shirley as being much like him. Shirley never married, blaming her single status on the horrible relationship she saw between her parents.

The first time Kiki went to meet the family she shared a bedroom with Shirley in their home. When she awoke in the morning she saw Lenny in bed with Shirley. They said, "We've been cuddling for years." Kiki was angry and confused. Shirley said they were always affectionate and those who mentioned incest were insane.

At dinner Lenny's elderly grandmother started to scream, "What does the shiksa want?" when Kiki asked for milk at a nondairy dinner. Things got worse when Kiki lit a cigarette from religious candles.

The following day, the Bernsteins left Kiki at home with Lenny's grandmother when the rest of the family went to make a condolence call. It was the Sabbath. So when Kiki opened the refrigerator door and the light went on, his grandmother slammed it shut. Then Kiki lit the stove to make coffee and his grandmother turned it off. She went to the piano to play and the lid was slammed down. Uncertain what she could do, Kiki just left and went back to Tanglewood.

On Sunday, Bernstein and Koussevitsky shared the conducting, with the younger man getting more applause than his mentor. Lenny continuously tried to mold himself in Koussevitsky's image. Koussevitsky wanted Bernstein to succeed him. He loved both Lenny and Kiki and wanted them to become engaged and announce their plans at Tanglewood. In preparation for the expected marriage, Kiki had been going to temple, presumably to convert to Judaism.

The day before the announcement, Bernstein suddenly appeared with a young musician. He told Kiki that the two men had had sex the night before and that Lenny was "in love with him." Kiki was astounded and asked what was going to happen to them. Bernstein told Kiki she would have to tell Koussevitsky not to make the announcement.

This was not the first such incident. Earlier that summer, a young female student came back to her room and found Bernstein in her bed with Aaron Copland. Her mother told her to say nothing.

The winter of 1941 brought on another problem. Bernstein wanted to stay out of the war. After Bernstein received a draft notice, Koussevitsky tried to help him by writing letters requesting a deferment. Bernstein said he was torn between the desire to promote his career and the need to fight

Marcia Henderson and Leonard Bernstein rehearsing for PETER PAN, c. 1950. (Photofest.)

for a cause, especially since Nazi persecution of Jews was already well known. As it turned out, he was deferred on the basis of asthma. It allowed him to claim over the years that he was "desperately disappointed" about not being able to serve.

Tanglewood closed for the duration of the war. Lenny got a job with the Harms Publishing firm doing arrangements for jazz composers. He was mostly bored by the experience. A few minor conducting opportunities kept him busy. He also began some serious composing.

Bernstein's *Sonata for Clarinet and Piano* was accepted for publication, and he wrote his first symphony, *Jeremiah*. Toward the end of 1942, Lenny heard of a competition Koussevitsky was holding with a deadline of December 31. Lenny worked nonstop for three days to complete the orchestration. He rushed by train to get it submitted by 10 p.m. It was a terrible disappointment to find that Koussevitsky did not like the piece. Bernstein did not win the prize.

However, one event would convert Bernstein from unknown to famous, overnight. The mover and shaker of the international conductors' network was Arthur Judson. Everyone knew that to get prime conducting positions it was necessary to give Arthur Judson 20 percent under the table. Years before, Koussevitsky's wife had bought the position for him. Now the position of conductor of the New York Philharmonic was available. Artur Rodzinski, a Judson client, was named to start in September 1943. Someone—no one knows who—had made a financial arrangement with Judson for Leonard Bernstein to be named his assistant. Koussevitsky had told Bernstein to ask for twelve thousand dollars for the year. Bernstein agreed to take only one hundred twenty-five dollars a week with no written contract. Bernstein didn't care. He was moving into the right circles.

Rodzinski gave Bernstein a huge amount of work to accomplish. He had to audition all potential guest artists and review compositions that were being considered for performance.

Artur Rodzinski's contract allowed him to take a two-week vacation after each full month of concerts. Bruno Walter had been hired as the guest conductor during those intervals. It was during such a period in November 1943 that Bernstein had several important career events occur. Opera singer Jennie Tourel was making her debut at Town Hall. Her program would include Bernstein's "I Hate Music." That same week arrangements were finalized for Fritz Reiner to conduct Bernstein's *Jeremiah* with the Pittsburgh Symphony early in 1944. Besides all that his *Sonata for Clarinet and Piano* was being recorded. To top it all off, he had been asked to write a new ballet for the Ballet Theatre. As a result, Lenny invited his family to come to New York City.

On Thursday of that week, Lenny took his family to hear Walter conduct. On Saturday, they went to hear Tourel perform his music. After her concert, a grand party celebrated the success of Bernstein's composition.

On Sunday morning, Lenny liked to say, he was awakened, bleary-eyed, by a phone call. It advised him that Bruno Walter was sick and that Bernstein would have to conduct the New York Philharmonic that afternoon. Others say that Walter got sick on Friday and had told the management, who notified Bernstein on Friday or Saturday at the latest. In either case there was no chance for a rehearsal. The orchestra had already been prepared by Walter. From his sickbed Bruno spent one hour helping to prepare Bernstein.

Bernstein later said that before the concert he went to a pharmacy and obtained both a phenobarbitol tablet and a Benzedrine, not being certain whether he need to be calmed down or energized. While standing in the wings, he heard the announcement of the replacement followed by groans. It angered him so that he discarded both pills before he strode out to the podium. By the time the concert ended the orchestra itself was overwhelmed and stood in unison to cheer him. His energy was dynamic.

Koussevitsky sent him a congratulatory telegram. Arthur Judson gave him an actual contract for a series of performances. Bernstein had conquered the symphonic world.

The media response was just as spectacular as he expected it to be. Numerous interviews were requested. At them, Bernstein learned quickly to portray an image of what he believed the world wanted to see. He made himself into the "youthful and enthusiastic boy next door" rather than the complicated personality that was the real Leonard Bernstein.

Some who knew him felt the emotions he expressed while conducting, as well as those he portrayed in his personal relationships, were not sincere.

Bernstein became the media focus of attention. Besides his music they wanted to know more about him, personally. His brilliance, even in activities as straightforward as crossword puzzles, amazed those around him. He drank and smoked excessively, believing that those abuses would never affect him. Benzadrine and black coffee kept him functioning without sleep. One person said of him that his life was sustained only by applause.

Previous assistant conductors at the New York Philharmonic had never conducted a single concert. In the 1943–1944 season Bernstein would conduct eleven times. The following year he would be listed as a guest conductor. Judson booked him in Chicago, Detroit, Rochester, Cincinnati, San Francisco, and Montreal. His *Jeremiah Symphony*, heard in Pittsburgh and New York, won the New York City Music Circle Award in 1944. All of this and he was only twenty-six years old.

His next project was to be a ballet created with Jerome Robbins for the Ballet Theatre (later known as the American Ballet Theatre). The subject was three sailors on shore leave, with a girl. Koussevitsky was not pleased that Lenny was "abandoning high art" for commercialism. FANCY FREE was a huge success with twenty curtain calls. It earned much more money for him than his symphonic works.

Rodzinski was not happy either with Bernstein's success or his lack of attention to his duties as assistant conductor. To avoid the friction, Judson began sending Bernstein from one major guest appearance to another. Wherever Lenny went there were record breaking crowds including 10,000 at Lewisohn Stadium, then on to Montreal, followed by the Hollywood Bowl for an all-Gershwin program with Oscar Levant. Wherever he went his sister Shirley was by his side, caring for his every need.

The years 1944 and 1945 would be busy ones for Bernstein. Besides participating in multiple philanthropic and political activities for FDR, he expanded FANCY FREE into the show ON THE TOWN with the help of his friends Betty Comden and Adolph Green. Robbins once again choreographed and George Abbott directed. It previewed in Boston, opened in New York and ran for 462 performances. For the five weeks of work he had earned one hundred thousand dollars.

Writers referred to him as a genius. Fan clubs were started and he was being called the Sinatra of Symphony. Marriage offers came in droves. All the while he traveled 50,000 miles conducting eighty-nine concerts. To the consternation of other conductors he appeared in *Harper's Bazaar* and gossip columns.

Helen Coates, an early teacher of his, assumed Shirley's role. She became his girl Friday. She moved to New York and took care of his every business need. She could handle money and she could say "No," two things that Lenny could not do.

Despite all his success, he had yet to be appointed conductor of a major symphony. So, when Fiorello La Guardia established a performance facility (eventually called City Center), an opportunity presented itself to Bernstein. He was offered the unpaid position of conductor, and he accepted it. The musicians got paid only five hundred dollars for a twenty-four week season providing low-price concerts for the masses.

Once in that role, Bernstein fought to get the orchestra members' salaries increased. He also established a custom by which any orchestra member could come talk to him privately about any problem, even personal.

As Bernstein came into the limelight, the reviewers began to examine his performance with greater scrutiny. No one was more critical of his wild flailing behavior on the podium than Virgil Thomson He felt Bernstein was just a showman who cared more for his career than for the music.

Oscar Levant once said of him, "I think a lot of Bernstein—but not as much as he does."

Bernstein continued as a guest conductor in many cities. There were always rumors that he would get a major appointment. The Boston Symphony passed on him when Koussevitsky retired. Bernstein attributed it to anti-Semitism, but the rejection was more likely due to the fact that he was an American. The orchestras seemed to be looking for an established, staid European. Bernstein was young, a Broadway composer, and a jazz enthusiast who once had been photographed dancing on tables in Tanglewood. His life did not fit the image they were seeking.

When Bernstein was given a seven-week residence in Pittsburgh, he became certain he was being groomed to replace Fritz Reiner. But nothing came of it. One by one every major orchestra passed him over. In 1947, when he was not yet thirty, he told a friend that he was depressed at having failed to accomplish anything when he was already "so old."

An opportunity presented itself in Rochester. José Iturbi was leaving as the conductor of the upstate New York city's philharmonic orchestra, and Bernstein had been their guest conductor many times, even once taking them on tour. He believed he had the inside track. He befriended Bettina Bachmann, the daughter of an older couple who were both members of the orchestra's board and visited their home continuously. The board chose Erich Leinsdorf. Bernstein claimed it resulted from a rumor that he was homosexual. Leinsdorf's autobiography, however, said that Judson had promoted him over Bernstein.

Many years later, his friend Bettina Bachmann's granddaughter was a college student at a school where Bernstein was invited to speak. After his presentation, she introduced herself, saying that when she was a child, Bernstein had come to her home many times in Rochester to visit her grandparents. He loudly responded, "No, you are wrong. I never was in Rochester."

With his fame his personal life was changing. His close associates said he had become extremely promiscuous, primarily with young men. Mitropoulos expressed to him that he felt that Bernstein was being very indiscreet in his behavior.

Bernstein remained with the New York Symphony because he was not getting the appointments he had hoped for. He was able to persuade some of the great international soloists to make appearances, although his budget was very small. Among them was the pianist Claudio Arrau. On one occasion, Arrau brought a guest to the concert, Felicia Montealegre y Cohn. Felicia was the daughter of a Costa Rican Catholic and an American, Roy Cohn (no relation to the infamous aide of Senator McCarthy). Cohn's grandfather was the rabbi who had founded Temple Emanuel in San Francisco. Cohn was a wealthy businessman in Chile.

Felicia had decided at an early age to live in the United States and was able to obtain immediate citizenship as her father was an American. The night she met Bernstein, Felicia decided she would someday marry him.

Felicia was extremely beautiful and elegant. In Bernstein's presence, she became quiet and retiring because he was so outspoken. Her speech pattern was lovely with a continental accent. Like the composer, she smoked heavily, but did not drink at all.

The beginning of their relationship was very difficult for Montealegre. Bernstein would appear to be serious and then vanish to conduct somewhere in the world with barely a good-bye.

In the fall of 1946, there was actually some talk of Bernstein being in a film about the life of Franz Liszt. Montealegre was making significant headway as an actor, getting roles in New York. In late 1946, she went to Hollywood with Bernstein for a month. On New Year's Eve their engagement was announced. The wedding was set for June 1947. Meanwhile his career was flourishing—a whirlwind of conducting activity culminated in a European tour. He also conducted the Palestine Symphony Orchestra in Tel Aviv. The response to this young, handsome Jewish American was overwhelming. He was surrounded by bobby-soxers.

When Bernstein returned for his opening Tanglewood concert in July he never contacted Felicia, not even to invite her to the concert. He seemed to ignore her completely and by the end of the summer the engagement was off.

Bernstein was in a poor frame of mind. He had been denied several major orchestras and resigned from his position with the New York Symphony. Kiki Speyer, who was now married, said that in his distressed state he asked her to get divorced and marry him. Bernstein's behavior grew erratic and he received some negative reviews for his conducting.

In 1950, he composed his symphony, *The Age Of Anxiety*, based on writing by W.H. Auden, who disliked Bernstein. Mixed reviews ensued.

Meanwhile, Felicia was advancing rapidly in her television career. She was also living with a young actor, Richard Hart. Bernstein's sister Shirley believed Felicia was still in love with Bernstein. He had been conducting in Europe, and when he returned with Shirley, Felicia met them at the dock. The three went out to dinner together. During the meal, Felicia received a phone call telling her that Hart had been hospitalized with a heart attack. Hart died that night at the age of thirty-six. Lenny commiserated with Felicia, and the couple reconciled.

In 1951, Bernstein and Koussevitsky were touring the country when Koussevitsky became ill with a chronic blood disorder. When they returned to Boston, Koussevitsky was hospitalized and got progressively worse. Bernstein visited him early on June 4, 1951. Koussevitsky had a stroke that night, when Bernstein was not there, and he died. Subsequently, Bernstein would say, "Koussevitsky died in my arms."

Bernstein proposed to Felicia again in the summer of 1951. He was still, however, tormented by the nature of his sexuality.

Bernstein's tie to Koussevitsky had been so strong that he altered one of Koussevitsky's white suits to wear at his September wedding. He even wore Koussevitsky's shirt, tie, socks, and shoes. For the remainder of Bernstein's life he would wear Koussevitsy's cuff links and kiss them before each performance.

In preparation for the upcoming marriage, Montealegre, who had been born Catholic, converted to Judaism. Religion always remained a source of conflict for both families.

After the wedding they went to Cuernavaca and stayed for several months while he began work on TROUBLE IN TAHITI, which was part of an evening of one-acts called ALL IN ONE. That show only ran for forty-nine performances. Felicia became pregnant and delivered Jamie in September 1952.

Bernstein spent that summer at Tanglewood. He had assumed Koussevitsky's role. In New York the couple moved into an apartment on the Upper West Side. Helen Coates, who was still managing all his affairs, moved into the building as well. Helen said that Felicia understood that she came second in his life; music always came first.

Felicia, however, offered something very important to her husband. She was his voice of moderation. She filled his life with class and style and encouraged gentler behavior.

Bernstein soon joined his friends, Comden and Green, in writing the musical version of MY SISTER EILEEN. The 1953 show, WONDERFUL TOWN, starring Rosalind Russell, was a hit. However, Bernstein was reproached because none of the songs had a popular appeal outside the musical itself.

Lenny went to Hollywood and wrote the score for ON THE WATERFRONT. He lost the Oscar to Dimitri Tiomkin for THE HIGH AND THE MIGHTY. Bernstein never wrote another film score.

In 1954, he decided he would write another musical, this time with Lillian Hellman doing the book. It was based on Voltaire's *Candide*. They were having so much difficulty with the writing that they lost their lyricist, John Latouche. Bernstein and Hellman decided to do the lyrics themselves. That did not work. So they called in a young poet, Richard Wilbur. Eventually, the entire project was shelved.

Interest turned in a different direction. Bernstein started to work with Arthur Laurents on WEST SIDE STORY.

After some time passed, Bernstein went back to CANDIDE. It finally opened in 1956 to fairly good reviews. The final production was not as Hellman would have liked it. Its punch was pulled for fear of political repercussions. The show ran for only seventy-three performances. It did have two great Bernstein pieces, the show's Overture and "Make Our Garden Grow."

Many years later, in 1973, Robert Kalfin of the Chelsea Theatre Center in Brooklyn persuaded director Harold Prince that CANDIDE could be revived in a new framework. They dropped the political overtones and made it into an "antic romp." Some lyrics were added by Stephen Sondheim and the book was rewritten by Hugh Wheeler, who had done A LITTLE NIGHT MUSIC. It was a grand success, moving to

Broadway, where it ran for 714 performances. Subsequently, it was revived in 1982 at the New York City Opera and again in 1988 by the Scottish Opera, this time in concert version. Bernstein believed it was his defining work in the theatre.

Though WEST SIDE STORY came to the stage later than CANDIDE, its origin went back to 1949 with Jerome Robbins. By the time interest in the show resurfaced eight years later, Arthur Laurents had written the book and Sondheim was hired to write the lyrics. Though he saw himself as both a composer and lyricist, Sondheim took the more limited assignment at the suggestion of Oscar Hammerstein, his mentor.

The show had very little appeal for investors. Almost everyone turned it down, certain that it would lose money. Hal Prince decided to take on the project as co-producer. Jerome Robbins, the show's director and choreographer, became its dominant force. It is generally felt that WEST SIDE STORY's success is as much due to Robbins as to Bernstein. It received critical acclaim, but achieved only a moderate level of financial success. Its great financial success came from the 1961 film, which received ten Academy Awards.

At last Bernstein was about to achieve his primary goal, which had been denied him so many times: to be named the conductor of a major orchestra. In 1957–1958 he was named co-conductor, with Mitropoulos, of the New York Philharmonic. He became sole conductor in 1958 and remained for ten more years. The choice of Bernstein had been unexpected as he had not even been asked to guest-conduct that orchestra for the previous eight years. However, most of the famous conductors were aging. Bernstein was only thirty-nine.

How this all came to be started with a story in the *New York Times*. The article stated that the New York Philharmonic was losing its position among the great orchestras of the world due to corruption in its management under Arthur Judson. He had held the position for decades. Distressed by what the orchestra had fallen to, the rattled Board decided on new, sweeping changes and chose Bernstein. He was young, energetic, and popular with the public.

Sono Osato, Leonard Bernstein and Mayor LaGuardia, 1945. (Photofest.)

Immediately Bernstein developed new ideas and programs. He appeared on the Ford Foundation's television show, *Omnibus*, explaining classical music to the masses. He was an astounding teacher. The presentations were so special and popular that they won Emmy awards. With great appeal, Bernstein was bringing music to ordinary citizens.

Bernstein's entire life seemed to have become much more wonderful. A second child, Alexander, was born in 1955. The household was bristling with constant visitors like Lena Horne, Harry Belafonte, Betty Comden, and Adolph Green. Helen Coates was there constantly to manage his career. Bernstein had reached the pinnacle of his success. He was sought everywhere in the world, and conducted the Israeli Philharmonic for the grand opening of the Mann Auditorium in Tel Aviv.

In his teaching, he had an amazing rapport with children. With that in mind his next adventure was not surprising. He became the centerpiece of a completely revitalized program, never to be forgotten, called the *Young People's Concerts*. Through it, he taught children to love the classics. For fourteen years he would mesmerize his audience. Through it, he reached live audiences of over three thousand, as well as the massive television audience. It was seen in twenty-nine countries, and received every major award for educational television. His performances were humorous, appealing to children and parents alike.

A decision by another conductor thrust Bernstein even further into the limelight. In 1959, the State Department scheduled Fritz Reiner to tour Russia with the Chicago Symphony. At the last moment Reiner cancelled the tour. The State Department asked Bernstein to take the New York Philharmonic. The tour was a gigantic success for Bernstein. The audience was enthralled wherever he went. He frequently appeared with the most famous Russian idols of the classical music world.

Wherever he went, Bernstein would make a dashing entrance, in the image of his mentor Koussevitsky, with a cape draped over his shoulders. His popularity grew beyond belief. The Philharmonic attendance rose to 98 percent, greater than it had been when Toscanini conducted. Bernstein's contract was extended to seven years. All this success was not just due to his conducting talent, but also his personal magnetism. However, with that, more outrageous behavior began to surface. It became so bad that once he was evicted from a hotel. Playwright and director Arthur Laurents described him as an "enormous-

Leonard Bernstein and Maximilian Schell, 1982. (Photofest.)

ly intelligent child." Nevertheless he had a constant entourage of those who loved him and believed his friendship was a gift.

As an educator, he had taken his art to the masses. But from the mid-sixties on, numerous critical complaints about his conducting style were lobbed against him. For his own part he expressed the need to return to composing, while having difficulty finding something worthwhile to follow WEST SIDE STORY.

Bernstein began getting depressed starting in 1963. John Kennedy's assassination had a significant effect on him. Besides that his elderly father had grown ill. Bernstein began having anxiety about his own aging.

He and Felicia were living in grand style. Felicia explored painting and rented a studio. She had become a close friend of the artist, Jane Wilson, and studied with her. Felicia was now less involved in acting and more focused on living the life of a wife of a famous conductor. Daniel Schwartz, who taught painting to the wives of many wealthy men, became her teacher as well. Schwartz once asked her why so many beautiful women were married to wealthy men who were homosexuals. She made light of that, remarking that her husband "was so handsome and talented" that she had been swept up by his enthusiasm and charm.

In the social world they now occupied, it was necessary to maintain one's success. Once fame was lost it was very easy to be dropped from the most-favored list. It's no wonder that Bernstein once wrote "to have is to be." Everything seemed to depend on what one had accumulated. Bernstein had everything. He went nowhere without his personal assistant, his chauffeur, and his valet.

Bernstein's friend, Roger Baldwin, founder of the ACLU, said that Bernstein was constantly distressed that, as a composer, he had not achieved the fame of Copland or Gershwin. Others said of him that he felt so insecure in his ability to produce high-quality compositions that he constantly found excuses not to compose.

In 1964, he took a full year's sabbatical from conducting for the express purpose of writing for Broadway. After he spent six months with his friends, Comden and Green, on a musical based on THE SKIN OF OUR TEETH, the project was suddenly, without explanation, abandoned. The same thing occurred in a separate project with Zero Mostel, based on a Brecht play. No reason was given for stopping the work on either. Obviously Bernstein was having difficulty completing a production.

During that same year Marc Blitzstein, a mentor of Bernstein, suffered a tragic end. He was on vacation in

Martinique, and as he had done in the past, sought out sailors at a waterfront bar. He was robbed and beaten and died the following day. Blitzstein was in the middle of three compositions. Bernstein, who was the executor of the Blitzstein musical estate, announced he would complete one of Blitzstein's works. He had the opportunity to do any of the three, but was able to do none.

Different theories have appeared to explain Bernstein's difficulty, ranging from insecurity within himself to a rejection of the change in the classical musical world. He did not like the move toward atonality and found he could not connect with it.

Bernstein, more and more, associated his professional life with that of Gustave Mahler. Like Bernstein, Mahler had been a very successful conductor. When he turned toward composition he found himself generally rejected. Bernstein felt that much the same thing had happened to him. Bernstein saw magic in Mahler's compositions and devoted himself to promoting them.

Bernstein's tenure at the New York Philharmonic had been so special that he was considered in a class with Toscanini. He held his position there longer than any previous conductor and performed more concerts than any other. In 1966, he announced that he would not renew his contract when it ended in 1969. That announcement only served to make him more of an icon.

After he left his post at the Philharmonic, he eschewed the opportunity to compose in favor of maintaining a hectic schedule of guest-conducting throughout the world. He was always claiming that there were a number of projects in the offing.

In 1971, he created quite a stir when his MASS was first seen at the Kennedy Center in Washington, D.C. There were complaints about it being sacrilegious, and demonstrations followed. However, most of the reviews were negative, but not on the basis of religion. They complained about the quality of the composition.

Aside from the professional changes in his life, there were other problems. Much has been written about the relationship between Bernstein and Felicia usually focused on how he was the center of all attention. It was generally believed that Felicia was the force attempting to keep him stabilized and in line, apologizing for him and frequently forced to be the butt of his humor. He could be extremely warm and personable or very cruel, especially to Felicia. In the eyes of all who wrote or spoke about her, she was a woman of great quality.

She felt stress as a result of his sexuality. As the years passed, there was no secret about Bernstein's pull back to homosexual activity. Many stories were told about times that he made advances on unsuspecting males.

With their growing affluence, the Bernsteins moved into the very posh apartment building, the Dakota. Other residents included Lauren Bacall, Polly Bergen, and John Lennon and Yoko Ono. By this point, Bernstein had met Tom Cothran, a young man from Indiana who was studying at Harvard. Sometime in 1976, according to a diary written by Helen Coates, Felicia found her husband at home in bed with Cothran. Angered, she threatened that she would create a scandal if Cothran did not leave New York. In October 1976, Felicia announced their separation. By that time she had already been diagnosed with breast cancer.

Bernstein announced he was moving into an apartment with "the love of his life." By April 1977, the Cothran affair was over and Bernstein was back home at the Dakota. In trying to understand Bernstein's relationship to both Felicia and Cothran, the noted psychiatrist Karen Horney said that individuals with such massive egos are so demanding of admiration, reassurance, and support that they become impossible to live with.

By July 1977, Felicia was diagnosed with lung cancer. She died at age fifty-six in June of the following year.

After Felicia's death, Bernstein sank into a deep depression, smoking and drinking even more. Friends like Copland and Sondheim believed he was slowly committing suicide.

Nevertheless, in the midst of his messy affair with Cothran and Felicia's illnesses, Bernstein continued to compose. He worked on a new musical, 1600 PENNSYLVANIA AVENUE, with Alan Jay Lerner. The Coca-Cola Company, the primary investor, had little experience in running such an operation. Arthur Laurents, realizing how bad the production was, quit. It wasn't long before the director, Frank Corsaro was fired. Bernstein and Lerner, on the other hand, had no understanding of how bad the show was, and refused to allow changes. It closed immediately after opening.

By 1980, Bernstein's public behavior was getting even worse. He appeared at an event at the Waldorf Astoria in a tuxedo so ill-fitting that all the buttons had split open and he was seen with a bare belly. At the event he loudly and drunklenly complained that all present had failed to mark the seventeenth anniversary of the Kennedy assassination.

During a concert in 1981, he left the podium in the middle of a piece coughing and did not return for five minutes.

His style of dress changed from what had been very chic during all the years with Felicia to denim jackets, bell bottom jeans, Indian bracelets, and Mickey Mouse watches. Some friends believed he was on cocaine.

Orchestra members said he had memory problems and that he was missing beat patterns in performances. He appeared to have become immune to embarrassment. With friends and associates he had become more sarcastic and cruel.

There was another side to Bernstein other than the brilliant conductor and the larger-than-life image he projected when not performing. He was also the consummate businessman. The entire operation controlling Bernstein's money was called Amberson Enterprises. It was managed

MAJOR WORKS

SHOWS:

ON THE TOWN **(1944)**
PETER PAN **(1950)**
WONDERFUL TOWN **(1953)**
CANDIDE **(1956)**
WEST SIDE STORY **(1957)**
1600 PENNSYLVANIA AVENUE **(1976)**

COMPOSITIONS:

BERNSTEIN WROTE THE MUSIC FOR 221 SONGS. FOR A FEW OF THEM HE WROTE THE LYRICS AS WELL.

by Harry Kraut from 1972 onward. He had come from Harvard with a background in both business and music. Initially, he worked in management for the Boston Symphony, where he had a reputation of great efficiency.

When he started working for Bernstein, Amberson was valued at about fifty-five million dollars. During his tenure it was estimated to have doubled. Kraut was known for his toughness in negotiations. A typical maneuver would be to notify the management of an orchestra, from which they had not yet received a check, that Bernstein was feeling under the weather, and possibly not able to perform. The check would be delivered immediately.

Kraut could be the butt of Bernstein's anger, or just as easily, the recipient of his generosity. Bernstein knew no matter how menial the request, Kraut could be depended upon to carry it out. There was a complete entourage of people ready to care for all of Bernstein's needs, no matter how demeaning.

Bernstein's depressive state now centered around his understanding that he had lost the opportunity to fulfill the enormous plans and desires he had as a young man. He knew he would never achieve the greatness he sought as a composer.

He had hoped to write an autobiography. Some friends were nervous about what he might include, since he was considering titling it *Blue Ink*. The book never materialized.

Bernstein's last opera was A QUIET PLACE. It was conceived to be a sequel to TROUBLE IN TAHITI. The reviews were universally poor. Bernstein, however, continued to believe that it was quite good.

In December 1989, CANDIDE was being performed in London. A recording was planned as well. Suddenly everyone in the cast and Bernstein, himself, came down with high fevers and the flu. Even though sick, Bernstein flew to Berlin to conduct a midnight performance of Beethoven's Ninth Symphony on December 23 at the torn-down Berlin Wall. It was to coincide with the first day that Germans could cross the border without visas. He considered it to be one of the most important events in his entire life.

In late 1989, Bernstein was diagnosed with a form of lung cancer. Though he was weakened, he insisted on continuing to conduct when he could. Radiation therapy was attempted, though its success rate with this particular illness was known to be poor. The treatment weakened him even more.

By 1990, Tom Cothran, with whom he had re-established a relationship, though they were not living together, was dying of cancer. It was never revealed whether it was HIV-related. Bernstein could tell from his own downward course that he was dying as well.

His schedule called for a Pacific tour, followed by Tanglewood, and a series of concerts in Europe. Since he was getting progressively sicker, the Asian trip had to be shortened. They decreased the number of scheduled concerts for him in Tanglewood. At summer's end, the plan was to make a very brief trip to Europe with the student orchestra.

Those who saw him then could hardly believe he continued to work. At times he could barely ascend to the podium. It was at Tanglewood that he performed for the last time, unable to complete his final concert. All further concerts were cancelled, though he continued to discuss the possibility of getting back to composing, and even conducting.

Leonard Bernstein had a heart attack and died on October 14, 1990. Up until the very end he never lost his enthusiasm for life and his plans for the future.

Some writers believed that Bernstein's feeling that he failed to reach the goals he wanted was due to his inability to separate his Broadway successes from his efforts at serious classical music. Crossing that barrier had been difficult for other composers as well. Only Gershwin had been able, to a modest extent, to find success in the transition.

Though in the latter years of his life his behavior was exasperating to everyone, even his closest friends, he possessed brilliance, charm, and exuberance that were admired by those around him. His death, though expected, was a shock to the world and to those who loved him. Up until the very end, with all his overwhelming medical problems, he never stopped smoking or drinking.

This was a man of great complexity. Not unlike some others who achieve great fame and position, he was larger than life. His demands for attention, love, and affection were massive. His behavior, in the earlier years somewhat controlled by Felicia, could be absolutely outrageous. Beyond it all, he brought to the world of music his own personal magic.

Hoagy Carmichael, c. 1947. (Photofest.)

HOAGY CARMICHAEL

ON WEDNESDAY, NOVEMBER 22, 1899, A MALE CHILD WAS born into the Carmichael family of Bloomington, Indiana. He was named Hoagland, which had been the last name of a railroad surveyor who was a family friend.

Hoagland's father, Howard, whose nickname was Cyclone, ran a horse-drawn taxi service for a while. He had learned about horses while serving in the United States Army during the Spanish-American War. As a horseman, Cyclone had made his way to the regimental championships. He married Lida Robison in May 1899, less than nine months before Hoagland was born.

Lida, only five feet tall, was an extremely accomplished pianist. After Hoagland was born, when silent movies began to be shown in Bloomington, she was the theatre's principal piano player. She also played frequently at fraternity and sorority parties.

Cyclone's taxi service vanished with the advent of automobiles, and he was generally unsuccessful at gaining other employment. He would frequently be out of town seeking work for weeks at a time. His spur of the moment decisions were probably the source of his nickname. In later writing, Hoagland would characterize his family as "poor white trash."

The family moved to Indianapolis in 1904, hoping to find better opportunities. Lida gave birth to a second child, Georgia, before the Carmichaels returned to Bloomington in 1906, where Hoagland was happiest. He loved small-town life, and his closest friends were from "Bucktown," Bloomington's black community.

With his father away much of the time, young Hoagy frequently sat next to his mother while she played at the movie house or the parties.

But Hoagy's happiness in Bloomington soon ended again. His father's lack of success and wanderlust led to a decision to go west, where there were new opportunities. The family moved to a remote area of Montana's Bitterroot Valley. There, Cyclone strung electric wires as a lineman. It was a dismal time for Hoagy. But, once again Howard Carmichael was unsuccessful. They returned to Bloomington where Lida resumed her role as the major breadwinner for the family.

With Lida's encouragement, Hoagy developed a desire to sing. Lida began to teach him, first to perform for the family and then for the public.

As the story goes, Indiana University in Bloomington installed a new bell tower that played the school's theme song. Hoagy, stranded one day at home due to inclement weather, listened and picked it out on the piano. That began a powerful musical relationship between him and his mother, who was quite capable of teaching him. Though he was still very young, he would play the theme as loudly as possible as the university's affluent fraternity members would pass by his house. He wanted them to look favorably upon his very meager existence.

Although playing the piano was considered an acceptable form of home entertainment, it was looked down upon as a profession for a man. Hoagy learned ragtime, the popular music of the time. It could be heard at the campus hangout played by Hubie Hanna with Hank Wells on the fiddle.

Two more sisters were soon born: Martha Claire in 1912, and Joanne three years later. Cyclone decided it was time to move to Indianapolis in 1916. Hoagy was enrolled in the Manual Training High School. If that was not bad enough, they moved into a rundown house across the street from the Central Indiana Hospital for the Insane. Hoagy spent a year in Indianapolis, which he described in his autobiography as "miserable." In 1917, he quit the school and began doing heavy manual labor for the remaining months there.

When he was not working, he and his cousin would go to hear ragtime music at what he called "fleshpots." There he met many African-American musicians. Among them was Reg Duvalle, who taught Hoagy a great deal about ragtime and improvising.

An incident occurred that would give him the incentive to vow forever that he would live a life better than his family's shabby hand-to-mouth existence. His baby sister Joanne was the apple of everyone's eye. In Carmichael's autobiography, he described a time she was crying uncontrollably. He went to her, kissed her, and said, "I love you." She kissed him back, said, "I wove you," and never had another tantrum. Even if apocryphal it indicated how much she meant to him.

At age three, Joanne suddenly became ill and in a few days she died. The diagnosis listed was diptheria. She had more likely fallen victim to the influenza epidemic of 1918, which killed so many children. Carmichael later wrote, "My sister Joanne . . . the victim of poverty. We couldn't afford a good doctor. . . . I vowed I would never be broke again in my lifetime. . . . It broke my heart that I didn't have the knowledge or the wherewithal to help her. It broke my dad's heart too."

The Great War was on. Hoagy actively wanted to serve and volunteered for the military. To his good fortune, however, the day after he was accepted for military service the Armistice was signed. He was never exposed to the war and was quickly discharged.

On his return Hoagy got a job to play at the Kappa Alpha Phi fraternity house, which represented a new beginning for him. His real goal was to become an insider at the Book Nook, a local establishment that started out as a hangout for high school students, before becoming the place to be for the college students. "The Nook" had an upright piano which only could be played with the approval of the regular customers. It was special for Hoagy because the most important young jazz musicians frequented the joint. Hoagy eventually got invited to join in with the others playing sax, trumpet, and drums. His playing was characterized as "enthusiastic," if not particularly good. Some of those who played there became quite successful in New York over the next decade.

Colleges had become the center for hot music. Every school had a band.

Carmichael's description of blacks and whites joyfully sharing music together did not reflect America. The KKK was on the upswing. Lynchings were at a record high, and the returning soldiers itched for a fight against the perceived threat of Communists, Jews, Blacks, and Catholics. Indiana was especially fertile ground for the KKK.

Hoagy remained a Republican all his life. Some of his associates have recalled his subtle anti-Semitic comments. Though a northern state, Indiana's southernmost areas had patterns not atypical of the South.

The music of the day, not surprisingly, was decried by parents, priests, pastors, and teachers. Jazz and the blues were buzzwords for sensuality. Indiana had become a dry state, so forbidden music went right along with prohibited alcohol to those just reaching the age of twenty to twenty-one. Young people who did not drink or smoke were considered uninteresting.

Hoagy had re-entered high school in Bloomington and was now a twenty-year-old senior, older than most of his classmates. At the end of the year he found himself two credits short of what was needed for graduation. He was living with his grandparents, as his parents had remained in Indianapolis. So Hoagy went back to Indianapolis to get Lida to tutor him and help him complete the subjects he needed. Once he passed his final exams, he registered as a freshman at Indiana University. Carmichael pledged to the Beta Theta chapter of the Kappa Sigma fraternity and felt he was on his way.

It made him feel particularly good to advance along with his new much-better-off fraternity brothers. With his mother's encouragement, he directed his education toward law. But even more important to Hoagy, he was hearing great music at a club called the Book Nook, and then at another place, the Friar's Inn. There he had heard for the first time a new young cornetist, Bix Beiderbecke.

An offer came up to go to Palm Beach to play the piano for "high society," to swim in the ocean and to meet "rich girls . . . plenty hot looking." Hoagy was faced with a critical decision. He knew that if he gave up his legal studies it would be terribly disappointing to his parents and grandparents. It was a pressure-packed decision he had to resolve.

Records at Indiana University show that he withdrew in January 1923 without completing a semester and went to Palm Beach. Other factors may have influenced his decision. The records also showed that he was delinquent in his payments to the school and as a result his grades had been withheld in June 1922. The bursar had granted an extension. It seems highly likely that those facts played a crucial part in his decision to go.

Hoagy found in Palm Beach all the glitz that had been promised. But the organizer of the trip had been more interested in women than in work. Worse than that, there was no work to be found. Completely disillusioned, Hoagy was back at the fraternity house and his law studies by the fall. He got occasional jobs playing the piano. With more and more famous musicians coming through town, Hoagy began thinking that music should be his ultimate direction. While he was in Palm Beach he had the occasion to hear Irving Berlin play the piano. Playing was known not to be Berlin's forte. Berlin played so poorly that Hoagy thought perhaps he should consider a career in professional music after all.

Carmichael's college education began in the early twenties and dragged on. He was often in and out of studies, usually unable to pay his tuition or student loans. He completed his schooling in 1926. There never seemed to be much urgency in reaching that goal. His time at Indiana University was mostly characterized by his intense interest in learning and playing the hot music of the day. Two people there had a lasting effect on his life. Both were younger than Hoagy.

One was William Ernest "Monk" Moenkhaus.

Monk, as he usually was known, had a father who was a professor of physiology at Indiana University. At age twelve, Monk was studying in Germany where his father had sent him. When the war broke out, Monk was moved to neutral Switzerland. By 1917, his father brought him back to Bloomington High School. Though he was only fifteen years old, his studies included piano and cello composition at the university. He was obviously brilliant.

Monk was tall, skinny, usually unshaven, and sloppily dressed. He had very large hands and long fingers. He was singularly homely.

Monk had spent his early years in Switzerland surrounded by a world immensely different from anything Hoagy had ever known. His days were spent in the Voltaire Café surrounded by the new Dada anarchic thinkers of Europe. Monk brought that world with him to Bloomington and converted the Book Nook into a space of philosophical ideas, and even some nonsense. Monk became the center of this new surrealistic atmosphere. The new hot jazz was part of this world. And Monk became a part of the music as well, even though his formal studies were in the classics.

He became a regular contributor to Indiana University's magazine, the *Vagabond*. His pseudonym was Wolfgang Beethoven Bunkhaus. The magazine published his verse, plays, and "treatises on nonsensical arcane subjects." Moenkhaus became a central focus of Hoagy Carmichael's life.

Monk appeared to show no inclination to graduate. It was not until 1929 when he was twenty-seven years old that he finally obtained a Bachelor of Music with high distinction. Hoagy was already gone, but they remained in touch. Monk went on to the Detroit Conservatory. There he taught and also wrote a symphony. Though no longer attending Indiana University, he still submitted plays and poems to the Indiana University *Vagabond*.

Less than two years later Monk suffered a ruptured stomach ulcer, and died shortly thereafter at the age of twenty-eight. Those who knew him said he had the talent for great genius in music, and also possessed great writing talent. He is buried, like Hoagy, in Rose Hill Cemetery in Bloomington.

It was during a summer between semesters at Indiana University that Hoagy first came across the other influential person during his college years. Carmichael had taken a summer job as a piano player. He heard about a great new group playing at the Friar's Inn. A young man from Davenport, Iowa, played the cornet in a way that he had never heard. A few years later, Hoagy got a phone call from the same person who had previously misled and persuaded him to quit school and go to Palm Beach to find work. This time, "his friend" was part of a new band that was looking for work. Hoagy, though wary, assured them that he could help with bookings at the university. They called themselves the Wolverine Band of Chicago. The band included the cornetist, Bix Beiderbecke, who Hoagy had previously heard at the Friar's Inn. Beiderbecke had a sound that Hoagy could hardly believe, and was also remarkable on the piano. Once Beiderbecke came to Bloomington, Hoagy was constantly at his side learning, even attempting to learn the cornet. Beiderbecke became his idol and teacher. Monk and Beiderbecke also connected well with each other, even though Beiderbecke was shy and retiring and Monk was an outspoken philosopher.

They both encouraged Hoagy to begin composing and in the spring of 1924, shortly after the Wolverines left Bloomington, the group held a recording session. Beiderbecke told the producer that they would be doing a song that a young kid in Bloomington had written. But that kid, who was Carmichael, did not know how to read or write music, so there were no sheets.

"Title?"

"Hoagy wanted to call it 'Free Wheeling.' But it's sort of a shuffle. So we call it 'Riverboat Shuffle.'"

It would be Hoagy Carmichael's first recorded song. But Hoagy was still uncertain what route he should take. Should he lean to the law and play music for fun? But music had a strong pull. Hoagy began to believe that there were songs waiting for him in the piano. All he had to do was sit in front of the keys and the music would pour out of him.

By 1925, Hoagy was ready to record. He had written two more pieces, "Washboard Blues" and "Boneyard Shuffle." "Boneyard" was a sequel to "Riverboat," but much better. "Washboard" was considered to be twenty-two seconds too short for the standard record. At the recording session, the band decided to go out for a cigarette while Hoagy wrote a solo portion for himself to be added to it. When they returned it was completed. "Washboard" turned out to be one of the most significant songs of that era. It was considered to be more important than "Tea for Two," "Five Foot Two," "I Never Knew," "If You Knew Susie," "Manhattan," "Yes Sir, That's My Baby" or "Remember."

The Collegians, Hoagy's group, completed a series of performances in May 1926 at the Indiana Theatre. He soon headed south to Florida, which, at the time, was the exciting place to be. Cyclone, Lida and the girls headed south also. Hoagy's first love, Kathryn Moore, married the trumpeter from the Collegians.

When the group achieved only modest success, Hoagy decided to put jazz behind him. He was going to practice law in Florida. He had decided to drive there after a slight left turn to New York City, where he was already somewhat known, thanks to the seven years he played in Indiana, and the composing he had done. After a few jam sessions he went to see the well-known music business wheeler-dealer, Irving Mills, who had been the publisher of "Riverboat Shuffle." After some negotiations Mills agreed to publish "Washboard." But as he so often did, he insisted on having his name added as co-lyricist, to keep some of the royalties for himself. Mills made Hoagy an offer to stay in New York and write more music. Hoagy declined, saying he'd think about it. But Hoagy had made up his mind to practice law in Florida.

Carmichael applied to take the Florida bar examination and, while waiting two months for the results, took a job with a collection agency. Hoagy soon took a job playing the drums for ten days on a cruise to Havana. He claimed that, upon his return, he heard that the famous Red Nichols had made a recording of his "Washboard Blues," and that this development led him to decide to choose music over law.

But there is more to the story. Records of the Florida Board of Examiners state that on June 26, Hoagland Howard Carmichael failed the bar exam.

Hoagy returned to Bloomington and moved back into the fraternity house. He began playing dates in the area. A new local band invited him to come join them in a jam session. Bud Dant, who was to become a lifelong friend, was only eighteen and in the group. He remembered that Hoagy played around with a melody during the session for about fifteen minutes. He said the music was what ultimately became Carmichael's greatest standard, "Stardust."

Carmichael fostered the friendship with Dant for his own personal advantage. Dant understood, yet it annoyed him tremendously. Carmichael still needed to learn a lot more about playing, reading music, and arranging. Dant had all those talents. Carmichael arranged for Dant and several others to go to New York for a job that he had booked for them. When they arrived there was no job, and it took them a month to find other work in order to pay for tickets to get back. It wasn't really Carmichael's fault. He had intended to go with them, until he passed the Indiana bar exam and started working for a law firm.

There are many stories about when "Stardust" was written. Carmichael says he worked it out in the Book Nook. Ernie Pyle, of World War II fame and a graduate of Indiana University, said Hoagy wrote it on the Pyle family piano. It was first recorded with Bix Beiderbecke and both Dorsey Brothers, because they were all members of Paul Whiteman's band, which happened to be in town. The first recording was not well arranged and by all accounts pretty ragged. But today, the song stands with the greatest works of Kern, Arlen, Rodgers, and others.

Immediately after that Carmichael was asked to come to Chicago to record "Washboard Blues" with the Whiteman orchestra. This time they wanted Hoagy to sing. He was so nervous about the prospect that he tried to

Left to right: Harold Russell and Hoagy Carmichael on the set of THE BEST YEARS OF OUR LIVES, 1946. (Photofest.)

get someone else to take his place. So Bing Crosby was asked to stand by should Hoagy not be able to pull it off. The recording was successfully achieved after two takes.

Hoagy began studying how to read and arrange music better. Despite all his success, he was having difficulty getting work. He was playing by ear and bands wanted musicians who could sight-read. Carmichael began calling Dant again for help. But Dant, fed up with Hoagy after having already been treated so badly by him before, rejected his calls, until Hoagy finally persuaded him to come to Bloomington to start a band. He promised Dant there would be lots of engagements and Hoagy would have him live at the fraternity house. But after Dant arrived he was told he couldn't stay unless he enrolled at Indiana University. Once again he had been misled. This time Hoagy and Dant's mother persuaded Dant to enroll at the university. In the long run the education turned out to be beneficial for Dant.

They did put together a successful group and made some recordings. At the end of 1928, the very fashionable Columbia Club booked them. The exclusive enclave for prominent and wealthy Republicans prohibited the band from playing anything too jazzy. After an unpleasant confrontation with a guest, Charles Lindbergh, they broke into hot jazz and were soon let go.

Around that same time, the law firm he was working for told him that they thought he would do better in a music career and fired him. With nothing going particularly well, Carmichael decided to try Hollywood. Through his contacts he met celebrities but no work was forthcoming. Beiderbecke was out there, but things were not going well for him either. He was sick, smoking and drinking too much, and not playing very well. By the fall, when the Whiteman band train left Los Angeles to go east, Hoagy stowed away onboard. He was back in New York.

He sought out Irving Mills, who immediately signed him to a contract, booking him for three dates. But Hoagy was not content. He had seen stockbrokers make huge sums of money while successful musicians struggled. Hoagy contacted a banking friend in Indiana and asked if he could get a job in the financial community. He believed his legal training and intelligence would make him a good candidate. He was also annoyed because he realize that his contract with Mills was completed tilted in Mills's favor. But when the Crash of October 1929 came, Hoagy, like the rest of society, lost all hope. Fortunately, he was able to get a low-level job with the Strauss firm.

A friend suggested he write a song about the South. He told Hoagy, "Nobody ever lost money writing songs about the South." It led Carmichael to write "Georgia on My Mind," even though he had never lived in the region. Talented people were actually recording his songs. Louis Armstrong's records of Carmichael's songs became classics. At one recording session, Hoagy saw Bix, who seemed to be regaining his strength. But shortly thereafter he heard that Bix was sick again. Hoagy went to visit him and found him even worse. Like Monk, Bix Beiderbecke died at the age of twenty-eight, in August 1930. Hoagy had lost the two people who had been musical and intellectual inspirations to him during his formative years. Now he was on his own.

Hoagy had heard about a wonderful clarinetist from New Orleans who was now in New York. He went to hear him play. His name was Sidney Arodin. When they befriended each other, Arodin asked Carmichael to work on a song that Arodin had started and together they wrote "Lazy River."

Though the economic environment was terrible, Hoagy was earning a good living through his music, while partying and having a very active social life. At the same time, Hoagy was significantly developing his talent as a lyricist.

Hoagy had been introduced to Johnny Mercer, who some consider America's greatest lyricist. Mercer later said he loved working with Carmichael, but didn't produce his best work in that collaboration, because he felt somewhat intimidated by the man from Indiana. Mercer believed that Hoagy had much greater lyrical prowess than any of the other composers he had worked with. Carmichael recalled that the two men took twenty minutes to write "Lazybones." Mercer's recollection was that it dragged on for months, with Carmichael waiting for Mercer to come up with a suitable lyric. Today some suggest that the song has racist overtones. But the historian Barbara Tuchman disagrees. She says that it must be viewed in terms of the time it was written. Not all would agree, based on a history of a subtle racism in Mercer's philosophy of life.

Things were going well for Carmichael as he went off on a six-week tour of Europe. Germany was in the beginning of upheaval and he was banned from performing "Lazybones" there. Interestingly the ban was not based on racism. Rather, the Nazi regime claimed that the song encouraged "idleness." Nevertheless it sold 15,000 copies of sheet music every day.

Mercer and Carmichael did not get along very well. Carmichael subsequently took the blame, because he admittedly considered himself the more important half of the collaboration.

In 1931, Mitchell Parish rewrote the lyrics for "Stardust." His lyrics for that beautiful melody are the ones we know today. And at the same time Carmichael began working on a project to compose something of a more classical nature for one of Whiteman's *Experiments in Modern Music*, much as Gershwin had done with *Rhapsody in Blue*. But, to his great disappointment, the performance of it was cancelled in the last minute.

Helen Meinardi, the daughter of a Presbyterian minister and a firebrand in her own right, had met Carmichael once in his time at Indiana University. She was quite beautiful, a very accomplished writer, and a highly successful model. She had a wealthy boyfriend who said he would like to meet Carmichael, which she assured him that she could arrange. When she made the attempt, Hoagy made a play for her affections. Advising him that she was already taken, she told Hoagy that she did have a beautiful younger sister, Ruth. Hoagy was thirty-six and Ruth was twenty-two, but the confirmed bachelor fell head over heels in love. In 1936, they were married in a grand ceremony with parties attended by the most famous celebrities. Warner Brothers came forth with a contract and the two of them and a pet monkey were off to Hollywood.

It seemed glamorous. He would be paid one thousand dollars a week and he didn't think that was too much. If the studio could afford four hundred thousand dollars a year for Crosby, they could afford fifty-two thousand dollars for the fellow who wrote "Stardust" and "Georgia on My Mind." Hoagy would soon find he was just a cog in a machine, instructed to write scripts and music and have no other input. There were seven studios fighting for power. They made and destroyed individuals at their whim. Because of that, Ruth was an important asset in meeting the right people, as she was much more outgoing than her husband. Hoagy, a staunch Republican, was disinterested in the left-wing causes espoused by so many of his associates. He preferred to stay at home and be at his piano. Politically, above all, he hated Franklin Delano Roosevelt, with a passion.

In the same year that he married and went to Hollywood, he also tasted Broadway success. He wrote "Little Old Lady" for a Broadway revue called THE SHOW IS ON, starring Bert Lahr and Bea Lillie. It became the show's hit song.

Carmichael was coming into considerable fame and affluence. He socialized with the highest society in California. He seemed to have lost his taste for intellectual thought and imagination that had been brought out in him by Monk and Bix. He was now in a world of drinking, golf, and tennis, a constant play world. His mind was not being nourished.

The following year, he wrote a song for the 1938 Paramount movie, ROMANCE IN THE DARK, "The Nearness of You," which became a big popular hit.

Soon Hoagy met Frank Loesser, a young struggling lyricist many found difficult to work with. Ultimately they wrote three hits together: "Heart and Soul," "Small Fry," and "Two Sleepy People," the last of which Hoagy recorded with Ella Logan.

Ruth gave birth to their first child, Hoagy Bix, in 1938.

Sometime during 1937 a friend sent Carmichael a poem. It came out of a magazine published many years earlier and was signed "J. B." Hoagy liked it and filed it away. It was titled "Except Sometimes." In 1939, he looked at it again and began changing some of the lines.

While most composers viewed music as the starting point, Carmichael focused constantly on lyrics. This predilection became one of his most important contributions to the musical literature. Alec Wilder, perhaps the most important of all music critics, expressed in his book *American Popular Song* that "I Get Along Without You Very Well" was unlike any other song he ever knew.

But a problem arose. The lyrics to this song were based on the poem by the unknown J. B., written fifteen years earlier. Walter Winchell pleaded with his readers to try to help him find the original author. Numerous people claimed ownership of the poem. After much legwork by two retired staff members of the magazine in which the poem was originally published, it was traced back to Ms. Jane Brown Thompson, a widow born in Indiana in 1867 and living in Philadelphia. Contracts were signed and the song was introduced by Dick Powell on January 19, 1939. On Wednesday, January 18, Jane Brown Thompson, ill for some time, passed away, twenty-four hours before the song was first heard.

We'll never know whether this was all true or if it had just been made up by the Hollywood publicity machine. A newspaper column found subsequently stated that the song was introduced on December 26, 1938, by the Guy Lombardo Orchestra. The fact that the date found on the contract was January 6, 1939, only confuses the picture further.

Another anecdote from the same period is definitely true. In March 1939, the Tommy Dorsey Orchestra performed at a giant concert in Indianapolis, featuring Hoagy Carmichael singing and playing his own music. Hoagy insisted that his mother, Lida, be added to the program because she had been his inspiration during his early years in Indiana. She played Scott Joplin's "Maple Leaf Rag" with such skill and enthusiasm that reviewers claimed she stole the show from Carmichael and Dorsey.

Around that time, interest grew around making a new movie or Broadway show about the life of Bix Beiderbecke. Burgess Meredith was being suggested as the possible lead. But the project was still to be many years off.

Work began in 1940 on a new production for Broadway, THREE AFTER THREE. The Shuberts were producing this show, to be written by Carmichael and Mercer. It started on the road in major East Coast cities, and was not well received. By the time it reached Broadway the title was changed to WALK WITH MUSIC. It lasted for only fifty-five performances. Carmichael's disappointment was palpable. It was not sufficient to have successes in Hollywood, where a triumph would be characterized as, for instance, a "Crosby movie." Whereas on Broadway a success was called a Kern, Porter, or Gershwin hit. The

Hoagy Carmichael, c. 1946. (Photofest.)

respect for the creator was quite different there.

With the outbreak of World War II, Californians actually thought that it might not be long before the Japanese attacked their state. In a panic, the multimillionaire Philip Wrigley put his luxurious Holmby Hills home up for sale. Hoagy, who had never owned a home in California, always renting, came up with an offer and bought the place. The property encompassed three acres and their neighbors included Crosby, Lana Turner, Judy Garland, Jennifer Jones, Alan Ladd, Humphrey Bogart, and Art Linkletter. They were now among the truly rich.

By this time the Carmichaels had their second child, Randy. Eva Ford had become their permanent housekeeper and remained continuously thereafter in that role. Much biographical information about Carmichael after his death, especially about the family dynamic, would be revealed by her.

Carmichael soon wrote "Skylark" with Johnny Mercer. Though Hoagy frequently worked on the words to his songs along with his lyricists, he generally left Mercer alone.

Ruth became close friends with producer-director Howard Hawks's wife, Slim, and introduced the two husbands to each other. Through this meeting, the idea surfaced to have Hoagy play the role of Cricket, the piano player, in a movie version of Hemingway's TO HAVE AND HAVE NOT. Carmichael immediately took to the laconic character and created a persona for himself as a movie actor. Lauren Bacall was to sing Carmichael's "Baltimore Oriole" in the movie, but found it too difficult. The filmmakers wanted her to sing his "How Little We Know." Due to her continued difficulty with the music, the producers decided to dub in another voice, choosing a very young Andy Williams. At the last minute, an insistent Carmichael taught Bacall the song and she wound up singing it herself in the film.

Carmichael was being asked more and more to sing his own songs, so he began recording with greater frequency. Hoagy Bix recounted that his father would be asked at every party to sing "Stardust," and that each rendition was slightly different from the last.

Hoagy's politics left him ill at ease at Hollywood parties. Once, Bogart chastised him for his right-wing philosophy. The two almost came to blows, before Ruth split them apart.

During the war, he wrote a number of patriotic songs, but none was very successful.

In 1944, Hoagy got his first regular radio show, Sunday night's *Tonight At Hoagy's*. It continued for two years when he switched over to NBC. Interestingly, considerable letters of complaint were written about the quality of his singing. It was of course his style, rather than a great voice, that made him appealing.

In 1945, he played a cab driver alongside George Raft in JOHNNY ANGEL. The following year, he was given the role of the piano-playing proprietor of a local bar in THE BEST YEARS OF OUR LIVES. His character taught Harold Russell's how to play "Chopsticks" with his prostheses. Similarly, he played the bandleader who helps Dana Andrews's blind pianist in 1947's NIGHT SONG.

In every picture he was in he somehow managed to play or sing one of his songs. He was a philosopher in 1946's CANYON PASSAGE and sang "Ole Buttermilk Sky," which remained on the Hit Parade for five months. It lost the Academy Award to Mercer and Warren's "On the Atchison, Topeka and the Santa Fe."

In later interviews his sons recalled him sitting for hours and hours working at an upright piano in his office, though there was a grand piano in the living room. When finished, he would pick himself up and go straight out to a golf course or a party.

In 1948, he decided to perform a series of one-man concerts throughout England and the response was wonderful. With so much success his attention turned to another challenge. He decided to try the classical medium

Hoagy Carmichael, c. 1953.
(Photofest.)

and wrote a tone poem called *Brown Country in Autumn*, played by the Indianapolis Symphony and in New York. It was panned by the critics, as had been Gershwin's and Ellington's first efforts in that direction. But where those two composers had rejected that criticism and continued their efforts, Hoagy gave up in that endeavor. He had been set back both on Broadway and in the field of classical music, mostly because his training was insufficient for either arena. But giving up seemed to come easily, as Ruth kept them constantly busy in a social whirl. Once again the idea for doing something about the life story of his dear friend Bix Beiderbecke surfaced.

In the new plans Hoagy would have a role as Smoke, the piano-playing friend to Bix Beiderbecke in YOUNG MAN WITH A HORN. Beiderbecke's character, to be played by John Garfield, was named Rick Martin. When that fell through, the role moved to James Stewart, then Dane Clark, Ronald Reagan, and, finally, the young Kirk Douglas.

As in the book, Beiderbecke's character was supposed to die of alcoholism. But Jack Warner thought that ending would be too much of a downer. So in the movie, Rick recovers and "trumpets away into the sunset" with his heart-of-gold girlfriend in the person of Doris Day.

An opportunity arose for Carmichael to play London's Palladium for a two-week engagement. He went there without Ruth. He sat on an empty stage with a hat on the back of his head, a cigarette hanging out the side of his mouth, and lazily played to the absolute joy of his audience. While he was there he fell madly in love with twenty-two-year-old Jean Simmons. She was beautiful and had a blossoming career in England. Some believed she saw Hoagy as her source of access to Hollywood. Though everyone in the community always assumed the Carmichaels had Hollywood's most perfect marriage, it soon became obvious that he was having an affair.

Carmichael began working on a project with Johnny Mercer for a movie starring Betty Hutton. It was to tell the story of Mack Sennett and Mabel Normand. The movie never got produced and its major song was put aside. At the same time, Frank Capra had decided he wanted to leave Paramount Pictures. The studio and he reached an agreement by which he could leave if he did one more film. It was to be HERE COMES THE GROOM with Bing Crosby and Jane Wyman. A friend of Capra mentioned having heard a song that had been put aside in the Hutton movie and that it was great. So Carmichael pulled it out and it was used in the movie. It was "In The Cool, Cool, Cool of the Evening" and it won the Academy Award.

By the 1950s, television was expanding rapidly. NBC broadcast the most successful programs, including *Your Show of Shows with Sid Caesar*. The network was looking for a summer replacement and decided on Hoagy Carmichael. The show turned out to be very stressful for him, and he wound up doing it for just one season. The record is unclear as to whether the change of hosts was his decision or NBC's. Eddie Albert took over the show in 1953.

It wasn't as if Carmichael wasn't busy. He kept acting in some movies and writing for others. But he didn't realize at the time that "In the Cool, Cool, Cool of the Evening" would be the last hit he would ever have. At the same time his role as a saloon pianist in 1955's TIMBERJACK would be his last in the movies. Like other composers of his time, Carmichael was being replaced by a new wave of artists and styles.

Articles in gossip magazines reported that his marriage was falling apart and that Carmichael was spending more time with alcohol than the piano. In September of 1955 Ruth filed for divorce. It wasn't just the philandering. Hoagy had become so stingy with her about all matters financial that she actually had to ask for money if she wanted to go out for lunch. Ruth was suffering from terrible insomnia, taking more and more drugs to sleep. She was charging thousands of dollars at I. Magnin's department store perhaps as a way of getting back at her husband.

When the divorce was finalized, Ruth married the much older Dr. Vern Mason, who had been supplying her with sleeping pills. When he died in 1965, she had no more source for the drugs and went rapidly downhill. At that point her children described her situation as "pathetic."

The Carmichael house was sold and she was given 30 percent of Hoagy's income, the equivalent today of about seven thousand five hundred dollars a month.

When they had been together, Ruth possessed all of the social skills and made all of the right contacts for Hoagy. But beyond that she had little balance in her life. So when there was an unexpected change in her life, it sent her over the edge, psychologically.

Hoagy began buying property and homes in Palm Springs. But his career was falling apart. His long-standing contract with Decca came to an end in 1956.

A small company, World Pacific Records, hired him to record albums for them, without any great success. He kept on writing, but his songs were unpublished. With no positive results forthcoming in music he accepted the role of a cook and handyman who would occasionally sing a song in a new television series, *Laramie*. The show debuted the same week as *Bonanza* did.

Hoagy's mother had grown old and sickly, so he purchased a house for her and his sisters to live in near his apartment in Los Angeles. On the day he signed the *Laramie* contract, his mother died at the age of eighty-one.

But Hoagy posed a problem to the television show. He was constantly pressuring the producers and writers to give him larger parts and play his music. Probably out of annoyance, at the end of the first season he was dropped.

1960 brought him a new success. Ray Charles record-

MAJOR WORKS

SHOWS:
THE SHOW IS ON (1936)
WALK WITH MUSIC (1940)

COMPOSITIONS
CARMICHAEL WROTE 298 SONGS WITH MULTIPLE LYRICISTS.

ed "Georgia On My Mind." It won two Grammy Awards and in 1979 Georgia adopted it as the official state song.

Carmichael did try once again in the 1960s to compose a classical piece about the life of Johnny Appleseed. There were several presentations of the twenty-minute orchestral suite, but it was not considered very good.

Hoagy's sister Martha died of an overdose, considered a suicide, in 1961. She had been severely depressed after her husband died. Carmichael had lost many people close to him around that time, including the pianist Buddy Cole, with whom he had a deep relationship.

He had no financial problems as the combined annual royalties from "Stardust," "Skylark," "Georgia on My Mind," and "Heart and Soul" brought him over three hundred thousand dollars.

All through the 1960s, he made guest appearances on television. He also became an exceptionally fine golfer, appearing regularly in pro-am competitions.

From the time of his divorce there were many women. A minor actress, Wanda McKay, became his permanent date. Her real name was Dorothy Ellen Quackenbush. They married in 1977 and his nickname for her was Dottie Quack. Their relationship was more one of companionship than passion.

Though receiving recognition for his past work, he was discontented. Carmichael wanted to be performing. At the drop of a hat, in strange locations, he would sit at a piano and play. While in his company, his sons were embarrassed by that. It was not that he wasn't great. They were embarrassed by his absolute need for attention.

After Dr. Mason's death, Ruth looked haggard, was hostile and remote from friends, and eventually committed suicide with a picture of Mason propped up next to her. Hoagy, himself, was in a terrible psychological state. He had been rejected so many times that he was withdrawing. All efforts by his sons to keep him active fell on deaf ears. Even things that they could readily arrange for him, such as teaching master classes on composing at UCLA, were rejected out of hand.

In the late 1970s, his disillusionment reached its peak. He was out to dinner with friends at a popular New York restaurant where a trio was playing. They recognized him and invited Hoagy to join in, playing and singing. The room remained noisy with no one paying any attention to him. Halfway through the song he got up and walked away, saying, "Well if they don't care, I'll be damned if I'm gonna perform for 'em."

All of Carmichael's friends were dying. He was frequently seen in public drinking excessively. All the while, his sons constantly sought his affection, feeling that they were always second in line to his music.

His health and especially his eyesight began deteriorating, leaving him unable to attend his seventy-fifth birthday party. However, he was able to be present for a giant eightieth birthday celebration at Carnegie Hall.

Using the stories of his early life with Monk and Beiderbecke, the Mark Taper Forum mounted a production about Hoagy, Bix, and Wolfgang Beethoven Bunkhaus in 1981. It subsequently moved to England and was the basis for an album titled *In Hoagland*, which received significant praise.

His last public appearance was on CBS in 1981, where he was interviewed by country star Crystal Gayle, who also sang his music.

By Christmas of 1981, he was diagnosed with prostate cancer. Hoagy, Dottie, and his two sons all had dinner together on December 26. The next morning, Hoagy collapsed, was rushed to the hospital, and died at 10:22 a.m. at the age of eighty-two.

With no formal training, Hoagy Carmichael had written some of the greatest songs in the repertoire of American popular music.

At the funeral, the Indiana University chancellor, among others, spoke. He recounted a story of once swimming in a pool in Lagos, Nigeria. As he was looking up into a beautiful sky, he told a young Nigerian pool attendant that a friend of his had once written a song about such a beautiful sky. He assumed the young boy had probably never heard of that song. With that the man began to sing, without missing a single lyric, "Ole Buttermilk Sky."

Left to right: Betty Comden, Adolph Green. (Photofest)

BETTY COMDEN & ADOLPH GREEN

BASYA COHEN WAS BORN IN BROOKLYN ON MAY 3, 1917, TO Rebecca and Leo Cohen. Apparently she was not the most beautiful of newborns, based upon the information provided to her by her ninety-eight-year-old spinster aunt, years later. Aunt Rose told her that her father and grandfather, on seeing her at birth, though they truly loved her, said she would have to marry a Rothschild, as they could never find a dowry large enough to entice a husband.

During her childhood, Basya was constantly tormented by her "friends," who called her Bahssie. It sounded much like the cow in the ads of that era, Bossie.

At age five, with the approval of her parents, she changed her name to Betty.

Her last name was another problem. Betty's paternal grandfather had arrived in this country with the surname of Astershinsky Simselyevitch-Simselyovitch. At Ellis Island, out of desperation, they converted it to Cohen. The family had no qualms about changing the name of Cohen, because it was not their real name. The young generation, with Betty's brother going to medical school and Betty interested in the theatre, wanted to change it. Their grandmother's maiden name had been Emden. So they combined the two and got Comden.

Betty's father was an attorney and her mother, an English teacher. Early in Betty's childhood, around age six, she was directed toward music, and began studying the piano.

Her first experience as an actor was in elementary school at the Ethical Culture School, where she performed in IVANHOE. She found that she loved the adoration she received for her portrayal. By the time she was in high school, Betty was doing more writing than acting. She went on to New York University and received a Bachelor of Science in drama.

Even as late as her college years, Betty lacked self-confidence, considering herself extremely unattractive. Once when she was out on a date, just as she expected him to give her a good-night kiss, her suitor placed his finger on the rather prominent lump on the bridge of her aquiline nose, and took off. She was left in a state of total despair.

A classmate at NYU encouraged her to get the nasal plastic surgery that her friend had already had done. Though at the time the surgery seemed rather frightening, Betty went ahead with it. The surgery went without complication and from that time on Betty's self-confidence changed remarkably. In later years, she wrote that the surgery completely transformed her life.

In 1938, she began acting in New York with the Studio Players, getting a number of roles and excellent reviews.

Throughout her NYU years, Betty would go back every summer to the country house that her grandparents had in Hunter, New York, where she had spent every summer of her childhood. While there, as a college student, she would take some roles in the local summer stock company. One day, her brother Nat invited her to play tennis with some of his friends. By her own description, that day she encountered the "most beautiful man she had ever seen." Nothing happened between them at that first meeting. He was an artist and his name was Siegfried Shutzman.

The following year they met once again, when her brother brought him to a party. Betty invited them all to a show in which she was performing. It was not very good and they all left rather early.

Finally, she decided to pursue him and they had a great date. Through some miscommunication of schedules, they did not get to see each other the next day. Betty soon became extremely ill with an upper respiratory infection. When Siegfried tried to reach her, he was told it was impossible due to her condition. Finally, they did get back together.

In her description of their courtship, she said they were living a wild and hectic life. Betty was performing at the Village Vanguard. There were so many performances that she couldn't take her make-up off between them. She would rush out to her cousin's apartment after a performance, strip out of her costume, and make love to Shutzman. He said as he gazed down at her, lying naked, she looked like a kewpie doll with red cheeks and long black eyelashes. Then she would quickly get up, jump back into her costume, and return to the Village Vanguard for the next show.

The outcome was that in January 1942 they were married and Betty's name changed. Baby Basya Betty Astershinsky Simselyevitch-Simselyovitch Cohen Comden was now Mrs. Siegfried Shutzman.

Like Betty, Shutzman changed his real name. His father's brother had come as a refugee from Russia and was taken in by a very kind German family when he arrived in America. He decided to take their name. When Siegfried's father followed, he assumed the same name as his brother.

Six months after Betty and Siegfried were married he was drafted. Having a German name at that time did not sit well with the Army. His family's original name had been Kyle. So he decided to anglicize it completely and changed his name to Steve Kyle.

The other main person in Betty Comden's life would turn out to be Adolph Green. Adolph's early life was not very different from Betty's. He was three years older than Betty, born in the Bronx in 1914. His parents were Helen and Daniel Weiss. Adolph had two brothers, and as in Betty's case, one became a physician. Adolph's interests in grammar school and beyond were directed toward writing, acting, and music.

After graduating from DeWitt Clinton High School, he started college. Green dropped out quickly. He wanted to be in the theatre. To support himself at that early stage he took jobs on Wall Street and with a carpeting firm.

In 1937, Adolph had the opportunity to play a role in THE PIRATES OF PENZANCE at a summer camp. A Harvard student was the music counselor there. When they met, the Harvard student decided to play a practical joke, one that he had pulled many times before. The Harvard student did not know how extremely knowledgeable Adolph was in all musical genres. He told Adolph that he was practicing a Shostakovich prelude. When Green asked which one, the Harvard student began to play a series of made-up notes. Green said he had never heard of such a prelude by Shostakovich. The Harvard student was thrilled. In the past when he had utilized that prank, the listener would always pretend he or she "recognized" it. The Harvard student turned out to be Leonard Bernstein. From that day on they would be fast friends.

Adolph returned to New York and joined a group called the Six and Company, performing a variety show with music and comedy routines, in the Catskills and Berkshires. One evening a seventeen-year-old in the audience, Judy Tuvim, came backstage to talk with Adolph after the show. She said she was interested in writing. Adolph asked if she would like to join the group and perform. She declined, stating she would be much happier filling in backstage needs. She remained with the group for

Betty Comden and Adolph Green, c. 1946. (Photofest.)

two weeks and, when she left, she and Adolph exchanged phone numbers.

That September, Judy got caught in the rain in front of a Greenwich Village basement club that had been a speakeasy. It was quite run-down. The owner, who was standing in the doorway, invited her to come in from the rain and have a cup of coffee. He had no liquor license. The club was the Village Vanguard, and the owner was Max Gordon. He told her that aspiring poets came there to read to a small audience every evening. Judy not only told him that she thought he needed a group to entertain, but also that she had one in mind. She assured him that they would be great there. Gordon agreed to try them. When she left, Judy immediately called Adolph Green.

The poets who regularly did their reading there, and those expecting to hear them, were quite annoyed. The performance did not go well for the Six and Company. The members, other than Adolph Green, refused to return.

Writers/lyricists Adolph Green and Betty Comden, 1947. (Photofest.)

Green had a friend, Alvin Hammer, who did monologues in the evening, while working as a shipping clerk during the day. Green asked him to join him. Soon after that, he bumped into Betty Comden, waiting in line for an audition for THE BOYS FROM SYRACUSE, a new Rodgers and Hart production. He had met her previously through mutual friends, when she was studying at NYU. Adolph wanted all the help he could get. As a result, besides herself, she recommended John Frank, whom she knew. He was a singer and played multiple instruments. Believing they needed another woman, they persuaded Judy Tuvim to put aside her anxiety about performing and join them. They changed their name to The Revuers.

At first they performed once a week and then more often. Even when they worked more frequently they received the same amount of money from Max Gordon. In the afternoon, they would meet at a diner, or one of their apartments, to write new material. They did a new show every week.

The heating in the building was terrible. So, in the winter, they frequently performed with their coats on. At times there were fewer people in the audience than on the stage. But one evening they arrived to find that the place was packed. A reviewer from the *New York Post* had been there the previous week and wrote that day that they were presenting "the most original material I have ever seen in a nightclub . . . so run, don't walk, if you want a night you'll always remember."

By the spring, business was so good that Gordon was able to buy a liquor license.

In the summer of 1937, Leonard Bernstein had just graduated from Harvard and his father had allowed him to have one last fling in New York City before coming to work in the family beauty-supply business. Everyone who heard him play the piano considered him a genius, but he was to spend his life in a different direction as far as the family was concerned. To the dismay of the Bernstein family, Leonard met Dimitri Mitropoulos,who insisted that he must study music. Leonard went to the Curtis School of Music in Philadelphia instead of entering the family business. That summer he had provided the accompaniment for a comedy recording the Revuers made.

Meanwhile, the Revuers were making progress. Betty Comden, writing about Adolph Green later in her life, described Green as brilliant and wildly eccentric. She believed that he was a creature who, as she described it, could only have been conceived by his amazing mind.

By 1939, they were doing two shows, five nights a week. They were getting good reviews from major publications. Their standard themes were parodies on films, theatre, and radio. They had become so successful that in the summer of 1939, they were featured in a variety show with Gene Kelly. In November, they were booked in the Rainbow Room at Rockefeller Center. The clientele there was "a little bit stuffy" for their satire and as Green described it, "We bombed!"

NBC hired them to do a weekly half-hour show, ordering twenty-five installments. For all their hard work, they received the meager sum of two hundred fifty dollars per week.

Next came the most grueling assignment of all. They performed at Radio City Music Hall between showings of the film—five shows a day for three weeks. Green missed one performance, showing up at City Hall instead and marrying Elizabeth Reitel.

By the end of 1940, the Revuers were back at the Village Vanguard and quite discouraged. It seemed they had made no progress at all in their careers.

The following year, after they landed some supper club appearances, an opportunity suddenly arose. Irving Caesar, the well-known lyricist, was doing a new musical titled MY DEAR PUBLIC and wanted them in it. There were out of town tryouts, but the show closed with terrible reviews.

They were about to go back to nightclubs when everything ended abruptly. John Frank, who had a serious alcohol problem, could no longer work. The group seemed to be breaking up. Betty Comden married Steve Kyle. Shortly after that he was drafted and went off to the war.

The four remaining members of the Revuers were offered a job in California. A movie based on the radio show *Duffy's Tavern* was being made. They took a train with Judy Tuvim's mother. But when they arrived on the West Coast, they were told the film had been cancelled.

Rather than return to New York, they took a job performing at the Trocadero nightclub, and received sensational reviews. Suddenly contracts were offered, but only to Judy Tuvim. Judy signed with Twentieth-Century Fox. Loyal to her colleagues, she convinced the studio to promise her that she would appear with the other three in her first film. If it was successful, the others would receive contracts as well. They completed the film. When it was released, however, the portion with Comden, Green, and Hammer had been cut out. Judy remained under contract and her name was changed to Judy Holliday. The other three never received contracts.

They were all discouraged. Betty went back East to see her husband Steve, who was out on furlough. Now there were only three left and Max Gordon offered them work at his new club, The Blue Angel. But Hammer declined, saying he was getting bit parts in movies in Hollywood. He believed that the Revuers would soon be breaking up. Ultimately, Gordon agreed to hire just Betty and Adolph.

While they were working there, their friend Leonard Bernstein came to see them perform, and brought along Jerome Robbins. They had just had a great success with FANCY FREE, a ballet written by Bernstein and choreographed by Robbins, about three sailors on leave in New York City. They came to ask Comden and Green if they would consider writing the book and lyrics for it to be expanded into a Broadway show. The title was ON THE TOWN.

When George Abbott agreed to direct it, it became easy to obtain the start-up money. ON THE TOWN ran for 463 performances and its hit song was "New York, New York."

Comden and Green, along with Jerome Robbins, immediately moved ahead with another show. Bernstein was not available, so Morton Gould was asked to write the music for BILLION DOLLAR BABY. It was only modestly successful, running for 220 performances.

It was time to try to Hollywood again. MGM brought them out to rewrite the screenplay for a new version of the film GOOD NEWS, considered one of the better college musical films of that period.

The 1940 marriage Adolph Green had rushed into during their performances at Radio City had already ended. Now he had fallen in love with an eighteen-year-old who was in the ensemble of ON THE TOWN. In 1947, when he was thirty-three, he married Allyn Ann McLerie.

When the film GOOD NEWS opened at Radio City, the team was already in rehearsal for a new show, BONANZA BOUND. Besides writing the book and lyrics, Green had a role in the show. It closed after two weeks of tryouts, never making it to Broadway.

Then it was back to Hollywood to write a screenplay called THE BARKLEYS OF BROADWAY for Fred Astaire and Judy Garland. Very quickly Garland began having personal problems and was soon replaced by Ginger Rogers. Astaire and Rogers, who had not starred together for a number of years, successfully reunited for this hit.

Before THE BARKLEYS OF BROADWAY opened Betty Comden gave birth to her first child, Susanna.

Comden and Green were asked to write a second screenplay for Gene Kelly called TAKE ME OUT TO THE BALLGAME. They had known Kelly in New York and it was through him that they began to meet people in Hollywood. Every Saturday and Sunday evening Kelly and his wife, Betsy Blair, would have an open house at their home. Food was served and everyone gathered around the piano. Frank Sinatra, Garland, Bernstein, Phil Silvers, Lena Horne, and Noel Coward all attended. One of the regular guests, Andre Previn, said of the gathering that there was more talent there than he could possibly imagine. He stopped going because he claimed it was so competitive, with each guest trying to outdo the others.

Kelly's film did not get good reviews but it was successful, probably due to the popularity of the cast.

ON THE TOWN was also released as a film in 1949, after Bernstein agreed to let MGM replace some of the music, which the studio felt was much too sophisticated for the film audience. Kelly, Sinatra, and Jules Munshin, who had starred in TAKE ME OUT TO THE BALLGAME, would be the leads in ON THE TOWN, and great reviews ensued.

In May 1950, Comden and Green were asked to write a screenplay for SINGIN' IN THE RAIN for Kelly, who had just finished AN AMERICAN IN PARIS. International film critics eventually voted SINGIN' IN THE RAIN, a combined effort of Comden, Green, Kelly, and Stanley Donen, the third-best film ever made.

Soon after, Comden and Green joined with Jule Styne for the first time on a Broadway show. Together they wrote TWO ON THE AISLE for Bert Lahr and Dolores Gray. The reviews were only fair, but it had a successful run of 281 performances. Comden and Green would go on to write seven more shows with Styne.

1953 brought them back out to Hollywood to write a screenplay based around the Schwartz and Dietz song catalogue called THE BAND WAGON. It was a great success, and their script even received an Academy Award.

That year Betty gave birth to her son, Adam Kyle. He was an unusual child who would ultimately bring her great heartache.

Bernstein wanted them to work with him once again. He had planned to do a show based on MY SISTER EILEEN, a Broadway play that had starred Rosalind Russell. The plan was to have her take the same role in the musical version, WONDERFUL TOWN. Together they wrote a marvelous score which won the Tony Award. The show had in it the songs "Ohio" and "One Hundred Easy Ways" as well as the lovely ballad "It's Love."

George Gaynes played the male lead. Adolph's wife, Allyn McLerie, met the actor, divorced Green, and married Gaynes.

In 1954, Comden and Green decided to write a sequel to ON THE TOWN. This time, the film would focus on three soldiers instead of sailors. Kelly signed on immediately. Sinatra, who was experiencing a career high after a major downturn, had just won the Academy Award for his supporting role in FROM HERE TO ETERNITY. He decided he didn't want to do any more musicals. Munchin was not available at all. As a result, Kelly joined with two other dancers, Michael Kidd and Dan Dailey. The film, IT'S ALWAYS FAIR WEATHER, received an Academy Award nomination for Comden and Green.

Thanks to their repeated successes, Comden and Green were in demand. A limited Broadway engagement of PETER PAN, followed by a live telecast, had been planned. It was written by the composer Moose Charlap and lyricist Carolyn Leigh. When it was completed, the producers felt that it still left something to be desired. They called in Jule Styne and Comden and Green to make changes. Carolyn Leigh was so furious that she refused to meet with them. Styne, Comden, and Green went ahead and added several songs. Both the show and the television production were extremely well received toward the end of 1954.

The following year, Comden and Green missed one of the greatest opportunities of their career. They made a decision that they were too busy to take on a show that was offered to them. Instead, book writer Arthur Laurents brought in a very young Stephen Sondheim to write the lyrics for WEST SIDE STORY.

Judy (Tuvim) Holliday had won the Tony and an Academy Award for her performances as Billie Dawn in BORN YESTERDAY. Now, in 1956, Comden and Green presented her with an idea for a new show. She had never sung on Broadway before. Once again, they joined with Jule Styne, this time to write BELLS ARE RINGING. It opened at the end of 1956 and once again Judy won the Tony Award. Two of Styne and Comden and Green's greatest hits are in the show: "Just In Time" and "The Party's Over." The show was on Broadway for almost three years.

In 1958, that trio created another Broadway show, SAY DARLING. It got mixed reviews, but based on their track record the advanced sales carried it for a year.

They were constantly busy. Hollywood soon called them to do just the screenplay for a film version of AUNTIE MAME.

Shortly thereafter a much more time-consuming and exciting project arose. A friend asked them to perform one night, as part of a series called MONDAY NIGHTS AT NINE, at the Cherry Lane Theatre in Greenwich Village. They were uncertain whether to take it on, but at Betty's husband Steve's insistence, they agreed. They did an assortment of their old material. It got such great reviews that it was brought to Broadway with the title, A PARTY WITH BETTY COMDEN AND ADOLPH GREEN. They did thirty-eight performances, then had to close as the theatre had other commitments. They re-opened when space was available for another forty-four presentations. They even received an Obie Award for their show.

During this run, they wrote the screenplay for BELLS ARE RINGING. It would be the last film that Judy Holliday would ever appear in, as she died of cancer in 1965.

A young woman, who had only had minor roles before, auditioned for BELLS ARE RINGING. Her name was Phyllis

Left to right: Adolph Green, Betty Comden, Gene Kelly c. 1950s. (Photofest.)

Newman and she got the job as Holliday's standby. Phyllis would come to all the rehearsals and sit on the back steps of the theatre so that Adolph Green would pass her every day. At last he asked her for a date. Once it became a regular thing he was introducing her to all his famous friends.

After a year as a standby, Phyllis got a role in a show called FIRST IMPRESSIONS that only lasted for ninety-two performances. During the tryouts in Philadelphia, Adolph made the trip to see her.

They traveled in Europe that summer. Wherever they went, Adolph would go on and on about his famous friends. She became so annoyed that she left him. Though he apologized, it seemed like their relationship had ended. Then one evening she went with a friend to see A PARTY WITH BETTY COMDEN AND ADOLPH GREEN, and decided that she definitely was in love with him.

Adolph and Phyllis were married in his apartment in January 1960. The following year, she gave birth to Adam. Their daughter Amanda followed three years later.

Comden and Green created another hit show in 1964. DO RE MI starred Phil Silvers, and featured the hit song "Make Someone Happy." The show ran for 400 performances.

During these hectic and extremely productive years Comden and Green constantly were on the go from coast to coast. Within that framework, the very unusual marriage of Betty Comden and Steve Kyle was trying to find its way. When asked, Comden would always say it was not the kind of marriage she would recommend for anyone else, but "it was successful for us." No one ever knows the inner working of anyone else's marriage, but by her description she was madly in love with this very handsome man. The way Betty put it, she "had never seen another man that beautiful." Once when explaining to an acquaintance how to recognize him on the occasion of meeting him at a train, she said, "Just look for the most beautiful man in the crowd."

Steve had been an artist. But after he got out of the Army he gave that up and opened a studio for fledgling artists. Obviously, Betty was the breadwinner in the family, leaving Steve primarily to care for the home and children. At an early age, their son Adam became deeply involved with drugs, and was in therapy for his emotional problems. They became so severe that he was in and out of school and rehab facilities. The situation became untenable for the family when Adam began stealing money and jewelry at home to pay for his habit. Ultimately disaster struck. He contracted HIV, most likely from the contaminated needles he used. Adam died in 1990.

In 1961, Comden and Green decided to write a show that would feature Phyllis Newman. The show's producer, David Merrick, balked at the idea, but finally gave in. The show was SUBWAYS ARE FOR SLEEPING. It did not get great reviews and ran for only 205 performances, but Newman won the Tony as Best Featured Actress for her performance. The show only lasted as long as it did thanks to the totally disreputable Mr. Merrick. He found individuals in the phone directory with the same last names as the leading theatre critics of the time. He persuaded them to use their names in ads in for which he wrote fake reviews. All of the newspapers but one caught on and refused to print the ads. No hit songs came out of the show.

In 1964, once again working with Styne, they wrote a screenplay for WHAT A WAY TO GO, a film that used a multitude of stars including Shirley MacLaine, Gene Kelly, Dean Martin, Paul Newman, Dick Van Dyke, and Robert Mitchum. The film was never made into a video or shown on television. However, a copy is available in the Library of Congress.

The reviews for the picture were universally bad, which probably accounts for why it was essentially discarded after its initial run, never to be shown again anywhere. But the amazing part of the story is that regardless of the reviewers' evaluations of it, the public loved either the picture or the cast, and it became that year's biggest money maker for Twentieth-Century Fox.

A second strange thing happened to Comden and Green in 1964. They had written a Broadway show for Carol Burnett called FADE OUT-FADE IN. Burnett was already a star on television. The spoof about Hollywood received excellent reviews and created expectations for a long run. Burnett began missing multiple performances, Betty Hutton was brought in to replace her for a full week. After 199 performances, Burnett quit, claiming she had exacerbated an old injury. A lawsuit was filed against her and the show was reopened for another seventy-two performances before she quit again. This time it was due to pregnancy. She had missed a total of sixty performances. The show actually closed and lost its investors half a million dollars.

Those were not the only problems during that year. After six months of work with Leonard Bernstein creating a musical version of Thornton Wilder's THE SKIN OF OUR TEETH, the project was cancelled.

It was not until 1967 that they had another show. With Jule Styne they wrote HALLELUJAH, BABY! featuring a largely African-American cast starring Leslie Uggams. It won the Tony for Best Musical, as well ones for Best Composer and Lyricist, and Best Actress (Uggams).

This was also the year that Green and Newman bought a house in East Hampton, Long Island, and planned to have Phyllis's niece's wedding there. As the guests arrived, the house caught on fire and was destroyed. They went ahead with the wedding on the lawn, and subsequently built a new house on the property.

In 1970, APPLAUSE, starring Lauren Bacall, based on the movie ALL ABOUT EVE, brought them their first real hit in ten years. It was truly a smash, running for 860 performances. The show, score by Charles Strouse and Lee Adams, Lauren Bacall, and book writers Comden and Green all received Tonys.

From 1970 to 1976, they wrote a series of unsuccessful productions until returning to the stage themselves for a revival of A PARTY WITH BETTY COMDEN AND ADOLPH GREEN, which was very well received.

In 1978, they had another hit show, ON THE TWENTIETH CENTURY, starring John Cullum, Madeline Kahn, and Imogene Coca. This time Cy Coleman wrote the music. They shared a Tony with him for the score, as well as winning a second one for the book. Betty Comden filled in for Imogene Coca for one week in January 1979 while the beloved star was on vacation.

Whatever joy that week brought to Comden would have little lasting effect in that terrible year. In October, her husband, Steve Kyle, died of acute pancreatitis. He had suffered with the ailment several years previously. This time the attack was rampant and caused his sudden death.

In later years Betty wrote a book about her private life offstage in which she characterized how strong her love affair with Steve had been. Comden never remarried.

The team were named to the Songwriters Hall of Fame and the Theatre Hall of Fame, both in 1980.

After Betty had corneal transplant surgery in 1982, Comden and Green taught a master class on writing musical comedy for NYU. To make it easier on Comden, some of the classes were taught in her living room.

They tried to write one more major musical, in 1982. A sequel to Ibsen's A DOLL'S HOUSE, it was titled A DOLL'S LIFE. But, it closed quickly.

All through 1984 and 1985 they both took a series of cameo roles in films and earned good reviews for their work. They soon participated in a very successful Lincoln Center concert production of Sondheim's FOLLIES, which resulted in a prolonged standing ovation for their performance.

It appeared as if their careers as lyricists had come to an end. They were still performing A PARTY WITH BETTY COMDEN AND ADOLPH GREEN with success around the country and doing some film work.

In 1991, they struck gold again with THE WILL ROGERS FOLLIES. Cy Coleman re-partnered with them, and the show lasted through 982 performances. It won six Tonys, including one for them.

That year they received both the Johnny Mercer Award for Lifetime Achievement and Kennedy Center Honors.

Still they continued their collaboration. Each day they would meet at Betty's apartment, have lunch and decide what they would work on that day. For six decades they had worked together, almost constantly. They had certainly spent more time together than with their spouses. They said of each other, "When one of them starts a sentence, the other finishes it." Their disagreements were confined exclusively to Comden's punctuality and Green's constant lateness.

More than any other description, their creations were known for the great wit they demonstrated. They generally made fun of what they loved the most, New York and show business. Because they adored their targets, the edge to their wit was never mean.

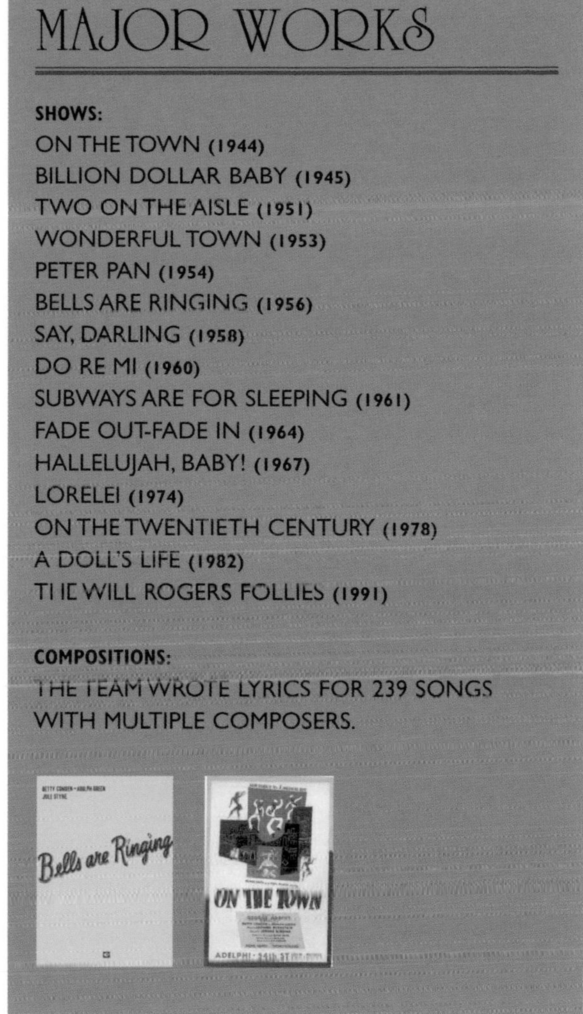

MAJOR WORKS

SHOWS:

ON THE TOWN **(1944)**
BILLION DOLLAR BABY **(1945)**
TWO ON THE AISLE **(1951)**
WONDERFUL TOWN **(1953)**
PETER PAN **(1954)**
BELLS ARE RINGING **(1956)**
SAY, DARLING **(1958)**
DO RE MI **(1960)**
SUBWAYS ARE FOR SLEEPING **(1961)**
FADE OUT-FADE IN **(1964)**
HALLELUJAH, BABY! **(1967)**
LORELEI **(1974)**
ON THE TWENTIETH CENTURY **(1978)**
A DOLL'S LIFE **(1982)**
THE WILL ROGERS FOLLIES **(1991)**

COMPOSITIONS:

THE TEAM WROTE LYRICS FOR 239 SONGS WITH MULTIPLE COMPOSERS.

In 2002, at the age of eighty-seven, Adolph Green passed away. A great tribute was held for him at the Shubert Theatre in December of that year, where Comden ended her reminiscences with "It's lonely up here." She died of heart failure in New York's Presbyterian Hospital in November 2006. She was eighty-nine years old.

In December 2002, Green's son Adam, a writer for the *New Yorker* and *Vogue*, published a column about Green's last day. Adam had dinner that last evening at his parents' apartment. They had brought in Chinese food. The conversation included their typical loving banter, packed with jokes and witticisms. Finally, Adolph, tired, asked to be taken to bed. Adam said that he might be in the neighborhood the next day and stop by for lunch.

Adolph responded, "Better call first. Miss Comden and I might be working."

One hour later he died peacefully in his sleep.

Howard Dietz 1974. (Courtesy Billy Rose Theatre Collection/The New York Public Library.)

HOWARD DIETZ

HOWARD DIETZ WAS BORN IN 1896 AND GREW UP IN Lower Manhattan. He apparently had little love or respect for his Russian-born father, who became a jeweler in New York.

Howard grew up like a typical child on the streets of New York, playing ball and getting into street fights. He had three older siblings, a brother ten years older and two sisters, five and three years older than Howard. Probably the most accurate description of the Dietz family dynamic was his mother's deathbed statement to her children:

"The ten years since your father died have been the happiest years of my life."

Early in Howard's life he fell in love with music and the theatre. But he could rarely afford to see or hear anything being performed.

He was accepted to Townsend Harris Hall, a preparatory school for New York's City College. He began writing a neighborhood magazine with Bennett Cerf and Merryle Rukeyser. They extorted local stores into buying it with the underlying threat that their parents, who patronized the stores, would not continue to do so otherwise. They did this, most likely, without their parents' knowledge.

At age fifteen, Dietz got a job as a copyboy, after school and during vacations, with the *New York American* newspaper. The income enabled him to see more shows. He idolized the famous reporters at the paper. Once he even had the temerity to submit an editorial, but it never got published.

One day the managing editor's secretary got sick, and Dietz persuaded him to allow Dietz to undertake those duties. He did quite a good job. He became so enthralled with the business that he decided to quit Townsend Harris and work full time at the newspaper. His boss told him that would be a terrible mistake. Dietz decided to cram all summer long and immediately take the admission examination for Columbia University. He was accepted and enrolled in the class of 1917. To his good fortune, the *American* hired him as a stringer, writing the Columbia news column for the paper. A friend of his, Francis Joseph Scully, was the stringer for the *Sun*. The two made an arrangement to share the stories they found, even though stringers competed to scoop one another for local news. *The Times* and the *World* had their stringers, as well.

On one occasion Dietz and Scully got the scoop on the results of a Columbia basketball team championship game. After they wrote it up and submitted it to their two papers they snuck into the press room that was shared by the other two reporters. They locked the door from the inside and climbed out the window so that the *Times* and *World* reporters could not get into their room to report the story. Dietz and Scully had their scoop.

While at Columbia, Dietz had the opportunity to meet an assortment of wonderful characters, many of whom would make their way in the literary world quite successfully. Among those he socialized with were included future book publishing giant Bennett Cerf, Merryle Rukeyser (who became a financial wizard), George Sokolsky (who became a political columnist), and lyricists Oscar Hammerstein II and Larry Hart.

In his junior year, Dietz won five hundred dollars in a contest for the best advertisement for Fatima cigarettes, and decided that advertising was his forte. As a result, he quit Columbia and went to work. This may not have been the only reason he left school. He was not doing too well academically, staying up carousing until the wee hours of the morning.

Dietz sent resumes to several advertising agencies and received the best offer from the Philip Goodman Company. The offer was for a small salary and specifically stated that there was little chance for advancement. But he took it and worked in a tiny cubby they provided for him.

Around this time, he met Ralph Barton, a very well-known illustrator at the agency. After a failed marriage, Barton married Carlotta Monterey, who left him to marry Eugene O'Neill. He fell in love with a department store heiress, Ruth Kindley, who also left him. She sailed away on the same day that Carlotta returned home from her French honeymoon with O'Neill. So Barton wrote farewell letters to Carlotta and Ruth. He tacked a drawing of his heart on a board, along with the two letters and drawings of the two women, placed the board on his chest, and shot himself with his revolver.

In 1917, America initiated the draft to prepare for their entrance into World War I, and it was of some concern to Dietz.. To avoid it, he persuaded his girlfriend Elizabeth (Betty) Bigelow Hall to marry him. She was four years older than Howard. They moved into a barn that had been converted into a makeshift dwelling. It was very cold, and due to the war effort it was difficult to purchase fuel, so they slept in their overcoats. The pipes burst and the living room became like an ice skating rink. Betty actually moved around on ice skates to sweep up. They tried making everything into a game to keep life bearable. They had an outhouse. But when it was too cold to go out they paper-trained themselves. They would fold up their newspapers like a gift package and place it outside the door.

One day when they returned from work a neighbor stopped them. She said, "A strange man came by . . . he took your packages and ran off. I hope they weren't valuable."

Like many others he knew at Columbia he was writing light verse, trying to get it published in Franklin P. Adams's column. Through a friend of Betty's, Dietz got the opportunity to write the lyrics for an operetta. Ultimately, it became popular in high school and amateur performances.

Unable to avoid it any longer, he was drafted into the Navy. Fortunately, due to his skills, he was given a job at the newspaper, *Navy Life*. Shortly before the end of the war, Howard became critically ill with fever, coughing, and vomiting, and fell into a coma. In the sick bay many of the other sailors died. It was the influenza epidemic. While in the coma, Dietz was accidently listed as dead in the Columbia newspaper. But he came out of it to be one of the few who survived.

At his discharge, he and Betty went on an all-night drinking binge, spending all the money he had received as his separation bonus.

Dietz was able to get a job at the newly-formed Goldwyn Pictures movie studio. Sam Goldwyn was actually born Sam Goldfish. When he combined his company with Edgar Selwyn, he changed his name. Goldwyn was not easy to work for, but Dietz was quite street-smart by then. He manipulated his way to get two hundred dollars a week, a lot more than others working there at his level. Later Dietz would say the stories told about Goldwyn's idiosyncrasies were really true. Once, a secretary asked the mogul if she could destroy documents that were more than ten years old.

He said, "Yes, but keep copies."

Howard and Betty were now living at 18 West Eighth Street in Lower Manhattan. Their landlords, Lou and Emily Paley, lived above them. Emily's maiden name before she married was Strunsky. Every Saturday evening there seemed to be a jam session going on there. The Dietz's chandelier shook so violently they were afraid it would fall. So one night, on their way out to the theatre, Howard told

Betty Comdon, Howard Dietz, and Arthur Schwartz, rehearsing for THE BAND WAGON. (Courtesy Billy Rose Theatre Collection/The New York Public Library.)

Betty to wait for him while he went up to ask them not to make such a big disturbance. When he knocked on the door, someone came, opened it, put his fingers to his lips to indicate "quiet," and gestured for Dietz to come sit on the floor with some forty others to listen to a man playing the piano. After a while Betty, still waiting, went up to get her husband. Once again, the fingers were on the lips, as she was led in to sit beside him. They skipped the theatre and became Saturday night regulars listening to George Gershwin, or when he was not available, Oscar Levant.

Even while working for Goldwyn, Dietz continued to stop by to visit with his old boss, Philip Goodman. By this time Goodman had gotten involved with producing. He was doing a show for W. C. Fields and asked Dietz to contribute some material. The show was successful, but Dietz got no credit in the program. Goodman was a fan of Dietz's writing, however, and gave him an important recommendation. One day Howard got a call and the person on the line said that Goodman had put in a good word for him. He then said his name was Jerry Kern. Dietz was rendered speechless. He finally responded sufficiently to discern that Kern wanted him to come see him the next day about writing a show together. When Dietz arrived, Kern gave him an armful of sheet music and asked that he return in two days. Dietz said what he then did was idiotic, somehow believing that Kern wanted him to write all the lyrics for the entire show in forty-eight hours. But that is precisely what he did.

When Dietz returned and showed him the first completed song, the more established composer expressed amazement. It was a comic song about polygamy titled "If We Could Lead a Merry Mormon Life."

Kern's response was, "That song alone will guarantee a great score."

Dietz decided he should only show him one other at that visit. Kern said they had better sign Dietz to a contract before it was too late.

Immediately after the show opened, Arthur Schwartz, a practicing lawyer who was just starting his career as a composer, asked Dietz if they could collaborate. Schwartz, born in 1900, was the son of an attorney who wanted Arthur to follow in his footsteps. Dietz responded that he didn't think a collaboration was a good idea until the two of them had established themselves in their own right. Schwartz had written that the only other person he knew who could write lyrics as well as Dietz had for the show with Kern, was Larry Hart.

Shortly after that, George and Ira Gershwin began working on a new show, OH, KAY! Ira became critically ill with appendicitis, which was often fatal at that time. George sought out P. G. Wodehouse and Guy Bolton to work on lyrics with him. He decided that the young Dietz would work for less money and credit.

Dietz got next to nothing. His first royalty check was

for ninety-six cents. Finally, they stopped all payments. Dietz later said that he was honored to work with George for nothing.

Dietz developed a relationship with the Round Table at the Algonquin. He started by going there and watching them. Gradually he became part of the circle. Once when he was at a party for them, given by the rather large Columbia football coach Joe Brooks, Dietz came to the defense of Dorothy Parker after Brooks had insulted her, at which time Brooks gave Dietz a severe beating. Parker took Dietz back to her apartment to treat his facial injuries. After awhile, Heywood Broun showed up at Parker's apartment in even worse shape. He said that he felt it necessary to come to their defense and was soundly beaten by Brooks as well.

Dietz was continuing to work for Goldwyn as a publicist and had to decide if he should stop and devote all of his time to being a lyricist.

In 1929, two men, Tom Weatherly and Dwight Wiman were considering producing a small musical revue in the style of the GARRICK GAIETIES. They were discussing it in a restaurant when Dietz overheard them. He advised them against it, saying it was a big risk. When they heard what he had done they asked if he would be interested in writing lyrics with the composer they had already signed. It was Arthur Schwartz, whom Dietz had previously rejected. The production was called THE LITTLE SHOW and it starred Clifton Webb and Libby Holman. The hit song of the show was "I Guess I'll Have to Change My Plan ."

Holman was a wild character who went to law school at age sixteen and then decided she would rather be in the theatre. She fell in love with Zachary Smith Reynolds, the son of the cigarette magnet, who was only twenty years old. He was insanely jealous and she was not exactly a faithful wife. They were not married very long when he shot himself to death. The size of his estate was twenty-five million dollars, but Libby received only seven hundred and fifty thousand.

Like Holman, Schwartz was a prodigy, getting into NYU law school at a very young age. But music was always in the back of his mind. He was born November 25, 1900. He supported himself all during his years of study by playing the piano. Larry Hart encouraged him to give up the practice of law and concentrate on composing.

Weatherly and Wiman wanted a second LITTLE SHOW written and Dietz and Schwarz agreed. But at the same time they began writing THREE'S A CROWD for another producer. The hit of that show was " Something to Remember You By."

Howard Dietz had always wanted a house in Greenwich Village. The specific house was on West Eleventh Street, and it was owned by Charles Merrill of Merrill Lynch. Mr. Merrill wanted sixty-five thousand dollars, but Dietz did not have that kind of money. Suddenly, with the success of THE LITTLE SHOW and THREE'S A CROWD he came up with forty thousand dollars in cash and got a twenty-five thousand dollar mortgage. He and Betty moved into the house in 1930. Dietz arranged to rent the second floor of the adjacent building and, with the consent of the owner, knocked down the wall between the two houses on the second floor. He had created a forty by forty-four foot room for giant parties and arranged for Richard Rodgers's wife Dorothy to decorate it.

Dietz started work on a new show with Schwartz, to be produced by Max Gordon and starring Fred and Adele Astaire and Frank Morgan. It was THE BAND WAGON and in addition to the song "I Love Louisa" it contained their greatest hit, "Dancing in the Dark."

A wonderful opportunity came up for Dietz to write sketches for the Marx Brothers. Every day that they were supposed to meet a different brother showed up, but none of the others. Realizing they were putting him on, Dietz gave up on the idea until one day he got another call to show up at a specific penthouse apartment at 9 a.m., with the promise that this time real work would be accomplished. When Dietz arrived he found a five-piece band playing music, and Harpo seated on a chair with a beautiful young woman on his lap. Harpo asked Dietz if he would like to play backgammon. When Dietz inquired what they would play for, Harpo indicated the young woman. Dietz won and the young woman moved over to his chair. The sketches never did get written.

In 1931, the team wrote FLYING COLORS. It had the songs "Louisiana Hayride" and "Shine on Your Shoes."

Despite all of this theatrical work, Dietz still felt that his primary occupation was as head publicist for MGM. He was earning a very good living from that and traveling back and forth between Los Angeles and New York.

Schwartz felt less secure. After the success of FLYING COLORS nothing was happening for him on Broadway all through 1933 and 1934. He was seriously considering returning to the practice of law. when a strange opportunity arose. A radio producer had a plan to do a musical comedy serial that would run for thirty-nine weeks. He told them it would take a great deal of work, but Schwartz and Dietz signed on. Over that period of time they wrote ninety-four songs.

They also tried writing an operetta in 1934, REVENGE WITH MUSIC. But it failed. It did have one great song—"You and the Night and the Music."

In that same year, Schwartz wrote a song with Yip Harburg, rather than Dietz. "Then I'll Be Tired of You," recorded by Fats Waller, became a hit.

Dietz felt none of the insecurity that Schwartz was experiencing. In his role as a publicity agent for MGM, Dietz was in the inner circle and knew everyone including Irving Thalberg, Norma Shearer, Joan Crawford, Hedy Lamarr, and every other important actor at the studio. Once, he was confronted by a friend who was a theatrical agent. He knew Dietz had a vast circle of acquaintances, and asked

Left to right: Jack Haley, Howard Dietz, Bea Little, and Arthur Schwartz, rehearsing for INSIDE USA, 1974. (Courtesy Billy Rose Theatre Collection/The New York Public Library.)

him to intercede with a vice president of a major radio network. The agent wanted Dietz to to persuade the radio bigwig to buy his idea of a new radio serial. Dietz said he couldn't. He had never met the executive, and worse than that, Dietz had once been a no-show for a scheduled meeting with him. Still, Dietz's friend persisted and Howard agreed to meet him at the vice president's office at 9 a.m. the following day, for a meeting that had already been scheduled.

That evening Howard was seated at a bar when Jean Harlow walked in with a date. Dietz and Harlow were dear friends. When her career seemed to be slipping away he created a publicity campaign that brought her back into prominence. Dietz sat down with Harlow and her date and completely monopolized the conversation to the point that her date picked himself up and left. Embarrassed, Dietz rushed after him, but for naught. He had already gotten into a cab and driven off. Dietz and Harlow spent the rest of the night bar hopping until at 7 a.m., when he realized he had an appointment with his friend and the radio vice president. He rushed home to shave and change clothes and made it to the office by 9 a.m. The meeting ended very abruptly when Dietz realized the vice president was Harlow's date from the night before.

Dietz and Schwartz went on to write two more shows in 1935 and 1937. The major songs from these productions were "By Myself" and "I See Your Face Before Me."

Betty and Howard rented a house at Sands Point on Long Island. Howard becoming an avid golfer. Their lives now consisted of golf and croquet in the daytime and party games at night. They developed a new circle of friends including Bill Paley, Irving Berlin, Abe Burrows, John O'Hara, Edna Ferber, and Marc Connelly among others. Dietz became enamored of boats and purchased three at one time, including one from Fred Astaire. The largest was seventy-two feet long and needed four as crew. One handsome friend, Nat Curtis, became a permanent crew member and eventually sailed in a uniform with braids.

Frequently Dietz would be called to Hollywood for stretches of two or three weeks. Curtis would remain at their home caring for the boats.

On one particular trip Howard met Tanis Guinness, an English beauty who had recently been divorced from royalty. He went out gambling one night with Tanis and Lupe Velez, the flamboyant Mexican actress. They had so much fun that he and Tanis agreed they would have a date every night unless one of them called to cancel it. They got together every night of the three weeks except one. It occurred to Dietz that although his marriage was still quite comfortable, he and his wife had become somewhat aloof. He and Betty had been married for eighteen years and had no children. Howard quickly realized that Betty had fallen for Curtis during Dietz's frequent trips away from home.

A problem did arise for Dietz. An Englishman by the name of Porchy Carnarvon persuaded Tanis that Dietz was permanently married and would never leave Betty. At his insistence she agreed to marry Porchy. The British press were notified that they would be going to Washington to be married by the British ambassador.

The night before the wedding, Tanis's French maid, Celia, found her distressed. She told her lifelong maid that she didn't really want to marry Porchy.

Celina told her, "Marry that nice Monsieur Dietz."

Betty and Howard got divorced, and Betty married Nat Curtis in Chihuahua, Mexico. Howard and Tanis also went across the border to Mexico. He bought Tanis a wedding ring there in the market for one dollar and got married in Juarez. The headline in the British press read, "Laborer Weds Heiress."

Tanis's family actually interviewed Dietz because she came from great wealth; she was the heiress to the Guinness beer fortune. Despite their inherent class differences, they accepted him because of his huge salary. Dietz later said the money didn't affect him because he remembered the old adage, "If you marry a drunk, you become a drunk. But, if you marry money, you never get rich."

As Dietz later described it, Tanis was a beauty who had would-be lovers everywhere. So much so that he was never certain where he stood in their relationship. They remained married for fourteen years and during that time, in 1938, his only child Liza was born.

Very shortly after Dietz became a vice president at MGM, he received a phone call from Sam Goldwyn. Goldwyn wanted to know if Dietz was a good friend of the people who ran the Loew's chain of theatres. When Dietz said he was, Goldwyn explained his problem. When he completed the film THE WESTERNER he didn't realize it was going to be better than GONE WITH THE WIND, in his estimation. He had sold it to them for 25 percent of the gross. But now he knew it would be worth 50 percent of the gross. Goldwyn wanted him to explain that to Loew's.

Goldwyn asked Dietz to persuade Loew's executive Nick Schenk to tear up the contract and write a new one giving him twice as much money. Dietz told Sam Goldwyn if he did that Schenk would ask Dietz whom he was working for.

Goldwyn's response was, "I guess you don't stand in so good with him!"

While Dietz was busy with his career in Hollywood, Schwartz was still trying to find his way. In 1938, he wrote a show with the lyricist Dorothy Fields called STARS IN YOUR EYES. But the show was not successful. As a result he continued to direct his efforts to Hollywood.

In 1941, Congress wanted the United States to remain neutral and began an investigation of the film industry to determine if they were making anti-German films. The industry hired Wendell Willkie, the losing candidate to Franklin Roosevelt in 1940. Dietz was named as Willkie's assistant, who was to provide Willkie with information for his testimony before Congress. Dietz testified on Friday, December 6, 1941. The rest of the hearings were cancelled when Pearl Harbor occurred that weekend.

Schwartz was spending all his time in Hollywood and, in 1943, he wrote a hit song with Frank Loesser as his lyricist. It was composed for Bette Davis to sing in the film, THANK YOUR LUCKY STARS. Her hit song was "They're Either Too Young or Too Old."

Meanwhile Schwartz was looking in another direction and began producing films in Hollywood. In 1944, he produced COVER GIRL and, two years later, he did NIGHT AND DAY, the rather weak film about the life of Cole Porter.

Dietz had two failed shows with Vernon Duke in 1944. Arthur Schwartz soon reappeared in his life. Schwartz had not had a show on Broadway for ten years, confining his work to Hollywood. In 1948, they got back together to have a big hit once again, INSIDE U.S.A., which ran for two years. The show had several successful songs including, "Rhode Island Is Famous for You."

His marriage to Tanis began falling apart. Soon, she left for good. Dietz began a new relationship with Lucinda Ballard, a theatrical designer. Ballard had two children from a previous marriage. Liza and Lucinda and her children hit it off wonderfully and Howard and Lucinda got married. The ceremony was held in an Espiscopalian church as Dietz said, though being Jewish, he had never been in a synagogue. All of them moved back into the house on West Eleventh Street in Greenwich Village where Dietz had now lived with three different wives. But after a while they sold the house and moved permanently to his place in Sands Point.

Some years later they read a story that the house on West Eleventh Street had been blown up by dynamite. Apparently renters turned out to be members of the radical Weathermen organization. They were building bombs there, which went off accidentally. Three of the radicals were killed.

His next important assignment was to translate to English several important operas. The first that he did was DIE FLEDERMAUS in 1950. It was so successful he was asked to do LA BOHEME in 1952.

Twelve years after Schwartz and Dorothy Fields collaborated on their failed show, the two reunited to write the 1951 musical version of A TREE GROWS IN BROOKLYN. Schwartz had worked with a number of different lyricists during the intervening years including Oscar Hammerstein, Ira Gershwin, Frank Loesser, and, of course, Howard Dietz. But most of Schwartz's productions had been revues. Once their run was over, there were few stage revivals, which provide the opportunity for audiences to become more familiar with the songs from the shows.

As far as Dorothy Fields was concerned, writing with Arthur Schwartz was "a pure delight." It is generally believed that A TREE GROWS IN BROOKLYN is the finest show she had ever written.

In 1951, she also wrote a film with Schwartz that did not get great reviews. It was EXCUSE MY DUST.

When MGM bought THE BAND WAGON for the movies, the Dietz family had to move back out to California. It was 1953 and Dietz rented Celeste Holm's house. Dietz and Schwartz were asked to add one song for the film score and it turned out to be a great addition, "That's Entertainment."

By 1954, Dietz began to develop Parkinsonism. He gradually became so ill that he had to resign his longtime position at MGM as its chief publicist. He had hoped to concentrate on writing with Arthur Schwartz. In 1961, they wrote THE GAY LIFE, which received fair reviews but only lasted for about three months.

Their final show, JENNIE, was written for Mary Martin in 1963 when Howard Dietz was sixty-seven years old. But Dietz was quite ill and had little control of the show. Martin and her husband, Richard Halliday, made constant changes and the show ended as a total flop.

Dietz had six operations over a one-year period, until he refused any others. By 1968, his condition left him barely able to walk. The pursuits he had expected would keep him active as he aged, like golf and bridge, became impossible. He could not even hold playing cards in his hands.

MAJOR WORKS

SHOWS:

DEAR SIR **(DIETZ AND KERN, 1924)**
MERRY-GO-ROUND **(DIETZ, RYSKIND, SOUVAINE, AND GORNEY, 1927)**
THE LITTLE SHOW **(DIETZ AND SCHWARTZ, 1929)**
THE SECOND LITTLE SHOW **(DIETZ AND SCHWARTZ, 1930)**
THREE'S A CROWD **(DIETZ AND SCHWARTZ, 1930)**
THE BAND WAGON **(DIETZ AND SCHWARTZ, 1931)**
FLYING COLORS **(DIETZ AND SCHWARTZ, 1932)**
REVENGE WITH MUSIC **(DIETZ AND SCHWARTZ, 1934)**
AT HOME ABROAD **(DIETZ AND SCHWARTZ, 1935)**
BETWEEN THE DEVIL **(DIETZ AND SCHWARTZ, 1937)**
TARS AND SPARS **(DIETZ AND DUKE, 1944)**
SADIE THOMPSON **(DIETZ AND DUKE, 1944)**
INSIDE U.S.A. **(DIETZ AND SCHWARTZ, 1948)**
THE GAY LIFE **(DIETZ AND SCHWARTZ, 1961)**
JENNIE **(DIETZ AND SCHWARTZ, 1963)**

COMPOSITIONS:

HOWARD DIETZ WROTE 198 SONGS WITH MULTIPLE COMPOSERS.ARTHUR SCHWARTZ WROTE 262 SONGS WITH MULTIPLE LYRICISTS.

He started taking an experimental drug, L-Dopa, and it brought about some significant improvement, though not enough to enable him to participate in the leisure activities he had hoped for. He had to give up swimming, which he loved. He began having intestinal problems related to the neurological ailments and needed to undergo abdominal surgery. Typical of his great sense of humor, Dietz explained "the surgeons reduced my colon to a semicolon." He remained on L-Dopa for a number of years and did not pass away until 1983 at the age of eighty-six. Arthur Schwartz died the following year at eighty-four.

Dietz's career was quite remarkable. As well as having some very significant success with Arthur Schwartz on Broadway, he was a major figure in the movie industry. Dietz was an intimate of all the great stars and power brokers in the industry. He was believed to have created Leo the Lion for MGM, as well as the studio's slogan, "Ars Gratia Artis."

Duke Ellington. (Michael Ochs Archives/Getty Images.)

EDWARD "DUKE" ELLINGTON

DAISY KENNEDY WAS THE FIRST OF NINE CHILDREN BORN to a Washington, D.C., policeman, James William Kennedy, on January 4, 1879. James had been a slave in Virginia. His parents were a slave and the son of a landowner.

James Edward Ellington was also born in 1879. His mother was a housekeeper and his father a driver, butler, and handyman to a prominent white Washington, D.C., physician.

Daisy and James were married in 1898 and their first child was stillborn. During her second pregnancy, Daisy was on a boat that sank in the Potomac River; still, she gave birth on April 29, 1899, to Edward Kennedy Ellington. Daisy intermittently suffered from depression during much of her life.

Due to the prominence of J. E.'s employer, Dr. Cuthbert, they were exposed to high society and much music. The Ellingtons actually had two pianos in their home and Daisy played quite well. Her son Edward began taking lessons at age ten, but did not take to it very well.

Edward was very close to his mother. They attended church regularly together. She believed he was destined for great things. As a result, at an early age, he was given the nickname "Duke."

Washington was the center of African-American society and culture in America. Within their own community there was class separation. The Ellingtons were neither the elite nor the impoverished. They were part of the black middle class.

It was a difficult time for African Americans. At the turn of the century, the Supreme Court effectively legalized segregation in the landmark decision Plessy v. Ferguson. "Separate but equal" was the accepted philosophy, but in fact it was separate and unequal.

Edward's early interest was in the visual arts, and he received a scholarship to the Pratt Institute. In 1914, his preoccupation with the piano developed. He would frequent a local pool room where he would hear a number of different fine piano players. Duke had the ability to hear what they were playing and reproduce it himself. His first composition was "Soda Fountain Rag."

Doc Perry, a professional musician, liked what he heard and brought him to his home to teach him more about the piano. Ellington quit high school and turned down the Pratt scholarship. However, his interest in art never waned. It may account for why so many of his song titles incorporate colors.

By 1919, he organized his first band, Duke's Serenaders. He was also working as a booking agent for other bands and between the two jobs he was earning between one hundred fifty and two hundred dollars weekly, quite a lot of money at the time.

His attitude about women was strange and conflicted. He had tremendous respect for his mother, but possibly because of his father's influence, he considered all other women to be little more than whores, to be used sexually, and he treated them terribly. In 1917, he married Edna Thompson after she became pregnant with his son Mercer. A second child died. Duke focused all of his energies on one thing only: the Duke Ellington Orchestra.

In Washington, Duke developed two very close relationships with musicians, one with Sonny Greer, a drummer, and the other with Otto "Toby" Hardwick, a saxophonist and violinist. In 1923, when Greer was offered a job in New York City, he said he couldn't take it unless it included Duke and Toby. Hardwick agreed. Duke, however, said he would stay behind in Washington. In March 1923, Duke finally agreed and joined them in New York.

Blues were the rage and the big names were Ethel Waters and Fats Waller. In the mid-twenties, Duke began meeting them through his work. Another major figure was Leonard Harper, the choreographer at the Cotton Club, Ciro's, and the Lido. Louis Armstrong, Cab Calloway, and Waters were among the artists who worked for him. Harper offered Ellington a job as rehearsal pianist. After a while Edna joined him when Harper hired her as a dancer. She left Mercer behind with his grandparents, and Duke and Edna moved into Harper's home.

Ellington became part of a new band that got a six-month contract at Harper's recommendation. It was called the Washington Black Sox Orchestra. Ellington had found a trumpeter, Bubber Miley, who would be important to his group in later years. Bubber had learned his style and technique from the famous King Oliver. Greer and Hardwick were also in the band. Ellington was listed as the pianist and arranger. Elmer Snowden was the business manager and leader of the band, but he soon quit and turned it over to Greer. Greer really didn't want that role and in turn passed it to Ellington.

They changed the name to the Washingtonians, and began performing at the Hollywood CAFÉ in New York's Theatre District. They were in good company. Up the street was the Paul Whiteman Orchestra, and in the same neighborhood were other nightspots such as the Winter Garden, the Plantation, and the Roof Garden.

A fire closed the Hollywood. Fortunately they got a quick booking at a club in Salem, Massachusetts, where the reviews said they were the biggest sensation ever. Around that time, Duke wrote one of his early songs, with lyricist Jo Trent, " Pretty Soft for You," and sold it for fifty dollars.

After the great reviews, they got booked for their first Harlem theatre engagement in March 1925. When Duke was told to write a revue for the next day, he wound up writing five songs that night. It was a skill he would continue to hone throughout his career. The show was called CHOCOLATE KIDDIES. Two months later the show was booked for a tour of Germany, England, and Russia, and met with huge success. The producer made a fortune from it, while Ellington and Trent split five hundred dollars.

The Hollywood Club reopened in 1925 with a new name, the Kentucky Club, and a new emphasis on black music. Again the reviews were spectacular. The result was an offer to go to the famous Cameo Club. Their very first night there the owner said they were "too tepid" and fired them. After a few weeks they persuaded the Kentucky Club to take them back. Over the years many great stars who came there wanted to sit in with the orchestra. They included Fats Waller, Al Jolson, George Gershwin, Irving Berlin, Ruth Etting, Bobby Clark, and Fanny Brice. Members of the Whiteman and Dorsey bands would sit in when off duty. Ellington remained at the Kentucky Club for four years while frequently playing other gigs at separate locations on the same night. Every few weeks on Sunday mornings they would go to Polly Adler's brothel and play there for tips.

Irving Mills, a well-known booking agent and entrepreneur, came there to hear the orchestra. He had been trying to get the Fletcher Henderson Band, the biggest at the time, under his wing. But negotiations had fallen through and Mills was taken by Ellington's group. Things would never be the same for the Duke, who, prior to their meeting, could not get recording contracts. Under Mills's management that would change. They had worked out an agreement which gave Mills 55 percent of Ellington's earn-

Duke Ellington. (Michael Ochs Archives/Getty Images.)

ings. Mills began making a lot of money through Ellington. Ellington realized, however, that Mills was getting things for him he could not get on his own. All during this time Ellington was assembling a group of very special musicians that he would keep with him through the thirties.

October 1927 brought a contract with Victor Records that continued for eight years. In the fall of 1927 he starred in JAZZ MANIA, and later that year had his first engagement at the famous Cotton Club. Harlem was exploding with white customers. Stories of Ellington's sexual escapades with white women, some of them socialites, soon abounded.

The streets of Harlem were packed with great clubs. One, called Mexico's, had a jam session every night after the musicians left their own clubs. One night the jam session would be all trumpets, and another all trombones, and so forth. The new use of mutes was making a very special difference in styles.

Most of the clubs were constantly being closed down and re-opened due to Prohibition. Others were never bothered because they made illegal payoffs.

Some of the clubs were owned by gangland figures. Owney Madden had just come out of Sing Sing after serving seven and a half years for manslaughter. He paid off journalists to keep his name out of the news. At that time, Jack Johnson, the great heavyweight fighter, had purchased a club in Harlem. He was not well liked due to his predilection for white women, which was not favorably looked upon at that time. As a result the club was doing poorly. In 1923, he sold it to Owney Madden, who wanted to operate a legitimate business while he was involved in gambling, drugs, and prostitution. It was made into the glamorous 700-seat Cotton Club.

In 1925, the Feds closed it down. But it re-opened in 1926. Dan Healy, a former performer, was hired to produce the shows. Healy tried several bands there, but was not pleased. Mills lobbied hard to get Ellington chosen, but Ellington was playing a show called DANCE MANIA for Clarence Robinson. Robinson threatened to sue if Ellington quit. So Madden sent one of his henchmen, Boo Boo Hoff, to see Robinson and advise him that it wouldn't be good for his health if he didn't release Ellington. Ellington was soon released from the contract.

At first there was some discontent with Ellington's sophisticated sound, nicknamed "jungle music." But it caught on and high society came to hear them. Once Fred Astaire showed up and jumped up on the stage and danced. Jolson, Helen Morgan, Eddie Cantor, and the Marx Brothers would also show up and perform. Even famous writers like F. Scott Fitzgerald and William Faulkner were seen there.

A young gangster, who packed a pistol and drove in the lead truck in caravans, would come and get up on the stage and dance. Next to Fred Astaire, he came to be known as the best dancer in New York. He became Mae West's lover and in five years he was in the movies. His name was George Raft.

One night Herman Stark, the manager, called Duke to his office and told him that Legs Diamond, the notorious gangster, was coming. Ellington was instructed to play "whatever music Diamond requested." Legs had just been released from the hospital after the second attempt on his life. He arrived with his girlfriend and requested "St. Louis Blues." He made the request repeatedly during the evening and Ellington continually acquiesced. At the closing, Legs stuffed a thousand dollar bill into Duke's pocket. He said, "Thanks kid. Buy yourself a cigar." He went into Stark's office. When he came out, Diamond put another thousand dollar bill into Ellington's pocket.

Ellington's reputation was expanding, and Irving Mills was keeping him busy. When the orchestra wasn't working at the club he had them in recording studios. On some recordings they were known as the Washingtonians and at other times as the Duke Ellington Orchestra. Mills was raking in money.

By 1927, Ellington and his Cotton Club Orchestra had achieved major stature. He brought in Barney Bigard, a clarinetist from New Orleans, and Johnny Hodges on the saxophone. Ellington had tried unsuccessfully to persuade Hodges to join him in 1925 and 1926. Hodges finally agreed in 1928 and remained with the orchestra until 1970. Hodges was featured in solos and wrote some music with the Duke. He did all of this despite the fact that he could not read music. Songs had to be played for him several times and that was all that was necessary. John Coltrane called Hodges the greatest of all saxophonists.

While his career was flourishing, Ellington's personal life was in a shambles. He was constantly unfaithful, having affairs, predominantly with wealthy white women. One night in bed at home he heard the click of a gun. Edna said she knew what he was doing and intended to kill him, but he lied his way out of it. Soon an incident occurred that led to their permanent separation. It was another confrontation about other women ending with Edna slashing him with a razor from his ear to his lip. It left a permanent scar on his face. He supported her for the rest of her life until she died in 1966. He would never mention her again and would throw a tantrum if a reporter brought up her name.

In 1928, Dorothy Fields and Jimmy McHugh wrote that year's annual Cotton Club revue. Duke was having trouble with Bubber Miley, his original trumpeter, who was constantly drunk. Ellington replaced him with the nineteen-year-old Cootie Williams, who stayed for ten years and was called by Benny Goodman the best trumpeter he ever heard.

Mills thought he had complete control of the orchestra, but the musicians didn't like him and kept telling Ellington that Mills was taking advantage of him. So Ellington found a way to sign a separate contract with Flo Ziegfeld. The orchestra would perform in a show for him called SHOW GIRL, with music by George Gershwin. Mills could do nothing about it, but he did arrange to have limousines at the stage door every night to take the orchestra directly to work at the Cotton Club. In the daytime before going to the theatre Mills had them in a recording studio.

Duke now had a new girlfriend, Mildred Dixon. He moved Mildred, his mother, his father, and his sister Ruth into his apartment. He put his parents into separate rooms, essentially ending their marital relationship, which was said to be his intention. Meanwhile, he lavished gifts on his mother.

Mills had arranged for a short subject starring the Orchestra. It was called BLACK AND TAN and was filmed in Astoria, Queens. The orchestra was traveling back and forth between Hollywood and New York. The shows at the Cotton Club were more successful than they had ever been and Stark was willing to accede to any wish from Ellington. Duke complained that his mother was able see him every night on Broadway, but was never allowed to see him at the Cotton Club, with its all-white clientele. Stark changed the policy to allow in, as he put it, "respectable negroes."

Another time Ellington wanted the band to be released for several weeks to go back out to Hollywood to make another movie. Stark agreed and allowed Mills to bring in a replacement, a great opportunity for whomever was selected. It was Cab Calloway. A contract was signed, giving 55 percent of the money to Mills and ten percent to Ellington. Calloway got only 35 percent.

There was so much traveling across the country that Ellington arranged to get a series of railroad cars outfitted for him and the musicians. Duke had his own compartment and each musician had a lower berth. But Duke was never in his compartment. He was out playing poker with his musicians. Ellington once said he could never write for musicians he hadn't played poker with.

Though they were extremely successful, racial prejudice still was strong. To prevent anyone from believing white musicians were in the orchestra, the producers of one of their movies actually forced the lighter-skinned musicians to have their skin darkened, so they would all appear the same.

In September 1930, the Cotton Club show was written by a new team, Harold Arlen and Ted Koehler. Everyone agreed their music perfectly suited the mood of the club. They understood the new black jazz. Ethel Waters said of Harold Arlen that he was "the blackest white man" she ever knew.

Ellington began reversing the roles of the clarinet, trumpet, and trombone and creating a new sound. Mills put some lyrics to a new song Ellington had composed, but the lyrics were mostly written with Mitchell Parish. Mills constantly was putting his name on Ellington's compositions. This first big hit was, "Mood Indigo."

The 1930 movie CHECK AND DOUBLE CHECK

was released in Manhattan and at the same time the Orchestra did a two-week concert at the Paramount Theatre, the first African-American orchestra to ever play there. Duke experimented with a more sophisticated style when he wrote *Creole Rhapsody*, reminiscent of Gershwin's *Rhapsody in Blue* and *Concerto in F*.

Duke ended his thirty-one consecutive month engagement at the Cotton Club in 1931. The orchestra began touring the entire country, from north to south, sleeping on their train to avoid problems in the South. Now his fame was established. That same year, he performed four times at Chicago's Oriental Theatre to packed houses, night after night breaking all records. A combined total of 400,000 people were in attendance. But wherever the Orchestra went they faced major discrimination in the form of threats, actual attacks from thugs, and constant denial of services.

He actually was writing his music live with the orchestra, allowing them to go off on different riffs during the composing. Billy Strayhorn, who became his most important associate, said of Ellington that he played the piano, but his instrument was the orchestra. It was a style similar to what Joseph Haydn used with the Esterhazy orchestra in his composing. Duke arranged everything he wrote, a significant part of his creative process.

The tour was better than he could possibly expect. They broke all records in every city. In February 1932, he recorded a new song with his lead vocalist Ivie Anderson. Ted Koehler wrote the lyrics for "It Don't Mean a Thing (If It Ain't Got That Swing)."

Duke added Lawrence Brown to the trombone section, and he stayed for nineteen years. It was also at that time that Duke got into a terrible fight with Irving Mills. Ellington's sister Ruth had won a dance contest put on by the NAACP. Duke was so happy he offered the orchestra to play for the award ceremony. Mills worked out an agreement to get a percentage of the gate receipts. When the band arrived Mills demanded five hundred dollars up front, which the NAACP refused to give him. Mills made the orchestra leave without playing. Ruth was devastated and Duke was so angry that he didn't speak to Mills for a year.

The Depression affected the entertainment industry throughout 1932. Though the Ellington Orchestra always had work, most clubs were closing. Every Wednesday morning unemployed musicians would come to see Duke and he would give each of them five or ten dollars.

In 1933, Paramount made a short subject film just with Ellington playing solo piano. Among the pieces Duke played in the film was his new ballad, "Sophisticated Lady." That year, the Cotton Club had Ellington back on the bandstand. He was filling in for the permanent occupants, Cab Calloway and his orchestra, while Calloway fulfilled a temporary obligation. Arlen and Koehler had written scat songs for Calloway that wouldn't work with the Ellington orchestra. So they started over and wrote the hit song "Stormy Weather," to be sung by Ethel Waters. It revived her flagging career. Everyone came to hear her including Sophie Tucker, Milton Berle, Jimmy Durante, Ethel Merman, Johnny Weismuller, and Irving Berlin. Irving Berlin asked for and got Waters for his new show, AS THOUSANDS CHEER, where she introduced "Supper Time" and "Heat Wave."

In 1933, Ellington started on the first of many European tours. It included in its many stops the London Palladium. The band stayed in the East End and Bloomsbury, but Ellington and Mills were put up in the luxurious Dorchester, where Ellington stayed every subsequent visit to London. London critics cheered, noting that the new jazz came from Harlem gin mills, Georgian backyards, and New Orleans street corners and that Duke was its first genuine composer.

Each performance started with huge applause as the curtain opened to the elegance of the orchestra dressed in pearl-gray suits, with Ellington in white tails. The applause at the end was a two-minute standing ovation. Ellington was deeply moved. He was the old man at thirty-four. His musicians were in their early to mid-twenties. Conservative London was shocked by the droves of white women waiting at the stage door for his autograph. The British adored him. He was feted not only by the elite, but by royalty as well. He frequently would be whisked off from his stage performance to a midnight show elsewhere with enormous crowds. He became close to the Prince of Wales, who became Edward VIII and later, after his abdication and subsequent marriage to Wallis Simpson, the Duke of Windsor. Theirs was a lifelong friendship.

Ellington and his musicians soon left for Paris. The demand for the Ellington Orchestra was so great that Mills was booking them for multiple concerts a day in Paris. From there they went to the resorts in Deauville. Mills was making more money than he could possibly imagine and took Ellington to a brothel, telling him to pick one, and that "the treat's on me." Ellington took two.

On their return the orchestra went immediately into a national tour. But the experience was not nearly as special. They faced significant prejudice throughout the South. The opportunity for African Americans to hear them was significantly restricted. And, although he had hobnobbed with European royalty, it was not to be the same at home. Although a native Washingtonian, he was ignored by the White House. Hoover refused to be seen with him and even the Roosevelt administration ignored him. He was not to be honored there for another thirty-five years.

In 1934, his mother Daisy was diagnosed with cancer. Duke seemed unwilling to face her illness and continued to tour without coming back to see her. ASCAP recognized his "Solitude" as the best recording that year. Finally, in May

1935, the family called to tell him Daisy was getting progressively worse. Instead of going to see her, he persuaded them to put her on a train and bring her to Detroit where he was performing. She died there on May 27, with Ellington going back and forth to the hospital before and after performances. He asked Mills for an advance of five thousand dollars to have a giant funeral and Mills refused. Maybe it was because of guilt about how he had handled the last year of his mother's life, whom he adored so much, that he became terribly distraught. He sat around constantly crying and getting drunk and finally fell into a deep depression.

From that time on Ellington no longer was out playing poker with the band. The door, always previously open, was now always closed and he could at times be heard crying behind it.

To honor Daisy, he began writing a plaintive, twelve-minute long piece called *Reminiscing in Tempo*. It provided none of the typical open spots where individual musicians could go into riffs. At first, the orchestra played it every night, then less and less. After five months it was played no longer, but remained in their book for the rest of Ellington's life.

By the mid-1930s, the combined effect of the economic Depression, the end of Prohibition, and the rise of radio was so damaging that many of the nightclubs were closing. Besides that, the people wanted more accessible swing dance music like that of Benny Goodman rather than Duke's sophisticated jazz. Instead of playing in New York, they went back out on tour. Late in 1935, Duke came out with new recordings including three great standards "Mood Indigo," "Solitude," "Sophisticated Lady," as well as his newest "In a Sentimental Mood."

A March 1935 riot in Harlem shut down the Cotton Club. It was moved to Broadway, because whites would no longer go to Harlem. Two years later, Duke opened a giant show there with Ethel Waters and the Nicholas Brothers. It was the tenth anniversary of his first appearance there. Life magazine named Duke one of the "twenty most prominent negroes" in America.

Late in 1937, his father died and he wrote another composition, as he had done at his mother's death, *Diminuendo* and *Crescendo in Blue*.

"I Let a Song Go Out of My Heart," one of the biggest hits he had ever written, followed in 1938. It also became a big seller for the Benny Goodman Orchestra.

Ellington, who had been with Mildred Dixon since 1929, met the beautiful Evie Ellis in 1938. Duke moved his sister and Mercer out of his apartment. They all moved in with Evie, who wanted him to divorce Edna and marry him. But he refused, continuing to support Evie, Mildred, and Edna.

In 1939, though things were bad in Europe, Duke and his orchestra made a six-week tour of the continent. But war seemed imminent, and they returned on the *Ile de France* jammed packed with people trying to get away.

Two major decisions were made in 1939. Duke brought Billy Strayhorn into the orchestra. Strayhorn would become his closest friend and co-composer. He even moved into the apartment with Evie, Ruth, and Mercer. The other major decision, made on the ship on the way home, was to sever his ties with Irving Mills. There was never any negative publicity or statement by either one about the other to the press, but private anger enveloped Duke.

Two other musicians, Jimmy Blanton and Ben Webster, joined the orchestra. They were such spectacular artists that historians have called the band of the 1940s Ellington's Blanton-Webster band, the greatest ensemble he ever assembled.

Ellington now had to find his way around a problem not of his making. ASCAP and the NAB (National Association of Broadcasters) got into a royalty battle. As a result no music written by an ASCAP musician could be played on the radio. Ellington told Strayhorn and Johnny Mercer, who were not members of ASCAP, to begin writing new songs for the band to record, which could be heard on the radio. It was then that Strayhorn wrote a great song frequently mistaken as written by Ellington. It was Strayhorn's "Take The 'A' Train."

Ellington began working on his first full musical, JUMP FOR JOY and wrote, "I Got It Bad (And That Ain't Good)."

The show opened in Los Angeles and ran for 101 performances, but could never get enough backing to bring it to Broadway.

It was not uncommon for Ellington to write music that had no lyrics. Some of these tunes would have lyrics added later. One such song was "Never No Lament" written in 1940. In 1941 Bob Russell added lyrics and it became the well-known song "Don't Get Around Much Anymore."

Immediately after JUMP FOR JOY closed, Duke's fantastic bass player Jimmy Blanton was hospitalized with tuberculosis and died in 1942. The war was on and Ellington's Pullman cars had been requisitioned by the government. Going on the road became so difficult that a number of his musicians quit.

Meanwhile Duke was working on one of his masterpieces *Black, Brown, and Beige*. It was considered to be in a class with Gershwin's *Rhapsody in Blue* and Ferde Grofe's *Grand Canyon Suite*. But the initial reviews were not good and Ellington took it hard. Like Gershwin's PORGY AND BESS and Rodgers and Hart's PAL JOEY, it would not be appreciated until much later.

In 1945, the band finally got a six-month-long engagement in New York City. It was the first time in years they were off the road. The show opened each night with Ellington being lowered from the ceiling, seated at the piano and playing.

Though some of his musicians remained for twenty to thirty years, there was still a constant turnover. Ben Webster, half the great combination with Blanton, became

Duke Ellington. (Michael Ochs Archives/Getty Images.)

more and more difficult. He wanted to control the orchestra. Ellington was strong too, and finally fired him. The day he left Webster slashed and destroyed one of Ellington's sport jackets.

Trumpeter Wallace Jones quit for an interesting reason. When asked, he just said "Mood Indigo." The song was played at every performance. It called for a sustained eight bars of high D for the trumpet. It is so difficult that Jones said he had nightmares about it every night and couldn't sleep.

Many sidemen just quit because of the stress of years and years of the one-night stands.

In 1945, they were the first African-American band to play at Ciro's in Los Angeles and two incidents occurred. John Garfield, who was a friend of Duke's, asked the musician to come sit at his table after the performance. Management showed up and told Ellington he was not allowed to sit there.

The following night, another friend, George Raft, came with a party of friends and asked Duke and Greer to sit at the table. Once again management stepped in. But Raft became furious. He had the table moved into an outside alley where he, his friends, and Ellington and Greer partied all evening. He told the maitre d' if it ever happened again he'd have him fired.

The recording strike finally ended in November 1944 after almost four years and Ellington wrote and recorded his latest hit, "I'm Beginning to See the Light."

When Mills was his manager the royalty checks all

came through him. Duke would get twenty-five hundred dollars. Now Ellington dealt directly with the recording companies and was shocked to receive the checks. They were for twenty-five thousand dollars. Only then did he begin to realize how much money he had been cheated out of by Mills.

In 1946, Ellington realized his dream, to write a show for Broadway. It was BEGGAR'S HOLIDAY. The original director John Houseman was replaced by George Abbott. Abbott said he never once saw Ellington during the preparation of the show. He dealt exclusively with Billy Strayhorn. That was because it was primarily Strayhorn who composed it. The reviews were mixed and it closed quickly.

Ellington was in a major slump. Big bands were disbanding and vanishing. Singers went out on their own. Young musicians started smaller groups that were cheaper for club owners. He began criticizing prominent public figures as being responsible for society's ills, and the FBI began monitoring him as a possible communist.

It was not until the 1956 Newport Jazz Festival, almost a decade later, that he began a resurgence. Once again he became the hit of Europe, and especially England and British royalty. He wrote the soundtrack for ANATOMY OF A MURDER, which won the Grammy award.

Duke started a three-month engagement at the Riviera in Las Vegas. There he met Fernanda de Castro Monte. They had a torrid relationship. When he left for Los Angeles she came to the train station dressed in a mink coat. As the train was ready to leave she opened her coat, completely naked, wrapped him in it and gave him a goodbye kiss. It became his fourth serious relationship. She took care of him like a personal manager for the rest of his life, making certain his every need was met. She spoke five languages. But, she was expensive, requiring costly gifts.

Another very important person in Duke Ellington's life was his son Mercer. Mercer had assumed many roles for his father over the years—companion, messenger, musician among them. In 1964, he was a successful disc jockey when Duke asked him to come with them on a European tour as the band manager. He asked Mercer to bring along his trumpet just in case. He filled in one night and remained in the trumpet section of the orchestra for the next ten years.

Even after Fernanda became part of Duke's life, his relationship with Evie Ellis continued. She stayed in New York and maintained their apartment, to which Duke regularly returned. In 1969, Edna, Ellington's wife of fifty-two years, developed cancer and died. He had supported her throughout her life.

In 1965, the Pulitzer Prize preliminary jury decided to award a special citation to him. But in an unusual action the full committee rejected the recommendation. It so angered two of the committee members that they resigned, suggesting racial prejudice. At the time he was composing symphonic music, performing with leading orchestras, and receiving other awards. He remained passive about the Pulitzer incident until later in the year when he was scheduled to do a concert with Mel Tormé. He was annoyed that Tormé was getting top billing. Tormé agreed to change it, but his manager would not. Ellington exploded with expletives, shouting that he had almost won the Pulitzer Prize.

Over the years his work became more and more significant. Some consider the works he created commemorating the history of African Americans, including *Black, Brown and Beige* and *Come Sunday*, to be his most beautiful compositions. *New World a-Comin'* had been written in 1945 and *My People* in 1963. He also wrote a series of pieces based on Shakespearean plays and spiritual music compositions that led to the *Sacred Concerts*.

In 1966, he was finally invited to the White House by Lyndon Johnson.

Billy Strayhorn had become his closest confidant and musical associate, But Strayhorn died of cancer in 1967 and Ellington was inconsolable. They had been together for twenty-eight years. Strayhorn was only fifty-one years old.

The white establishment was giving Ellington more and more recognition. He received seventeen honorary Doctorates of Music including one from Yale. International honors were coming as well. Ultimately, President Johnson invited him to the White House seven times.

On April 29, 1969, President Nixon gave him a giant seventieth birthday party at the White House and presented him with the Presidential Medal of Freedom. He was even given the opportunity to invite fifty guests. The party was a glorious celebration that went on until 3 a.m.

In the spring of 1970, the orchestra made an exciting tour of the Far East featuring his lifelong friend and great sax player Johnny Hodges. But immediately after their return Ellington got the news that Hodges had suddenly died at sixty-three. They had worked together for forty years. Ellington gave the eulogy, comparing him with Strayhorn, Tatum, and Sidney Bechet.

Ellington was now so important that the State Department commissioned him to tour Russia as part of a cultural exchange program. He performed there with an orchestra conducted by Dimitri Shostakovich's son, who told Ellington his father was very sick in the hospital. After the concert the two of them went to see the great Russian composer. From there it was on to one-night stands all over Europe and South America, twenty-four concerts in as many days.

Ellington and his musicians were getting older and sicker. Smoke-filled nightclubs had taken their toll. Many had emphysema and Ellington now was diagnosed with lymphoma.

In 1973, working with Stanley Dance, he wrote his autobiography, *Music Was My Mistress*. The story sounded like nothing but wonderful things had ever happened in his life.

His editor responded, "Accuracy was never a part of an autobiography. They are just a picture of what the subject wanted you to believe."

Though Ellington was getting sicker he was invited to London to perform the *Third Sacred Concert* at Westminster Abbey. Mercer recalled walking into Duke's dressing room and finding him lying down and barely breathing. But when it was announced that Princess Margaret was approaching the stage door, Duke rose and put on his tails. He went out to greet Margaret and escort her to her seat. He looked nothing like the fatigued man Mercer had seen just moments before. After the concert, Ellington stayed at the party at 10 Downing Street for only fifteen minutes. The next day he was off on a twenty-seven day, twenty-seven concert tour through Europe and Africa. Mercer was concerned about his father's health and arranged for Duke's close friend and physician, Arthur Logan, to meet the plane when it returned to London.

The day before he was supposed to leave New York, Logan left his apartment to visit the site of a new clinic being built for him by the city and to see his patients at the hospital. Forty-five minutes later, his wife received a phone call from the police informing her that he had been mugged. His body was thrown 100 feet off a viaduct and he was killed.

Mercer felt he couldn't tell Duke as he was going directly to do a command performance for Queen Elizabeth II and Prince Philip.

When they finally told Ellington, he was more distraught than he had been with the death of his mother or Billy Strayhorn, as Logan had been such a close friend. The perpetrators were eventually caught.

In March 1974, Ellington collapsed after a concert and was admitted to Harkness Pavillion in New York City. His sister Ruth arranged for Frank Sinatra to get Dr. Michael DeBakey to fly there from Texas in Sinatra's private plane. Debakey said nothing more could be done other than what they were doing. An electronic piano was put in his room and he and Mercer continued composing. Mercer said afterward that Duke knew he was dying because he was instructing Mercer on how pieces should be completed if Duke was not around.

Evie Ellis visited him every day but didn't tell him she herself had been diagnosed with lung cancer. It became urgent for her to have surgery, so it was left to Mercer to explain why she no longer visited. Ellington's women visited him in shifts to avoid confrontations.

He was still in the hospital on his seventy-fifth birthday. President Nixon called to wish him "Happy Birthday" even though it was the very day he divulged on television the existence of the Watergate tapes.

His sister was with him the night Ellington died. He demanded of her kisses and more kisses before he lost consciousness. Edward Kennedy "Duke" Ellington passed away at 3:10 a.m. on May 24, 1974.

MAJOR WORKS

SHOWS:
JUMP FOR JOY **(1941)**
BEGGAR'S HOLIDAY **(1946)**
SOPHISTICATED LADIES (REVUE BASED ON HIS WORK: **1981)**

COMPOSITIONS:
IT IS ESTIMATED THAT ELLINGTON WROTE OVER 1,500 PIECES.

More than 60,000 people came to the funeral home. They were lined up four abreast for two city blocks. Around Ellington's neck were the Presidential Medal, the Emperor Star of Ethiopia, and the Legion of Honor from France. At St. John the Divine Church, 10,000 people attended the funeral with another 2,500 in the street. Along with the eulogies, Ella Fitzgerald sang "Solitude." Harry Carney, a friend and musician of his for decades, left the funeral saying, "I have nothing to live for," and died a few months later.

A memorial service in London at St Martin-in-the-Fields ended with his friend Larry Adler playing "Mood Indigo" on the harmonica.

Evie died of lung cancer in less than a year. Mercer left his wife of thirty-five years, moved to Denmark, and had a child with a woman there. His wife claimed he would never have done that were Duke still alive. But Duke's history with women did not set any such example.

Duke Ellington had multiple mistresses and five musicians in his band were married to women with whom he had previously had affairs. He left no will, just a note for Mercer. It said, "I'm easy to please. I just want everyone to be in the palm of my hand."

Duke performed 20,000 times in the United States, Europe, Latin America, and Asia in his more than fifty-year career. He made thousands of recordings and wrote several thousand compositions. His son Mercer kept all he could find in a Manhattan warehouse. In 1986, four people catalogued it for the Smithsonian Institution. There were 200,000 pages. In 1991, they received a thousand additional pieces of music from his sister Ruth. And in 1993, there was a giant exhibition in his honor.

More than anything else, Ellington was jazz music's greatest orchestrator. When Stravinsky came to the United States, he said his first priority was to hear Ellington at the Cotton Club.

In April 1999, on the centennial of his birth, thirty years after he had been denied recognition by the same body, Duke Ellington was finally awarded the Pulitzer Prize for his body of work.

Dorothy Fields, c. 1930s.
(Photofest.)

DOROTHY FIELDS

DOROTHY FIELDS WAS BORN IN ALLENHURST, NEW Jersey, on July 15, 1905, even though her family lived in New York City. They were at a house on the New Jersey coast, which they had rented for the summer. It was Rose Fields's fourth child, and she was in very active labor. They went searching for a physician, but could only find a midwife who owned a newsstand in town. Dorothy was delivered by her in the Fields's rented house.

The infant's three siblings were Herbert, age six, ten-year-old Joseph, and eleven-year-old Frances.

The family was quite well to do, living in the affluent Upper West Side. Lew, the father, was a famous performer and a Broadway impresario. They lived in a world with a chauffeur, a cook, a maid, a governess, and a laundress.

Lew had grown up in poverty in the Lower East Side. His parents, the Schoenfelds, had come from western Poland near the German border.

Lew arrived in America when he was five years old. Throughout his life he claimed to have been born here. He was actually part of an influx of Jews that come earlier than the Eastern European Jews who emigrated around the turn of the century. The earlier, central European Jews considered the Eastern Europeans to be second-class.

Lew's father was a tailor. He survived economically by using the labor of everyone in the family.

It was as a student at the Henry Street School that Lew first met Joe Weber. They began their act at age twelve in what were called "dime museums," in the company of other variety and freak acts. They performed ten shows a day, for which they received three dollars a week. That came to about five cents a performance. For his stage career, Lew shortened his name from Schoenfeld to Fields. The two of them did their comedy act with German Jewish dialects.

Over time, they progressed to Oscar Hammerstein's Olympia Theatre and then to Tony Pastor's upscale vaudeville theatre, where the entertainment was deemed to be suitable for families. In 1893, Lew married Rose.

Weber and Fields soon became famous not just as performers, but also as impresarios. They bought theatres and offered shows of every variety. Among others, Lillian Russell, Marie Dressler, Irene Castle, and Helen Hayes worked for them. In 1904, after a dispute, Weber and Fields dissolved their partnership.

Lew was a dynamo in the world of theatre, while Rose ran the home without question. She was known as the Queen. When at home, Lew was warm, kind, and passive. His career was so active that he was, however, rarely there and spent little time with the children. Both Lew and Rose had decided they did not want their children to have theatre careers. As a result, Lew rarely invited business associates or performers to their home.

On the other hand, the children loved the opportunity to go to the theatre and introduce themselves as Lew Fields's children. In the process they came to know performers like the incomparable Lillian Russell very well. Her huge collection of wigs was extremely impressive. One day her backstage dressing-room door was opened a crack. As the children peeked in, they screamed in shock. Miss Russell was totally bald. On hearing the screams, Miss Russell swore them to secrecy.

Lew Fields's downfall was an addiction to gambling which frequently brought him severe financial distress. This problem led Rose to leave him on two occasions, taking the children with her.

Lew frequently tried to hide his terrible financial state from Rose and the children. At times he was forced to return to performing to get urgently needed cash. Ultimately, the stress caused him to have a nervous breakdown. He went begging to the Shuberts for help. The family's personal lifestyle had to be significantly cut back. Fortunately, their eldest child, Frances, married into a wealthy family and her husband Charles Marcus bailed them out.

Dorothy later remembered that when she was fourteen, a young college student, Richard Rodgers had come to their house to play music he had written with Larry Hart. The entire family was there as an audience and Rodgers was smitten by young Dorothy. That was not strange because Rodgers was frequently smitten and a womanizer his entire life. Lew was impressed by the work of Rodgers and Hart and bought "Any Old Place with You." He immediately put it into a show.

That meeting started a working relationship between Dorothy's brother Herb and Rodgers and Hart. In their first show for the philanthropic Akron Club, Dorothy had a starring role. She was only fourteen and even received mention in a theatre magazine.

The three of them, Rodgers, Hart, and Herb Fields, continued writing essentially amateur productions for either charity or Columbia University varsity shows.

Lew Fields was offered the opportunity to produce GARRICK GAIETIES but declined. It became Rodgers and Hart's first hit show in 1925. Fields lacked confidence that the team could make it on a professional basis. But following that success Lew Fields produced their next five shows. During that time, Dorothy dated Dick Rodgers a few times.

Dorothy's parents were firmly committed to keeping her out of show business. They had been relatively successful in this pursuit until she accidentally met J. Fred Coots on a golf course. He thought that she was talented and introduced her to Jimmy McHugh, who, aside from composing, had a salesman's job at Mills Music.

Her early lyrics were influenced by Larry Hart. But she soon realized that she had to find her own style.

Their personalities were quite different. McHugh was outgoing while Dorothy was quiet and shy. But they learned to work together and did so for a decade. McHugh arranged for the two of them to create the music for the new and important Cotton Club shows. The Cotton Club was where the affluent white society went to hear African-American performers. But African Americans were not welcome as patrons.

On opening night of the first show McHugh and Fields had written for the Cotton Club her entire family was in the audience. Aida Ward sang the opening number. It was the most lewd song anyone had ever heard at the Cotton Club. Lew was shocked until Dorothy told him that she knew nothing about it and had not written that song. Even though the management was known to be made up of gangsters and murderers, Lew went backstage to complain angrily. As a result, an announcement was made that the opening song was not written by McHugh and Fields.

Following that success, a producer, Harry Delmar, hired them to write the songs for his next vaudeville show. They wrote one for Bert Lahr and Patsy Kelly to perform. On opening night, Delmar hated the song so much he demanded they remove it permanently from the show.

Subsequently, they were hired to write the music for

Lew Leslie's BLACKBIRDS OF 1928. They put the same song back and it was panned in reviews. But Leslie was not deterred and kept the song in. The show ran for 519 performances, and was the first show to have its score in an album. Now their frequently maligned song, "I Can't Give You Anything But Love (Baby)" was becoming a hit.

By the late 1920s, the song had become so popular that its sheet music could be found in almost every household. Cliff Edwards recorded it and it became the number one song in America. It was later recorded by Billie Holiday and Teddy Wilson, ending up high on the charts.

The song was used in multiple musical films and even two non-musicals. In one case, Katherine Hepburn and Cary Grant sang it in the movie, BRINGING UP BABY. Judy Holliday also sang it in BORN YESTERDAY. And even on Broadway it was heard in both AIN'T MISBEHAVIN' and SUGAR BABIES.

Dorothy and Jimmy wrote their first book show, rather than a revue, in 1928. It was HELLO, DADDY. It was only moderately successful, with no lasting music. They were still writing revues at the same time.

In 1924, Dorothy had married Dr. Jack Wiener, a physician and chest specialist. He was ten years her senior. It was a marriage only in the legal sense, and lasted almost ten terrible years. Wiener had moved into high society and was well liked, but their relationship was disastrous.

In her own right, Dorothy had moved into a very important position in the music world, earning thousands of dollars weekly. Broadway was dying during the Depression, however, which led composers and lyricists to head for Hollywood. Other members of her family were in deep financial difficulty. Lew was practically bankrupt. Her sister Frances's husband's family, in the banking business, had been very hard hit. Frances's husband Charles was indicted, and his brother Bernard would go to prison. Frances and Charles gave up their luxurious lifestyle and ultimately were divorced. Dorothy's brother Herb had invested heavily in his brother-in-law's bank and lost his entire investment.

Hollywood, offering cheap and diversionary entertainment, was booming. Some of the composers and lyricists detested the lifestyle and the working environment, where the studios controlled everything. But others were very happy there. As an example, Burton Lane stayed for years. McHugh and Fields had an arrangement that allowed them periodically to return to New York City to work in the theatre. In 1930 and 1931 they went back and forth between the Coasts. On Broadway they contributed music to four revues. But everything written for Broadway at that time wound up a flop for all the composers. The one that looked the most promising was Lew Leslie's INTERNATIONAL REVUE. Even that lasted only three months, which was pretty good for the Depression. McHugh and Fields did write two lasting hits for that show. One was "Exactly Like You." The other became one of the most popular songs ever written and was ultimately used in seven movies. The song was "On the Sunny Side of the Street."

Their life in Hollywood was extremely pleasant. Everyone was being very well paid and living in high style. Her brother Herb had signed with Warner Brothers and Dorothy and Jimmy McHugh with MGM. Herb and Dorothy rented a house in Beverly Hills. Soon brother Joe got a job with Republic Studio and moved in with them. They were living lush lives with pool parties, parties around the piano, multiple automobiles, and lots of drinking. With Lew now in retirement, they persuaded their parents to come out West and move into their spacious home. Once again, Rose controlled everything and insisted they all have Sunday dinner together. Lew even got a few cameo roles in films. The parents and children had reversed roles as Lew and Rose got an allowance from their children. Lew was even subsidized by his children as he made frequent trips to the racetrack.

Even though Lew, most of all, had resisted Dorothy's entry into show business, ultimately, of all the siblings, she had become the most successful in the business.

A new opportunity was about to come Dorothy's way. In 1932, Radio City Music Hall was completed. Its construction was funded primarily by the Rockefellers. The Hall possessed the largest stage in the world and a gigantic opening night celebration was planned. There were more than six thousand seats. In attendance would be the Rockefellers, the Berlins, Gene Tunney, Alfred Smith, Leopold Stokowski, and Amelia Earhart.

Dorothy and Jimmy McHugh were asked to write two songs and perform them for the live audience. Lew Fields and Joe Weber were reunited for a special performance. The show went on until 12:30 a.m. There may have been some indication that it was overlong and not terribly great by a reviewer who stated it was the first time she "ever saw 3000 people sleeping together."

Fields and McHugh wrote several movies in 1933, including MEET THE BARON. It included the song "Don't Blame Me," taken from a failed show CLOWNS IN CLOVER. The song became a big hit.

By 1935, Dorothy began working with others besides McHugh. It was a big year for her. Fields wrote the scores for eight films. Two of the songs from EVERY NIGHT AT EIGHT would become standards. They included McHugh's and Fields' most famous ballad, "I'm in the Mood for Love," which remained on the Hit Parade for weeks. The other was "I Feel a Song Coming On."

By then Dorothy's marriage had been dissolved and she was dating some of Hollywood's most eligible bachelors, including producer Felix Young.

This was also the time of big hits by Fields with

composers other than McHugh. Jerome Kern had been one of Dorothy's longtime idols. In 1935, she got to work with him on the film version of ROBERTA, for which Fields provided some new lyrics. Together they produced "Lovely to Look At" and "I Won't Dance."

The opportunity to work with Kern came about in a strange way. Though Kern had a fine relationship with Oscar Hammerstein II, he had a reputation for being difficult. Some considered him to be pompous and pedantic. Kern had openly stated that he refused to work with anyone he didn't like. After finishing work on the film ROBERTA, he left a melody with the studio and went to New York. Pandro Berman, the head of production at RKO, invited Dorothy to write lyrics for this unusual melody. It was a risky thing to do because he had not asked for Kern's permission. Berman took the lyrics and shot the scene in the film without Kern knowing about it beforehand. Fortunately, Kern loved it and was impressed with Dorothy's work. The song was "Lovely to Look At." Kern told her that he wanted to collaborate more with her and a longterm relationship was established.

They were an odd pair. Kern was quite short and Dorothy towered over him. Kern was also nineteen years her senior. And most amazing of all, although many others were intimidated by him, Dorothy called him Junior because of their height difference. Kern was not upset by that at all. He was crazy about her and Dorothy became almost like a member of his family.

When ROBERTA was done, Kern was signed to write a film called I DREAM TOO MUCH. He insisted that Dorothy be the lyricist. But he was still a very tough and stingy businessman. He arranged to receive five thousand dollars weekly, while Dorothy was paid one-fifth that amount.

Dorothy learned a lot from Kern about how to combine lyrics with melodies. One of the reasons he loved her so much was that she was not intimidated by him. She apparently saw through the front he presented to the public, considering him cute, rather than ferocious. There was constant laughter when she was in his home. Kern's wife Eva was always aloof or shy with her. However, Dorothy had a very close relationship with his daughter Betty. They spent a great deal of time together.

Kern and Fields both were immaculate dressers and had a common interest in antiques. Kern taught her a great deal about the subject. Frequently, they would be seen together at auctions.

The only argument Dorothy ever recalled having with Kern centered around an automobile. George Gershwin had been teaching Dorothy how to play golf. One day he drove her to the course in his new flashy Cord. Gershwin was a lot more fun-loving than Kern. He encouraged Fields to buy a Cord as well. The day that she obtained the blindingly bright blue car, Dorothy rushed to Kern's home to show it to him. He saw it and refused to drive with her, claiming it was "vulgar." He insisted that she have it painted black, which she did. He told her to sell it because it wasn't any good. She unhappily agreed, and sure enough the Cord Company shortly went out of business.

An opportunity arose for her to write a Rogers–Astaire film with Kern. Through the 1930s, the screen pair's films had been the repository for one hit song after another, for multiple composers and lyricists. The project started in 1936. It was initially called I WON'T DANCE, then NEVER GONNA DANCE, and finally it became SWING TIME. For the first time, Dorothy wrote the lyrics before the melody. It would be the peak of her work in Hollywood.

For that one film, she wrote "Pick Yourself Up," "A Fine Romance," and the Academy Award–winning "The Way You Look Tonight." She was only thirty years old and the first female songwriter to win the Best Song award.

Dorothy also wrote a song that year with Fritz Kreisler, the world-renowned violinist. His response to the lyrics she supplied for him was a simple, "Thank you, Miss Fields."

Dorothy's world in Hollywood consisted of a lively party life with many afternoons spent at the Gershwins' home playing tennis. In the evenings, the parties frequently centered around a piano. George Gershwin would always be playing and at the center of attention. Kern and composer Sigmund Romberg were resentful that everyone wanted to hear Gershwin play rather than either of them. They never really understood that the guests loved their music as well, but that no one could play the piano like George Gershwin.

Two disasters cast a pall over the entire community. Initially, Jerome Kern had a severe heart attack followed by a stroke, which incapacitated him for months. Immediately afterward, George Gershwin died suddenly of a brain tumor at thirty-eight. Dorothy was a particularly close friend of Gershwin, and she was devastated by the death. Her brother Herb, who had worked with him, actually went into a deep depression.

With these events, life changed completely in Hollywood. Dorothy went back to New York and eventually married again. This time it was to a clothing manufacturer. Like her first husband, Eli Lahm was significantly older than she was—there was a twelve-year difference between them.

They moved into an apartment across the street from Carnegie Hall. Now getting older, she found herself much more domesticated in this marriage. She and Eli had two children, David in 1940, and Eliza in 1944 when Dorothy was thirty-nine years old.

In 1938, Dorothy collaborated with Arthur Schwartz to write the show STARS IN YOUR EYES. No longing working primarily in Hollywood, she reflected on lyrics in a different way. In movies, the goal was to write songs that could even-

Dorothy Fields, c. 1950s. (Photofest.)

tually become pop hits. On the stage, Hammerstein had been in the forefront of constructing songs that would be an integral part of the story, much less likely to result in hit songs. Stephen Sondheim, probably more than anyone, would become a part of that philosophy of songwriting.

Dorothy also began writing just the librettos for a series of shows with her brother Herb. Three of the shows were by Cole Porter, who wrote all of his own lyrics, and they were all hits: LET'S FACE IT, SOMETHING FOR THE BOYS, and MEXICAN HAYRIDE. During this time, Ethel Merman, who had become one of Porter's favorite leading ladies, became Dorothy's close friend.

After not writing lyrics for five years, Dorothy began a new project in 1945 with producer Mike Todd. She and her brother Herb signed on to write both the book and the lyrics. Sigmund Romberg eagerly accepted the job of composing the show, as he had not had a hit for ten years. The show was called UP IN CENTRAL PARK, a spoof on the corrupt New York City politicians in Tammany Hall. It ran for a year and a half.

In her marriage to Eli, Dorothy experienced a new kind of life. She was now an integral part of New York City's social elite, and became a part of the trio known as "the three Dorothys," the wife of Richard Rodgers, the wife of Oscar Hammerstein, and Dorothy Fields. Her social life mainly centered around those couples and the Berlins.

Dorothy's father died while she was writing Porter's LET'S FACE IT. As a result, Rose moved back east to be near her two daughters, Frances and Dorothy. Even Dorothy's brother Joe had come to New York to write two major shows for Broadway, MY SISTER EILEEN and JUNIOR MISS.

Dorothy suddenly got an idea that a show could be written for her dear friend, Ethel Merman, about the life of Annie Oakley and her love affair with Frank Butler. Merman loved the concept, so Fields took the idea to Mike Todd, who rejected it completely.

During that period, Rodgers and Hammerstein had not only been extremely successful with their own shows, OKLAHOMA! and CAROUSEL, but they also had begun producing others' shows. Close to both men, Dorothy brought them her Annie Oakley idea. They immediately found it exciting. However, the style of a comic musical was not something they relished writing themselves and decided that they would prefer to be the producers. When Fields suggested Kern as the composer they grew ecstatic. They had tremendous respect for his work. Kern was still writing in Hollywood and winning Academy Awards. Rodgers and Hammerstein wrote him a very solicitous letter and in it, as an added perk, Hammerstein suggested that when he came east that they should start working on a rewrite of SHOW BOAT for a Broadway revival.

Adding the perk was unnecessary. Kern loved both the theme and the idea of working once again with Dorothy Fields. He agreed and made immediate plans to come to New York.

Jerome and Eva Kern moved into the St. Regis Hotel and, in the morning, Jerome left to meet with Hammerstein. He left a note on the bathroom mirror, reminding Eva that she had a luncheon date with Dorothy Fields.

After window shopping in some antique stores for a piece of furniture as a gift for their daughter Betty, Kern collapsed, unconscious, on the corner of East Fifty-Seventh Street and Park Avenue.

As he was carrying no identification, the ambulance took him to the city hospital on Welfare Island, where the drunks and derelicts were cared for. Someone noticed that he had an ASCAP pin in his lapel and called there. An immediate identification was made. Eva, Hammerstein, and Dorothy Fields raced to his bedside. Betty came from California. Kern had suffered a stroke, was comatose, and in critical condition. He rallied sufficiently to be transferred to Doctors' Hospital in Manhattan. On November 11, Kern died.

Once the terrible loss was fully accepted, the question of what to do about the show arose. When the suggestion was made to ask Irving Berlin, Rodgers and Hammerstein left the answer to Dorothy. It was understood that if Berlin agreed it would only be on the basis that he could write both the music and the lyrics, as he always did. Dorothy urged them to make the offer.

Berlin took Dorothy and Herb's libretto with him to Atlantic City to try to work on a score. He returned after one weekend with three songs: "You Can't Get a Man with a Gun," "There's No Business Like Show Business," and "Doin' What Comes Natur'lly."

The division of royalties for a show is standard. One-third goes to the composer, one-third to the lyricist, and one-third to the librettist. Berlin said he based all of his titles on the material provided by Dorothy and Herb. He was so impressed with their book that he suggested they divide the royalties half and half. That was quite amazing as Berlin was noted for being an extremely frugal and tough businessman.

Everyone agreed through all the production and rehearsals that they had never seen such a smooth preparation for a show. It was devoid of arguments, fights, or disagreements of any type. Due to a physical problem with the theatre, it opened temporarily in Philadelphia. During the first act, on opening night, there were no laughs, applause, or audience reaction. At the intermission, the show's principals were certain they were stuck with a complete flop. But something happened to the crowd during the intermission and they became very receptive during the second act. The reviews were mixed. But, it became one of the biggest hits Broadway had ever seen.

The show ran for 1147 performances. At that time, it

had the second-longest run in Broadway history, behind OKLAHOMA! Many of the songs became standards. It is generally considered to be Berlin's finest show and was a huge financial success.

When it was made into a film, sadly, Merman was replaced by Judy Garland. Garland developed many personal problems and was replaced by Betty Hutton. Even with these conflicts, the movie became a big hit. Still today, the license to perform the show is one of the most frequently granted. In 1966, it was revived successfully at Lincoln Center with Ethel Merman once again in the lead. It is considered, with SWEET CHARITY, to be one of Dorothy Fields's finest works for the theater.

Dorothy soon took on a project for the Theatre Guild. They had produced a play in 1934 called THE PURSUIT OF HAPPINESS and decided to convert it into a musical. The Guild hired Dorothy and Herb to do the book and lyrics and arranged for Burton Lane, who had just completed the successful FINIAN'S RAINBOW, to compose the music. Lane and Dorothy were old friends and he came to her house to read the libretto. After dinner he took it to bed with him.

As he read it he felt certain that it was inadequate, but as an old friend felt embarrassed to tell them. Nevertheless, in the morning Lane withdrew from the project. As a replacement they hired Morton Gould, who had had very limited success in the theatre. The show, ARMS AND THE GIRL, turned out to be extremely weak, as Lane had predicted. It opened in early 1950 and closed after a few months.

The following year brought an opportunity and a strong comeback for Dorothy. George Abbott selected her to write just the lyrics, not the book, for A TREE GROWS IN BROOKLYN. It starred Shirley Booth and opened in April 1951 to rave reviews. The music was composed by Arthur Schwartz and is generally considered the best score he ever created for Broadway. A TREE GROWS IN BROOKLYN also had one of Dorothy's finest songs, "Make the Man Love Me." The show, even with great reviews, was a disappointment, as it never clicked with the public. It ran for less than one year.

It was a good time for Dorothy. She, Eli, and the two children moved to a larger apartment on Park Avenue. They also had a second home in Brewster, New York, and divided their time between the two residences throughout the 1950s. She greatly enjoyed the company of her two other Dorothy friends, Rodgers and Hammerstein, and devoted her days to much charity work. Primarily she worked for the Girl Scouts of America and the Federation of Jewish Philanthropies. When her name appeared in newspaper columns, she was often noted as being the most elegant dresser among important women, with a very tailored wardrobe.

Dorothy Fields was not very political, but she did follow in the footsteps of her husband and closest friends. They were all acknowledged supporters of the Republican party.

In 1953, another possible assignment came her way as she was hired to write the lyrics for CARNIVAL IN FLANDERS, but was replaced. It was a fortunate loss for her, as the show was a complete failure and closed after six days. Intermittently she was also taking assignments in Hollywood with Arlen, Harry Warren, and Arthur Schwartz. But none of these films had any lasting quality.

A TREE GROWS IN BROOKLYN had been such a critical success that Dorothy and Herb were encouraged to write a sequel for Shirley Booth. It was titled BY THE BEAUTIFUL SEA. The show was not considered to be as good as A TREE GROWS IN BROOKLYN. However, possibly because of the popularity of Shirley Booth, it ran just as long.

In 1958, in Dorothy Fields's estimation, she wrote one of her poorest shows, REDHEAD. However, she won her first Tony award for it and found it difficult to understand why other productions of hers had not received that recognition. Similarly, Fred Ebb, who wrote with John Kander, felt that the best things he wrote failed and the worst received awards.

It is not difficult to understand why she wrote what she considered to be her worst work in 1958—it was an extremely difficult year for her. In March, her brother Herb died of a heart attack, and four months later her husband Eli died of a stroke. Her son was already in college and Dorothy was left at home with a teenage daughter. Dorothy had already been known to have a drinking problem, but these events exacerbated it. All of this was occurring while she was writing REDHEAD.

The show's problems included the frequent recasting of the leading lady. Finally, the role was given to Gwen Verdon, who agreed to do it only if her husband, Bob Fosse, was named the director and choreographer. Verdon and Fosse's work resulted in the show becoming a hit, running for 455 performances. Fosse was not easy to work with and forced Fields and Albert Hague, the composer, to rewrite almost the entire score. As it turned out, it became the most successful of Dorothy Fields' shows, winning nine Tony Awards.

Dorothy Fields never developed an ongoing collaboration with the composer of REDHEAD, Albert Hague. By this time, Arthur Schwartz, her longtime collaborator, was no longer available to her either, as he had moved to London. She had no one to write with and seemed to fall out of the loop.

Fields sold both her Brewster home and the Park Avenue apartment, moving to West 81st Street. There was no work for her and she was drinking more than ever.

Friends were at their wits' end trying help. She occasionally went to the theatre with a friend, Earle Earl.

Out of nowhere, Cy Coleman, who had composed

Dorothy Fields and
Jimmy McHugh, c. 1930s.
(Photofest.)

LITTLE ME with Carolyn Leigh, contacted her. He was twenty-five years younger than Fields. He asked in 1965 if she would be interested in writing a show with him.

Fosse had selected a Fellini film, NIGHTS OF CABIRIA, to adapt for a new show. It told the story of a kindhearted prostitute who is repeatedly mistreated. Catering to the sensibilities of the American public, the role of the prostitute was converted into a dance-hall hostess. The show became SWEET CHARITY, with a jazzy burlesque format. When they began their collaboration, Fosse, who would direct and choreograph, Neil Simon who wrote the book, and Gwen Verdon who was the star, were all in their late thirties, while Dorothy Fields was sixty.

Suddenly, Fields's life had turned around. The show was a huge success with two blockbuster hit songs, "If My Friends Could See Me Now" and "Big Spender." Gwen Verdon had become the leading light on Broadway and the show ran for 608 performances. There was a London production and a revival in 1985 on Broadway. Dorothy was back on top, personally and financially. However, another seven years would pass before she and Cy Coleman were back on Broadway with another show, SEESAW.

During that interval, several projects, some with Coleman, began and ended. It was a new era on Broadway. Shows had become much more expensive to produce and, as a result, investors were more wary of risks. Dorothy also felt her style of writing was no longer relevant, as the new genre of rock musicals had taken hold.

In 1972, Fields and Coleman began working on an adaptation of Willaim Gibson's play, TWO FOR THE SEESAW, retitled GITTEL, about a Jewish bohemian dancer and her uptight Midwestern boyfriend. The name of the show was quickly changed to SEESAW. The two worked on it for seven months. There seemed to be constant problems all through the production and rehearsal period. Lainie Kazan, the lead, created innumerable difficulties, because of her inability to control her weight and trouble remembering her lines. Ultimately, the producers fired her and almost everyone else associated with the show.

By January 1973, Michael Bennett was brought in to take over the production. He hired Tommy Tune to do the choreography. Bennett forced Coleman and Fields to discard half the songs they had written and start over. Neil Simon was hired to rewrite the book. The level of firings went all the way down to the chorus, where many were replaced.

The producers panicked as all the changes had blown the budget up to over one million dollars. The main personnel like Bennett, Coleman, and Fields took salary cuts. They even began putting up some of their own money to help sustain the project. The show opened Sunday, March 19, 1973. Although the reviews were great, the production lacked sufficient funds to pay the performers and a decision was made to close after the first week. Dorothy put up thirty thousand dollars and the cast accumulated another six thousand to buy a radio advertisement. In a public relations coup, they got Mayor John Lindsay (who resembled the show's lead, Ken Howard) to make a cameo appearance one night. Finally, by the end of the first week, advanced sales started to accumulate. The show ran for nine months. But Dorothy felt weary from the difficult struggle. She worried about where the future of Broadway was going.

A year later rehearsals were on for the national tour. On Thursday, March 28, 1974, Dorothy Fields left the rehearsal hall early to return to her apartment to rest, and then dress for a fund-raising event that evening. Before that evening came she died of a stroke at the age of sixty-eight.

ASCAP named her the most important woman in the history of the organization. In her career she had written nineteen Broadway musicals, the lyrics for thirty movies, and a total of almost two hundred and fifty songs. In the latter years of her life, Dorothy Fields received many awards.

Five years after Fields's death, the 1979 show SUGAR BABIES came to Broadway, starring Mickey Rooney and Ann Miller. Once again the public heard the stunning music of Dorothy Fields and Jimmy McHugh.

MAJOR WORKS

SHOWS:

BLACKBIRDS OF 1928 **(1928)**
HELLO, DADDY **(1928)**
ZIEGFELD MIDNIGHT FROLIC **(1929)**
THE INTERNATIONAL REVUE **(1930)**
THE VANDERBILT REVUE **(1930)**
CLOWNS IN CLOVER **(1933)**
STARS IN YOUR EYES **(1939)**
UP IN CENTRAL PARK **(1945)**
ARMS AND THE GIRL **(1950)**
A TREE GROWS IN BROOKLYN **(1951)**
BY THE BEAUTIFUL SEA **(1954)**
REDHEAD **(1959)**
SWEET CHARITY **(1966)**
SEESAW **(1973)**

COMPOSITIONS:

FIELDS WROTE LYRICS FOR 250 SONGS WITH MULTIPLE COMPOSERS.

George Gershwin, c. 1930s. (Photofest.)

GEORGE GERSHWIN

MORE BOOKS, MAGAZINE AND NEWSPAPER ARTICLES, speeches, and published letters have been written about the young man born Jacob Gershwine, to Morris and Rose Gershowitz in 1898, than about all of America's other great composers put together. Each year, more Gershwin scholarship emerges. The latest book on him actually lists more than 150 sources in its bibliography.

Starting from an immigrant Russian Jewish family in the Lower East Side of Manhattan, Gershwin's early life was nothing like that of Irving Berlin, who grew up alone in abject poverty. Morris made a decent living moving from one small business to another. They lived modestly, in more comfort whenever the business was successful. Rose had better business acumen than Morris and was a lot more aggressive and ambitious. As a result, the marriage was not great, which may partly explain why George never married. But, the marriage triumphed over its problems and lasted.

George, as he was always called, not Jake or Jacob, was preceded into the world by his brother Israel, two years his senior. Izzy, or Ira, was a good student, bookish and introverted. George was by comparison a poor student, somewhat delinquent and a street fighter. He was no child prodigy. But when a piano was bought for Ira, George, who was about twelve, became interested in music for the first time. After he showed signs of talent, his parents arranged for him to have lessons with local teachers, but he advanced too rapidly. So, at age fourteen, he began studying with Charles Hambitzer, a successful performer and teacher. When Hambitzer's wife died suddenly he became depressed and alcoholic, thus ending George's early studies.

Gershwin hated school. At fifteen, he heard there was an opening for a song plugger on Tin Pan Alley. He was able to convince his parents to allow him to quit school and go to work. He stayed for three years, but found, like school, that the job was dull. He was making friends in the industry and during this period tried composing a little. To earn extra money he also cut piano rolls—120 of them over a ten-year period. Many were recovered over the years. In 1917, with no specific prospects of employment, he quit his job as a song plugger. Ira was floundering at work as well. At times Ira submitted articles to magazines with little to no success. There were also two other siblings. Arthur was two years younger than George, and Frances, the youngest, later called Frankie, had the earliest success when at ten she was singing semi-professionally.

By the end of 1917, through his contacts on Tin Pan Alley, George worked as a rehearsal pianist for shows composed by Jerome Kern, Sigmund Romberg, and Victor Herbert, along with collaborators such as P. G. Wodehouse and Guy Bolton. At a rehearsal he befriended the new young star, Vivienne Segal, who, decades later, ultimately starred in PAL JOEY. She agreed to add two songs he had written with lyricist Irving Caesar into a show she was headlining. George was acting as a rehearsal pianist for the show. In this era, songs by multiple composers might be interpolated into someone else's production. And one of those two, "You-oo, Just You" was published.

Left to right: George Gershwin and Jerome Kern posing in a broadcasting studio, June 1933. (Photofest.)

He soon met Max Dreyfus, the head of Harms Publishing, who hired him to write songs for thirty-five dollars a week and a three-cent royalty for any piece of his that was sold. He was now only nineteen. George worked at the same time, with Max's permission, as the rehearsal pianist for the 1918 ZIEGFELD FOLLIES.

The one-step was the dance craze at the time. One evening during his father's weekly poker game, George and Irving Caesar pounded out a song for the one-step in the other room of the apartment, to the distraction of the poker players. They completed it in just fifteen minutes.

Meanwhile Gershwin had several songs interpolated into a show called HALF PAST EIGHT, but it flopped. He tried to persuade Irving Berlin, who could not read or write music, to hire him as his musical secretary. Berlin turned him down saying George "was too talented to subordinate his talent to that of another songwriter."

Another show with some of his music, LA LA LUCILLE, closed immediately as well. Then the song he wrote with Caesar in fifteen minutes was used in a show called DEMI-TASSE and completely ignored. During that run, Al Jolson also opened a new show and Gershwin was hired to play at its cast party. While playing he included his one-step song and Jolson was crazy about it. He put it in his own show, recorded it, and sold one million copies. The unknown George Gershwin earned ten thousand dollars for the song written with Irving Caesar, "Swanee."

Gershwin entered his twenties as a known composer. But he continued studying as he did through the remainder of his life, always feeling a little insecure in his knowledge of harmony, orchestration, and other elements of musical theory.

George White was beginning to produce his SCANDALS to compete with Ziegfeld. White was originally a dancer. Ziegfeld tried to stop the competition by offering to give White, and his wife, dancer Ann Pennington, a major dancing spot in the FOLLIES, if he would forego his plans to produce the SCANDALS. Ziegfeld, a non-performer, was married to Billie Burke. So as a sarcastic counter-offer, White told Ziegfeld if he would stop producing the FOLLIES, White would give him a big role acting with Billie Burke in the SCANDALS. White obviously was moving ahead and offered Gershwin a contract to write all the music for the SCANDALS, an assignment that wound up lasting for five years. Gershwin took the job for just fifty dollars a week. Even by the end of five years his salary had only risen threefold. But it took only a small portion of his time and kept his name in lights on Broadway. During that time he wrote "I'll Build a Stairway to Paradise" and "Somebody Loves Me"

It was during that time he also began to write with Ira, who did not want to capitalize on his brother's name. As a result he used the pseudonym Arthur Francis, combining the names of his two siblings. The Gershwins sold

The Gershwins c. 1937. *Left to Right:* Fred Astaire, Ira Gershwin, George Gershwin. (Photofest.)

one song for two hundred and fifty dollars. But the show closed and they didn't get paid. Instead, George persuaded the producer to pay Ira one hundred fifty dollars by concocting a story. He told him Arthur Francis was just a college student "who really needs the money."

George got a job for Ira writing lyrics with a young friend, Vincent Youmans. The show they wrote together was successful, which meant Ira had a hit on Broadway before George did.

Toward the end of 1921, George collaborated with lyricist Buddy DeSylva and they wrote "Do It Again."

Now George was being invited to Broadway parties as a guest, instead of a paid piano player. Still, it became known that as soon as he arrived he would sit down and monopolize the piano for the rest of the evening, just for the joy of playing. At one party Irene Bordoni heard "Do It Again" and, like Jolson with "Swanee," she wanted the song interpolated in her show, THE FRENCH DOLL. It became Gershwin's biggest hit in 1922.

A violinist named Paul Whiteman was hired for the 1922 SCANDALS. In 1924, he and Gershwin would strike gold. An entrepreneur, Whiteman soon developed his own orchestra and wanted to make a splash on the jazz scene. Whiteman advertised a special EXPERIMENT IN MODERN MUSIC with an Irving Berlin tone poem, a Victor Herbert suite, and a Gershwin concerto. Vincent Lopez, a competitor of Whiteman, booked Carnegie Hall for a similar event around the same time. With Carnegie Hall's schedule filled before Whiteman could arrange for the performance, his concert would be held in Aeolian Hall, half the size.

Gershwin began writing on January 7, 1924, and was finished in three weeks. During that period, Ferde Grofe, Whiteman's orchestrator, went to the Gershwin apartment every day to pick up the latest material. Completed on February 4, it was performed for the first time on February 12. It was a cold snowy day, but the hall was packed. The program was long, with Gershwin near the end. By the time they reached that point, disenchanted with both Berlin's and Herbert's offerings, the crowd began wandering out, until a thin man appeared on the stage, sat down at the piano, and nodded to Whiteman. The clarinet cadenza began . . . and by the end the audience was ecstatic. What they heard was Gershwin playing *Rhapsody in Blue*.

It was an exciting year, with Gershwin performing at Carnegie Hall and with major symphonies around the country. In July, he left for London and wrote the musical PRIMROSE specifically for a British audience. It was a big hit, but never brought to America. He sailed back with Alex Aarons, who was to produce George's next show. Aarons wanted to persuade Otto Kahn, one of the wealthy passengers on the ship, to invest. Kahn appeared disinterested, until Gershwin played a number from the show and Kahn immediately changed his mind. The song was "The Man I Love."

The song was ultimately dropped from the show, the hit LADY, BE GOOD!, starring Fred Astaire, before it opened. (It was interpolated into the 1927 flop, STRIKE UP THE BAND, before achieving success as a purely commercial release.) Nonetheless, LADY, BE GOOD! had its own big hit song, one of Gershwin's greatest, "Fascinating Rhythm."

Gershwin developed the habit of writing mostly at night and mostly in the winter so as not to take him away from his spring and summer outdoor activities: tennis, golf and swimming. He was a fine athlete.

The following year, 1925, began with composor Igor Stravinsky coming to the U.S. for a Carnegie Hall performance. A glamorous Fifth Avenue party after the concert was held in his honor. Who else would immediately be at the piano but Gershwin? Suddenly everyone wanted them to play a duet. Neither was pleased with the idea, but they took seats looking like boxers challenging each other when they started playing. However, not a sound was heard. It was a special electronic piano, but the switch was in the wrong position. Later in the evening the piano was fixed. By then Stravinsky had left, so Gershwin played alone for hours.

In the spring Gershwin completed a show called TELL ME MORE. It suffered by comparison to LADY, BE GOOD and closed quickly, only to re-open to a successful run in England. Around that time, Walter Damrosch, the conductor of the New York Philharmonic, commissioned him to write a concerto for a classical concert. Damrosch explained that though *Rhapsody in Blue* was quite lovely, it did not take the truc form of a concerto. Many advised him not to do it as sticking to the form would destroy his free style. Gershwin had to go to the library to find out what a concerto actually was. Most historians, as well as the reviewers of his time, considered Gershwin to be a composer with insufficient formal training. It is at least part of the reason that George never stopped studying with major teachers. Gershwin agreed to the commission even though he was committed to compose a musical comedy, TIP-TOES, with Ira, and an operetta with Hammerstein and Harbach, SONG OF THE FLAME.

The summer was hot and Gershwin was getting little privacy. To help him, his friend, the dean of the Juilliard School of Music, took George to a place called the Chautauqua Institution, a self-contained cultural center. He was provided a cottage and a practice shack in the woods. But Juilliard had graduate students there as well, and it was impossible to keep the students and Gershwin apart. So Hutcheson, the dean, put down a rule. "No communication until 4 p.m." Every day at four the students and Gershwin would congregate and it was music for as long as they would last. There Gershwin finished the first movement and half the second before returning to Manhattan. The *Concerto in F* was completed in November and debuted in December. Reviewers commonly complained that Gershwin had lost some of the spontaneity of *Rhapsody in Blue*. Meanwhile, TIP- TOES and SONG OF THE FLAME opened within one week of each other, between Christmas and New Year's, and only TIP-TOES yielded a memorable song, "Sweet and Low-Down."

In the fall of 1926, the Gershwins moved. George bought a five-story building on West 103rd Street. The first floor contained a kitchen and game room. The second floor had a large living room and dining room, and a bedroom for George's parents. The third floor was for Frances and Arthur. On the fourth floor were accommodations for Ira and his new wife Leonore. The fifth floor belonged to George, with a bedroom, a study and a grand piano. There was an elevator of course. Visitors might find a crowd on the ground floor playing pool or ping-pong. Asking for George or Ira, they would be told "upstairs." Another group would be found on each floor pointing up. When Ira and then George were reached and asked who were the people downstairs, their comment would be, "I don't know. I think they're friends of Arthur's." It was actually just a constant open house.

George was now the central figure in New York's whirlwind social circle. He always brought his close friend, Bill Daly, to the many parties he attended. Bill was his favorite conductor at his shows, orchestrator of his theatrical compositions, and advisor for *Concerto in F*. At parties they would sit at two pianos playing duets. On Sunday evenings at West 103rd Street a regular gathering convened. Frankie, George's sister, would sing while he played. Frequently she would dance with George, a remarkable dancer, who had been taught steps by his friend Fred Astaire. George took Frankie to the socialite parties as well. It was around this time that George became acquainted

George and Ira Gershwin departing New York for George's last trip to Los Angeles, August, 1936. (Photofest.)

with Oscar Levant, who became a lifelong friend

Another very important friendship began that year. James Paul Warburg, scion of a wealthy banking family, and his wife, Kay Swift, invited George to a party at their home. George sat at the piano. He suddenly rose from the seat, said, "I've got to go to Europe now," and left. Kay witnessed that and was completely taken by him. No idolizing fan, she was extremely accomplished in her own right. A fine pianist, she subsequently played with him regularly at home. At times she served as a musical secretary so he could continue to compose without pause. She composed as well and wrote a well known standard for jazz vocalists, "Can't We Be Friends?"

In London, he was working on the British premiere of LADY, BE GOOD! and making a deal with Gertrude Lawrence for a new show. It has been claimed that at that show's cast party, Gershwin played the piano until 8 a.m. He was never happier than when he was sitting at the piano playing. There was no conceit. He merely loved to play for people.

Lawrence's show in the United States was titled OH, KAY! Ira was critically ill with appendicitis during the writing. In that pre-antibiotic era, appendicitis was frequently fatal. He was hospitalized for six weeks. His friend, press agent, and part-time lyricist Howard Dietz, who would later work with Arthur Schwartz, agreed to step in. In their separate autobiographies they give different accounts of Dietz's contribution to the show. Dietz said he had written a great deal of the lyrics and got paid practically nothing, but, that he would have worked for nothing for the chance to collaborate with George Gershwin.

The huge hit of that show was "Someone to Watch Over Me," written by Ira and George in only thirty minutes. Lawrence sang it to a rag doll; there wasn't a dry eye in the house.

George was working on another classical part of his repertoire, piano preludes. It had always been thought that he had composed five in total. But at a concert in Boston with Bill Daly, members of the audience swore that they played six. The sixth one has never been found. Some have even suggested that the two of them improvised it on the spot that night.

Early in 1927, Gershwin rented an estate in Westchester to work with Ira and George S. Kaufman on a new project, STRIKE UP THE BAND. It was a new type of show with an extremely caustic book. It did not go well and the show closed before reaching Broadway. It was rewritten in 1930 and George conducted opening night. Remarkably, before they became famous, Glenn Miller, Benny Goodman, Jimmy Dorsey, Gene Krupa, and Jack Teagarden all played in Gershwin's orchestra that night. This time the show was a hit, but the only lasting songs were "Strike Up the Band" and "I've Got a Crush on You."

That year, Gershwin also had a major falling out with Paul Whiteman about how Whiteman was trying to jazz up *Rhapsody in Blue*. They never resolved this conflict and their friendship ended. But the year was salvaged at the end with FUNNY FACE, a show starring Fred Astaire. It looked weak during rehearsals, but turned out to be very successful. A great song was pulled, to be used in a subsequent show. It was replaced by another hit, "He Loves and She Loves."

Meanwhile Gershwin had forgotten a promise to write a show for the great star Marilyn Miller. He finally agreed that if Romberg would write part with Wodehouse, the Gershwins would supply the rest. The show, ROSALIE, was a hodgepodge and one of Gershwin's worst. But it was a tremendous hit. To cut down on the work, the Gershwins used the song that was taken out of FUNNY FACE, "How Long Has This Been Going On?"

Late in 1927, he began working on his classic, *An American in Paris*. Gershwin went to Paris with Ira and Frankie. There he met Maurice Ravel and, always trying to learn more, he asked to study with him. Ravel turned him down, fearful that he would cause Gershwin to lose his gift, but gave him a letter of introduction to the famous teacher Nadia Boulanger, a mentor of Aaron Copland. In London and Paris, Gershwin experienced a frenetic life of party after party, with British royalty mixing with theatre and music royalty, including Noel Coward, Gertrude Lawrence, Bea Lilly, Prokofiev, Stravinsky, and Cole Porter. Gershwin played the piano every night. He was on the cover of *Time* magazine and it was said that Gershwin had become for music what Lindbergh was to aviation. At a party, Porter, listening to George and Frankie, asked if Frankie could be in his new revue, singing Gershwin tunes. She stole the show, and soon received requests to perform in London and Madrid. George and Ira, always extremely protective of her, said no to that. She had to return to the U.S. when they did.

Gershwin also asked Stravinsky if he could study with him. Stravinsky wondered how much money Gershwin was making. When Gershwin answered honestly "in the six figures," Stravinsky's response was "I should study with you."

Diaghilev asked if he could create a ballet set to *An American in Paris* and turn it into the composition's premiere. Stokowski asked to get the premiere for the Philadelphia Orchestra. But Gershwin had promised it to Damrosch and the New York Philharmonic. In Paris, George wanted to find real taxi horns for the piece and he returned with a stack of them. At a giant welcome home party he was re-united with Rosamund Walling, a cousin of close friends. She was twelve years his junior, and he hadn't seen her since she was a child. Now she was attending Swarthmore College. Ultimately she became one of the few women he considered marrying.

George could not have been busier. Besides completing *An American in Paris*, he had promised another show for Gertrude Lawrence. It was TREASURE GIRL, a complete flop closing quickly. Its only saving grace was the song "I've Got a Crush on You." (which was later re-used in the 1930 version of STRIKE UP THE BAND.)

Kay Swift and Warburg soon provided Gershwin a guest house right on the grounds of their estate. George was with Kay constantly. He completed *An American in Paris* on November 18, 1928, and the New York Philharmonic performance was on December 15 of that year. Kay and Rosamund were both at the premiere. The next day he and Kay went to a shop on Madison Avenue, where he bought her two lovely bracelets. Finally, Kay and Warburg got divorced.

Not only did the world change in 1929, but Broadway did as well. The Gershwins had been working on a project for Ziegfeld, EAST IS WEST. Ziegfeld suddenly told them to stop and write a different show for his new young star, Ruby Keeler, in just two weeks. The nineteen-year-old had just married Al Jolson. Ziegfeld wanted to start as soon as they returned from their honeymoon. It had the Duke Ellington Orchestra; Clayton, Jackson and Jimmy Durante; a ballet; and Eddie Foy Jr. It was a terrible show except for one great song. With Keeler dancing, suddenly Al Jolson would stand up in the third row of the orchestra and blast out a few choruses of "Liza." It closed after three months and Ziegfeld refused to pay the Gershwins. They sued but to no avail. Ziegfeld had lost everything in the stock market collapse.

That summer George performed his first concert at Lewisohn Stadium in front of 18,000 people. He played *Rhapsody in Blue* and conducted *An American in Paris*. It was the beginning of his conducting career and from then on he conducted opening night for all his shows.

George and Ira subsequently wrote a show with all newcomers. Ginger Rogers was just starting out, and it was Ethel Merman's first show. The book was weak but the score was divine. Among the hits were "Embraceable You" and "Bidin' My Time." Additionally, GIRL CRAZY contained the song that rocketed Merman to stardom, "I Got Rhythm." The show was a huge success, quite a feat when almost every other show on Broadway was failing. It also had a song that some say is the most beautiful ballad ever written, "But Not for Me."

Like the rest of the Broadway composer-lyricist teams, George and Ira were being wooed to Hollywood. Meanwhile sister Frankie was being wooed by Leopold Godowsky Jr., a violinist who Rose Gershwin thought was not a suitable husband for her daughter. The rest of the family secretly made plans for a wedding in George's new apartment. Even George didn't know about it. His parents came thinking they were there to say good-bye to their sons, who were off to Hollywood. When they arrived everything was ready and George, still in his pajamas, went to the piano and played "The Wedding March" and an excerpt from *Rhapsody in Blue* for the wedding.

But things didn't go well for the Gershwins in Hollywood. Their lives were fun enough, but the quality of movie musicals was poor. They wrote one called DELICIOUS and made a movie version of GIRL CRAZY. Both were unsuccessful. But DELICIOUS had the beginnings of *Manhattan Rhapsody* in the picture. It was later expanded to be his *Second Rhapsody*.

Life in Hollywood was not all work. In January and February 1931, he met and constantly dated the silent movie star Aileen Pringle, whom he called Pringie. But he was writing plaintive letters to Rosamund all during this time. When he left at the end of February, the Pringie romance ended. He went back to write a new show with the hit title song, "Of Thee I Sing."

It opened in New York City for its premiere on exactly the same day that the movie DELICIOUS opened there to poor reviews. The response to the two of them was like night and day. Other hits from OF THEE I SING were "Love Is Sweeping the Country" and "Who Cares?"

While 1931 ended on an upbeat note, the following year would not quite be the same. Premieres for the *Second Rhapsody* in January and February with the Boston and New York Orchestras received lukewarm reviews. Gershwin was also feeling very negative about his health,

Ira Gershwin and George Gershwin, 1938. (Photofest.)

his romantic relationships, and even money. He was always mildly hypochondriacal and stopped smoking for a few months during that year.

A story about his up and down love life was told by publishing giant Bennett Cerf, with whom George had taken a Hawaiian vacation. They were both single and, while there, they met two very attractive women. Cerf reported that one stood Gershwin up. When he bumped into her the following day and asked her why she had not shown up, he was terribly upset by her response. She said she wanted to call him, but couldn't remember his name.

DuBose Heyward had been discussing his book *Porgy* with George since 1927, but Gershwin said he was so busy he couldn't consider anything until early 1933. Heyward was from a famous family, which included a signer of the Declaration of Independence. Heyward was two when his father died and his family fell into poverty. After growing up without a formal education and suffering a crippled right arm from polio, he worked the docks. Always an avid reader and writer, Dubose was published for the first time at thirty-seven. It caused him to sell his insurance business and become a full-time writer. *Porgy* was published in 1926 and performed as a play in 1927.

In 1932, Gershwin began studying with Joseph Schillinger, a famous teacher who advocated the application of mathematical concepts to the art of orchestration. From 1932 to 1936 they met for three hours weekly. After Gershwin's death, Schillinger claimed he was deeply involved in Gershwin's compositions from 1932 on. Oscar Levant, also Schillinger s pupil, said the claim was nonsense, because Schillinger had never composed anything of consequence.

George played at a gigantic outdoor concert in 1932, with Bill Daly conducting and Levant playing as well. They did all of his major works and a selection from his shows.

Also in that year, Gershwin agreed to do a series of free concerts to provide work for musicians. All the receipts went to the Musicians' Fund. Daly conducted. A violist and part-time composer named Langley was in the orchestra. He did not like Gershwin and was jealous of his success. During rehearsal, when Daly heard an error, Langley claimed to have heard Daly mumble, "Did I write that there?" Langley claimed that Daly was the true composer of Gershwin's music and orchestrated his classical pieces. Langley had studied with a known racist and anti-Semitic teacher. Daly wrote a piece in the *New York Times* saying that, like every other composer, their Broadway productions were always orchestrated by someone else. It was known that *Rhapsody in Blue* was orchestrated by Ferde Grofe, because he was Whiteman's orchestrator. But Gershwin himself had orchestrated and written every piece of his own classical music since then. Daly ended by saying that if anyone should be offended it should have been him, because Langley said the music he accused Daly of writing wasn't even any good.

The 1933 sequel to OF THEE I SING, LET 'EM EAT CAKE, was a failure. Critics said it had a good score and a terrible book.

During this period, George developed an extremely close, non-romantic friendship with Mabel Schirmer, wife of the sheet music magnate. Their correspondence over the next few years provided much of the most important information to biographers about his life.

Jolson, Kern, and Hammerstein had been approached by the Theatre Guild to make a musical out of *Porgy* as well. There are many versions of what happened, but the most likely one is that the project fell through due to financial problems. That possible production put off an agreement between Gershwin and Heyward until late in 1933, and Gershwin still was not ready to work on it. In February 1934, he finally came up with his first song for the show, "Summertime."

George was preoccupied with a weekly radio show and Ira was writing a Broadway revue with Harold Arlen and Yip Harburg. But the story of the development of PORGY AND BESS has both an exciting and a dark side. Heyward wanted desperately for George to come south and experience the environment. Unsuccessful in his request, Heyward came to New York for several weeks of work. Finally, in the summer of 1932, George and his cousin, painter Henry Botkin, left for Charleston. They rented a ramshackle house on the beach at Folly Island where there were swamps, wildlife, and no telephones, and the locals spoke Gullah dialect. Gershwin was deep into the atmosphere of the story's setting. The experience for George was glorious. He mingled with the locals, heard gospel music, and went to the churches. He would make several such trips. On his return the casting was done. Unknowns, like Todd Duncan of Howard University, were used. Some were from Juilliard. The only famous performer was John Bubbles of vaudeville's Buck and Bubbles dance and comedy team. Bubbles was difficult to work with, but Gershwin demanded he be kept in the cast as Sportin' Life. Other beautiful numbers began to take shape like "My Man's Gone Now" and "I Got Plenty of Nothin'."

Gershwin was still doing his radio show and Ira was completing LIFE BEGINS AT 8:40 in August 1935 when they got down to their duets, "I Loves You, Porgy" and the beautiful "Bess,You Is My Woman."

The show went to Boston at the end of 1935. It was four hours long and took the form of a true opera. The reviews were amazing, but the director Rouben Mamoulian said they needed to cut it substantially. Heyward and the Gershwins accepted his decision and began to cut ruthlessly. By the time it got to New York it had changed. The audience reception was the same, but not the reviews. That plus the bad economic times were a devastating combination. Even with lowered ticket prices it had a short run and closed. Gershwin, depressed, knew he had created something special. Not until after his death was that adequately acknowledged.

In August 1936, Hollywood beckoned again. Bill Daly, Kay Swift (now divorced), and Mabel Schwirmer threw a farewell party for him. None would ever see Gershwin again. Daly died suddenly of a heart attack. Schwirmer was on a cruise when she heard of Gershwin's death. Kay Swift's story is the most intriguing. She was extremely talented herself and though romance tied them together, music did as well. Possibly, her having three children kept him from pursuing her further. One of them held George responsible for her parents' divorce. But George had difficulty with the concept of marriage. On his departure for Hollywood, George agreed with Kay not to communicate with each other for a year. But George's letters to Mabel contained many requests for information about Kay.

In Hollywood, George and Ira were told to begin writing songs without a script for a new Astaire movie. First they came up with "Let's Call the Whole Thing Off." The producer was thrilled but still had no script and told George and Ira to keep going. Another of their hits, "They All Laughed," soon emerged.

When they finished another great number, they rushed over to Harold Arlen's house to play it for him. The Berlins, the Cantors, the Edward G. Robinsons, and the Arlens all lived in the same neighborhood in Beverly Hills. The song Arlen heard was "They Can't Take That Away from Me," and it became part of the film SHALL WE DANCE.

Life was good. Gershwin was playing tennis, golf, and poker with friends as well as performing at concerts. He wrote to Heyward saying he wanted to do another opera with him, intimating that he viewed Hollywood as a means to make enough money to free himself for his true passion, writing classical music.

In November 1936, he complained of a dizzy spell during a haircut and in February of the following year he almost fell off a podium while conducting. Shortly thereafter, he shockingly played some wrong notes at a concert, but a complete physical failed to reveal any problems. He and Ira started into a second picture for RKO, A DAMSEL IN DISTRESS, which was completed in the spring of 1937. Ira had a reputation for being a slow and dogged writer of lyrics. But it was said that they wrote "A Foggy Day" for the movie in less than one hour.

Around that time George went to a dinner party given by Edward G. Robinson. He was seated next to Paulette Goddard, who had recently married Charlie Chaplin. George was mesmerized by her. They began having secret trysts that were almost comical. Chaplin was having them followed.

They would drive around and, with the assistance of friends, switch cars repeatedly. As though in a silent movie, they were attempting to get away to a secret rendezvous.

George and Ira started to work on THE GOLDWYN FOLLIES. Goldwyn was difficult, harassing them constantly. They were writing but George complained of fatigue and headaches that became worse. But a physical on June 9 again failed to reveal any serious medical issues. While with Goddard on June 22, he became so disoriented he was admitted to Cedars of Lebanon Hospital, where he unbelievably received a diagnosis of stress and hysteria. He developed photophobia, an extreme sensitivity to light, and started to smell strange odors. Skeptical friends ignored his complaints. In a horrible incident, especially in view of what was found subsequently, when he fell to the ground outside the Brown Derby, an acquaintance said, "Leave him there. All he wants is attention."

Still George and Ira completed several songs for THE GOLDWYN FOLLIES, including "Love Walked In."

As things got worse, a psychoanalyst was brought in to consult. George was dropping silverware and knocking over glasses and could not play the piano. His friend, playwright S. N. Behrman, stopped by to see him and could not believe the deterioration. He insisted it was not emotional and wanted to take George back to New York to see doctors. But it was too late. A few days later Gershwin went into violent shaking spells, was brought to the hospital, and immediately fell into a coma. A spinal tap revealed the diagnosis. Only then were extraordinary efforts mobilized. They tried to reach the most famous neurosurgeon in the world, who worked out of Johns Hopkins. He was out on a yacht during that weekend. They went through the White House to get a Coast Guard cutter to find the yacht and bring him back. While the process continued, George got progressively worse. A local neurosurgeon in Los Angeles was called in and after a conversation between the two physicians, they decided there was not sufficient time for the first to travel from Baltimore to the West Coast. So the surgery was started. It began after midnight and lasted more than five hours. A large, highly malignant glioblastoma was found. An earlier diagnosis probably would have given Gershwin a little more time, but it is almost certain that it would still have been fatal. He was back in his room at 7 a.m. Within two hours. his temperature was at 106.5, the brain surgery and tumor obviously destroying his body thermostat. His pulse was 180. He died at 10:35 a.m. on July 11, 1937, at the age of thirty-eight.

He had reached the position of being a national icon. He was bigger than life. He adored music—writing it, conducting it, and, most of all, playing it. He could never turn down an opportunity to play, whether it was a gigantic concert or anyplace he might find a piano.

Never to be heard were the symphonies, quartets, ballets, concertos, or a second opera he had contemplated with DuBose Heyward.

The very last song he wrote, which was for THE GOLDWYN FOLLIES, has always been one of his most special compositions, "Our Love Is Here to Stay."

MAJOR WORKS

SHOWS:

LA, LA, LUCILLE **(1919)**
GEORGE WHITE'S SCANDALS **(1920)**
GEORGE WHITE'S SCANDALS **(1921)**
GEORGE WHITE'S SCANDALS **(1922)**
OUR NELL **(1922)**
THE RAINBOW **(1923)**
GEORGE WHITE'S SCANDALS **(1923)**
SWEET LITTLE DEVIL **(1924)**
GEORGE WHITE'S SCANDALS **(1924)**
PRIMROSE **(1924)**
LADY, BE GOOD! **(1924)**
TELL ME MORE **(1925)**
TIP-TOES **(1925)**
SONG OF THE FLAME **(1925)**
OH, KAY! **(1926)**
FUNNY FACE **(1927)**
ROSALIE **(1928)**
TREASURE GIRL **(1928)**
SHOW GIRL **(1929)**
STRIKE UP THE BAND **(1930)**
GIRL CRAZY **(1930)**
OF THEE I SING **(1931)**
PARDON MY ENGLISH **(1933)**
LET 'EM EAT CAKE **(1933)**
PORGY AND BESS **(1935)**

COMPOSITIONS:

GERSHWIN WROTE JUST UNDER 700 PIECES.

E. Y. Harburg.
(Courtesy of
The Estate of
E. Y. Harburg.)

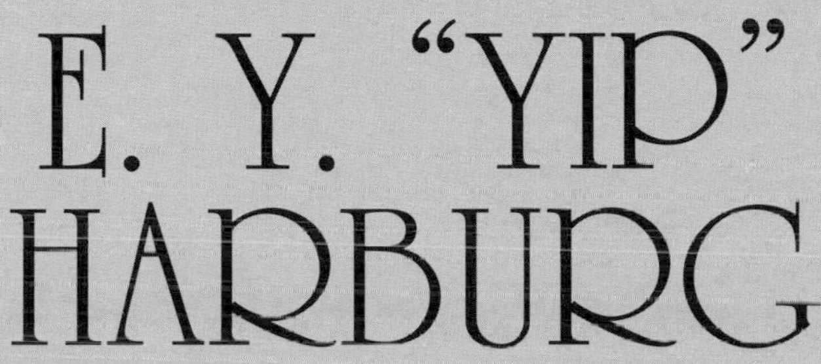

E. Y. "YIP" HARBURG

E.Y. "YIP" HARBURG, ORIGINALLY ISIDORE HOCHBERG, WAS born on April 8, 1896, in the crowded dirty world of New York's Lower East Side. He was raised in a sixth-floor walkup, sleeping in chairs instead of beds. His family survived primarily by working in sweatshops. Of all the great Broadway composers and lyricists born around the turn of the century, only Irving Berlin lived in greater poverty.

As a young boy he was fast and athletic and was given the nickname Yipsel, which in Yiddish meant squirrel. Over time it was shortened to Yip.

The family were Orthodox Jews. They had a deep involvement in social issues, undoubtedly due to their own poverty. Yip attended religious services regularly with his father until a tragedy occurred.

Yip had a brother, Max, who was twelve years his senior. He was a brilliant scientist and Yip idolized him. Max had already obtained his masters and doctoral degrees from several New York universities and was writing major papers in physics and mathematics when he suddenly died of cancer at the age of twenty-eight. The entire family was devastated. Yip lost all faith, and became an agnostic.

He turned his thoughts to theatre, frequently attending the Yiddish theatre and seeing Boris Thomashevsky, who was the grandfather of Michael Tilson Thomas, the conductor of the San Francisco Symphony. He also visited the vaudeville stages to see stars such as Al Jolson, Bert Lahr, Fanny Brice, and Ed Wynn.

On his own, Yip had become a favorite as an actor in high school, where he was also writing light verse and getting it published in the school newspaper.

One day a classmate saw him reading some verse and asked if he knew that it had been put to music. The young man brought Yip to his apartment and played the recordings to which Yip had no access. The family was much more affluent and the young man was Ira Gershwin. After that they began writing a high school column together and continued it into college. It was signed "Yip and Gersh." They styled themselves after Franklin P. Adams, the foremost writer of light verse at the time, and the mentor of Benchley, Kaufman, Parker, E. B. White, and Thurber among others. Eventually, Harburg's pieces would actually appear in Adams's columns. But, by the 1920s lyricists were moving away from his style to writing for theatre.

In 1917, Yip got a job in Uruguay, which especially pleased him because he was against the First World War and it got him out of the draft. He was working for Swift and Co., but was also making a name for himself writing for an English language newspaper there. Yip, during his time in Uruguay, sent money home for his impoverished parents.

When he returned from Uruguay the economy was booming. Yip went into the electrical appliance business and was so successful that by 1929 he was worth a quarter of a million dollars. All the while he continued to write light verse.

In 1923, he had married Alice Richmond, changed his name from Hochberg to Edgar Y. Harburg, and had two children. Still immersed in writing, he dreamed of making more money, selling the business, and devoting himself to a life of literature. Then, in 1929, the Depression came along and destroyed everything. Harburg saw it as a release from the world of business that he hated.

Here the story takes a strange and confusing turn. Harburg wrote that after the crash he went to Ira Gershwin, who loaned him five hundred dollars and put him in touch with Jay Gorney. Gorney had just lost his lyricist partner, Howard Dietz, who had joined Arthur Schwartz. Harburg sent his wife and children to California, saying he would follow once achieving success. But history shows that Yip wrote a radio show with Gorney all through 1929. They also wrote a portion of *Earl Carroll's Sketch Book* on Broadway in July 1929, all before the crash.

Had the business folded before the stock market? Had he sent his family to California because the marriage was already dissolving, not because of his career? What is certain is that at sometime toward the end of 1929 or the beginning of 1930, Harburg was destitute and alone in New York, working in a watch company by day and writing with Gorney by night.

All through the early 1930s, Yip was not in a class with his fellow lyricists Ira Gershwin or Larry Hart. He was just getting introduced to the composers Gorney, Burton Lane, and Vernon Duke. Gershwin and Hart had years to practice their craft and Yip was just starting.

Gorney, like Harburg, had come from Russian Jewish ancestry. But his family went to the Midwest. After college he became an attorney. Unhappy with the practice, he left and went to New York to write. Nine years later he met Yip. They wrote the previously mentioned radio show and the revue for Earl Carroll.

Yip began jumping from composer to composer in an effort to find his voice. Over the years he would write with forty-eight composers, thirty-one of them between 1929 and 1934, when he met Harold Arlen. Only a few of the others became major composers, such as Jerome Kern, Burton Lane, Arthur Schwartz, and Vernon Duke.

Broadway, like the rest of the country, was struggling in 1932. Yip was writing some comedy material for Bert Lahr, Ed Wynn, and Fanny Brice when he got his big break. It was the opportunity to write AMERICANA, the first socially-conscious show dealing with the Depression. Vincent Youmans, a rather strange person, got a ten thousand dollar advance to be the show's composer. He wrote an opening chorus and vanished. So Harburg got Gorney, Arlen, and Burton Lane to compose the necessary music.

There were breadlines throughout New York. Gorney wrote a melody straight out of his Russian Jewish heritage. It sounded like a chant. Harburg, reaching an intensity he had not previously achieved, wrote the lyrics for "Brother Can You Spare a Dime?"

The Shubert Brothers, who were the co-producers, had to approve the song. They hadn't spoken to each other for about fifty years. They met to hear the song with intermediaries. One said to an intermediary, "Ask him if he likes it." The response was, "I don't." Then through the intermediary, "Ask him why." The response was, "It's too sorbid." But Lee Shubert, the brother with the most clout, ignored the misused word, and decided to put it in the show anyway.

The show was panned. But the song became a massive hit. One reviewer said it was the most important social commentary of the time. Jolson and Bing Crosby recorded it.

Harburg had a much bigger success two and a half months later with Vernon Duke. The show was WALK A LITTLE FASTER. Harburg continued writing with Duke from 1930 through 1934. As distinct from many other theatre artists of Russian descent, Duke, born Vladimir Dukelsky, had actually grown up in Russia. An excellent composer, he had written for symphony and ballet. In the U.S. he became a protégé of Gershwin, who was very impressed by his work. For his part, Duke was unimpressed with Harburg when he first met him. They were complete opposites, Harburg a Jewish socialist and Duke a social-climbing elitist White Russian.

Unlike Gorney, Duke had no ethnic sound to his music. He wrote American pop. Their show was very sophisticated, with Beatrice Lillie and Bobby Clark starring. Monty Woolley directed and S. J. Perelman wrote the sketches. Subsequently Duke wrote that he was sitting in Tony's restaurant reminiscing about Paris when a tune suddenly came to him. No mention was made of Yip writing any lyrics. Harburg later wrote that he was sitting in Lindy's with brochures about Paris. Duke's music is never mentioned. It was always a cold collaboration between them. But it resulted in the masterpiece, "April in Paris."

Harburg had reached the big time. The *New York Times* gave him high praise and Larry Hart sent an enthusiastic telegram.

WALK A LITTLE FASTER was only one of two shows to open with Harburg lyrics that week. The other, Ben Hecht's THE GREAT MAGOO, was not a musical, but its producer, Billy Rose, wanted Harburg and Harold Arlen to contribute one song. Rose, with his terrible reputation, was up to his old tricks. He had his name added as co-lyricist. The show folded quickly, but not the song. "It's Only a Paper Moon" was the first of Harburg's lyrics to illustrate his belief in love.

In 1933, Harburg wrote his last show with Vernon Duke. It was to be the first ZIEGFELD FOLLIES since Ziegfeld's death. Billie Burke had sold the rights for his name to the Shubert Brothers for only one thousand dollars. It was a flop and the year in general was terrible for Harburg as he got divorced as well.

It was a time of great friendship between composers. George and Ira Gershwin were writing PORGY AND BESS. Yip had been asked to write a revue with Harold Arlen called LIFE BEGINS AT 8:40. Since Yip had just completed the FOLLIES, and was tired, he asked Ira Gershwin to join him in writing the lyrics. It was a great opportunity for Harburg, as by then Arlen was recognized as a genius in a class with George Gershwin. The lyrics and political satire were reviewed as brilliant. It was a big hit and the beginning of the period from 1935–1939 during which almost all of Harburg's work was with Arlen.

By 1935, while Broadwy was hurting badly, Harburg found himself in California, like most of his fellow songwriters. But, for the most part they were writing for inferior movies. Arlen had written a melody while still in New York, which he showed to George Gershwin, who told him it was too complicated to have lyrics added. Kern looked at it and said it was "too esoteric for public consumption." When offered to Johnny Mercer he said, "a lyric could not be written for it." Finally, Harburg got his hands on it.

The most important of all Broadway historians, Alec Wilder, wrote of that song that "it goes far beyond the boundaries of popular music." When offered to Hollywood for a movie, it was rejected, and, later in the 1940s, Judy Garland and Frank Sinatra also initially turned it down. Both ultimately recorded it and, years later, Sinatra's version was reviewed by the *New York Times* as "being transplanted to the center of the earth." Even until his death it was Arlen's favorite of all the songs he had written. It was the only song in which Harburg wrote of the irrevocable loss of love. The song is the beautiful "Last Night When We Were Young."

In 1936, Vincente Minnelli was doing a new revue for the Shuberts and asked Harburg and Arlen to return to New York to write it. Advised that Broadway was dead, they agreed to write only two songs for it. Minnelli added music from Duke, Gershwin, Schwartz and Dietz, Rodgers and Hart, and Hoagy Carmichael. The out-of-town trials were poor so Harburg was brought to New York to fulfill a role he was to assume a number of times, that of "show doctor." Broadway soon hailed a new smash, called THE SHOW IS ON. And, the biggest hit song was one of those written by Harburg and Arlen, "The Song of the Woodsman." Bert Lahr performed this slapstick number, which was eventually considered a classic.

Traveling back and forth between New York City and Hollywood, Harburg and Arlen wrote a new show for Ed Wynn titled HOORAY FOR WHAT? Harburg was at his peak. Aside from the lyrics, he had conceived the show and written the book with Howard Lindsay and Russel Crouse. It ushered in a small wave of political musicals of the late 1930s and early 1940s. The show was an antiwar farce about how great nations of the world were vying for an invention by a small-town American inventor. He had discovered a gas that would allow the user to conquer the world. The show was successful. Even its hit love song, "Down with Love," was satirical.

Arthur Freed was working on plans in Hollywood to do a very special musical. Everyone wanted the assignment. He had considered Kern to compose the music. But, after having seen HOORAY FOR WHAT?, he changed his mind. Freed offered it to Harburg and Arlen. The score was for THE WIZARD OF OZ, and it was to be MGM's prestige movie, and no expense was to be spared.

The story behind the movie is quite special. Irving Thalberg had been the unifying power behind MGM when he died suddenly in 1936. Louis B. Mayer, trying to find a replacement, chose Mervyn LeRoy, a successful director who couldn't meet the standards Thalberg had set. Arthur Freed, a part-time lyricist who had written with Nacio Herb Brown, was named his assistant. But with time Freed assumed a larger and larger role, enabling him to select Harburg and Arlen for OZ. At the time almost no one realized that Frank Baum's tale was not a children's story.

Historians later revealed it as an allegory for the powerlessness of the common man (the Scarecrow), the industrial worker (the Tin Woodsman), and the failed populist leader William Jennings Bryan (the Cowardly Lion). The Wicked Witch represented the economic leaders, and the federal government was the Wizard. It would be the beginning of Harburg's use of movies and the theatre to show, through allegories, the world as he saw it.

The film had a rocky start. Four days after signing a contract, George Cukor, MGM's premier director, quit, saying it was not a serious work.

Throughout the course of the movie's production, Harburg achieved power. There was no consistent producer and eleven separate scriptwriters. He insinuated himself and became the script editor, thereby controlling the story. Yip created the first integrated movie musical in which the story and the music were intertwined, much as SHOW BOAT and OF THEE I SING had done on Broadway.

They had completed the score but were unable to find the song to describe Dorothy's discontent with her bland life in the beginning of the story. The schedule was tight and they were given fourteen weeks to complete the score. They still were missing that one number. On the way to a movie, supposedly, Arlen suddenly got an inspiration, jotted it down and when he got home he completed it by midnight. He called Harburg to come over immediately. Harburg listened and said "No! That's for Nelson Eddy." Arlen went back to work on it for two more weeks and, without changing it, insisted it was right. So Harburg called in his close friend Ira Gershwin to act as an intermediary. Gershwin believed it was fine and just needed a tempo change. But it still wasn't done because Arlen couldn't find the melody for the bridge.

Arlen had a funny little dog called Pan who frequently couldn't be found. He had developed a whistle that he used to get him to return. So Harburg suggested he use his Pan whistle notes. From that Arlen got the musical phrase that matched with the lyrics "Some day I'll wish upon a star."

Harburg was having difficulty lyricizing the first two words, "some day," "some time" and finally found, "somewhere over the rainbow."

The operetta portion in the middle of the film in Munchkinland includes all the city fathers and workers singing "Ding Dong, the Witch Is Dead," and culminates with the new friends heading off down the Yellow Brick Road singing, "We're Off to See the Wizard."

Harburg and Arlen were shocked to discover at the first preview showing that "Over the Rainbow" had been cut. Arthur Freed was furious. He went to see Mayer, who didn't like the song. Freed threatened to quit if it wasn't put back. It didn't appear until the third preview night. But it was so well received it remained in. The movie opened in 1939 to mixed reviews. But "Over the Rainbow" won the Academy Award for Best Song. It took another ten years for the movie to make its money back.

At that point, CBS and MGM were negotiating a deal for GONE WITH THE WIND to be shown on television, but could not reach an agreement. So MGM offered OZ as a consolation prize. It was a ten-year contact. Each year OZ was shown the ratings got higher and higher. Twenty-five years later, it was still being broadcast in prime time, and it had been seen more than three times as often as the next most popular prime-time show. By then it had made multiple millions for MGM.

It took years before the genius of Harburg and Arlen was recognized for their work on OZ. But in a way it was too late. By that point, Harburg was already blacklisted from movies.

After OZ, Harburg and Arlen split for a while. Arlen started writing with Johnny Mercer while Broadway was calling for Harburg to write a show for a comic named Joe Cook. It was an old-fashioned musical comedy he would create with Burton Lane, titled HOLD ON TO YOUR HATS. The producer ran out of money and Al Jolson, who hadn't been on Broadway for nine years, stepped in to finance it and take the lead role. It turned out to be a strange project. At the end of the show no one remembered the songs of Harburg and Lane because about three-fourths through the evening, Jolson would come to center stage and start belting out his old standards like "Sunny Boy," "Swanee," and "April Showers" while saying, "You ain't heard nothin' yet." The show was still barely a financial success.

Harburg went back to Hollywood, married Edelaine Gorney, and wrote some insignificant songs with Lane and Arlen. He even tried writing one with Kern. But Kern was difficult and inflexible. Harburg had trouble grasping the beat of Kern's music due to the quality of his piano playing. At times he took the music to Burton Lane asking him to play it for him.

Producers as well as composers had a problem with Harburg introducing his personal philosophy into his lyrics. He was one of a very few who felt compelled to integrate his politics into their work. But because fondness for Harburg was so widespread, no one rejected him for this propensity.

In 1943, Harburg and Arlen wrote additional songs for CABIN IN THE SKY, their only successful movie musical after OZ. It featured an all African-American cast, and was a perfect vehicle for Arlen, whose career had been built at the Cotton Club. He understood the blues and music of the African-American community better than any other white composer. Arlen had generally preferred writing that style of music with Ted Koehler and Johnny Mercer. But with Harburg he wrote the great song, "Happiness Is Jes' a Thing Called Joe."

OKLAHOMA! introduced a new form of musical play in March 1943. Eighteen months would pass before Harburg would bring his next musical play to Broadway. For the first time he would be in charge of everything.

E.Y. Harburg. (Courtesy of The Estate of E.Y. Harburg.)

BLOOMER GIRL concerned itself with racism and women's equality at the time of the Civil War.

The song "The Eagle and Me" from the show is thought to be the first civil rights song heard in the theatre. The lyrics, according to Stephen Sondheim, are some of the greatest ever written. But the musical arrangement did not seem to be right. Forty years later it became a civil rights anthem when the arrangement was changed in a recording by Lena Horne.

The biggest battle during the production of the show centered around a ballet created by Agnes de Mille, demonstrating the effect of war on the women left behind. It lasted a full ten minutes and Harburg was insistent that it be removed. He had the support of the producer, but not Arlen, who stuck by de Mille. They compromised by agreeing that it would be removed after the out-of-town tryouts. But it was such a rousing success on the road that Harburg and the producer relented and it stayed in.

Sketch of E.Y. "Yip" Harburg drawn by George Gershwin. (Courtesy of The Estate of E.Y. Harburg.)

Harburg and Arlen traveled from coast to coast for money-raising auditions. Louis B. Mayer, whom they disliked immensely for his efforts to remove "Over the Rainbow," became one of the major investors.

When BLOOMER GIRL opened in the fall of 1944, it was the first show since the beginning of World War II to have a formal dress opening night. It was a smash hit, running for 654 performances. Interestingly, not one review commented at all about its political statement. Not until a 1981 regional revival was the message fully understood.

Immediately after the opening, Harburg went headlong into politics. He was a founder of the Hollywood Demonstration Committee, enlisting support for Franklin Delano Roosevelt. On the eve of the 1944 election, he produced the national radio broadcast for Roosevelt. He commissioned several composers to write songs for the show, including Earl Robinson.

Harburg's ultimate problem was that Robinson was

a known member of the Communist Party and director of the Worker's Theatre. He had written songs for unions including his most famous, "The Ballad of Joe Hill." Harburg was moving away from Arlen, who had very conservative views. Harburg felt he had reached the pinnacle as a lyricist spokesman for the liberal left.

In the spring of 1946, Yip presented a program on the radio in association with the formation of the United Nations, titled UNITY FAIR, emphasizing a one world theme. But the Cold War was on, and it would be the last time any network would allow Harburg to express his political views.

Immediately after BLOOMER GIRL had opened, Yip presented the idea of FINIAN'S RAINBOW to Arlen. Arlen refused, advising him to separate his politics from his writing. But Harburg wanted to explore politics further in the theatre. The split between Harburg and Arlen would last for ten years. Harburg thought he would do the show with Robinson. But Robinson was really not capable of composing an entire score. So Harburg turned to Burton Lane, and in 1947 they wrote FINIAN'S RAINBOW.

Harburg and Lane had first met when Yip was just leaving the business world and starting to write. Lane was a teenage protégé of George Gershwin. He had limited Broadway success up until then, writing mostly for Hollywood. Ultimately, Lane would write ON A CLEAR DAY with Alan Jay Lerner, for which he received rave reviews.

In 1951, with complete creative control, Yip would write FLAHOOLEY with Sammy Fain. All three of Harburg's postwar musicalss would have powerful political overtones, but the most strident was FINIAN'S RAINBOW. The fable, considered a theatrical masterpiece, presented a true assault on capitalism and racism. It resulted from Harburg's anger with Mississippi's Senator Bilbo and Congressman Rankin and their racist statements on the floor of the Senate and the House. He remembered an Irish fairy tale about a leprechaun, three wishes, and finding one's wealth through gold in America. In the show, a white racist gets transformed into a black man.

Harburg delves into the political subplot in which the racist senator plans to drive the black sharecroppers off the land where the gold has been found. But when the senator is in conversation with Sharon, who had come with Finian from Ireland, she is distressed by his attitude. While standing over the magic crock, from which the leprechaun has granted three wishes, she inadvertently says to the senator, "I wish that you were black, so that you would understand!" And, of course, he turns black.

As did Harburg, Finian looks to a utopian future, with a constant state of optimism. He believes in the end he will finally reach his dream, Finian's rainbow. Some of the very strident positions Harburg wanted to take in the story were softened by Lane. But one that remained was the attempted lynching of the senator who had been turned black. He was accused of having sexual relations with a white woman, who was, in fact, his wife. Eventually, some of Harburg's pointed barbs were removed or toned down. He was able to combine his attack on these fronts in a framework of humor and folklore, quite a challenge, successfully achieved.

Yip controlled FINIAN'S RAINBOW as the senior and more successful half of the team. Once, he introduced Lane at a backers' audition as his pianist, greatly offending his collaborator. Their relationship was not a good one. But Lane had developed a sound in his work that combined old European and American jazz, perfect for this show. The score became one of Broadway's greatest.

Harburg introduced an old story he had remembered from Irish folklore. He felt he needed an Irish song at the beginning, which Lane worked on unsuccessfully for four weeks. One evening, Harburg went to Lane's home teling him they must have the song completed. Lane took out the reams of material he had been developing. He was frustrated and began playing a tune. Immediately Harburg was attracted. He began writing a lyric. Together, they had come upon their great hit, "How Are Things in Glocca Morra?"

All the songs in the show are sung by the protagonists, for in Harburg's words, "Racists may not sing!"

Several love stories weave their way through the multiple narrative threads. One musicologist said that Lane and Harburg created one of the greatest love songs ever by combining tremendous desire with romanticism in their beautiful "Old Devil Moon." They also constructed a typical song-and-dance production number for the character of Susan in the wonderfully lilting "If This Isn't Love."

When the sharecroppers hear of their gold bounty, they want to know when it will be theirs and they sing, "That Great Come-and-Get-It Day."

Harburg used that development to demonstrate the rule of unintended consequences, by showing how they change when overwhelmed by material things in the song "When the Idle Poor Become the Idle Rich."

But Harburg didn't believe in creating villains. He held fast to the idea that everyone is basically good. So in the story he wanted to make sure the senator learned his lesson and changed his ways.

Another subplot is about Og, the leprechaun, who is only half human and has never felt the draw of sex. He is confused about his feelings for Susan, who is mute. To theatricalize this, Harburg created the song that Stephen Sondheim says is the greatest eleven o'clock number (referring to a song placed near the end of the performance) in the annals of musical theatre, "When I'm Not Near the Girl I Love"

The public response to FINIAN'S RAINBOW was enormous, and the show ran for 725 performances. It prodded others to write about human rights including Rodgers and Hammerstein in SOUTH PACIFIC. The day after the open-

E.Y. Harburg. (Courtesy of The Estate of E.Y. Harburg.)

E.Y. Harburg. (Courtesy of The Estate of E.Y. Harburg.)

ing, Harburg received a telegram from Oscar Hammerstein. It said, "Yip, I love you. . . . Will you marry me?"

In 1950, Yip was working with Burton Lane on a musical version of *Huckleberry Finn* for MGM's Arthur Freed. Lane had agreed to work with Harburg only if they would get equal billing. He was no longer willing to write with him for Broadway. Harburg had gotten permission to leave when they were only half done to go write FLAHOOLEY for Broadway. Lane had turned him down for that project and Arlen did as well. They felt it was far too political. So he turned to Sammy Fain, who had written only for Hollywood and was known for his song "I'll Be Seeing You."

It was while Harburg went to New York that the anti-Communist fever hit Hollywood and Harburg was blacklisted. As a result, HUCKLEBERRY FINN never was completed. Yip resisted fiercely, writing letters about his patriotism, claiming truthfully that he had been nothing more than a Roosevelt Democrat with a deep conviction in support of the underdog. He had a hatred of Stalin and totalitarianism. He was no wild political activist. He was a lifelong idealist, naively committed to a utopian society where men and women could be the best they could possibly be. But, as a result, for twelve years he was excluded. He swore honestly that he had never been a member of the Communist Party. His problem was that he was pushing his liberal philosophy at the height of Senator Joseph McCarthy's power.

Some studios tried to use him. But as soon as he was named, the project would be stopped. Harburg was heartbroken. He had been asked to write HANS CHRISTIAN ANDERSEN but the offer was withdrawn. Garland and Arlen arranged for him to do A STAR IS BORN, but the studio said "No!" Around him, some who were blacklisted committed suicide. But Harburg still had the good fortune to be receiving significant royalties. So he sent money to others, including Dalton Trumbo.

In 1956, he was asked to write a movie with Arlen, NELLIE BLY, and once again it was stopped. Even after the heyday of McCarthyism, many powerful individuals still maintained an informal blacklist. Arthur Freed wanted Harburg and told him he would have to see Roy Brewer, the head of the American Legion and the International Alliance of Theatrical Stage Employees, to be taken off the blacklist.

Harburg said to Brewer that he had called Harburg a Communist, but no one had, in fact, ever testified to that.

Brewer's response was, "But you did things."

Harburg asked, "Like what?"

Brewer asked, "Well did you write a song called "Happiness Is Jes' a Thing Called Joe?"

"Yes, a big hit."

"Which Joe were you talking about? Was it Joe Stalin?"

Harburg said he didn't know whether to laugh or get mad, so he just began laughing and left. Brewer had also asked if Harburg had given money to the Spanish Loyalists. He said he had and asked if Brewer would preferred that Nazi Germany had won? NELLIE BLY was never made.

Finally, in 1956, he got to write the Broadway show JAMAICA with Arlen, starring Harry Belafonte. But Belafonte got sick. Producer David Merrick hired Lena

Horne, locked Arlen and Harburg out of the production phase, and completely changed the show into a type of nightclub act for his new star. The book was discarded. It was the poorest score that Arlen had ever written.

The show was bad, but Merrick's instincts were financially correct. It became a hit because of Horne, though the critics panned it. Harburg had lost complete control of his project.

By 1960, the blacklist was over and he and Arlen wrote the music for the animated picture GAY PURR-EE. Harburg's lyrics were increasingly out of synch with popular tastes.

Hart and Hammerstein had died. Ira Gershwin had retired and Dietz had written his last show. There was no one left to write with. Arlen had become depressed since his wife's death. And Yip and Burton Lane had grown more and more apart. Harburg tried unsuccessfully to develop projects.

Finally, in 1961 he wrote THE HAPPIEST GIRL IN THE WORLD. With no collaborator available he tried to do what Hammerstein had done when converting CARMEN into CARMEN JONES. He used the music from the 1880s written by Offenbach and the Greek story of *Lysistrata*, where the women refuse to have sex with the men unless they stop fighting wars. It closed after ninety-seven performances.

Still feeling a strong social pull, he continued writing light verse and satire, but encountered no great demand for his work.

A film version of FINIAN'S RAINBOW was made, but Harburg and Lane were excluded from the production and the result did not get high praise.

In 1968, when he was seventy-two, Yip Harburg wrote his last show, DARLING OF THE DAY. He did not write the book, conceive the idea or direct it, all things he had done in the past. But composer Jule Styne insisted on getting Harburg for the lyrics. They could not get any of their choices for the lead and had to settle with Vincent Price, who was awful, and panned by everyone. The score and the lyrics got great reviews, but it could not survive and closed after thirty-two performances.

Through the 1970s, Harburg continued writing. There were a few songs with Arlen and Lane and with a young rock-oriented composer named Phil Springer. They reflect his feelings about aging, friendship, and love. One even memoralizes Jimmy Durante, called "Goodnight Mrs. Calabash, Wherever You Are."

In March 1981, just before he reached eighty-five years of age, his car slowly drifted across Sunset Boulevard into oncoming traffic. His death was reported inaccurately as a traffic accident; he had suffered a massive heart attack and was already slumped over the wheel at the time of his crash. The driver of the car he struck was uninjured and stated he saw no one at the wheel of the car that hit his. Harburg was on his way to a conference about a possible new movie titled TREASURE ISLAND.

In Harburg's greatest show, FINIAN'S RAINBOW, Finian is characterized as the person who is never down. No matter what difficulty he faces, he will find an answer to his problem. As Harburg stated, "That's the rainbow!" In his work, he constantly returned to the concept of the rainbow. But in FINIAN'S RAINBOW instead of looking beyond it, as in "Over the Rainbow," he looked to it. That was his dream. That was Harburg's idealism. The song he wrote was one of his greatest, but has never been fully acknowledged as such. Nevertheless, "Look to the Rainbow" describes him and was one of his favorite songs.

MAJOR WORKS

SHOWS:

EARL CARROLL'S SKETCHBOOK **(1929)**
THE GARRICK GAIETIES **(1930)**
EARL CARROLL'S VANITIES—EIGHTH EDITION **(1930)**
THE VANDERBILT REVUE **(1930)**
BILLY ROSE'S CRAZY QUILT **(1931)**
ZIEGFELD FOLLIES OF 1931 **(1931)**
SHOOT THE WORKS **(1931)**
BALLYHOO OF 1932 **(1932)**
AMERICANA **(1932)**
WALK A LITTLE FASTER **(1932)**
ZIEGFELD FOLLIES **(1934)**
NEW FACES OF 1934 **(1934)**
LIFE BEGINS AT 8:40 **(1934)**
CONTINENTAL VARIETIES **(1934)**
THE SHOW IS ON **(1936)**
HOORAY FOR WHAT? **(1937)**
HOLD ON TO YOUR HATS **(1940)**
BLOOMER GIRL **(1944)**
BLUE HOLIDAY **(1945)**
FINIAN'S RAINBOW **(1947)**
FLAHOOLEY **(1951)**
JOLLYANNA **(1952)**
JAMAICA **(1957)**
THE HAPPIEST GIRL IN THE WORLD **(1961)**
DARLING OF THE DAY **(1968)**

COMPOSITIONS:

HARBURG WROTE LYRICS FOR 537 SONGS.

In rehearsal for HELLO DOLLY: Carol Channing and composer Jerry Herman, 1964. (Photofest.)

JERRY HERMAN

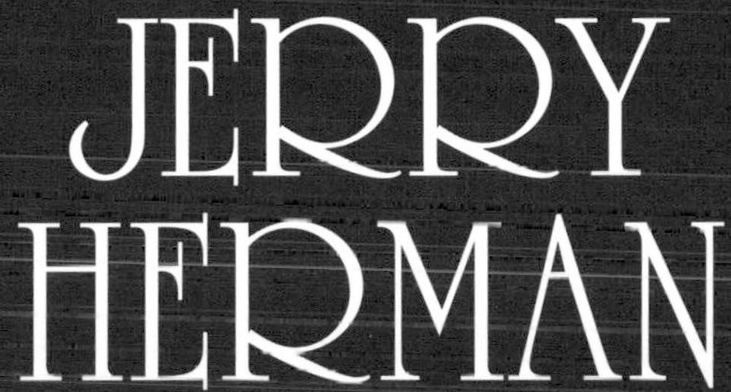

DAVID HERMAN WAS BORN IN 1880 IN POLAND IN A small town near Minsk. He sang in the synagogue but was mainly interested in the visual arts. Because of the constant pogroms his little community was subjected to, he left at fifteen to make his way to England. There he became an apprentice decorative artist, painting faux draperies and marble on the walls of churches and synagogues. He advanced sufficiently enough to come to America.

Extremely bright, fluent in Polish, Russian, and Hebrew, David moved in with the Rosenfeld family in a tenement on New York's Lower East Side. There he met their daughter, Ida, three years older than David. She was running her father's saloon in the Bowery. Crazy about David's brilliance and good looks, she married him three months later.

Ida was ambitious and persuaded David they should move to the rapidly growing city of Galveston, Texas. But there was little work for him in Galveston and she disliked the city. So she persuaded David to move to Los Angeles. Harry, their first child, was born in 1901.

Ida opened a bar in Los Angeles. After ten years of little financial success, she decided they should return to the East. Since New York City was very expensive, they moved to Jersey City, New Jersey. They moved from apartment to apartment so frequently that their children said they could come home from school only to find a note with instructions concerning where their new home would be.

Harry had two valuable attributes. He was a very fine athlete and very funny as well. He became a gym teacher and, in the summer, a tummeler—the entertainment director whose job it was to keep all the guests happy—in the Catskills. There he met Ruth Sachs, a singer, pianist, and music teacher. Two years later in 1928, just after she received her teaching certificate, they got married. They moved in with her parents, who adored Harry.

The first summer after they married they went to Camp Colang. Harry served as the sports director and Ruth as a music counselor. They worked at several camps hoping someday to own their own and create something special. At forty-five, Ruth's father had a stroke and died. Her mother and Aunt Belle moved in with them.

On July 10, 1931, Ruth gave birth to Gerald Sheldon Herman. It was a loving home in which Gerald was surrounded by women: his mother, Grandma Pauline, Aunt Belle, and at times even his great-grandmother. From them he learned to speak pidgin Yiddish.

Herman's great-grandmother on his mother's side, Dora Jacobson, had come to America with nine immigrant children. Her youngest, Willie, Jerry Herman's great-uncle, became an important physician. When this warm and close family gathered, as they did frequently, music was always a part of the occasion. Herman always believed that a section of his family on his mother's side was responsible for his ultimate musical success. His father on the saxophone and his mother on the piano and accordion played Rodgers and Hart, Kern, Porter, and Gershwin continuously. And, in the beginning, Jerry's only teacher was his mother.

In 1936, Harry and Ruth fell in love with Stissing Lake Camp. They became counselors and then head counselors. The owners had invested in the stock market, but the Hermans had not and were saving money. In 1937, with the owners in financial trouble, the Hermans bought a share of the camp. As the years went by, Harry and Ruth bought a larger and larger share. The camp's clientele was upper middle class and continued to attract families while other camps closed during the Depression. From age six to twenty-three, Jerry spent every summer at Stissing Lake. Finally, when the original owners retired, the Hermans assumed complete control.

The Hermans moved to a nicer neighborhood in Jersey City and met new neighbors, the Perlmans. Claire Perlman, who was three years older, became Jerry's best friend.

Jerry was showing a great talent for music. After going to shows with his parents he could play the songs by memory when he came home. Ruth finally got him a teacher who started him with the standard classical books. But he resisted those lessons. Another teacher advised them to leave him to his own devices, and on his own Jerry began creating very interesting chords. Like Irving Berlin and Noel Coward, Herman could not read music.

Meanwhile, his father, who had very different interests, was attempting to push him into sporting activities, for which Jerry lacked both interest and ability. He was small and frail. Significant friction developed between them.

Even at school he did not participate in musical activities like the orchestra because he had no formal training. He was a loner, preferring to be just left to his piano.

In 1946, when he saw ANNIE GET YOUR GUN, he decided he wanted to be like Irving Berlin. The following year, he met Phyllis Newman at the Jewish Community Center. She was a very talented singer and dancer. He became her accompanist and she learned the songs he would write for her.

Life at Camp Stissing improved immensely. His father came to realize the true nature of Jerry's talent. A Broadway-style show was done every year at the camp with Jerry in charge of writing the music, designing the scenery, and directing. Because of his artistic talent he decided that upon graduating from high school he wanted to go to the Parsons School of Design. During the first semester, Ruth arranged for him to have a meeting with Frank Loesser and show him his work. Loesser encouraged him to leave school and write music. He persuaded his parents to let him leave Parsons and study theatre at the University of Miami. At least partly it was to get away from Ruth and Harry.

At Miami, Jerry came out of his shell, becoming outgoing instead of shy. There he met Carol Isaacson, who would remain a lifelong friend. Jerry became a member of the ZBT fraternity and would entertain at parties and dances.

By his sophomore year, he met Sally Singer. He, Sally, and a fraternity roommate and his girlfriend rented a hotel room for a weekend and discovered sex in a wild orgy.

Herman was writing show after show and winning awards. Eventually, the shows were produced not just for the fraternity but the university as a whole. The first university-wide production was set for March 1953. It had a cast of ninety-six and a stage crew of twenty-two. They rented the Dade County Auditorium. Herman wrote nineteen original songs, which were rehearsed for six weeks. The title of the program was SKETCHBOOK, and it is still performed at the school every year, with the same title.

Jerry and Sally became engaged. Though they were sleeping together, he felt something was wrong. During his sophomore year, while waiting offstage for an entrance, he was kissed by a young male actor. They went back to his place after the show and Herman had his first homosexual experience. He knew he felt more comfortable with that.

He was afraid to explain the truth to Sally. At graduation, he told her he had decided to go to New York to try to write. Rather than honestly discussing his sexual dilemma, he told her it wasn't the right time for him to make a commitment.

Jerry Herman with two of his "Mames," Angela Lansbury (left) and Ginger Rogers, August 25, 1966. (Photofest.)

The summer of his twenty-third birthday, he was back at Camp Stissing when he got drafted into the Army. He was a terrible soldier, losing weight rapidly, falling under a hundred pounds. He received a medical discharge.

By this time his father had changed his attitude about Jerry's future, and provided his son with financial and emotional support for his theatrical goals. Herman wrote a new show and it starred his old friend Phyllis Newman. It was called I FEEL WONDERFUL and it was performed at the Theatre de Lys, which is now known as the Lucille Lortel Theatre, running for forty-nine performances. The *New York Times* review was terrible, but the *World Telegram* was positive.

Priscilla Morgan became his agent. But tragedy fell upon him as his mother was diagnosed with cancer and died in three months at the age of forty-four. Jerry and his father were devastated. Grieving, Herman could do no work until finally he was pushed into playing again at cocktail lounges. He became the pianist for Mabel Mercer's nightclub engagements at ninety dollars a week. Celebrities who came to hear Mercer soon found that Herman could compose, and hired him to write special material. Included in that group were Tallulah Bankhead, Ray Bolger, and Hermione Gingold.

After one year Jerry heard of a new venue, The Showplace, in Greenwich Village. It was similar to the Upstairs at the Downstairs. Customers could come in and sing with an accompanist on the first floor. On the second floor, where Herman wanted to work, there was a full revue. The owners said they were already booked, but if he would take the job on the first floor, when an opening appeared they would give him a chance at the revue. He accepted the job. The pianist he replaced was Warren Beatty.

He finally got his chance with a revue called NIGHTCAP, for which he wrote the music and did the

sets, staging, and directing. Phyllis Newman choreographed. The cast included Charles Nelson Reilly, Dom DeLuise, and Estelle Parsons. Frank Loesser saw it and wanted to sign Herman to an exclusive contract with his publishing firm, but Priscilla Morgan wouldn't let Herman sign. A producer wanted to take it to Off-Broadway. Herman added some songs and Dody Goodman was added to the cast. It was given a new title, PARADE. The *New York Times* panned it, but it lasted for ninety-five performances and was his first real step toward Broadway.

There were many different individuals who claimed responsibility for the idea of Herman's first big hit, MILK AND HONEY. What is definite is that Herman wanted to be on Broadway, so his agent connected him with Don Appel, twelve years his senior, to write the book. She knew they were both gay and Jewish and thought they would make a good team. Seed money was found and some of it came from the Israeli airline El Al. It was used to send Herman and Appel to Israel to research the project. They were most impressed by the sight of a green and fertile land which had once been barren. Herman wrote a score with a Middle Eastern flavor. Several songs start in a minor key, then modulate into a major.

It starred Molly Picon of the Yiddish theatre, Robert Weede of THE MOST HAPPY FELLA, and Mimi Benzell of the Metropolitan Opera. It opened in New Haven with problems. It was too long, and had to be cut so much that one cast member quit because his part had become so small. Herman frequently reprised songs, a technique he used in his later shows as well. He believed the audience needed to hear a song multiple times to retain it. By the time it reached Broadway in October 1961, it looked promising. A party was arranged at the Four Seasons to wait for the reviews, which would be out at 2 a.m. The reviews had minor complaints but were essentially wonderful.

It was a great hit for the first thirty weeks. But then Molly Picon got an offer to make the movie COME BLOW YOUR HORN and left the show. Ticket sales dropped markedly with her stand-in, so they brought in Hermione

Gingold. Gingold helped slightly but by the thirty-fourth week they were down to half-price tickets. Mimi Benzell soon got sick. She left the show and died shortly after that.

Things got even worse, as a problem arose that almost every Broadway composer has faced: a lawsuit stating the material had been stolen. The suit was thrown out, but was a major annoyance. When her movie was done, Picon returned to the show, but she soon got appendicitis. The show closed in January 1963, after 541 performances. But it was so expensive to produce that it actually lost money, the first time a long-running Broadway show had done so. The music in the show was daring and different and some believe the best Herman ever wrote.

Once MILK AND HONEY opened, Jerry was back at work at another show, MADAME APHRODITE, derived from an unproduced radio script. The score was well reviewed but the book was panned and it closed after thirteen performances. It was a major disappointment for him after the success of MILK AND HONEY.

A man who would create a great deal of distress and turmoil for Jerry Herman soon entered his life. David Merrick was born in 1911 as David Margulois. He studied law but really loved the theatre. When his wife received a major inheritance he invested her money in a show yielding a significant profit, which he subsequently deposited into his own private bank account.

After some failures, Merrick obtained the rights to FANNY, and had a score written by Harold Rome. With clever publicity and advertising he turned it into a two-year hit show. From 1955 on, he had an array of hits.

Jerry Herman went to see him and persuaded Merrick to allow him to turn Thornton Wilder's THE MATCHMAKER into a musical. When Merrick received the preliminary score his first decision was to call Ethel Merman to ask her to take the starring role. She refused, stating she was going to retire. After several other choices failed, Merrick decided on Carol Channing. Herman and Channing hit it off immediately. David Burns, who had been a hit in THE MUSIC MAN and A FUNNY THING HAPPENED ON THE WAY TO THE FORUM, was chosen for the role of Horace Vandergelder, but didn't want it. He asked his friend Jack Gilford to help him find a way out of it without offending Merrick. Gilford suggested he ask for more money, but Merrick agreed to it. So Gilford told him to ask for star billing. And Merrick gave it to him. Finally Gilford told him to demand a piece of the record because the producer was bound to say "No!" but Merrick gave it to him. So Burns took the role of Horace Vandergelder and remained in HELLO, DOLLY! for two years, introducing Herman's great comic song "It Takes a Woman."

Gower Champion was chosen as the choreographer-director. Champion hated Merrick, who had been so abusive to him during the production of the show CARNIVAL. But Champion accepted because he wanted a hit show.

HELLO, DOLLY! was not considered by some to be Herman's best, but the music historian Martin Gottfried disagreed. He felt it was quite special. He said it evoked showmanship and warmed the audience. It culminates with Channing and the chorus doing a spectacular presentation of the title song.

HELLO, DOLLY! began its out-of-town tryouts in Detroit. Merrick had just had a flop on Broadway and came to Michigan abusive to everyone. He told Herman the music was terrible. Herman protested to no avail that it was the same music Merrick had loved when he first presented it to him. Merrick privately asked Bob Merrill to come in to rewrite the score, telling him that Herman wanted him to do it; this was a complete lie. Merrill added very little, but the experience for Herman would be the worst he had ever known or would know in the theatre.

Merrick went to the team of Charles Strouse and Lee Adams and asked them to write a closing number for Act One. When the song was presented to Champion, he didn't like it and gave Herman the chance to write a new song for the scene in question. In forty-five minutes, Herman used the Strouse and Adams title, but came up with his own "Before the Parade Passes By."

Herman woke up Channing and Champion in the middle of the night to play it for them. Though no one had ever claimed that Strouse wrote anything for the show, Merrick gave away 50 percent of Herman's royalties for "Parade" to Strouse, claiming that Strouse had written it. Herman was so angry he asked for and received a signed letter from Strouse stating that Herman had written the song by himself. With the addition of that song, Champion became a complete supporter of Herman in any struggles with Merrick.

In January 1964, HELLO, DOLLY! opened on Broadway. Herman's father, grandmother, and Aunt Belle were in the audience. With its great success at last Herman would begin making a significant amount of money. As a result Herman bought Edward Albee's townhouse on Tenth Street in New York. Numerous performers recorded the title song, including Louis Armstrong. The publisher underestimated the recording's appeal, assuming it would sell one million copies. Armstrong's version alone sold three million copies. There are 350 recordings in 22 languages, and it is in the top ten of all time at ASCAP.

HELLO, DOLLY! won ten Tony awards, the record until THE PRODUCERS won twelve. It also won Drama Desk, Outer Critics Circle, and Grammy Awards. The same problem rose again. Mack David claimed that the opening notes of "Hello, Dolly!" had been taken from his 1948 song "Sunflower."

Herman received support from everyone in the lawsuit, including Richard Rodgers and Jule Styne—except Merrick.

Merrick said he was negotiating the rights to a movie of

HELLO, DOLLY! and that nothing could be accomplished "while there is a legal cloud over the property." As a result, Herman was forced to settle a "bogus suit" for two hundred thousand dollars, just to save Merrick's opportunity for a film.

When Channing left she was replaced by Ginger Rogers, who rarely sold out the house and missed many performances. Merrick would close the box office and start the overture before any announcement that Rogers would be replaced by an understudy.

Rogers was followed by Martha Raye, who was angry that Herman never came to any of her performances. In truth, he was in the hospital with hepatitis during most of her run.

The next lead was Betty Grable, a childhood idol of Herman. She would come to his house on Fire Island on her days off and wash dishes wearing a schmata in his kitchen and swim in his pool. It was a very happy time for him.

As ticket sales dropped off, Merrick switched to an all-black cast, starring Pearl Bailey and Cab Calloway. Merrick sold the movie in February 1968. It starred Barbra Streisand. She was actually too young for the role and fought with everyone including the director Gene Kelly, costar Walter Matthau, and the clothing designer.

In December 1969, Phyllis Diller undertook the Broadway role and did it quite well. Even though he had been initially rebuffed, following Diller's run, David Merrick was able to persuade Ethel Merman to be the final leading lady. She was supposed to take the role for three months but actually stayed for nine months. It broke the MY FAIR LADY record by reaching 2844 performances in just under seven years. Over the next twenty-six years, Carol Channing starred in several revivals, even into her late seventies.

Mary Martin toured with the show in the United States, London, Japan, Vietnam, all over Europe, and Russia. Even with all of its success, it certainly caused Jerry Herman more heartache than any other show he ever wrote due to the constant fights with Merrick, the disputed origins of songs, and the charges of plagiarism against him.

Many twists and turns led up to Herman's next show. They started with a young man, Edward Everett Tanner III, who so hated his name that he changed it by selecting an alternative from the telephone directory, Patrick Dennis. He went on to write the book titled *Auntie Mame: An Irreverent Escapade*. It was rejected by nineteen publishers before being bought by Vanguard and becoming a two-year best-seller.

The producers of WONDERFUL TOWN, starring Rosalind Russell, were certain that she was the perfect lead for the theatrical version of Dennis's book and negotiated with Frederick Brisson, her husband and manager. He had a reputation for being extremely difficult to deal with, so difficult that his nickname was "The Lizard Of Roz." Irwin Shaw, Noel Coward, Moss Hart, and Truman Capote all turned down the offer to adapt AUNTIE MAME. Finally, Jerome Lawrence and Robert E. Lee of INHERIT THE WIND agreed to adapt it for the stage. It ran for two years. The movie based on the play also starred Rosalind Russell, and it became the highest grossing film of 1958.

On Broadway, the starring role was taken over by Greer Garson, Sylvia Sydney, Beatrice Lillie, Constance Bennett, and Eve Arden.

It was then that the idea of making it into a musical came up. Its working title, MY BEST GIRL, was subsequently changed to MAME.

Roz Russell and Merman both turned down the lead. Gwen Verdon was occupied doing SWEET CHARITY. Interest turned to Mary Martin. The producers chose Joshua Logan to be the director because he had a long-time relationship with Martin. Jerry Herman was chosen by Lawrence and Lee to write the score, which thrilled him. He agreed to go to Brazil to persuade Martin to take the role, but Martin also turned it down. The Winter Garden Theatre had already been engaged and they were desperate. They considered and either rejected or were turned down by Eve Arden, Patrice Munsel, Bette Davis, Katherine Hepburn, Greer Garson, Lauren Bacall, Susan Hayward, Arlene Francis, Tammy Grimes, Constance Bennett, Ann Southern, Doris Day, Ginger Rogers, Olivia de Havilland, Lucille Ball, Irene Dunne, Beatrice Lillie, Julie Harris, Margaret Leighton, Elaine Stritch, Lena Horne, Jane Morgan, Geraldine Page, Dinah Shore, Maggie Smith, Georgia Brown, Kitty Carlisle Hart, Nanette Fabray, Giselle MacKenzie, Simone Signoret, Dolores Gray, Janet Gaynor, Phyllis Diller, Lisa Kirk, Barbara Cook, Kaye Ballard, and Judy Garland.

Suddenly, Angela Lansbury decided she wanted the role and offered to pay her own way to come from California for an audition. It took place in a terrible location and didn't go very well. But Jerry Herman was certain that she was right for the role. Meanwhile the producers were becoming less enchanted with Joshua Logan and replaced him with Gene Saks. So Lansbury got a second audition with him. He expressed concerns about her weight and her dancing ability. Saks began to consider his wife, Beatrice Arthur, for the lead and then changed his mind, selecting her for the second lead, Vera.

In a subsequent television special, Arthur jokingly said that they wanted to change the name of the show to VERA, but Jerry Herman was not able to think of anything to rhyme with Vera. After a long laugh she said, "Stephen Sondheim could have."

Meanwhile, terribly furious with the indecision, Lansbury said she could no longer wait for them to decide and was going back to California. They finally agreed and offered her the part. She immediately went on a diet and began rigorous singing and dancing lessons.

The title song of the show is considered by musicologists to be far superior to the title song for HELLO, DOLLY! It is part of the wealthy southern plantation owner Beauregard Johnson Pickett Burnside's marriage proposal. Another great

Left to right: Alexander Cohen, Lucia Victor, Angela Lansbury, Jerome Lawrence, Robert E. Lee, and Jerry Herman (at piano). (Photofest.)

song from the show was "If He Walked into My Life."

When the show opened on Broadway, the reviews were mixed, but the audience response and word-of-mouth praise were great. It was a hit and had expectations of winning the Tony. They were disappointed when MAN OF LA MANCHA swept the awards including that for score. But Angela Lansbury had converted her image from supporting Hollywood player to Broadway star. Lansbury won a Tony for Best Actress, and Arthur won for Best Featured Actress.

Lansbury continued to play the role for two years. Garland begged to follow her and although her audition was fabulous, the producers decided that healthwise she was too risky. Janis Paige took the role for one year, followed by Jane Morgan. Finally, they brought in an aging Ann Miller. She did a great job and remained for a year before catching pneumonia. It closed in 1970 after 1508 performances. The producers agreed that Lansbury was the perfect lead of them all for the role, and it would be necessary to have her in it to run the show any longer.

A revival in 1982 had mixed reviews except from Frank Rich, whose review was devastating.

When the decision was made to make it into a movie, Hollywood erred as it had on many other occasions. They wanted a Hollywood star and gave the role to Lucille Ball. The movie was a disaster.

Overall the 1960's were the Golden Age for Jerry Herman and his three great hits, MILK AND HONEY, HELLO, DOLLY! and MAME.

With all of his success, Herman decided to go on a vacation to the Virgin Islands with a friend, Sheila Mack. She had a friend there who owned a restaurant. The owner was blue-eyed, sun-tanned, and handsome, and Jerry began his first serious gay relationship. With George living in St. Thomas and Jerry in New York, their three-year-long liaison faced inherent difficulties.

Herman decided to write a show based on the play THE MAD WOMAN OF CHAILLOT. He and producer Alexander Cohen planned on doing a small-scale production. Herman wanted Angela Lansbury. She turned him down initially because the director Gene Saks had not supported her when she was trying to get the role she created in MAME. But when Saks dropped out of the show she agreed and commanded a large salary based on her success in MAME. As it progressed, the show became much larger than originally conceived. The bigger it got, the worse it got. The title was changed to DEAR WORLD. It had a typical Parisian flavor much in the style of Edith Piaf and Jacques Brel. It closed after only 132 performances. Herman and Lansbury were both devastated, and Herman went into semi-seclusion. To this day Herman and many others believe, because the score was so good, a much smaller production would have been a success.

Before the run ended, Herman finally came out of seclusion. He developed a routine. He would go to the Mark Hellinger Theatre at 8:30 p.m. to hear Lansbury's great performance of "I Don't Want to Know." Following that, he would go straight to the Winter Garden to see the first-act closing of MAME, and spend the intermission with the cast. From there he would head over to hear the second-act showstopper of HELLO, DOLLY! and after the show have dinner with the leading lady.

Herman also began having a relationship with a male cast member of DEAR WORLD, which lasted for a year.

Herman was approached with the idea to write a musical about two real people, Mack Sennett, the great silent movie producer, and his girlfriend and leading lady Mabel Normand. In real life it was a sad story with Normand dying at thirty-seven of alcoholism, drug addiction, and tuberculosis.

David Merrick would be the producer with Gower Champion directing. Mistakes by Champion caused the show to get terrible reviews. MACK & MABEL opened in October 1974 and closed in eight weeks. The show, Herman's favorite of all his works, became a cult hit with revivals all over England and the United States.

In 1982, when the ice-skating champions Torvil and Dean used the music it brought MACK AND MABEL back into the spotlight. Ten years after its opening, the cast album was re-released and reached number six on the charts, unheard of for an old show. The 1995 production in London won the Evening Standard award for Best Musical. And in 2000, it was a success in Los Angeles. Some consider it Herman's finest score.

His next show was to have no such success. Jerry's style was stuck in the mold of the older musicals. Michael Stewart had repeatedly approached him to do a musical based on S. N. Behrman's JACOBOWSKY AND THE COLONEL. Once Herman began writing, a number of technical problems arose. But not much attention was paid to them until just before the previews were to begin. The title had been changed to THE GRAND TOUR. In a panic Stewart shortened it drastically and completely changed the flavor of the show. Another problem was that Herman preferred writing for strong leading ladies and there was no such character in the show. It received mixed reviews and, without a producer as aggressive in promotion as David Merrick, it closed after sixty-one performances. One number, "I'll Be Here Tomorrow," became the theme song of the Gay Men's Health Crisis, an organization committed to the fight against AIDS.

Jerry believed that had he been born thirty years earlier, all his shows would have been hits. But the time had come for rock musicals and the shows gaining huge audiences were HAIR, GODSPELL, and JESUS CHRIST SUPERSTAR. With two failures in a row, Herman was losing interest in the theatre and decided to turn his attention to interior design. He began buying properties and redesigning them. He considered completely changing his career.

A great story about that relates to Herman's decision to purchase, for the outrageous price of one million dollars, the honeymoon home of Richard Burton and Elizabeth Taylor, which was in a state of severe disrepair. It had a spectacular view of the Pacific Ocean. When his restoration work was completed, the housing market totally collapsed and there was no way to recoup his investment. At the same time, DOLLY was opening in London. Herman flew there and was coerced by Carol Channing's husband to escort Lady Rothermere to the opening. Rothermere's husband owned the newspaper, the *Daily Mail*. She was enormous and wore an even larger gown of layer after layer of pink tulle. When he saw her he was horrified and felt suffocated by her in the taxicab. But Bubbles, as the Lady was known, turned out to be a lovely companion for the evening. And on the way to the theatre he sold the California house to her for two million dollars.

When Herman first saw the movie LA CAGE AUX FOLLES he decided immediately that he wanted to make it into a musical. Herman felt if MILK AND HONEY, HELLO, DOLLY! and MAME were big hits, the possibilities for LA CAGE were even greater. But the next day he had a terrible disappointment. He found out that the rights had already been obtained and the project had already progressed quite far. Maury Yeston, who was working on NINE, had been chosen for the score. Mike Nichols was to direct. Tommy Tune was the choreographer and the book was being done by Jay Presson Allen, the writer of the stage version of THE PRIME OF MISS JEAN BRODIE. Discouraged, he put it out of his mind to work on the production of JERRY'S GIRLS, a revue of his past musical successes, which was to run for two years.

Alexander Cohen came back into his life asking Jerry to be a musical doctor to straighten out a show in trouble for Tommy Tune, A DAY IN HOLLYWOOD/A NIGHT IN THE UKRAINE, to which he added three songs. The producers felt during the tryouts that there was something missing in the show. The changes Herman made as a "show doctor" were so significant it was said they enabled the show to be a success, run for one year, and even win two Tonys.

Then one day a producer asked Herman to meet with him. He thought the meeting concerned putting JERRY'S GIRLS on tour. Instead, four years after he had first wanted to do LA CAGE, Herman was asked if he was interested. They had run into difficulties with Nichols, Tune, and Yeston, who was busy with NINE. Herman was ecstatic. They wanted him to start from scratch and asked him who he would like to write the book. He suggested Arthur Laurents, who had already had successes with WEST SIDE STORY and GYPSY. Instead, Laurents asked to direct and recommended Harvey Fierstein, who had been successful with TORCH SONG TRILOGY, to be the librettist.

The result was that the librettist, the composer, and the director who would be responsible for the first musical about a gay couple would all be gay.

Both the stars, Gene Barry and George Hearn, were heterosexual. In fact Hearn's wife at the time was a member of the show's chorus. The show was a huge hit with great reviews and Tony Awards for the show, George Hearn, and Herman's score. Two of the best numbers from the show were "The Best of Times" and "I Am What I Am."

LA CAGE walked away with all the awards over SUNDAY IN THE PARK WITH GEORGE. Herman made a comment in his acceptance speech about hummable music still being acceptable. It offended some of the theatrical community, who interpreted it as a slur about Sondheim's complicated intellectual style.

Herman's success had reached its pinnacle. He now had unlimited access to the gay community and met Marty Finklestein, who was to become the great love of his life. Finklestein was sixteen years younger and had been living in Philadelphia with a physician. But after several months passed, he told Herman that he was leaving the physician, and they began a seven-year relationship.

They started a business in Key West, buying old homes and restoring them. They called the company Majer, using the beginnings of their two first names.

In 1986, Marty got word that the physician he had been living with was dying of AIDS. A few months later, Marty got sick, and Herman tested positive for HIV. By 1989, Marty died of AIDS.

Over the next few years, Jerry involved himself in several projects including an album with Michael Feinstein called the *Jerry Herman Songbook*, and writing a Christmas musical for television. Called MRS. SANTA CLAUS, it starred Angela Lansbury on Hallmark and is frequently reshown.

Herman developed a severe heart problem in 1997 and had a successful triple bypass operation.

In Palm Springs, in August 1999, he met Terry Marler. Herman was sixty-eight and Marler fifty-three. Marler maintained his home in Palm Springs while Herman stayed in Beverly Hills, but as permanent partners. His HIV status remained under control. Still capable of working, he was asked by Mel Brooks to write the music for the show THE PRODUCERS. But Herman knew the music that Brooks had already written for the original film, and encouraged him to write it himself.

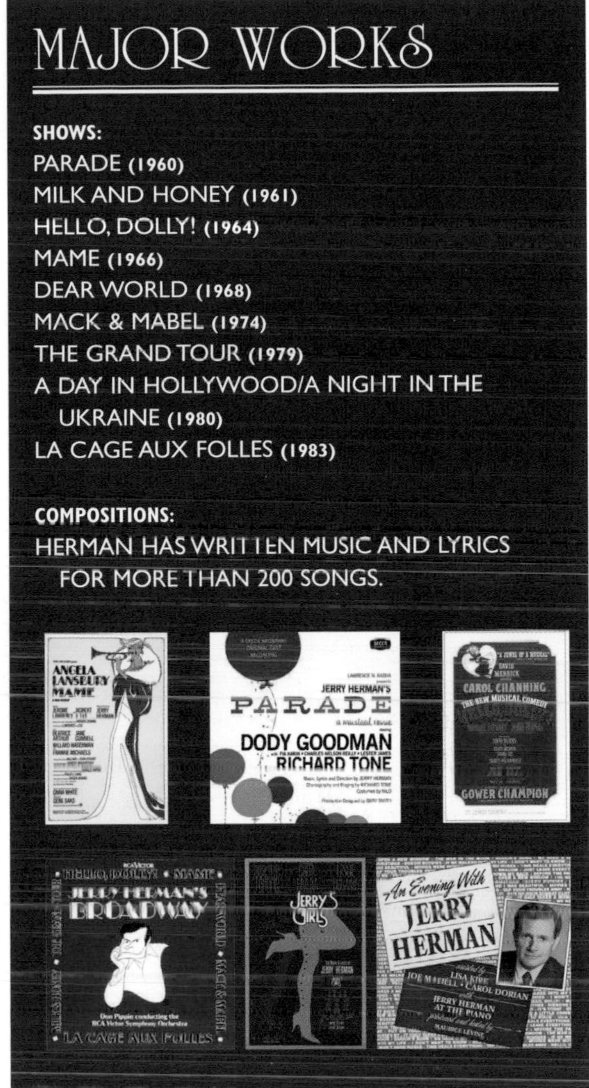

In 1998, Steve Wynn created a spectacular hotel in Las Vegas and signed a half million dollar contract with Herman to write a show specifically for the Las Vegas environment. Everyone who heard the score deeply admired the show Herman created. But, just before it was ready for production, Wynn sold all his hotel rights in Vegas and it was never produced. It was called MISS SPECTACULAR and Herman still has a hope that some other Las Vegas hotel will want to produce it.

In the pantheon of geniuses of the American musical theatre, Herman falls into that very special group who wrote both the music and lyrics for their shows. That places him in a very distinguished category which includes Irving Berlin, Cole Porter, Frank Loesser, and Stephen Sondheim.

Left to right: Fred Ebb, John Kander, and Florence Henderson. (Photofest.)

JOHN KANDER & FRED EBB

FRED EBB WAS BORN TO HARRY AND ANNA EBB IN APRIL 1936. They lived in Manhattan where Fred went to NYU, and then to Columbia for a Master's degree in English.

John Kander had a totally different beginning. He was born in Kansas City, Missouri, in 1927. John took piano lessons from the age of six. He began studying at Oberlin College, well known for its music curriculum, and also ended up at Columbia getting a Master's degree.

Unlike so many of the other great composers for Broadway, Kander was a relatively slow starter. From 1955 to 1950 he was the choral director of the Warwick Musical Theatre in Rhode Island. He was already twenty-nine years old when he got the job as a pianist for the pre-Broadway run of THE AMAZING ADELE and AN EVENING WITH BEATRICE LILLIE in Florida.

At thirty-five, Kander made his composing debut on Broadway in 1962 with A FAMILY AFFAIR (with lyrics by James and William Goldman).

Meanwhile, Ebb was writing for nightclub acts and reviews, and the television show THAT WAS THE WEEK THAT WAS. In 1962, when Fred was twenty-six, they met.

They were both from Jewish homes, but completely different environments. John's family was almost non-religious, celebrating only the major holidays. What his family was committed to was music. None were professionals, but all could sing and play instruments. It was a major part of the family's entertainment. Aside from the music at home, the children were brought to music appreciation classes and children's concerts in Kansas City. It was a very warm and affectionate family life.

Ebb had quite a different childhood. His father had a tedious job as a salesman. He came home and shared little with his family. There was no loving relationship between his parents nor any interest in theatre, music, or books. The family wanted him to be a doctor or lawyer. His exposure to theatre was as an escape, and he went alone to the theatre, paying fifty-five cents for standing room tickets. Even though he lived in New York he didn't see his first musical until he was fifteen, when he asked for tickets as a birthday present.

Ebb had an assortment of jobs including working for a trucking company and a hosiery company, and even bronzing baby shoes. At NYU, he got a Bachelor's degree in English literature before receiving his Master's from Columbia.

Kander's family by comparison was quite well off. They had a very successful poultry and egg business. By the time John was twelve, the family was taking annual trips to New York, specifically to go to the theatre.

Kander would sit with his elderly piano teacher's mother and listen to recordings of Wagner, which he loved. In high school and college, he occasional performed on the piano, but performing was not something he enjoyed.

Ebb loved writing poetry, especially limericks. A girl he knew suggested that he visit a friend of hers who was a professional composer. On his way there he decided that he should bring an example of his writing. On the bus ride, he wrote out a lyric on the back of a matchbook cover. Phil Springer, the composer, seemed impressed and asked if Ebb could write lyrics to a melody he played. Ebb wrote a lyric titled "I Never Loved Him Anyhow." Springer said he wanted him back there every day from nine to five so that they could work on it. They did and it was recorded by Carmen McRae. Ebb earned eighty dollars.

Once John Kander decided to make his career in musical theatre he began playing in summer stock and for auditions. After the opening night of WEST SIDE STORY in Philadelphia he met a man at a party. His new acquaintance played piano in the pit for the show. So, when the piano player went on vacation, he asked Kander to fill in for him.

The stage manager for WEST SIDE STORY, Ruth Mitchell, was involved with the casting for GYPSY at the same time, and asked Kander if he would like to play for Jerome Robbins at the auditions. After a couple of weeks, Robbins asked Kander if he could do the dance arrangements for the show. Kander, of course, agreed. To this day Kander believes that if it weren't for that WEST SIDE STORY party he never have had a career in the theatre.

Meanwhile, Ebb worked with Springer for about a year. Among other things they wrote together was "How Little We Know." Ebb began writing with Paul Klein for a revue called FROM A TO Z and an off-Broadway show, MORNING SUN, but it closed quickly.

Both Kander and Ebb knew an up-and-coming publisher, Tommy Valando, who made the suggestion that they should meet. Neither Kander nor Ebb had been particularly successful up until Kander arranged to go to Ebb's apartment. Ebb was very nervous about the meeting. A show called TAKE HER, SHE'S MINE was opening. So as an exercise they decided to write a title song for it. No one ever heard it or bought it, but they liked the way they worked together. They continued writing other songs, all with a comic flair, until one day Kander asked, "Why don't we treat this new idea of yours seriously and write a ballad instead?"

They wrote a song that they showed to their mutual friend Kaye Ballard, who was working on THE PERRY COMO SHOW. She thought she might be able to get Sandy Stewart to sing it. She did and the result was 20,000 calls and messages the following day. The song was "My Coloring Book."

Many others, including Barbra Streisand and Kitty Kallen, subsequently recorded it.

They began getting work writing special material for Judy Garland and Carol Channing for nightclub acts, but they knew that they wanted to write for the theatre. Best of all they found that writing together was fun and easy. Even when songs were not working out, they never felt stressed or agonized in the process. They would just throw them out and start over. They never seemed to get writer's block. They became so close that writing with anyone else seemed an anathema to the creative process. Once Richard Rodgers asked Ebb to join him in writing a show to be called REX. Although it was tremendously difficult to say no to someone of such great stature, he said that he just couldn't do it. In subsequent years, Ebb had said that the only other composer with whom he thought he might be compatible was Cy Coleman.

Though Kander hated performing, Ebb was just the opposite. Once when they were asked to perform at the Palace in support of a political candidate, Ebb was enthralled, but John Kander refused, expressing his disdain for the politician. Ebb insisted, "It's the Palace. Imagine standing where Sophie Tucker and Jolson once stood."

Kander replied, "You'd entertain for Adolf Hitler if it was at the Palace . . . but not me."

Since Kaye Ballard had given up "My Coloring Book" to Sandy Stewart, they wrote another song for her. Ultimately, the song, "Maybe This Time," became a hit for Liza Minnelli in the 1972 film version of CABARET.

Their first Broadway musical together was FLORA, THE RED MENACE, a satire. Produced by Harold Prince and directed by George Abbott, it opened in May 1965. It

Left to right: Fred Ebb and John Kander, 1987. (Photofest.)

had a relatively short run, but won a Tony for Liza Minnelli. Actually, the first show that Kander and Ebb had written was called GOLDEN GATE. It never got produced, but they used what they had written as an audition piece for Harold Prince in the effort to get the assignment to write FLORA, THE RED MENACE.

One day, while they were writing GOLDEN GATE, Kander was at the piano trying to work out a song, when Ebb said that he was going in to take a shower. After a few moments, Ebb came rushing out of the shower saying, "That's the best thing I've ever heard in my life."

Kander looked at him and said, "Thanks! That's Puccini . . .*Turandot*."

When they got to the casting of FLORA, THE RED MENACE a friend brought Liza Minnelli to them. She was only seventeen, but Ebb was certain that she was perfect for the part. He presented her to George Abbott who immediately decided he didn't like her and left it to Ebb to tell her so. Abbott had Eydie Gorme in mind, but she never showed up when they were supposed to meet. So Abbott gave in to Ebb's choice. Subsequently Abbott became Liza Minnelli's greatest supporter.

Kander and Ebb developed what was to become a long personal relationship with Liza. They wrote a great deal of music for her including the title song of her theatre concert, LIZA WITH A "Z."

Kander, Ebb, and Prince ultimately came to the realization that it was Abbott who did the most damage to FLORA, THE RED MENACE. He was very strong and would never allow Minnelli the freedom she needed for the role. Abbott really never understood the framework of the show. Prince actually said later that if he had been more secure in his role, he would have insisted on directing it. He said he would have changed the entire feeling of the show. But he was very early in his career.

The fact that FLORA didn't work was very difficult for them, as both Kander and Ebb had already had a failed show. This made them even more insecure. But George Abbott was very professional and taught them a great deal. He was not in any way difficult to work with, so it was a good experience for them. It also helped to establish their work habits.

They would always write at Ebb's apartment. Fred liked staying home and John liked going out. They never worked independently, like some other teams who would present completed music or lyrics to one another. They always created the songs together. And, they always start-

Left to right: John Kander, Fred Ebb, Jill Haworth, Hal Prince, and Ronald Field in rehearsal for CABARET. (Photofest.)

ed with the opening number.

Ebb didn't play the piano or read music. He was always amazed at how Kander could construct a melody. Kander's explanation was that he heard it in his head and felt it in his hands.

Their next project was CABARET. It was produced and directed by Prince, and opened in November 1966. It was a huge success. They credited Prince with conceiving the idea of the show, which was so different from anything that had previously been done. It ran for three years and won eight Tony Awards. A 1987 revival lasted for only about nine months. But in 1998, a totally new production was developed at London's Donmar Warehouse. It was a great hit and in some ways even more daring than the original.

The story of CABARET was told through an Emcee, originated by Joel Grey. Grey's role evolved slowly as Kander, Ebb, and Joe Masteroff, who wrote the book, together developed the story and the songs. Kander and Ebb finally had their first big hit.

Among the great songs that came out of that show were "Cabaret," "The Money Song, and, for the film version, "Maybe This Time."

The result was that David Merrick selected them to write the score for THE HAPPY TIME. Director Gower Champion turned the show into an extravaganza at a huge expense. It ran for close to a year and won Tonys for Champion and Robert Goulet, but, due to its massive overhead, it lost a great deal of money. When the show was revived in a much smaller way at the Goodspeed Opera House, it turned out to be much better.

ZORBA was started while Kander and Ebb were working on THE HAPPY TIME, and they were having difficulty with it. The original production, which opened in 1968 and starred Herschel Bernardi, seemed too heavy. Though it ran for almost a year, it was not a financial success. But in 1983 a revival starring Anthony Quinn appeared on Broadway. Quinn had originally starred in the film adaptation of the original novel. Quinn's powerful personality overwhelmed everyone else in the production. Although Kander and Ebb preferred the original, this production was far more successful. Part of the problem for Kander and Ebb was that Quinn believed that he could do anything. But in truth Quinn really had great difficulty with rhythm and dancing. In the film there were scenes of him dancing which showed only his lower body. That's because the film's producers employed a stand-in to cover the dancing.

The next show they wrote had the shortest run of any of their productions, only thirty-five performances. 70, GIRLS, 70 was much lighter than ZORBA. It was overwhelmed by that season's hit, Sondheim's FOLLIES. 70, GIRLS, 70 was a story about elderly New Yorkers who aspire to a life of crime. They believed it was a small show that should be produced Off-Broadway, but were persuaded to go big. David Burns was in it. It opened in Philadelphia and in its last act, Burns, who was a comedian, fell to the floor and got a big laugh. The audience believed that was part of the show. In actuality, Burns had suffered a fatal heart attack.

Ebb delivered the eulogy at his funeral and said it was the perfect ending for Burns, as the last sound he heard was a laugh.

Kander and Ebb didn't have another show from 1971 to 1975, but they kept busy doing other projects, primarily television specials and movies. They were responsible for Frank Sinatra's OL' BLUE EYES IS BACK, a return after a brief retirement. The show featured Gene Kelly along with Sinatra. The experience soured them on the legendary singer. They found him mean and self-centered. And, though they acknowledge that his version of "New York, New York" brought them a great deal of recognition, they disliked him immensely. They also felt that Liza, for whom they had written several shows, performed the song much better than Sinatra. Among their complaints about him was that he would change a song to whatever he wanted it to be. He did it not just with Kander and Ebb's music, but also with that of Berlin, Porter, and many other greats. They were extremely distressed about how cruel he constantly was to Gene Kelly throughout the production, nicknaming his costar "Shanty," to mock Kelly's Irish roots. On the other hand they had great admiration for Kelly.

During this period, they realized that they much preferred working in New York's theatre environment to California, where they felt little community spirit.

They began work on CHICAGO. They had worked with Bob Fosse before (on the film of CABARET and Minnelli's concert), and as was well known in the theatrical community, he could be extremely difficult. In the middle of the production, Fosse had a heart attack, and he was out for three months. The movie ALL THAT JAZZ is based on that incident. In it, the character based on Fosse is always victimized by others. Kander and Ebb felt that was a distortion, and that Bobby, as they called him, was always paranoid. They recalled that when he returned to work after the attack, he was even more unpleasant.

Ebb told of how Fosse interviewed him in preparation for making the movie and asked him an amazing question. He wanted to know how people felt when he had his heart attack.

"I was horrified," Ebb answered. "Disappointed and sad."

Fosse's strange response was, "Was anybody happy?"

Fosse went on. "When you went to Hal Prince to have him to take over the show . . ."

Kander was shocked. "Neither Fred nor I ever did such a thing. It was your show and your idea. I don't know who your sources are. If someone went to Hal Prince, it wasn't us."

Kander and Ebb had a reputation throughout the industry of impeccable honesty. But, nevertheless, that story became part of the film ALL THAT JAZZ. Hal Prince did not like CHICAGO, and in fact sent a very terse and unpleasant note to them that he believed CHICAGO was just a rip-off of CABARET. He said that Chicago in the 1920s was not Berlin—the city, not the composer.

The production of CHICAGO was very tense and difficult for everyone. There was no concern about Fosse's talent. But, he was very mean, even toward his wife, Gwen Verdon, who played the lead, Roxie Hart.

Ebb recalled Fosse admitting to him that the director-choreographer was indeed picking on him. Fosse asked Ebb if he understood why. Ebb had no answer. Fosse replied that the reason was, "Because you are vulnerable, and vulnerable people drive me crazy!"

The entire experience became so intolerable that Kander and Ebb almost quit the show. One day Fosse yelled at Ebb, "Why didn't you give me that rewrite of the Roxie number?" He had never mentioned it before, and Ebb was ready to respond vehemently when Kander took him by the shoulder and marched him out of the room. John felt there was no better way to deal with a bully than to ignore him and not play by his terms. Kander wanted to leave because he felt no show was important enough to die for.

The show got mixed reviews, and lost all the Tonys to A CHORUS LINE, but it did run for three years. Critics did not like the heaviness of the theme, much as PAL JOEY had been rejected in its initial run. The *New York Times* said nothing good could come of such bad people.

But a 1996 revival enjoyed smashing success, thanks in part to Ann Reinking's turns as both the star and choreographer (incorporating Fosse's style). Kander and Ebb saw the revival and were blown away. They said it was their greatest night in the theatre.

As Ebb thought back, he said that with all the problems and the meanness, he loved and missed Bob Fosse. He had learned so much from him and taught him as well. Ebb felt that his relationship with Fosse was a major force in his life.

In 1977, their show THE ACT, a huge star vehicle for Liza Minnelli, opened. Martin Scorsese was the original director but had so much trouble that he was replaced by Gower Champion. Champion pulled it together for a modest success running 233 performances.

Kander and Ebb were truly amazed by the fact that something really good that they wrote could be panned and forgotten, while a mediocre work of theirs could wind up

Left to right: Fred Ebb (lyricist, Best Original Score), Chita Rivera (Best Actress), John Kander (composer, Best Original Score) with their 1993 Tony Awards for KISS OF THE SPIDERWOMAN. (Photofest.)

winning Tony Awards; their next musical was a case in point.

The team felt they never should have written WOMAN OF THE YEAR. They were not particularly proud of that work, but did it out of their great fondness for Lauren Bacall. It opened in 1981 and won Tony Awards for Bacall and Kander and Ebb. Subsequently Raquel Welch and Debbie Reynolds took over the lead role. Kander and Ebb had to keep rewriting the show to suit their individual personalities. Debbie Reynolds, who was the final leading lady, would constantly ad-lib during the show. They found her to be much like Eydie Gorme (for whom they had written material), changing the feeling of the show at almost every performance.

In another case they had a completely opposite experience. The show was THE RINK, starring Liza Minnelli and Chita Rivera. The believed it was one of their best, and yet it was not well received. It opened in 1984 and Rivera won the Tony, but the show ran for only 204 performances. Minnelli, though she begged for the part, was actually miscast. Frank Rich, in the *New York Times*, demolished her and the show in his review. Minnelli, who was trying to make a comeback, was devastated and got deeply into drugs. After she missed many performances, an intervention led her to enter a treatment center.

In KISS OF THE SPIDER WOMAN, something very unusual happened. Kander and Ebb had arranged to create the show, based on a successful movie starring William Hurt. In a workshop at the State University of New York at Purchase it was in its earliest stages. They had begged the *New York Times* not to review it, as it was changing every day. The *New York Times* refused and Frank Rich wrote a scathing review. So Kander and Ebb closed the workshop. However, they did continue to rewrite it for two years and in 1992 brought it to Broadway. It was a smash hit, winning seven Tonys including one for Chita Rivera and one for

Kander and Ebb. The show ran for 906 performances.

In between THE RINK and KISS OF THE SPIDER WOMAN, they got involved with some new, up-and-coming talents. Director Scott Ellis, choreographer Susan Stroman, and librettist David Thompson came to them asking to do a new, smaller version of FLORA, THE RED MENACE. It was very well received. After that, the same team put together a revue that was a huge success, AND THE WORLD GOES 'ROUND: THE SONGS OF KANDER AND EBB. It ran for 408 performances Off-Broadway.

Over the years Kander and Ebb had created a family of people they loved to work with, over and over. They included Liza Minnelli, Chita Rivera, Rob Marshall, Karen Ziemba, and Susan Stroman.

So once again they combined the efforts of several of these friends and wrote STEEL PIER in 1997. Like THE RINK, it was strong, emotional, and they felt it was very good. And, like THE RINK, it got panned. Both shows were about deep personal relationships. They sincerely loved the two shows probably more than anything else they had written, and as a result they were the biggest disappointments of their careers. Everything about the shows, including the casts, were very dear to their hearts. Ironically, Stroman lost the choreography Tony that year to Reinking for her work in Kander and Ebb's CHICAGO. They were saddened by Stroman's loss, but they had great affection for Reinking.

Kander and Ebb's spectacular contribution to the world of theatre was recognized in the presentation of their body of work at the Kennedy Center Honors in 1998.

In 2002, twenty-five years after the original production of CHICAGO opened on Broadway, a movie version of the show was released and won six Academy Awards. Kander and Ebb had met Fosse at a funeral years earlier, and he told them that he had figured out how to do the show as a movie. But he died shortly after without another word on the subject. No one ever knew what Fosse's idea had been.

There were a few bad reviews for the movie. One said there would be no audience for this type of material. But Kander and Ebb had reconciled themselves to bad reviews with the philosophy, "You get over death. You get over love and you go on."

They began working on two other shows, CURTAINS and THE VISIT. They wanted to move out of the framework of big expensive extravaganzas. Sadly, Fred Ebb died of a heart attack in September 2004, ending a long and wonderful Broadway partnership that went on for forty-two years.

In February 2007, CURTAINS, a musical comedy detective mystery, came to Broadway, with Kander finishing the show with librettist/lyricist Rupert Holmes. It ran for 511 performances and won a Tony for its star, David Hyde Pierce.

There were three other shows that Kander and Ebb nearly completed at the time of Ebb's death. With other artists, Kander has moved ahead to attempt to bring them to the stage.

MAJOR WORKS

SHOWS:

FLORA, THE RED MENACE **(1965)**
CABARET **(1966)**
THE HAPPY TIME **(1968)**
ZORBA **(1968)**
70, GIRLS, 70 **(1971)**
CHICAGO **(1975)**
THE ACT **(1978)**
WOMAN OF THE YEAR **(1981)**
THE RINK **(1984)**
KISS OF THE SPIDER WOMAN **(1992)**
STEEL PIER **(1997)**
FOSSE **(1999)**
THE VISIT **(2001; REGIONAL AND OFF-BROADWAY)**
CURTAINS **(2006; KANDER/EBB/HOLMES)**

COMPOSITIONS:

KANDER AND EBB WROTE MUSIC AND LYRICS FOR 496 SONGS.

One titled ALL ABOUT US is a musical version of THE SKIN OF OUR TEETH. It has already played in repertory theatre as OVER AND OVER AGAIN. A second show, THE VISIT, was performed in 2008 at the Public Theatre Off-Broadway. The last one, THE MINSTREL SHOW, was intended to be performed in blackface. It tells the sad story of the Scottsboro Boys, who were falsely accused of rape in Alabama.

Like almost all creative individuals, Kander and Ebb both agreed that there was a style to their work. They believed their shows conveyed a message to survive, because somehow things will get better, sometime in the future. It was an optimistic approach to life.

They worked together without conflict as practically no others ever had on Broadway. Through their flawless partnership, they made a huge and lasting contribution to Broadway.

Jerome Kern, 1930s.
(Photofest.)

JEROME KERN

JEROME KERN WAS THE LAST OF NINE SONS BORN TO HENRY and Fanny Kern, who were of German-Jewish descent. It was 1885. Only three of those sons survived. Joseph, the eldest, was in real estate like his father. Edwin had sheet music stores. Fanny had wanted Jerome to be a girl, so she dressed him as one for the first three years of his life.

Fanny was very cultured and a pianist. She began teaching Jerome to play the piano when he was five. He was the center of attention in the family and was showered with love. Like Richard Rodgers, he was still in high school when he began composing musical scores. When he was sixteen, the Newark Yacht Club made Kern an honorary member so that he could write a show for them. The original score was a spoof on *Uncle Tom's Cabin*.

Jerome was a mediocre student, but his exceptional ability at the piano gave him stature at school. After graduating high school in 1902, he went to work for his father in the family department store. On one occasion his father gave him the responsibility to order some stock for the business; Jerome was directed to purchase two pianos, but by accident bought two hundred instead. His father decided that Jerome was not going to be a successful businessman and as a result allowed him to attend music school. After graduation he persuaded his parents to send him to England to further his career. There he had the opportunity to write songs which were fill-ins in London shows. One was called "My Little Canoe."

He also wrote a number of the songs for MR. WIX OF WICKHAM. It came to America and failed immediately. However, Kern was favorably mentioned in the reviews.

Kern came back home and became a song plugger in Wanamaker's Department Store, as well as a sheet music salesman in the Lyceum publishing firm. At the same time, he attended the New York College of Music. In 1905, he began working for Max Dreyfus at Harms Publishing, where he ultimately became a partner. During that time Jerome sold his first hit song for a show, "How'd You Like to Spoon with Me?"

During the first few decades of the twentieth century, producers would routinely put any songs they wished, from any composer they wished, into their own shows. From 1905 until 1912, Kern had more than 100 songs interpolated into other composers' shows. So by 1910, at the age of twenty-five, he was already very successful financially.

Kern was the senior member of a group of great new American composers. In 1905, when he was twenty, Richard Rodgers was only three, George Gershwin and Vincent Youmans were seven, and Cole Porter was twelve. Gershwin and Rodgers, by their own admission, were significantly influenced by Kern's work. He was the supreme melodist.

In 1907, Kern's mother died suddenly after a brief illness. His father died the following August. Jerome was only twenty-two. In his father's obituary, Kern was already spoken of as a Broadway composer.

Kern had a 1908 love affair with Edith Kelly, who subsequently married the millionaire Frank Jay Gould. In the summer of that year, he visited a friend in London, who took him for a weekend to the Swan Hotel at Walton-on-the-Thames. At the hotel, he met the owner's daughter, Eva, who was seventeen years old. After he left England he began writing to her, against her father's wishes, until finally Jerome was able to convince him to allow them to marry. Though they were completely different in family background and temperament, in October 1910 he returned to England, and he and Eva were wed.

The newlywed Kerns moved to New York. Very shy and retiring, Eva went to no social business functions, did all her own housework, never disturbed her husband while he was working, had contact with very few people, never went to openings, and knew nothing at all about their business affairs.

Kern dressed immaculately. He looked and talked like a college professor. On the other hand, he was a strange contradiction. Bright, sophisticated, and erudite, he was also an inveterate gambler at both cards and horse races. He loved playing parlor games with friends. A consummate baseball fan, Kern attended games in New York every weekend. Kern was far from the poor businessman that his father perceived him to be. He was an avid book and silver collector. In 1929, just before the Depression, he auctioned off his collection for over two million dollars, quite a sum at that time. Among other things, the proceeds enabled him to buy a yacht that would take him to and from Palm Beach, Florida.

He could be very generous, or sometimes cold and calculating. When an early collaborator of his, librettist Guy Bolton, suggested they work on a fifty-fifty basis, Kern ended the conversation and never wrote with him again. When Ira Gershwin, after the death of George, wrote with Kern he also asked for an even split. But Kern insisted on taking 55 percent of their earnings, even though Ira was by then also very famous.

In 1911, he wrote for his first songs for THE ZIEGFELD FOLLIES, as well as his first full score, THE RED PETTICOAT the next year. And though it was a failure, Kern was not discouraged.

The war in Europe was having a significant effect. European-born composers and lyricists and their operetta style had monopolized Broadway. But, suddenly tastes changed, and Americans wanted more homegrown talents. The beneficiaries would be Kern, Hammerstein, Berlin, and the Gershwins.

In 1914, Kern had his first big success, THE GIRL FROM UTAH. Among the songs was one of Kern's biggest hits, "They Didn't Believe Me."

Most of the shows at that time were based on a concept still around today, the big production number. Often shows relied on large-cast numbers, extravagant scenic effects, or a combination of both. To cut back on the exploding production costs, one producer, Bessie Marbury, built a small theatre seating only 299, where she hoped to produce small plays. Because she was somewhat obese, Ms. Marbury was known as the "charming and benign elephant." She was the daughter of a prominent attorney. Marbury became a copyright expert and then a theatrical agent. Her new venue was the Princess Theatre, and it began an era known as the Princess Theatre productions. In 1914, with P. G. Wodehouse, Kern wrote for her the hit show VERY GOOD EDDIE, which ran for a year. It was followed by OH BOY! for a year and a half. In it was Kern's "Till the Clouds Roll By."

That was followed by another hit, OH LADY! LADY!! with Wodehouse and Bolton. A song was written for it which was discarded before the opening because it wasn't right for the performers in that show. It was revived many years later when it was felt to be just right for Helen Morgan in SHOW BOAT. The song was "Bill."

OH LADY! LADY!! was the last of Kern's Princess Theatre productions. Kern had become fantastically successful and was reportedly earning five thousand dollars a week. In the latter part of the century's second decade, he wrote show after show, including ROCK-A-BYE BABY, which was his favorite until SHOW BOAT.

In 1916, the Kerns moved out of New York City to the suburbs in Bronxville, where they lived for the next twenty years. They kept dogs, cats, sheep, and horses. Kern also

Jerome Kern, early 1940s. (Photofest.)

began collecting cars including a Rolls Royce. But he hated driving, and by 1923, and for the remainder of his life, chauffeurs drove him. He also bought a speedboat and a house boat.

Betty, his only child, was born in 1918. The couple spoiled her terribly with governesses, private teachers, a nurse to escort her to school, and constant trips around the world during the school year, severely disrupting her education. As an adult, she had two failed marriages, one of them to Artie Shaw, before a successful marriage in 1947. In retrospect, she blamed her divorces on her upbringing, feeling that she was ill-prepared for a shared life. For a while, she functioned as her father's escort in place of her introverted mother.

From 1920 through 1926, Kern wrote eleven more Broadway musicals, but the era of the great musicals had not yet arrived. Many of these shows failed. The Broadway musical was in a downturn and Kern was in a slump. In 1919, a show of his called ZIP actually closed during its tryouts. Ziegfeld wanted Kern to write a musical for the big star Marilyn Miller. That show was SALLY. So Kern put a song in the show which had originally been in ZIP. It was "Look for the Silver Lining."

Kern again tried using "Bill," which he had removed from OH LADY! LADY!! but thought once again it was not right for Miller. So it was again removed. Ultimately, a chorus girl in SALLY, Helen Morgan, was the one who finally sang it.

In 1925, competing with Ziegfeld, Charles Dillingham asked Kern and Otto Harbach to write a new show. Harbach had five shows running on Broadway, including Gershwin's

Jerome Kern and Dorothy Fields, SWING TIME, 1936. (Photofest.)

SONG OF THE FLAME and Youmans's NO, NO, NANETTE. Harbach had worked with the young lyricist Oscar Hammerstein II in 1924 and asked him to join in the new project with Kern. It was the start of an important collaboration. The show was SUNNY. Kern presented Hammerstein with an interesting problem: "Write lyrics for a song with a high note held for nine beats." Kern said in later years that Hammerstein's answer was brilliant and the song was "Who?"

Kern and Hammerstein were enthralled by Edna Ferber's 1926 novel Show Boat and began working on an idea for a musical version even before they ever approached the writer. She was concerned it would be the typical extravaganza with chorus girls. Kern promised that songs, dances, sets, and humor would be secondary to the story, so she agreed.

Ziegfeld, not known for being trustworthy, vowed to open the show in February 1927 at his brand-new theater, the Ziegfeld. But at the last minute, he decided to book in another one of his shows, RIO RITA, and it was completed first. Kern was furious that Ziegfeld broke his promise. That was only one of many battles among Ziegfeld, Kern, and Hammerstein during the development of SHOW BOAT.

Rehearsals didn't begin until the fall of 1927. Its first tryout performance in Washington, D.C., ended at 12:30 in the morning. Kern and Hammerstein worked feverishly to cut it down. By the time of it opened in December, it was still a half hour too long. During that month, two songs were added to a score that already included "Ol' Man River," which brought tears to Edna Ferber's eyes the first time she heard it.

Just before the end of the tryouts, another great song was added. It was "Why Do I Love You," and the song "Bill" was finally used. Though the show was written by Kern and Hammerstein, the program listed that the lyric for "Bill" was credited to Wodehouse. SHOW BOAT also introduced "Make Believe" and "You Are Love." One of the biggest hits turned out to be "Can't Help Lovin' Dat Man."

Eva suffered a nervous breakdown in 1927. Some attributed it to Kern's hectic lifestyle and the imperious manner in which he treated her.

SHOW BOAT became the biggest hit Broadway had ever seen. A landmark of American musical theatre, it began an entire new Broadway era and created the stylistic basis for some of the great subsequent shows on Broadway. It ran for two years in New York, toured Europe until March 1930, and was revived on Broadway two years later. It opened in Paris and in London in 1928. In 1941, Kern wrote a symphonic version debuted by the Cleveland Orchestra.

SHOW BOAT was revived once again in New York in 1946. In that production one song was added, "Nobody Else But Me," which turned out to be the last song that Jerome Kern ever wrote. By the time the revival opened Kern was dead. It ran for more than a year and grossed two million dollars. That revival toured for a year and returned to Broadway. SHOW BOAT was made into movies in 1929, 1936 and in 1951. Another Broadway revival opened in 1994 and ran for 947 performances.

The 1929 collapse of the stock market diminished the original production's financial success. Even the quality of Broadway musicals was affected by the economic crisis. Light escapist entertainment was in vogue. No works of great stature would follow for almost two decades, until the production of OKLAHOMA!

Interestingly, although Kern and Hammerstein had discovered something new in SHOW BOAT, they didn't necessarily understand what they had accomplished at the time. Two years later, they wrote a show of no great significance at all, in the old style, SWEET ADELINE. But in it, Helen Morgan sang one of their great hits, "Why Was I Born?"

Kern found no work in 1930. He spent the year cruising across the Atlantic or on his own yacht. It was also a time of great stress due to a lawsuit filed against him centering on the authenticity of a rare book he had sold.

The following year, Otto Harbach and Kern wrote THE CAT AND THE FIDDLE, which had no songs of any great consequence.

Sigmund Romberg was one of Kern's closest friends. Romberg was very open, warm, jovial, and well liked. He was, among other things, Jerome Kern's regular bridge partner. A great story is told about their relationship. Kern was a serious card player. In bridge it is important for the players to count, in their heads, the number of pieces of trump that have fallen in each hand. This is to be performed silently. Romberg in his casual manner would actually count the number out loud during each hand—"One, two, three"—and on up to thirteen as they fell. In this friendly regular game the others would disregard his strange behavior. But once, as Romberg counted, Kern realized his partner was making a mistake and had missed one card. Anticipating that Romberg would end up making a serious misplay and lose the game, Kern began humming. Romberg ignored him and went on to lose the hand. At the end, Kern, furious, asked, "Ziggy, do you know what I was humming?"

"Sure, one of my songs!"

"Well didn't you listen? The song is 'One Alone' and you miscounted by one."

Romberg looked at him and responded, "Who knows from lyrics?"

In 1933, Kern wrote another show with Hammerstein, MUSIC IN THE AIR. Finally, they had another success with two great hits, "The Song Is You" and the lilting "I've Told Ev'ry Little Star."

That same year, Kern wrote ROBERTA with Otto Harbach. It was not considered to be especially good, but it is remembered because it introduced a number of new actors who became very famous including Bob Hope, Fred MacMurray, Ray Middleton, and George Murphy. It did have some great songs including "Yesterdays," "The Touch of Your Hand," and a song which became one of Kern's most important hits, "Smoke Gets in Your Eyes."

There is, however, a lasting sour note about the song. Harbach claimed that Kern had written it in an up tempo, which Harbach insisted he should slow down to a ballad, as it is now known. Kern angrily denied the story, which resulted in permanent friction between them.

Meanwhile Kern and Hammerstein wrote another musical, THREE SISTERS, which was first seen in London. The reviews were so bad it never opened on Broadway. Kern found it so discouraging that he stopped writing for Broadway and didn't return for five years.

In 1935, ROBERTA achieved greater success on screen than it did as a show. The film version featured Fred Astaire and Pandro Berman, the producer for the movie, wanted more songs added. Two great songs were added, with Kern collaborating with Dorothy Fields: "Lovely to Look At" and the Astaire classic "I Won't Dance," which was taken directly from the failed show, THREE SISTERS.

Kern wrote his last Broadway show with Hammerstein in 1939. It was VERY WARM FOR MAY. Kern had had a very bad experience with the producer Max Gordon and did not like him. But Hammerstein persuaded Kern to allow Gordon to produce the show, even though Gordon was preoccupied with several movies he was in the process of making. Kern and Hammerstein worked with director Vincente Minnelli without Gordon present at all. The tryouts in Wilmington earned rave reviews, which continued in Philadelphia and Boston. Gordon saw it for the first time in Wilmington and hated it. He fired Minnelli, demanding Hammerstein rewrite the book. Kern and Hammerstein were quite insecure due to their recent failures and caved to his demands. The rewrite was long and tedious. Sadly, Kern's last show received terrible reviews when it arrived in New York. Its saving grace was that it had one fabulous song, "All the Things You Are." Today, some critics consider it to be the most perfect ballad ever written.

The show also contained one of Kern and Hammerstein's most poignant songs, "All in Fun." It boasts the most sophisticated lyrics in the entire Hammerstein repertoire, and sounds much more like the work of Hart or Porter. It has become a staple in the performances of many of the greatest jazz vocalists.

While Kern wrote thirty-eight Broadway shows, he just missed working on four great ones.

When George and Ira Gershwin began creating PORGY AND BESS, the Theatre Guild, in severe financial distress, had asked Kern and Hammerstein to write a show with the same story and have Al Jolson as its star. The Gershwins were asked to forego their project for the good of the Theatre Guild. The brothers agreed and put the show aside. But the Guild was unable to raise the money, so the effort was cancelled and the Gershwins went back to writing the show. The rest of that story is history as it became one of the great triumphs of American musical theatre.

In 1937, MGM asked Kern to compose the music for their new movie THE WIZARD OF OZ. He rejected the offer and what happened to Harold Arlen as a result is well known.

Six years later, he missed out on another opportunity. Oscar Hammerstein II came to Kern and asked him to compose a musical based on the story of GREEN GROW THE LILACS. Kern looked it over and told Hammerstein he didn't think it would ever work as a musical. He not only rejected the idea but suggested to Hammerstein that he not pursue it any longer. Hammerstein didn't take his advice. Once again Hammerstein was in the forefront of changing the theatre when he and Richards Rodgers used the story to create OKLAHOMA!

Finally, Kern had been signed to write ANNIE GET YOUR GUN when illness ended his career.

In 1939, Kern turned to Hollywood. Many of his Broadway hits had already been converted to movie musicals. But he was signed to create new properties. Most were disappointing. Up until then there had been one movie he worked on that both he and the critics really liked, 1936's SWING TIME. With a screenplay by Howard Lindsay and Allan Scott and lyrics by Dorothy Fields, it starred Astaire and Rogers. Among its big hit songs were "Pick Yourself Up" and "A Fine Romance."

The film had a comedy routine for Ginger Rogers with Astaire singing about her unsightly appearance as she shampooed her hair. It brought an Academy Award to Kern. Today the song is no longer performed as a comedy routine. It is done as a romantic ballad, "The Way You Look Tonight."

Kern was highly respected, but not content. Dinner parties in Hollywood were constant and he was always invited with Romberg and Gershwin. But George would always usurp the piano and play his own music all night. No one would ask Kern to play. Kern thought his music was unappreciated. But actually it was Gershwin's genius at playing and performing that held sway. Kern was not a very fine pianist, and Gershwin's overwhelming desire to perform kept him at the piano all night.

In January 1935, Alexander Woollcott, who had a nationwide radio show, told Eva to be certain Jerome listened to it at 4 p.m. Eva had difficulty getting Kern to a radio without suspecting anything, but once Kern got there, he heard a live tribute to himself including an orchestra playing a medley of his hits. Luminaries such as Noel Coward, Franklin P. Adams, Walter Slezak, and Ethel Barrymore honored him. Then Woollcott had his biggest surprise for Kern. There was a knock. Kern opened the door. The delivery person was his friend Irving Berlin. "They fell on each others' necks," Woollcott later wrote.

Kern was becoming more and more frail by 1936, and was soon diagnosed with pernicious anemia, the disease from which his father had died. Things were not going well as his movie HIGH, WIDE AND HANDSOME did poorly at the box office.

In May of the following year, the morning after a dinner at the Berlins' home, Kern suffered a mild heart attack and three weeks later had a stroke, which paralyzed him on one side. Depressed, he was certain he would never play again. He was in such a bad state physically that no one was willing to tell him that George Gershwin had died in July. Not knowing, Kern repeatedly complained that even his friend George Gershwin was ignoring him during his illness. But after nine months of recuperation and therapy, he began playing the piano again. In the following six years, he produced some of the finest songs he ever wrote for Hollywood, including "Long Ago and Far Away."

Paris fell to the Germans in June 1940. Hammerstein, who had spent so much time there in his youth, expressed his heartbreak in a poem. Immediately afterward he flew to Los Angeles to meet with Sigmund Romberg about a collaboration they were planning. Before leaving L.A. he brought the poem to Kern and asked him to write music for it. By the time his flight arrived on the East Coast, Kern had written the music for the haunting "The Last Time I Saw Paris."

Kate Smith obtained an exclusive on the song and performed it on her show. No one else was allowed to use it for six weeks. In the last minute it was added to a movie, LADY, BE GOOD, and won the Academy Award. Kern always felt he didn't deserve it, and that it should have gone to Harold Arlen for "That Old Black Magic" because "The Last Time I Saw Paris" wasn't written specifically for the movie. To Kern's credit, he was instrumental in changing the rules rules requiring that a song nominated for the award must be written for the specific film in which it appears.

Kern built a lovely home in Beverly Hills. There was a studio with a grand piano. It became a meeting place for him and Eva and their friends the Berlins, the Gershwins, Cole Porter, Harold Arlen, Johnny Green, Harry Cohn, and Arthur Schwartz. On the piano were busts of Wagner and Liszt. The room was filled with books—first editions—and photos of Kern with famous people. A mess with stacks of papers all over, spilling out into the living room., it constantly irritated Eva. One day to please her he brought her into the room to show her it had been cleaned up. To her dismay, she found he had just moved all the stacks of scores to another room.

Life in Hollywood was very different from Broadway. In New York, he had command of his shows and major responsibilities. The Hollywood system did not allow that. He submitted the songs they requested and was then out of the picture. Producers didn't need or want his presence or his ideas. He had a tremendous amount of time available for recreation. He played poker at least once a week with his friends. Sometimes they would rent a room or even an apartment at the Beverly Wilshire Hotel to play all night. Kern even had a special room added on to his home for poker games. But he was an awful player and lost almost every time. Gambling remained a passion for him, especially betting on horse races.

He gave up regular golf and played on a pitch-and-putt course with Harold Arlen, Gus Kahn, and Harry Warren. Then it was off with them for lunch at the Farmer's Market and dinner parties in the evenings. Eva's life changed in Hollywood as well. She became much more outgoing socially and involved in Kern's business affairs.

In the 1940s, Arthur Freed, a Hollywood producer, persuaded him to be involved in the making of a picture about his own life, TILL THE CLOUDS ROLL BY, starring Robert Walker as Kern. The music was wonderful, but the picture was generally considered terrible.

Shortly after that he declined Hammerstein's offer for what would become OKLAHOMA! Instead he wrote an insignificant movie, YOU WERE NEVER LOVELIER for Astaire and Rita Hayworth that featured the song "Dearly Beloved." (The lyrics were by Johnny Mercer, who was collaborating more frequently with Kern.)

It was in 1943 that Kern wrote "Long Ago and Far Away" (lyrics by Ira Gershwin) for COVER GIRL, a movie with Rita Hayworth and Gene Kelly.

1945 was a very special year for him. He reached sixty, and enjoyed a weeklong celebration of his work, which took place all over the country on radio and in theatres and nightclubs. His latest movie, CENTENNIAL SUMMER, though not too successful, had in it "In Love in Vain."

Jerome Kern was headed to New York to work with Oscar Hammerstein on a new SHOW BOAT revival. He had also signed on to compose a new show, the first in many years for him. Rodgers and Hammerstein would be the producers. It was to be about Annie Oakley, and Dorothy Fields was to be his lyricist.

He looked vigorous, healthy, and happier than he had for years. He arrived in New York on Friday, November 2. On Saturday, he felt strange, changed his mind about going to a movie, and returned to his suite at the St. Regis Hotel. The following day, he went to the cemetery where his parents were buried, as he always did whenever he returned to New York. In the evening, he was off to a small dinner party with some friends.

Early Monday morning, he went to a gallery looking for a breakfront to give as a gift to his daughter Betty. He had a 2 p.m. appointment with Hammerstein to work on casting for SHOW BOAT. At noon, Jerome Kern, unrecognized, collapsed on the sidewalk at East Fifty-Seventh Street and Park Avenue. An ambulance took him to the public ward on Welfare Island, where alcoholics and derelicts were treated. He carried an ASCAP card, which helped identify him. Word got back to Hammerstein, who rushed to the hospital. Gradually everyone was reached and came to Welfare Island. Finally, by Wednesday, Kern was stable enough to be transferred to Doctors' Hospital in New York. The following Sunday, November 11, 1945, Jerome Kern passed away. He was only sixty years old.

Jerome Kern was generally recognized as the father of this great era of Broadway musicals. Many of those who followed him claimed that he was an early inspiration for their subsequent theatrical success.

MAJOR WORKS

SHOWS:

THE RED PETTICOAT (1912)
OH, I SAY! (1913)
THE GIRL FROM UTAH (1914)
90 IN THE SHADE (1915)
VERY GOOD EDDIE (1915)
ZIEGFELD FOLLIES OF 1916 (1916)
OH, BOY! (1917)
LEAVE IT TO JANE (1917)
ZIEGFELD FOLLIES OF 1917 (1917)
OH LADY! LADY!! (1918)
TOOT-TOOT! (1918)
HEAD OVER HEELS (1918)
OH, MY DEAR! (1918)
SHE'S A GOOD FELLOW (1919)
THE NIGHT BOAT (1920)
HITCHY-KOO (1920)
SALLY (1920)
THE CABARET GIRL (1922)
THE BUNCH AND JUDY (1922)
STEPPING STONES (1923)
SITTING PRETTY (1924)
DEAR SIR (1924)
SUNNY (1925)
CRISS CROSS (1926)
LUCKY (1927)
SHOW BOAT (1927)
SWEET ADELINE (1929)
MUSIC IN THE AIR (1932)
ROBERTA (1933)
VERY WARM FOR MAY (1939)

COMPOSITIONS:

KERN WROTE MORE THAN 1,050 COMPOSITIONS.

Alan Jay Lerner, c. 1960.
(Photofest.)

ALAN JAY LERNER

JOSEPH LERNER WAS BORN IN 1887 IN PHILADELPHIA TO Sophia and Charles Lerner. Financially comfortable, they moved to Brooklyn when he was sixteen. Joseph studied dentistry and set up his office in Atlantic City, New Jersey. Wanting to change his life by age thirty, he joined with his brothers to establish the Lerner Corporation, which became the Lerner clothing stores for ladies' fashion. They prospered through the Depression.

In 1916, he married Edith Adelson. They had a son and then another, Alan, in 1918. A third son was born in 1921. They occupied a seventeen-room apartment on Park Avenue. The marriage was always rocky and ended in the late 1920s when Edith discovered he was having an affair.

Alan began studying piano at age five. His father loved the theatre and Alan was obsessed with the idea of being a part of it from his early childhood. When Alan was twelve, his father sent him to boarding school in England to improve his English. Alan was obviously his father's favorite. Though his father didn't believe in religion, the occult, or an afterlife, Alan was introduced to many issues of spirituality during his semester in England. It showed itself in some of his work later. While his mother was primarily responsible for her sons, taking them to Europe every summer to expose them to museums, churches, and culture, his father was more interested in theatre and sports. Alan always felt closer to his father than his very strict mother and barely mentioned her in his autobiography.

The family was affluent enough for him to study at Choate, Harvard, the Sorbonne, in Spain and Italy, and for a time at the School of Foreign Service at Georgetown. He was expelled for smoking when he was a senior at Choate, though he had been extremely successful there. To please his father, he joined the boxing team at Harvard. He was struck in the eye, needed emergency retinal surgery, and lost the sight in that eye. It was replaced by an artificial one. The accident permanently cancelled his plans to become a pilot. Instead he joined the Hasty Pudding dramatic society at Harvard, and with two other sons of famous fathers, Nathaniel Benchley (son of humorist Robert Benchley) and Benjamin Welles (son of FDR's Under-Secretary of State, Sumner Welles), he wrote a spoof about Hitler and Mussolini titled SO PROUDLY WE HEIL. It was performed at Harvard and later at the Waldorf-Astoria Hotel in an amateur production.

While summering in Europe with his mother and brothers he met a young woman, Ruth O'Day Boyd. At his graduation from Harvard, Lerner was denied his diploma because a local shopkeeper accused him of leaving a bill unpaid. Lerner ultimately received his diploma after the opening of MY FAIR LADY, many years later. After graduation in June 1940, he married Ruth Boyd in a Catholic ceremony and had a daughter three years later. Alan Jay started writing for an ad agency, got bored, and switched to radio. He tried writing songs and a play. Over the years he wound up writing more than 500 radio shows. His marriage was deteriorating and he moved from his apartment to the bachelor quarters at the Lambs Club. One day while there, Fritz Loewe, an unsuccessful composer and pianist, stopped by his table, introduced himself and asked whether Lerner would be interested in writing with him. Lerner agreed. Loewe was forty-one years old, and Lerner was not yet twenty-four.

Loewe was born in 1901, the son of a Viennese opera tenor. He studied piano early and composed by the age of five. He was a symphony guest artist in Europe in his teens. His composition *Katarina* was a huge hit in Europe when he was only fifteen. In 1924, his father had a heart attack and died, leaving Fritz and his mother penniless. Fritz came to the United States and tried getting work, but found it difficult getting used to American jazz tastes. As a result, Fritz did all types of nonmusical work like punching cows and working at the post office. In the thirties, he went to New York and worked as a pianist in Yorkville, a German enclave. Around that time, he married. But the union dissolved rather quickly due to his womanizing.

In 1935, Dennis King liked a song of Loewe's and interpolated it into his show PETTICOAT FEVER. Loewe received twenty-five dollars. The next year, Loewe sold a song to be used in a revue whose songs were mostly written by Frank Loesser. In 1937, he wrote his first complete show for summer stock, SALUTE TO SPRING. The next year, Loewe wrote his first Broadway show, GREAT LADY, which ran for only twenty performances.

By the time Lerner and Loewe met in 1942, the older man had received an offer to rewrite a show seen the year before in San Francisco. He told Lerner they were to get a five hundred dollar advance and Lerner agreed. It was called PATRICIA, and it ran for nine weeks in Detroit, but was never brought to New York. From the very beginning their style of writing was to work together rather than for one to write the music or the lyrics first.

The year after their initial meeting, they tried writing a lighthearted show called WHAT'S UP?. It only lasted for sixty-three performances, so Lerner went back to radio and Loewe took odd jobs. Lerner had befriended Larry Hart, who was at the end of his career, and they frequently met at the Lambs Club.

Loewe also knew Hart. In fact, it was Loewe who found Hart drunk, sitting in the cold rain, without a coat, the night of the revival of A CONNECTICUT YANKEE in 1943. In a few days Hart was dead of pneumonia.

In 1945, Lerner and Loewe tried again, writing THE DAY BEFORE SPRING. This time the reviews were mixed and they had a mediocre success, with the show running for 165 performances. The movie rights were sold, but the film was never made.

Lerner's early tie to spiritualism and the occult as a student in England led him to the writer J. M. Barrie and the idea for BRIGADOON, in which an entire Scottish town emerges from the mists of the past once every one hundred years. When BRIGADOON was completed they offered their new show to the Theatre Guild, but the Guild showed no interest. After that they went from producer to producer, but all said "No." They tried the producer Billy Rose, who was enthusiastic. He demanded the right to control casting, however, and to change the composer or lyricist if he felt it was necessary. He said, "Sign or else." They decided not to accept. They finally got Cheryl Crawford to produce the show. She had to find fifty backers to get sufficient money. It opened in New Haven and Boston to unfavorable reviews, but the audiences loved it. Due to word of mouth, it was sold out by the second week. From there it went to Philadelphia where it got great reviews. It opened in New York in March 1947. Ironically, the theatre in New York was owned by Billy Rose.

George Jean Nathan, a famous critic at that time, developed a crush on the female lead, Marian Bell. But she was unwilling to go out with him because she was having an affair with Lerner. In a fit of pique, Nathan wrote a column saying that Lerner had plagiarized his writing of BRIGADOON. That accusation died when the *New York Times* gave Lerner an opportunity to refute it. The show included the beautiful songs "The Heather on the Hill," "Come to Me, Bend To Me," and the hit "Almost Like Being in Love."

Because he was angry with Lerner, Nathan tried rallying support for FINIAN'S RAINBOW to win the New York Drama Critics Circle award for the most outstanding musical over BRIGADOON. But BRIGADOON won and Lerner did as well, winning the affection of Marian Bell. With the show's success, Loewe was off to Paris to vacation with a young woman. Lerner on the other hand was eager to get back to work.

In April 1947, Lerner was introduced to Kurt Weill, and they begin working on the idea of a vaudeville show that told of the dissolution of a marriage. It was called LOVE LIFE. Though it ran for 252 performances, it was not considered a success, in part because it did not receive critical acclaim. Most of the blame was placed on Lerner's book and lyrics. But Weill and Lerner liked each other and wanted to do more work together. That plan would not come to pass. In 1949, while they were playing tennis together, Kurt Weill collapsed. The following year Weill died suddenly of a heart attack before any further collaboration could be achieved.

Around that time, movie musicals were suffering because of television. Arthur Freed persuaded Lerner to come to Hollywood to write the film version of BRIGADOON. Freed also wanted him to write a new musical for the movies, and introduced him to Burton Lane, who had written FINIAN'S RAINBOW with Yip Harburg. Lerner and Lane would write ROYAL WEDDING. Problems with the film were compounded by a succession of stars being hired and fired, starting with June Allyson and then Judy Garland. Finally, Jane Powell assumed the lead role. The reviews were mediocre but it was a box office success. Included in the score was "How Could You Believe Me When I Said I Loved You When You Know I've Been a Liar All My Life."

By 1947, Lerner's marriage to Marian Bell, his second wife, was falling apart. It ended in 1949 when he began romancing the twenty-one-year-old actress Nancy Olson, whom he would marry the following year.

At that time, Arthur Freed wanted to make a movie based on Gershwin's *An American in Paris* ballet. Gershwin's brother Ira suggested they use all Gershwin music for the score. They asked Lerner to write the story for a movie starring Gene Kelly, Leslie Caron, and Oscar Levant.

A wonderful scene features Levant in the film. Levant, a known wit but not an actor, was disappointed at how small a part he had received. He made a suggestion to Lerner that was accepted, and Lerner wrote a scene called "the ego-fantasy." Levant is seen playing Gershwin's *Concerto in F* on the piano. The camera pans to the orchestra, where each of the musicians and even the conductor are also Oscar Levant. The piece ends as Levant acknowledges wild applause and then shifts to the audience with a thrilled Oscar Levant in the audience. Finally, it dissolves to Levant daydreaming on a cot.

When filming began, Lerner and his new bride moved to New York City. He and Lane had a song nominated for an Academy Award, but it lost. He was not present due to his father having his forty-ninth operation for cancer. But he was surprised to hear that his movie, AN AMERICAN IN PARIS, had won for Best Picture.

In 1950, his marriage was still good. He had signed contracts for three movies, including BRIGADOON, as well as a musical with Burton Lane based on HUCKLEBERRY FINN , and another one, as yet unnamed. Loewe, meanwhile, was living high, surrounded by young women all over the world. He had been unable to write while Lerner was working with Lane, Weill, and Freed. Back in 1948, when Americana themes came to the forefront in the theatre with OKLAHOMA! ANNIE GET YOUR GUN, and HIGH BUTTON SHOES, Lerner got an idea to do a show about the Gold Rush. But Loewe wasn't interested. The idea floundered until 1950.

The show was PAINT YOUR WAGON. It was fraught with problems, cast changes, arguments between lyricist, composer, and producer, and an announcement before opening by Billy Rose that he was selling his shares. In the end, it met with poor reviews. It ran for 289 performances, thanks mainly to advanced sales. But it still lost money. Louis B. Mayer wanted to make it into a movie, but Loewe wasn't interested, so arrangements were made for Arthur Schwartz to add some songs. During this process, Mayer suddenly died and the project was cancelled. Ultimately, in 1969, the film was made with Lerner as the producer. Many of the original songs were dropped and an entirely new story written. Andre Previn wrote the new music. But the movie was not successful.

Nancy gave birth in November 1951 and again in 1953.

In 1952, a flamboyant film producer named Gabriel Pascal had three George Bernard Shaw plays on Broadway. In April of that year, when Shaw was ninety-four years old, Pascal obtained the musical rights to PYGMALION. Shaw insisted the program have the following note: "With apologies to Mr. Bernard Shaw for an unauthorized parody of one of his comedies." Pascal contacted Lerner asking for a luncheon meeting. He told him he wanted Lerner to write the musical version of PYGMALION, as no one else in the world was capable of doing justice to the show. After they lunched and waited in front of the restaurant for their cars, Pascal unzipped his fly and emptied his bladder at the curb. Lerner later said nothing would ever be able to embarrass him again after such an episode.

The Theatre Guild had already agreed to co-produce. Lerner and Loewe met with Pascal and then tried with no success to come up with a story. One day, Lerner had lunch with Oscar Hammerstein II and was told that Pascal had given the assignment to Rodgers and Hammerstein. He told them the same story he had told to Lerner—that only they could be capable of writing it. But Rodgers and Hammerstein gave up on the project. Subsequently Lerner and Loewe also gave up on it. Following that Coward, Porter, Schwartz and Dietz, and Yip Harburg all gave up on the play.

Lerner and Loewe stopped working together again. Loewe unsuccessfully tried collaborating with Harold Rome and Leo Robin.

Though Lerner was not happy with it, the film version of BRIGADOON was released and financially successful. HUCKLEBERRY FINN was well underway when Gene Kelly quit. Lerner believed the picture promised to be wonderful, but it was never made. On top of that, an adaptation of GREEN MANSIONS was dropped.

In 1953, Lerner had tried writing LI'L ABNER with Arthur Schwartz but without success. Lerner was depressed. He had developed encephalitis, meningitis, and a temporary paralysis of his left leg. His father also finally succumbed to cancer after more than fifty operations. Lerner told Nancy, "I may never work again. I should be working with Fritz and he won't have me." Nancy disagreed and suggested to him that he invite Loewe to lunch. Around the same time, Lerner read that Pascal had died and Nancy arranged the luncheon. Somehow, with exhilaration over the prospects for PYGMALION, they clicked again.

First they called Rex Harrison and began writing songs to fit his character and non-singing voice. But they had not yet secured him. With the word out, they suddenly got a call from Mary Martin's husband, Richard Halliday. She was in PETER PAN and they wanted to hear what Lerner and Loewe had written, hoping to land her the leading female role, Eliza Doolittle. They came to the arranged meeting, listened to them play and sing, and left without a word. After a week, Lerner called Halliday. He agreed to meet with Lerner and told him that it had been a terribly sad night for him and Mary. They had left saying, "How could it have happened? Those dear boys have lost their talent." Lerner was horrified but Loewe ignored them and took it in his stride.

The next battle was to get the rights, still owned by Pascal's estate. Meanwhile, with Mary Martin out of the picture, they found their Eliza Doolittle. She was Julie Andrews, a nineteen-year-old British girl who made her American debut in THE BOY FRIEND in 1954. No contracts were signed, but she agreed to accept nothing else that would tie up her time. The major problem was Harrison. Lerner sold one hundred and fifty thousand dollars worth of gold stocks to finance a five-week trip to London. After multiple meetings they persuaded Harrison to accept. They were also able to sign up, as Eliza's father, Stanley Holloway, now a movie character actor. He had not appeared on stage since 1942.

For Holloway's character, a ne'er-do-well, they wrote the great song, "With a Little Bit of Luck."

When he returned home from London, Lerner sat at his typewriter from 6:30 a.m. to 6 p.m. every day, writing nothing. After four barren weeks he had lost eight pounds and was in a panic. He went to see Dr. Bela Mittleman, a psychiatrist, who told him it was a reaction to the statement by Halliday that he had lost all his talent. By the next day, he was writing again and by the day after that, he had written "Wouldn't It Be Loverly?" for Eliza.

CBS was persuaded to be the full producer and Moss Hart to be the director. One problem was that Rex Harrison was starring in a very successful run of BELL, BOOK AND CANDLE in London. To get started with their production that show would have to close. Lerner made a deal to force BELL, BOOK AND CANDLE to close by November 1955 with a cash settlement of fifty thousand dollars and the right to produce the new show in London, if it came to that.

Lerner and Loewe wanted to write a song to demonstrate Eliza's elocution success and claimed that in ten minutes in their new Manhattan offices they came up with "The Rain in Spain."

By November, they had written and discarded six songs to describe Eliza's feelings for Higgins. When auditions began, they were still missing critical songs and a complete libretto. Moss Hart demanded that Lerner come with him to Atlantic City and write in solitude all day long. They stayed four days and everything was completed, including "I Could Have Danced All Night" for Eliza.

They needed to write a song describing Higgins feelings after finding out that Eliza was going to leave once his project with her was completed. It resulted in one of the most beautiful songs they ever wrote, "I've Grown Accustomed to Her Face."

Not until the second week of rehearsals was the title MY FAIR LADY selected.

In February 1956, the show opened in New Haven. Harrison was nervous about the singing and complained about the orchestra. A big snow storm beset opening night. Harrison said he was not ready and would not go on. Using the storm as an excuse, they cancelled the performance and sent home the cast. But huge crowds showed up. So the theatre manager threatened Harrison that if he did not go on, he would go to the media and tell them the real reason for the cancellation. Harrison gave in, but the remainder of the cast had to be gathered up again, just in time for the curtain. The first act was too long and several songs were cut. But Lerner wisely resisted removing "On the Street Where You Live." It ultimately became one of the most popular songs in the show. It reached number one on the Hit Parade and remained there for fifteen weeks, thus vindicating Lerner.

The reviews in New Haven, Philadelphia, and New York were among the most spectacular ever seen. At that time, it was considered the finest musical ever written. It ran on Broadway for six and a half years and 2,717 performances, and in London for 2,281 performances. The cast album earned forty-two million dollars for Columbia records. Lerner and Loewe were on top of the world. After the opening Loewe was immediately off to Paris and the Riviera for gambling and

Shown from left: Frederick Loewe and Alan Jay Lerner, c. 1950s. (Photofest.)

women. Lerner was eager to work, neglecting his marriage and a very domesticated Nancy Olson.

Arthur Freed wanted them to write the film GIGI, but Lerner had to wait for Loewe. Loewe refused to return, so Lerner said under the circumstances he would just write the screenplay. Loewe finally agreed, if Lerner would come to Paris to write with him during the hottest summer in years, without air conditioning. They began casting with Maurice Chevalier and Hermione Gingold. Audrey Hepburn turned them down, and they got Leslie Caron. They wanted Dirk Bogarde for the male lead, but he couldn't get a release from J. Arthur Rank. So they turned to Louis Jourdan.

One day while working, while Loewe was in the bathroom, he heard Lerner playing a melody and rushed out with his pants around his ankles saying, "That's beautiful." They completed the entire song, "Gigi," in one hour except for the

Alan Jay Lerner and Frederick Loewe scripting BRIGADOON for Hollywood, c. 1952. (Photofest.)

Left to right: Frederick Loewe and Alan Jay Lerner, 1962. (Photofest.)

last two lines, which were finished within three days.

While in Paris, Lerner's marriage was disintegrating. He was bored with Olson and attracted to a prominent Parisian attorney, Micheline Muselli Pozzo di Borgo. She, at age thirty, had been the youngest person ever accepted to the French bar. Lerner was thirty-nine. An announcement in the *New York Times* said he and Nancy had separated. In 1958, when GIGI opened in California, Lerner attended with Micheline.

An anecdote told about their return trip to the United States related that Lerner and Loewe stopped in London at a Rolls Royce dealership. Lerner, always extravagant, decided to buy a new model that was on the showroom floor and not yet available. He persuaded Loewe to purchase one too. And, as the apocryphal story goes, Lerner took out his checkbook and said, "I'll get this. You paid for lunch!"

Work progressed on GIGI, and when it was done they both were horrified. They struggled to get the studio to redo the picture, even offering up their own money. Finally, the studio agreed and it was markedly improved. It won nine Oscars, plus a lifetime achievement award for Chevalier. Ultimately the three million, three hundred thousand dollars it went over budget yielded thirteen million for the studio. It was released in 1959. Fourteen years later it was converted into a Broadway musical, which closed in three months, losing all its money. But Broadway was in such a downturn that it still won a Tony for Best Score.

Alan and Micheline moved into a glamorous Sutton Place apartment in New York. Burton Lane once said that Lerner spent more money than some countries. Nancy Olson and her daughters moved into more modest quarters on the Upper West Side.

The summer of 1958 brought the great success of the London production of MY FAIR LADY, followed by a six-month tour through England. Loewe had a heart attack and after recuperating returned to his sybaritic lifestyle. Meanwhile Lerner and Moss Hart were seeking out new projects. Lerner became interested in a new novel about King Arthur and the first ideas for CAMELOT began. Lerner decided to write the book without Moss Hart. Loewe was being difficult following his heart attack and required Lerner to travel to New York, Cannes, and Palm Springs if he wanted to write together. By the following summer, a half dozen songs were done.

In the winter of 1959–60 it was time to get some serious work done. The team rented two houses on Sands Point, Long Island. Micheline was not happy because it was too far from Manhattan and boring. Not understanding their work process, she kept interfering and getting on everyone's nerves. Rehearsals were set for September 1960, with an opening in November. In March, the pressure increased as the *New York Times* published a sixteen-page supplement on the fourth anniversary of MY FAIR LADY with ads for the CAMELOT opening and the release of the music. In April, ticket sales began with the advance reaching three million dollars.

Lerner fought constantly with Micheline, and in July she said she was taking a trip to Europe with their son, Michael. Michael was two and Lerner was deeply attached to him and missed him very much, but his work production increased significantly. One week later his work was totally paralyzed when Micheline notified Lerner she was not returning. A psychiatrist provided him with medication so he could work and he wrote the beautiful "If Ever I Should Leave You."

The show was to open in Toronto in a new theatre. Lerner thought that would help them avoid the spotlight until corrections could be made. To his dismay the impresario Alexander Cohen arranged for New Yorkers, Bostonians, and even Europeans to be at the opening. Suddenly Micheline came back to harass him.

The show was far too long, with opening night ending at 12:25 a.m. But the reviewers were kind. Though not particularly liking the show, they said massive changes would be made before reaching Broadway. The second performance, even with cuts, still went to midnight.

Lerner suddenly became ill with a bleeding ulcer and was hospitalized for a week. Meanwhile, Moss Hart held the show together. As Lerner left the hospital, a gurney was rolled in with Moss Hart. He had suffered a major heart attack, his second. Lerner was devastated. Hart asked Lerner to assume the directorship. Loewe disagreed, wanting someone else to be brought in. He felt it would be impossible for Lerner to rewrite lyrics and the book if he were directing as well. Richard Burton and Julie Andrews both agreed that Lerner could not do it. Lerner and Loewe stopped talking and Burton essentially assumed the role of the director. When the show left Toronto the ending time was still at 11:50 p.m.

At the hotel in New York they took suites on different floors. Lerner had Micheline and Michael. The fifty-nine-year old Loewe, who looked older, had a twenty-fouryear old companion. The team that had been so close now worked in constant tension. At Micheline's insistence she would be present at their work sessions. Loewe, furious, threatened to bring his young girlfriend to the work sessions as well. Bud Widney, Lerner's assistant, was also there constantly. Loewe did not like Widney either.

The Boston tryout was extended to four weeks with rewrites every day. The pressure was constant. Lerner once asked Andrews if she would be willing to sing a new song for the first time on opening night in New York. Andrews, so easygoing, replied that it was okay, but asked if she could get the music the night before. When the opening-night reviews came out it was obvious to a dejected Lerner that, although it would be a financial success due to the massive pre-sale, it was an artistic failure. Lerner left immediately for a Swiss ski resort where he spent his time morosely sitting alone in the hotel lobby. Just when CBS was contemplating closing the show a miraculous thing happened.

Ed Sullivan said he wanted to do an hour-long show to commemorate the fifth anniversary of MY FAIR LADY. Lerner suggested that as part of the show they do a twenty-minute segment of CAMELOT with Burton, Andrews, and Robert Goulet. It was a smash. Ticket sales boomed. The show ran for two years and then one and a half years in London. It was made into a film, which was an artistic and financial failure.

Life was good again. In the spring of 1961, his marriage to Micheline, his fourth wife, was back in shape. They vacationed in Europe and returned to a townhouse on East 71st Street. Moss Hart wanted to write a straight play with Lerner. But Lerner was thinking of finding a new musical partner. Hart moved to California and in December 1961 had another heart attack and died. Loewe decided he wouldn't work anymore and confined his life to Paris, Cannes, and Palm Springs.

While Lerner was working on CAMELOT, the show that Lerner believed would be Loewe's last, various newspapers reported that Lerner would next be joining Richard Rodgers, as Hammerstein was dying. They began working on I PICKED A DAISY, which later became Lerner and Lane's ON A CLEAR DAY YOU CAN SEE FOREVER, but little was accomplished.

Lerner had promised Rodgers that he would work all Labor Day weekend on I PICKED A DAISY, but Lerner was always unreliable. When Rodgers tried to contact him, he was told that Lerner had left for a trip to Capri. Lerner also wanted to do a show about French couture designer Coco Chanel but Rodgers wasn't interested. So Rodgers began working on NO STRINGS, which he would write alone, and Lerner worked on a screenplay for MY FAIR LADY. By July 1963, the arrangement was dissolved.

Micheline was living in high style with glamorous parties, Dior gowns, and expensive jewelry. Lerner was interested in volunteer activities, including his role as president of the Dramatists Guild, his work with ASCAP, and various charity functions.

Lerner was getting into the habit of using designer drugs. Dr. Max Jacobson was developing a reputation for treating the affluent with shots that provided euphoria and sharpened concentration. He was injecting Methedrine, a form of speed.

Lerner had contacted Burton Lane and got him to agree to take Rodgers's place and write ON A CLEAR DAY with him. They started by writing "What Did I Have That I Don't Have?"

In May 1964, Lerner and Micheline's marital problems resurfaced in the media and the two were in court constantly up through March of the following year. Articles appeared about drug addiction, infidelity, and wild spending sprees. Most of the ruthless attacks were initiated by the attorney Roy Cohn. Finally an agreement was signed while Lerner secretly bought a house on Long Island. He was having affairs.

One day, Lane, a man not easily perturbed, showed up for a 10:30 a.m. meeting. By 11:30 a.m., Lerner had not yet appeared. Lane was about to leave, when Lerner walked in, sat down, and fell asleep. Lane left. Not hearing from Lerner for several days, he began calling around and found him in Dr. Jacobson's office, receiving drugs. Lerner apologized, but on a number of occasions Lane considered quitting.

Among the affairs that Lerner was involved in was one with Jean Kennedy Smith. Jean, the youngest Kennedy daughter, was married to Stephen Smith, an important cog in the Kennedy election apparatus. They had four children, but there were lots of rumors of his infidelity. When Micheline moved to California with five-year-old Michael, Alan and Jean began the affair. In June 1965, Lerner presented a partially completed script for ON A CLEAR DAY. Auditions were scheduled for early summer with rehearsals in August. Immediately after submitting it he flew off to Venice with Jean.

Against Lane's better judgment Lerner insisted on Louis Jourdan for the lead. The score was delivered late and the Boston tryouts in September didn't go well. It was too long and Jourdan was having difficulty with the part. Finally Lerner agreed to replace him with John Cullum. It was an expensive settlement. Jourdan would receive four thousand dollars per week if he was not working on any other project, and twenty-seven hundred dollars per week if he was working. This arrangement would last for eighteen months. By comparison Cullum received only twelve hundred dollars per week for actually playing the role. Lerner became hostile and critical because Jourdan was a friend.

Meanwhile, Doris Warshaw Shapiro, Lerner's personal assistant, had been getting treatments with Lerner from Dr. Jacobson. She had to be hospitalized for detoxification. Her husband took her to California to get away from Lerner permanently.

The relationship between Lerner and Lane soured even more. Lane did not even stay for the cast party after the opening in New York. Finally, when a movie contract was signed, Lane contacted Lerner's agent, Swifty Lazar, to say he would be willing to write some additional songs for the movie if necessary. He was told, "Alan doesn't want you." The film was not successful.

A 1965 news article stated that Lerner was embarking on a project with Rosalind Russell's husband, Frederick Brisson, to create a show about Coco Chanel. Lerner had been thinking about that since he first suggested it to Richard Rodgers in 1961. By 1965 Loewe was totally out of Lerner's life.

Lerner had worked with Andre Previn on GIGI and the movie of MY FAIR LADY. Previn was an up-and-coming star. From age twenty-one he was a successful pianist, arranger, and conductor. He had written some songs with his second wife, Dory Langdon, who had written with many composers. The team was set for a 1966–67 opening for COCO. Brisson hoped Russell would play the lead.

Meanwhile Lerner began dating Karen Gundersen, a beautiful young journalist whom he met while she was writing about ON A CLEAR DAY. He had now been a bachelor for a year, the longest stretch in his adult life. In November 1966, he married Gundersen. His fifth wife was seventeen years younger than he. Work on COCO was slow, which distressed Previn. It was at least partly because Lerner was also writing screenplays at the same time for CAMELOT and PAINT YOUR WAGON. Also there was a twenty-fifth anniversary celebration planned for Lerner's work on Broadway. Interestingly, neither Loewe nor Lane made an appearance at the celebration.

After many delays Katharine Hepburn was named as the lead in late 1968. COCO opened in December 1969 with poor reviews for everything except Hepburn. When she was replaced by Danielle Darrieux the show closed. Lerner provided Hepburn with many caustic lines, possibly reflecting his own personal life. At one point Hepburn says in the show, "One doesn't get married to escape boredom. One gets divorced." Lerner's fifth marriage, was also not going well.

But Lerner was ready to move on. His new project would be taken from LOLITA, the provocative novel by Vladimir Nabokov that had been followed by a commercially unsuccessful movie. He no longer had access to Loewe or Lane and sought out a young composer who had never written a musical before, John Barry. LOLITA, MY LOVE received terrible notices and closed in Boston after four performances. The show does not even get mentioned in Lerner's autobiography.

In the spring of 1971, Lerner actually coaxed Loewe out of retirement by sending him a fully written book for a musical based on THE LITTLE PRINCE. Loewe agreed. But before they could start they got an offer to convert GIGI into a show. They agreed and wrote four new songs. It opened in San Francisco in July 1973 and came to New York in November, closing after 103 performances.

In mid-1972, Lerner left his fifth wife and started dating Sandra Payne, an English actress.

When GIGI failed they went back to THE LITTLE PRINCE. It was seen at Radio City in 1974 as part of the Christmas show and was panned. Lerner unfairly blamed it on the director, Stanley Donen, when everyone agreed that the problem was a very poor screenplay.

An announcement was made that Lerner would write a new show with Leonard Bernstein. It would be a political musical called 1600 PENNSYLVANIA AVENUE. The CEO of Coca Cola was one of Lerner's Harvard classmates, and the company decided to back the entire show. They provided no supervision. Who needed supervision with a team like Bernstein and Lerner? However, both were busy with other projects. Lerner was writing his autobiography and Bernstein was doing a rewrite of CANDIDE, which this time would be successful.

On December 9, 1974, Lerner divorced Gundersen and married Sandra Payne the next day. His sixth wife was twenty-nine years his junior.

Bernstein and Lerner starting collaborating in 1975 and both said it was the finest work they had ever done. The show opened in Philadelphia in February 1976 and was changed every day until it arrived on Broadway in March, where it lasted only seven performances. Even

Lerner's new marriage wasn't going well, as Payne returned to England to pursue her career.

It had been ten years since their falling out, but Lerner contacted Lane to ask if they could meet to discuss a new idea. Lane agreed but presented a list of rules. No other projects. No vacation trips. Lyrics must be completed before rehearsals. The idea was based on a film, BUONA SERA, MRS. CAMPBELL, which itself had not been successful. Then one night at a dinner party Lane heard that Lerner was leaving for a vacation in Australia. Lane's wife once said of Lerner, "He never told the truth in his life." Lane had no choice but to continue working with Lerner on the show, which was now called CARMELINA.

By the end of 1976, Lerner was divorced for the sixth time. He was now constantly in and out of court for non-payment of child support. In April 1974, while still married, he was seen at a party with Nina Bushkin, daughter of jazz pianist Joey Bushkin. Bushkin himself was two years younger than Lerner. In 1977, Alan and Nina got married. He was thirty-two years her senior. She was his seventh wife.

CARMELINA opened in 1979 and lasted only seventeen performances.

In 1979, Lerner was sued for the fourth time by his fourth wife Micheline and the judge awarded her fifty thousand dollars. By December, he was already separated from Nina Bushkin. She was quoted as saying that his age (sixty-one) was no problem, but his friends were all in their eighties. In 1981, Micheline sued him again.

In 1980, he was asked to come to London to direct a revival of MY FAIR LADY. The lead would be Liz Robertson. Lerner fell in love again. He and Robertson, wife number eight, married in August 1981. Multiple projects were announced, but none came to fruition.

Lerner persuaded Charles Strouse, who had written BYE BYE BIRDIE, APPLAUSE, GOLDEN BOY, and ANNIE, to write a new show with him based on Robert E. Sherwood's IDIOT'S DELIGHT. The new title would be DANCE A LITTLE CLOSER. It opened and closed the same night in May 1983. Lerner not only wrote the book and lyrics, he directed and Liz Robertson played the lead.

In 1984, the IRS said that he owed them two hundred fifteen thousand dollars.

Friends in London arranged for a young composer, Gerard Kenny, to work on a new show with Lerner, called MY MAN GODFREY. It was during that time that he took time out to receive the Johnny Mercer Award for a lifetime of excellence. He was honored at the Kennedy Center in December 1985. His wife, Liz Robertson, sang his songs to honor him that night.

Over the years, Lerner's collaborators often made note of the white gloves he constantly wore. Some knew the reason why was that his nervous tension caused him to bite his nails to the point where they would bleed.

MAJOR WORKS

SHOWS:

LIFE OF THE PARTY **(1942)**
WHAT'S UP? **(1943)**
THE DAY BEFORE SPRING **(1945)**
BRIGADOON **(1947)**
LOVE LIFE **(1948)**
PAINT YOUR WAGON **(1951)**
MY FAIR LADY **(1956)**
CAMELOT **(1960)**
ON A CLEAR DAY YOU CAN SEE FOREVER **(1965)**
COCO **(1969)**
LOLITA, MY LOVE **(1971)**
GIGI **(1973)**
1600 PENNSYLVANIA AVENUE **(1976)**
CARMELINA **(1979)**
DANCE A LITTLE CLOSER **(1983)**

COMPOSITIONS (MOSTLY LYRICS):
MORE THAN 250 SONGS.

Work stopped on MY MAN GODFREY in February 1986 as Lerner began receiving treatment for lung cancer. In April he went to Sloan-Kettering for further treatment. Alan Jay Lerner died June 14, 1986, with the IRS still pursuing him. He was sixty-seven years old. His wife was virtually penniless and, as she stated, Lerner left her only "a taste for champagne." Shortly after Lerner died, his daughter from his first marriage, Susan, died of cancer as well.

While working on MY FAIR LADY, Lerner and Loewe needed to write a song describing Higgins's feelings after finding out that Eliza was going to leave once his experiment with her was completed. He realized, by then, that the one thing he would never allow to happen, had in fact happened. He had fallen in love with Eliza Doolittle. It resulted in one of the most beautiful love songs ever written, "I've Grown Accustomed to Her Face."

It was fitting that Lerner would be identified by a very beautiful love song. With a record of so many great accomplishments on Broadway, this highly neurotic lyricist is probably best known for his unusual love life, which resulted in eight marriages. But that made him no less a genius of the theatre.

Frank Loesser, c. 1940s. (Photofest.)

FRANK LOESSER

BERTHA EHRLICH WAS ONE OF SIXTEEN CHILDREN BORN to Josef Ehrlich. His first wife delivered eleven children and died during the last birth. A second wife bore him five more children. They lived in the Yorkville section of Manhattan, a German enclave. They practiced no religion, but by birth they were Jewish. In 1892, Bertha married Henry Loesser, who was a piano teacher by trade. A son, Arthur, was born in 1894. In 1898, Bertha's sister Julia, eleven years younger, left Germany and moved in with them, but a problem ensued. Henry fell in love with Julia. So Bertha sent her away to live with another brother. Fortunately for Julia, Bertha soon died in another attempt at childbirth. Henry brought Julia back to live with him and raise Arthur. In January 1907, they married and in December, Julia gave birth to Grace, and Frank came along three years later.

Arthur was the special child of the family. He became an accomplished pianist and went on to become a critic, musicologist, and teacher at the Cleveland Institute of Music. Henry realized that Frank also had talent at the piano, but Henry died suddenly when Frank was sixteen, thus ending the family's income. Arthur, who was giving concerts, had to give that up to become a full-time teacher and support the family. Frank, who was writing songs as an amateur, went to work for a newspaper, in restaurants, and as a cartoonist.

He even took a job for a while as a process server. But Frank wanted to be a Tin Pan Alley songwriter. Finally, Frank and a friend got hired for one hundred dollars a week for all the songs they could write, plus royalties for any that were published. Over a full year's time not one song was published.

Frank soon began writing with another friend, William Schuman, who went on to become a great classical composer. They were hired to write material for specific performers. Schuman would write the melody, and Loesser a set of lyrics. Then they would switch the role of composer and lyricist and complete two pieces of music. Almost everything was rejected.

Because of his exposure to Tin Pan Alley, Loesser began developing a distinctly urban accent with some intonations of Yiddish. His mother and brother were embarrassed by Frank's speech patterns as they perceived themselves to be at a higher cultural level. They told him that he sounded as if he had been raised on the Lower East Side.

By the mid-1930s, Frank was going to see every musical that came to New York, of course in the least expensive seats. At the time he was writing with multiple composers and singing his own songs in small clubs.

A woman from quite a different background soon entered Frank's life. Mary Alice Blankenbaker was born in Terre Haute, Indiana. In 1917, wanting to be an actress, she came to New York and changed her name to Lynn Garland. One night she went to the Back Drop Club where Frank and Irving Actman were performing. She met Frank, who was short and intense, with a ready laugh and a ready temper. She also soon realized that his language was foul, but they fell in love. At first this tall thin gentile blonde was not well accepted by Frank's family. For her part, she resented how his mother and brother looked down on him.

Loesser and Actman were hired by Universal Studios. They moved to Hollywood and earned two hundred dollars each per week. It was a typical Hollywood deal. Everything they wrote belonged to the studio. If it was published the studio got its share. And if they weren't any good their option wouldn't be picked up. Under those circumstances they would get return tickets to New York City. But the return tickets would be provided only if they left town within a week of losing their jobs. After a short while they did lose their jobs, but decided to stay in California and forego the tickets. Frank asked Lynn to come out to California and marry him, though he had nothing. She did and they were wed in a judge's office. Irv was the witness and they celebrated in a local restaurant. His mother's response was to write and tell him that he was a failure at music and to get a real job.

In July 1937, Burton Lane, who had heard some of Loesser's lyrics, persuaded Paramount to hire him. It was just in time, as Frank and Lynn were broke. To celebrate his employment, they invited Lane to share their dinner, an apple and a can of baked beans. Frank started at $166.66 per week plus royalties. Now his songs began to sell and by the end of 1937 he was earning quite a good living. He began sending money to support his mother. Even with her lack of emotional support, he provided financial assistance to her for the rest of his life.

Loesser remained with Paramount all the way until 1949. His first big hit, written with Alfred Newman, was "The Moon of Manakoora." It was for Dorothy Lamour in the picture HURRICANE. Following that, he wrote the Crosby hit "Small Fry" with Hoagy Carmichael. Frank and Hoagy also combined on "Heart and Soul."

One night, when the Loessers were having dinner at the Carmichaels, Frank and Hoagy decided to try to write a song. They worked until the wee hours of the morning, with little success. They gave up, and while the Loessers were leaving, Lynn said that the pair of couples looked like "four sleepy people." Those words clicked for Loesser and they went back into the house and worked until dawn. They came up with "Two Sleepy People." The sheet music actually reads, "Title suggested by Lynn Garland."

Over the next year Frank wrote with composers such as Burton Lane and Matty Malneck, wrote the theme song for bandleader Lawrence Welk, and had eight songs that reached *Your Hit Parade*.

Now Frank was becoming a musical force. He became widely known for his hyperactive personality, pacing, cursing, and smoking with constant nervous energy while at work.

Meanwhile, Lynn was having little success. At times she got small roles in New York City. Whenever they were in separate cities, Frank wrote wonderful letters full of advice. His career was growing. He had become so successful by 1939 that they had hired two live-in domestics to help at home.

In 1940, Paramount borrowed John Wayne for a picture and in return had to give a return of services to Republic Studios. They put Frank together with Jule Styne and together they wrote "I Don't Want To Walk Without You." That was followed by another hit, "Jingle, Jangle, Jingle." Loesser was still only writing lyrics.

By 1941, like many other composers and lyricists, he got the urge to write something patriotic. It was at that time that he had his first success writing both music and lyrics for a song. He had tried in 1939, but seemed to lack confidence, until he made another go at it in 1942 when he wrote "Praise the Lord and Pass the Ammunition."

In 1940, brought together by their wives, Frank and John Steinbeck became fast friends. That close bond continued for the next thirty years. During all that time they constantly planned collaborations, though none ever occurred, with Steinbeck dying just shortly before Loesser.

In 1942, Frank enlisted in the Army to join the Radio Productions Unit with the cream of Hollywood. Frank shared a house with actor–comedian Peter Lind Hayes. Lynn and Peter's wife, Mary, would come to visit them on week-

Left to right: Frank Loesser, Patricia Waterhouse, and Harry Bluestone. (Photofest.)

ends. Frank wrote a song for Mary with her name in the title. Six years later he changed the woman's name in the song and with that Ray Bolger stopped the show WHERE'S CHARLEY? when he sang "Once In Love with Amy."

Loesser wrote songs for all the armed services including a gripe song titled "What Do You Do in the Infantry?" For the movie SEE HERE, PRIVATE HARGROVE Loesser wrote the biggest hit gripe song of the war, "In My Arms," but the military wanted him to write a more serious song. To try to do that he went through the list of Congressional Medal of Honor recipients to find a name that would rhythmically fit well for lyrics. He was somewhat embarrassed that his choice of whom to write about was based on nothing more than what scanned best. The result was his very famous "Rodger Young."

When he presented the original manuscript to President Truman he had to explain the little drawings on it were due to his habit of doodling while he was composing. He was, in truth, quite a fine artist.

He remained a private throughout his stint in the Army and was discharged when he came down with pneumonia. All the money received from his songs about the war was contributed to charities.

While in the service he continued to write for

Left to right: Frank Loesser (Best Song, "Baby, It's Cold Outside"), presenter Cole Porter, and Paramount music director Louis Lipstone at the 1950 Academy Awards ceremony. (Photofest.)

Left to right: Marlon Brando and Frank Loesser, 1955. (Photofest.)

Hollywood. In 1941, he wrote "Dolores," which was nominated for the Academy Award. Two years later, he got another nomination for a song written for Bette Davis, "They're Either Too Young or Too Old." Also in 1943 he wrote "Murder, He Says" with Jimmy McHugh. But in 1944 he was back to writing both the music and lyrics and produced the beautiful, "Spring Will Be a Little Late This Year."

When in 1947 he wrote "I Wish I Didn't Love You So," it was nominated for the Academy Award. But he lost again. He would write home to his mother "still a bridesmaid, never a bride."

After the war, he and Lynn moved back to Hollywood, even though she thought he should try writing a Broadway show. They lived a glamorous life in a house they bought from Veronica Lake. In 1944, their daughter Susan was born. Like so many others in Hollywood they hired a nurse to be their daughter's constant companion. Ida, the nurse, was a warm, nurturing person and most important, she was always there for Susan, while Frank and Lynn often were not. Susan became friends with Vicky James, the daughter of Harry James and Betty Grable, Candy Bergen, daughter of Edgar Bergen, and with Liza Minnelli, daughter of Judy Garland, but never met their parents, only their nurses.

Loesser's daughter remembered him as funny and delightful, but frightening when he lost his temper. Afterward he would act as if nothing had happened. There were constant parties at their house with other famous friends, and heavy drinking and hangovers abounded. Parties were the center of their lives and arranged for at the drop of a hat. The Loessers even erected an outdoor tent for the larger celebrations. They would work at creating special entertainment. Marc Connelly of the famed Algonquin Roundtable once created an opera for Frank Loesser, Abe Burrows, and himself to perform.

Children's parties were massive as well, with the different parents trying to outdo each other. Lynn once rented the entire Beverly Hills Amusement Park.

In 1944, Frank wrote a song that he and Lynn performed at one of their parties. It became their song and the hit, "Baby, It's Cold Outside."

In 1948, it saddened Lynn immensely that he sold the song to MGM. It became his first and only Academy Award winner, sung by Esther Williams and Ricardo Montalban in NEPTUNE'S DAUGHTER.

Earlier that year, producers Cy Feuer and Ernest H. Martin bought the rights to make a musical of the British comedy CHARLEY'S AUNT, and changed the name to WHERE'S CHARLEY? They wanted Harold Arlen to compose the music and Loesser the lyrics. At the last minute Arlen suffered a major house fire and withdrew. Loesser wanted to write both the music and lyrics. The producers said they would agree if the director, George Abbott, okayed the plan. He did and Loesser wrote both the music and lyrics. The show was in trouble in rehearsals and tryouts in Philadelphia. George Balanchine quit as the choreographer and the hot tempers of Loesser, Feuer, and Martin exploded constantly. Only Ray Bolger held it together. Bolger sang the lyrical "My Darling, My Darling" and the big hit, "Once in Love with Amy."

The show was off to a poor start, when at the first Saturday matinee Bolger forgot the lyrics to "Once in Love with Amy." He stopped the conductor and said, "Let's start again, what are the words?" Cy Feuer's seven-year-old son was in the audience. He had been coming to the rehearsals and knew all the music. He stood up and started singing it to him. Bolger, a little flustered and a little annoyed, said, "Okay, everybody, let's all sing." After the show Bolger thought it would be great if he brought the audience in every night. Word spread about the audience participation. Rodgers and Hammerstein came, loved that bit, and told everyone to come see the show, which ended up running for two years.

Loesser was at the top of his game, with a Broadway hit, an Academy Award, many hit songs, and significant wealth. But all was not perfect. His mother and brother had little respect for his accomplishments, which they considered to be beneath Arthur's classical work and his mother's cultural tastes. Even though Frank was supporting her, he never received the approval he desperately wanted.

Loesser was a much more broadly talented person than they gave him credit for. Besides his musical and artistic abilities, he was a master craftsman of furniture. In his workshop he created furniture for himself and for friends in Hollywood.

Meanwhile, Feuer and Martin were negotiating with Paramount to get the rights for a musical based on a Damon Runyon story they owned. Jo Swerling, a Hollywood writer, was hired to write the book and work with Loesser. But Loesser was certain that the book wasn't right. It wasn't funny and it didn't sound like Runyon.

At a party, Loesser met Abe Burrows, who was writing DUFFY'S TAVERN for the radio. He loved the opening lines. "Hello! Duffy's Tavern, where the elite meet to eat. Duffy's not here. Archie speaking. Oh hello! It's you, Duffy." Loesser and Burrows improvised parodies for several hours and became fast friends. Together they wrote songs like, "I'm Strolling Down Memory Lane Without a Single Thing to Remember" and "The Girl with the Three Blue Eyes."

At one party they wrote the following song:

"You haven't got cheeks like roses
You haven't got eyes like stars
Your sigh doesn't sound like music
The music of soft guitars
You haven't got lips like rubies
Your hair doesn't even curl
But, baby, it makes no difference to me
Cause you're not my girl."

Loesser suggested that Feuer and Martin bring Burrows in to work on their project. Burrows wrote a book with a Runyonesque quality that demonstrated a kind of dignity. The underworld characters took pride in their very specific way of enunciating. They were noble and lovable. The show became GUYS AND DOLLS.

George S. Kaufman directed and Michael Kidd did the choreography. The casting began with Vivian Blaine as Adelaide and Robert Alda as the male lead, Sky Masterson. Stubby Kaye, as Nicely-Nicely Johnson, would be sensational singing the fabulous hit song "Sit Down, You're Rockin' the Boat."

They still had to cast one of the gangsters, Big Jule. The casting director said he had the perfect person, but he couldn't come for a few weeks. Feuer, with his hot temper, said, "A couple of weeks! What do you mean? Have him come in now."

"Well he can't come in now."

"Why the hell not?"

"Because he won't be getting out of jail for a couple of weeks. But really, he's very good."

B. S. Pully had been put in jail for doing a very raunchy nightclub act. When he was released he joined the cast. They also got Sam Levene for Nathan Detroit. Levene couldn't sing. So in "The Oldest Established," a choral number, he was specifically instructed just to mouth the words. The big problem was his solo, "Sue Me." He could not find the right note to start. So Loesser added a five-note ladder in the beginning to get him started right. The song now began, "Call a lawyer and sue me, sue me. What can you do me? / I love you."

During rehearsal in Philadelphia Lynn went back to the West Coast to have her second child, a boy, John. She returned to New York in three weeks, leaving Susan and the new baby with Ida.

GUYS AND DOLLS featured spectacular music that meshed perfectly with its book. It opened with the "Fugue For Tinhorns" in which a trio of gangsters sang about horserace betting. The score also included "A Bushel and a Peck," "Luck Be A Lady," "If I Were A Bell," "More I Cannot Wish You," "Take Back Your Mink," and one of the greatest show tunes ever written, "Adelaide's Lament." The main love song was "I've Never Been in Love Before."

Today, many consider GUYS AND DOLLS to be the greatest musical ever written for Broadway. "I'll Know," perhaps Loesser's loveliest song, comes from that show.

The movie, however, presented new problems. Loesser was unhappy with the way Frank Sinatra was singing "Sue Me." At a rehearsal the two of them got into a major shouting match using every four-letter word imaginable. In the end Sinatra did it his way. Loesser never went to see the movie and the two of them never spoke to each other for the rest of their lives.

Meanwhile, the Loesser marriage was falling apart. Loesser, who had such a short fuse, could not tolerate that Lynn was late for every engagement. She was always meticulous and spent a long time getting made up with a drink by her side, while Frank would scream and yell and curse at her to get ready and get out.

They maintained separate bedrooms supposedly because he snored so loudly. But it was more than that. They slept different hours. He was up at the crack of dawn. She slept away most of the morning. By the time she got up he was taking an afternoon nap. She drank more and more, and took Demerol for back pain. What had brought them together when they met, the sexual attraction of a beautiful, tall, blonde non-Semitic looking actress, seemed to have vanished for Frank.

For Lynn the feeling was quite different. As extreme as was his temper and use of foul language, Loesser still exhibited the same ebullience and could be seen as charming and lovable. Perhaps as well she saw his tremendous potential. But whatever had brought them together was now long lost for him.

In 1951, Samuel Goldwyn wanted to do a movie about Hans Christian Andersen. First he wanted Gary Cooper, then decided on James Stewart and Moira Shearer for the two leads. He hired Sylvia Fine to write the movie and she suggested Stewart wasn't right for the part. She asked Goldwyn to consider her husband, Danny Kaye. Goldwyn agreed and Loesser was selected to write the score. With a screenplay by Moss Hart and a great performance by Danny Kaye, HANS CHRISTIAN ANDERSEN became a big hit and a financial success. Kaye performed wonderful simple tunes like "The Inch Worm" and "Thumbelina," as well as a great story song "The King's New Clothes," and the charming, "The Ugly Duckling." In it there was also the lovely ballad still done by pop singers today, "Anywhere I Wander," and the lively duet, "No Two People." Possibly its biggest hit song was the marvelous up-tempo waltz, "Wonderful Copenhagen."

In 1920, a drama, Sidney Howard's THEY KNEW WHAT THEY WANTED, won the Pulitzer Prize. Revived in 1939 and 1949, it did poorly. Loesser decided he wanted to make a musical out of it and began writing the book himself. He worked on it for five years. The form he was conceiving was semi-operatic. It probably was an attempt on his part to demonstrate to his critical mother and brother what he was capable of composing.

He had already established the Frank Music Corporation to maintain control of the properties he was writing. Lynn was running the business end of the operation. She persuaded the producer Kermit Bloomgarden to join with them in the production of the new show. She also designated herself as the casting director and went looking for the proper people for the parts. After a complicated and at times fruitless effort to find the right lead, auditioning over 2000 people around the world, she came upon Robert Weede of the San Francisco Opera. Lynn knew she had made the right choice.

With all the success she was having in running that operation, her personal life was still a problem. She was not drinking any less and certainly would be considered an alcoholic. She became loud and boistcrous, and was the first one at the theatre bar at intermission and after performances. She was spending less and less time with Frank.

It was Lynn who selected Jo Sullivan to be the female lead. Raised in a small town in Illinois, Sullivan had studied piano and voice and tried unsuccessfully to get into Juilliard. She got a job on the GODFREY TALENT SCOUT SHOW, a part in the chorus of OKLAHOMA! and did a small nightclub act. In 1950, Jo landed an offbeat show called LET'S MAKE AN OPERA. It ran for five days with the reviewer writing, "Let's not!" Then all of a sudden she won the major role of Polly Peachum opposite Lotte Lenya in Kurt Weill's first American production of THE THREEPENNY OPERA. Lynn brought her in for an audition with Frank and she got the lead role in THE MOST HAPPY FELLA.

Lynn was no longer the sweet demure girl seen in the early home movies and photos with Frank. She was now the hard-driving businesswoman, her long flowing hair pulled back in a tight bun. She wore business suits and drank very hard. But she had worked feverishly for THE MOST HAPPY FELLA.

She soon recognized, like everyone else in the cast and crew, that Frank Loesser was falling in love with Jo Sullivan. But at forty, she stood by and watched, because she could not walk away from this project.

Another operatic singer was originally cast as the second male lead, the foreman on the farm. It was just not the proper fit and he was replaced at the last moment by a pop vocalist, Art Lund, who was a tremendous hit as he sang his big solo, "Joey, Joey, Joey."

Just a few weeks before Loesser's show premiered, MY FAIR LADY opened to absolutely rave reviews, ultimately winning the Tony awards with good cause. It had a very subduing effect on the opening of THE MOST HAPPY FELLA.

In the opening act, two beautiful songs are performed by the leads. The female lead sings "Somebody, Somewhere," and the male lead performs "Rosabella." The darling song "Ooh! My Feet!," originally written for GUYS AND DOLLS but cast aside, was reworked for the second female lead of THE MOST HAPPY FELLA, a waitress. Shorty Long and three others sang the wonderful quartet, "Standing on the Corner." The really great dance number for the entire cast was "Big D."

Most of the reviews were excellent, but some had misgivings. The most painful review came from Frank's brother, Arthur, published in the *Cleveland Press*. While the review was positive, it contained an undercurrent of, "Anyway, you don't really care or know whether a show is 'good.' All you care is whether it is successful." The review hurt Frank as did most everything that came from his mother and Arthur.

Nevertheless, the show ran for two years and has been revived on Broadway several times.

In 1956, when Frank was forty-six, and Lynn was forty, they got divorced. Susan was twelve and John was six. The children would go to live with their mother. The house in California was sold and Jo and Frank moved in together the following year. Lynn tried to make it on her own as a producer, but unsuccessfully. She had a new boyfriend who turned out to be an alcoholic and violent as well. All of their friends migrated to Frank. The children developed problems in school and in their personal lives.

Loesser began a new project, a folk fairy tale called GREENWILLOW. It was fraught with problems, repeated rewrites, cast changes, quitting, and ultimately terrible reviews. It lasted ninety-seven performances based only on advanced sales. Frank and Jo had gotten married in 1959 and during that first year, with GREENWILLOW going so badly, there was nothing but arguing and bickering between them. When the show folded they left for an extended trip to Europe. Loesser didn't see his children for six months.

When the couple returned in September 1960, Feuer and Martin presented Frank with the idea of doing a score based on the book HOW TO SUCCEED IN BUSINESS WITHOUT REALLY TRYING. The musical's book would be written by Abe Burrows. Though unenthusiastic about the idea, Loesser completed the score by January 1961. The show was a spoof and did not have a traditional love ballad, but the satirical song, "I Believe in You" became an admired classic. But the show was fun and a huge success. It ran for four years and at the time was the fifth longest-running show of all time. In 1962, it won the Pulitzer Prize for Drama.

Life was now going well for Frank and Jo, and they bought a townhouse on East 70th Street in Manhattan. In 1962, Jo had a baby girl.

Loesser wanted to become a better businessman in relation to his music. He knew that Irving Berlin had controlled everything he had ever written. Also Rodgers and Hammerstein had produced many projects they themselves didn't write. So Frank Music took on performers with big hits such as "Unchained Melody" and "Cry Me a River." He befriended the creators of KISMET, Wright and Forrest, and published everything they ever wrote during Loesser's life. Loesser published the scores of both THE PAJAMA GAME and DAMN YANKEES for Adler and Ross, and everything that Meredith Willson wrote from THE MUSIC MAN on.

For three years early in his career, Alfred Uhry, the writer of DRIVING MISS DAISY, was under contract to Loesser writing lyrics and television commercials. Loesser even entered the advertising business, producing jingles for major corporations.

In the 1960s, Loesser became disenchanted with the music business. He did not understand or like rock music and was offended by young people smoking pot and demonstrating against the war in Vietnam, somewhat out of synch with his times.

In 1964, he began working with Bob Fosse and Sam Spewack on making a musical from a comedy. As a play, ONCE THERE WAS A RUSSIAN had closed after just one performance. For the musical, the title was changed to PLEASURES AND PALACES. It never came together well. There were tryouts in Detroit, which were extended for six weeks in an effort to doctor it and then it closed, never reaching Broadway.

Frank and Jo had their second baby, another girl, in June 1965.

Budd Schulberg wanted to make a musical of his book SENOR DISCRETION HIMSELF. They started work in December 1965 and continued on it all the way until March 1968 when finally Loesser finally gave up on it. The songs Loesser contributed to this show were the last he ever wrote.

In January 1969, Frank's brother died suddenly of a heart attack. Arthur was seventy-four and his non-biological eighty-eight-year-old mother had lost her favorite child.

Only weeks before, Loesser's dearest friend, John Steinbeck, had died.

Around this time Frank first began complaining of abdominal symptoms and fatigue. Hospitalized twice for tests, he was chagrined when no explanation could be found for his symptoms. He was sick, his friends were dying, and he couldn't write. All these factors were depressing him. By the spring he was feeling worse and an abdominal operation revealed nothing, but he was unable to eat. The problem was that he had undiagnosed lung cancer that had now moved into his esophagus. In June 1969, the diagnosis was finally made.

On June 29, the family celebrated his fifty-ninth birthday in the hospital, but Frank Loesser was barely conscious. When he died on July 26, a letter left with his lawyer requested that there be no ceremony or official notice. Nevertheless it made the front page of the *New York Times*. The following Sunday that paper's Arts & Leisure section contained a eulogy by Abe Burrows.

No doubt Frank Loesser's greatest legacy was GUYS AND DOLLS. However, it is his total body of work that certainly places him in the class of geniuses of the American musical theatre.

Johnny Mercer, c. 1950.
(Photofest.)

JOHNNY MERCER

GEORGE ANDERSON MERCER WAS AN ATTORNEY, REAL estate developer, and prominent public citizen of Savannah, Georgia. He had a stern Victorian manner about him. His wife Mary bore him two sons, George Jr. and Walter. In December 1900, Mary died in childbirth at the age of twenty-nine. She had given birth to Hugh, their third son, whom George Sr. blamed for her death. George banished Hugh from the home to be raised by his aunt, Katherine.

Eight years later George married his secretary, Lillian Ciucevich. Her father had run through the Yankee blockade during the Civil War to bring supplies into Savannah. She was melancholy but warmhearted and insisted that George bring his banished son, Hugh, back into the family home. In November 1909, Lillian bore him a fourth son, John Herndon Mercer. Though there was always music in the household, John inherited his mother's melancholy temperament.

Johnny grew up in an environment quite different from all of the other composers and lyricists of that golden age. Like Cole Porter, he was raised in affluence. He had none of the early exposure to Broadway that so many of the other composers and lyricists did in their childhood. Rather, he was exposed to the music of the family's black servants and the black children with whom he played. Their dialect—rather like the Gullah dialect that Gershwin heard when he went to South Carolina to prepare to write PORGY AND BESS—was uniquely indigenous and was called Geechee. But he also heard the music on recordings of Berlin, Gershwin, and Porter. At an early age, though he loved music, he rejected learning to play the piano. Instead he sang in the church choir. When old enough he would go into the African-American sections of town to listen to and buy what were called "race records" and "coon records." He learned to dance well and he used his musical talents to attract girls.

Young Johnny was sent to Woodbury Forest Prep School and had a substantial education in literature and classics. Though he was known as the class clown, he was also a fine student and he began writing quite a bit. His fellow students recognized him for his overwhelming knowledge of music. Later in life he said that during that time he had a huge sexual appetite and sublimated it through music. To his dismay Johnny claimed that in his social circle the girls protected their virginity like a "rare jewel."

By tradition the Mercers all went to Princeton University. One of the most important of American generals during the Revolution was Hugh Mercer. A statue of him stood on the Princeton campus. But in September 1927, Johnny's mother wrote to him that his father's real estate business was one million dollars in debt and that they could not afford to send Johnny to college. So Johnny got a job and went to night school to learn typing to make himself more employable.

He had a friend by the name of Dick Hancock who played the piano on boats between Savannah and New York. They concocted a scheme for Johnny to stow away because he couldn't afford to travel to New York. He had met a girl in Savannah who lived there and he wanted to see her. But soon after departure he was discovered and put to work in a filthy environment below deck for the three-day trip. He never did get to see the girl in New York, but fell in love with the city.

He came back to a better job but dreamt of returning to New York. Two girls persuaded him to try out for a part in a play in Savannah. He got the part and the troupe won a prize that would send them to New York in May 1928 to compete with other acting companies. After getting favorable reviews Johnny decided he should make acting his career. His parents weren't pleased, but they were supportive. While there he went to Broadway, to see vaudeville, and to hear the music in Harlem. Mercer was overwhelmed by all he took in. He quit his job in Savannah and moved to New York. A performer he had met sent him to two elderly women who booked actors out of a small office. They got him bit parts in Theatre Guild productions. The experience of traveling from town to town performing in these productions was grueling.

Once, on his return, he found that the landlady had sold the house in which he lived and he would have to move out. Another actor invited him to share quarters. But when he returned one evening he found the other actor in bed with a man. He knew many of the other actors were homosexual. But he moved out saying, "I couldn't see living in a menage-a-trois, unless the third member were (sic) a girl."

He moved into a one-bedroom apartment with three other actors and a piano. With jobs hard to find he began working at the piano, although he was untrained. He got some gigs singing at clubs but was unable to pay his share of the rent and had to move again. He was eating only oatmeal for meals and ironing his shirts with a pot heated on the stove.

With things getting worse he snuck in backstage where Eddie Cantor was performing in WHOOPEE! Cantor was shocked that the doorman had let him in, but was kind to him. Mercer played a song he had written. Cantor said he was going on the road and would like to hear more of his material. They continued to communicate and though Cantor never bought or used any of his work, his interest sustained Mercer's spirit.

The market crashed that October 1929, and Mercer returned to Savannah at Christmas time, destitute.

After the holiday he returned to New York City into a ramshackle apartment. Although he had grown up in affluence with servants, he was living in abject poverty. He began trying to write lyrics. A friend gave him an eight-bar melody, with no bridge. Without knowing how to read music, he composed the bridge and wrote the lyrics to his first song, "Out of Breath (and Scared to Death of You)." Amazingly, it was accepted for the 1930 edition of THE GARRICK GAIETIES and sung by Sterling Holloway. In 1925, Holloway had introduced Rodgers and Hart's "Manhattan" in the original GAIETIES. Other composers for the show included Aaron Copland, Vernon Duke, and Marc Blitzstein. Rosalind Russell performed in the show as a newcomer. But the big surprise was that Mercer's song got great reviews.

In the meantime, eighteen-year-old Anna Meltzer had emigrated from Russia. She traveled by foot across Europe to join her husband, Joseph, who had preceded her. When she arrived in New York she moved in with his family. After they had three daughters, Joseph committed suicide. Anna started her own business as a seamstress of elegant children's clothing. She wanted her middle daughter, Rose Elizabeth, to study piano. But Rose Elizabeth was more interested in dancing and became a chorus girl.

In 1927, the theatre was prospering. Twenty new musicals opened. As a result, Rose Elizabeth immediately got a job in a road company of HONEYMOON LANE. Another dancer and friend was Mary Meehan. Rose Elizabeth Meltzer decided to change her name to Ginger Meehan. She moved in with another friend, Dolores Reade, who ultimately married Bob Hope. In Philadelphia, HONEYMOON LANE appeared at the same time as Bing Crosby and the Rhythm Boys were playing. Crosby and his partners were a wild, carousing bunch and drunk most of the time. But Crosby

Walt Disney and Johnny Mercer. (Gene Lester/Hulton Archive/Getty Images.)

met Ginger and they quickly became serious.

Ginger got a job in the new Broadway show GOOD NEWS. Ginger always claimed that Crosby was pursuing her. But just how serious Crosby was is in considerable question. At the same time he was taking many of the other chorus girls to bed. One seventeen-year-old chorus girl, Dixie Lee, who knew his reputation, refused to date Crosby. Ultimately, she married him. Dolores, Dixie, and Ginger all remained lifelong friends. So did their husbands—Bob Hope, Bing Crosby and Johnny Mercer.

Ginger's next job was in THE GARRICK GAIETIES, where she met Mercer. Johnny had decided to concentrate on writing lyrics and a few songs got interpolated into shows. A successful operetta written by the European composer, Emmerich Kalman, was to be brought to the United States. The producers wanted someone to write English lyrics and to work cheaply. They hired Mercer. They required him to come to California. But before he left, he and Ginger slept together for the first time. From subsequent letters between them it appears that it was Johnny Mercer's first sexual experience, but not Ginger's.

Mercer disliked the music for which he was writing lyrics, but enjoyed going to the clubs hearing musicians such as Louis Armstrong.

Meanwhile, he was writing passionate letters to Ginger about how unbearable it was to be without her. She wrote less frequently and with little passion. She was going on the road with the GAIETIES and with his work being completed for the Kalman operetta, PARIS IN THE SPRING, he was madly looking forward to a reunion in Chicago. But the producers told him that he couldn't leave town. He had to do rewrites for a San Francisco opening. So the Chicago meeting was canceled. Besides that he heard, through third parties, that Ginger was dating others. The one-sided relationship depressed him.

Mercer came back east, but work was difficult to find. Finally, a small publishing house, Miller Music, hired him at twenty-five dollars per week. It wasn't that bad, considering the Depression was in full swing. Ginger finally agreed to marry him, though her family felt that he had no future. The sexual awakening he experienced with her, as well as his desire to solidify his life, certainly led him to put constant pressure on Ginger to become his wife. He was only twenty-one when they married in 1931. But Ginger was self-centered and frequently made Mercer feel insecure with her constant reminders that she could have married someone much more successful, someone like Bing Crosby. After a few years, the marriage began to deteriorate.

Mercer got a job to write the show JAZZ CITY, which was soon cancelled. It was a difficult time. He would plug songs for performers, frequently having to add their names to the credits. Sometimes Mercer would make all sorts of backdoor deals to get work, giving up royalties. He jumped from composer to composer. Things got so bad that he entered a talent contest Paul Whiteman was holding nationally. Whiteman, taken by his performance, declared Mercer the winner. As a result he performed on Whiteman's national radio broadcast, for which he got paid nothing, and it never led to anything, either.

A break came in 1932, when Vincent Youmans skipped out of a contract to write a show with Yip Harburg called AMERICANA. Harburg went scrambling to find composers and lyricists to help complete it. Among them were Harold Arlen and Johnny Mercer, who combined to write one of the show's hit songs, "Satan's Li'l Lamb."

Mercer was soon introduced to Hoagy Carmichael, who was already successful and became a good taskmaster for Johnny. Together they wrote, over a full year's work, Mercer's first real hit, "Lazybones."

As a result he was admitted to ASCAP and got to meet those he had admired so much for years: Berlin, Porter, Gershwin, Hart, and Coward. Whiteman offered Mercer a real job to sing with the orchestra. He took it because he loved performing and would receive the princely salary of seventy-five dollars weekly. Carmichael was distressed by Mercer's career choice, saying, "Johnny and I could have flooded the market with hit songs. We were atuned . . ."

RKO offered Mercer five hundred dollars a week to come to California. Whiteman, a shrewd businessman, required that RKO pay Whiteman another five hundred dollars a week to allow Mercer to break his contract. Mercer went, although he was sad to leave the friends he had made in the Whiteman Orchestra: Glenn Miller, Benny Goodman, the Dorsey brothers, and Artie Shaw.

Early movie musicals were so bad that by 1932 they had almost ceased to exist. But, in 1933 they made a comeback with RKO in the forefront. Mercer's writing and performances were not particularly good, but his southern hospitality endeared him to everyone. He began drinking heavily and for the first time it became obvious how terribly mean he became under the influence of alcohol. He was starstruck by the famous actors around him, but when drunk he would insult everyone, even the most famous among them, such as Helen Hayes. Recognizing his own terrible behavior, he would frequently send flowers and an apology the following day to those aggrieved. Anger always seemed to be in the background. He was involved with a heavy-drinking crowd including the Crosbys. But his work at RKO was poor, and the studio did not renew his contract. Now he was out of a job and he and Ginger drove back to New York. It took three days just to go across Texas. Without knowing how to read music or play the piano, he wrote the music and the lyrics during that ride for "I'm an Old Cowhand (from the Rio Grande)."

Even though he lacked musical training, like Berlin, Mercer could hear everything in his head and was angered at the suggestion that musical secretaries wrote his songs.

On the way back they spent time with his family in Savannah where Ginger never felt comfortable. She never really considered herself Jewish, but to them she was a Jew from Brooklyn. With Johnny's vibrant personality, wherever they went, he was the center of attention. For Ginger, Savannah proved a difficult world to break into. There was a strong Christian tradition and Ginger was not even allowed to join the most exclusive club there. It began a trend of Mercer returning to visit Savannah alone.

Crosby put "I'm An Old Cowhand" into a movie in 1936, which was a big help to Mercer. Another big success came that year when a song he had written with Matty Malneck during the years he was with Whiteman was recorded by Benny Goodman. This tune, "Goody! Goody!" was number one on the Hit Parade for four weeks.

He then got an offer to go to London to write a show, BLACKBIRDS OF 1936, which ran for six months. But the most interesting thing that happened there was that he learned about his family heritage. Hugh Mercer had been a young surgeon in Scotland and, in 1746, had fled to the colonies when he was on the wrong side of a battle between England and Scotland. Before dying at the Battle of Princeton he had five children. Ann, the eldest, married Robert Patton. A grandson of theirs, a colonel in the Confederate army, was killed in the Civil War. His wife and two children fled to Virginia, where they hid in a deserted house. There they found two dead Union soldiers. To escape being erroneously blamed for killing them, they buried the bodies and subsequently moved to California. On that site, years later, the Woodberry Forest Prep School, which Johnny Mercer attended, was built. The young boy who buried the bodies would grow up to have a son who became the great World War II general, George S. Patton.

On his return, Warner Brothers hired Mercer, though he was under verbal contract to Jack Robbins. The competition was fierce. On the day Robbins heard of the signing, his daughter-in-law had called him in a panic about her little son vanishing. It was the time of the Lindbergh kidnapping. Robbins offered this response to her: "Don't worry about it! Today I lost Mercer to Warner Brothers. More children you can have. Losing Mercer, you can't have."

Warner Brothers had been successful with Harry Warren and Al Dubin. Dubin was an alcoholic, which created problems. So they needed more songwriters. When asked whom he would like to work with, Johnny suggested Dick Whiting, for whom he had tremendous respect. The movie they made was READY, WILLING AND ABLE. They came up with the hit "Too Marvelous for Words."

It became Mercer's happiest collaboration. Mercer's other favorite was that with Harold Arlen. He and Whiting had several unsuccessful movies but their other big hit song was "Hooray for Hollywood."

Whiting was always sickly and, in February 1938, while they were working on their fourth movie, Whiting suddenly died of a heart attack at the age of forty-six. He had been more than a collaborator. He was a father figure who guided Mercer through the complexities of Hollywood.

Warner matched Mercer up with Harry Warren. They wrote "You Must Have Been a Beautiful Baby" and the song that got Johnny his first Oscar nomination, "Jeepers Creepers." It lost in 1938 to "Thanks for the Memory," which became Bob Hope's theme song.

Harry Warren soon switched to 20th Century Fox, which also took many of Warner's stars. Mercer was left once again in a lurch at Warner Brothers, until his singing career revived in the late 1930s. Bing Crosby, Johnny Mercer, Pat O'Brien, Jerry Colonna, Fred MacMurray, Andy Devine, and Bill Frawley began putting on private shows for themselves and friends. They were so funny that Mercer was asked to join the cast of the radio show CAMEL CARAVAN. Soon he was the emcee and began writing songs with multiple composers. His first new hit came when he gave a lyric to Jimmy Van Heusen. The result was "I Thought About You." He and Rube Bloom soon wrote "Day In—Day Out."

With Benny Goodman as the show orchestra leader, they began a gimmick in which Goodman said he would play a melody and see if Mercer could write a lyric by the time of the next show. Goodman asked Ziggy Elman to play a melody. It had a Klezmer quality. Mercer said "Okay, but slow it down." The following week they presented "And the Angels Sing."

In 1940, Mercer had another hit with Bloom. It was "Fools Rush In."

He became so prolific that at one point in 1940, five of the ten songs on the Hit Parade were by Johnny Mercer.

Radio began making a great deal of money based on its use of music, and ASCAP, as with nightclubs and theatres, demanded more in royalties payment. It was receiving four and a half million dollars annually and distributing it to composers, lyricists, and publishers, but still believed it was being underpaid. Mercer had been elected the youngest member of the ASCAP board, and when the contract was to be renewed, the radio broadcasters refused, so all ASCAP music was removed. As a result, the broadcasters set up their own competitive organization, BMI. They signed up 110 composers from the South, the Midwest and the West and country music received national exposure for the first time. ASCAP finally capitulated and rather than get an increase, they were decreased to three million dollars annually. By 1952, 80 percent of all composers and lyricists were with BMI rather than ASCAP.

In 1940, he tried writing another Broadway show with Hoagy Carmichael called WALK WITH MUSIC, which closed quickly. The following year he joined with Buddy Morris to enter the music publishing business in a firm called Mercer Morris. It had a very short existence.

He received a lovely melody from Jimmy Van Heusen, but didn't get the lyrics done in time. So it was given to Johnny Burke and the beautiful "What's New?" was written. As a result Burke got the job of writing all Jimmy Van Heusen's lyrics including the Crosby-Hope movies. With all these things going wrong Mercer was dejected, never really feeling that he was successful. He was off the ASCAP Board. His radio show was off the air. And war was now looming in Europe.

In November 1940, he and Ginger illegally adopted a child, Amanda, in Georgia. They adored her. But their marriage was deteriorating. Just before the adoption they had experienced a major car accident. Ginger had some serious injuries and asked Johnny to swear that he would never leave her.

Though he was still only thirty years old and had accomplished quite a bit, he felt unfulfilled. He envied the stardom of his friend Bing Crosby, and Ginger would taunt him with it. But he had become important enough not to have to sign with any studio. He could pick and choose his own collaborators. So he chose Jimmy McHugh, who had been writing with Dorothy Fields. Mercer found him a difficult collaborator though they got an Oscar nomination in 1941 for "I'd Know You Anywhere." He also tried writing with Walter Donaldson.

In November 1940, Mercer received a call from his mother saying that his father was very sick. Mercer's

Johnny Mercer and Jo Stafford in the studio. (Photofest.)

father had helped support Johnny through all the years of struggling, even after he was married, by sending him fifty dollars every month. Though horribly frightened by airplanes, Johnny flew on four separate flights only to arrive shortly after his father had passed away. George Mercer had gotten progressively sicker after the Depression and had gone into bankruptcy. He suffered from depression triggered by his sense that he had let his investors down, and remained deeply committed to paying them back.

Mercer's grief was uncontrollable at the funeral. It had been a year since his father came to New York to visit him. After that visit George Mercer wrote a letter to Johnny in which he stated that he believed that his son was a genius. Mercer returned to California in a terrible emotional state.

Judy Garland had just completed THE WIZARD OF OZ. She was eighteen years old and had fallen in love with Artie Shaw. But he had broken her heart when he ran off and married Lana Turner. She rebounded with a writer, but was deflated when she found him in the embrace of another man. Around this time, she met the composer David Rose.

Johnny Mercer had met Judy Garland two years earlier at a party where he dueted on the song "Friendship" with her. In June 1941, she and Rose became engaged and Johnny and Ginger were invited to a party in their honor. Mercer and Garland danced together and whispered in each other's ear that they had always had a crush on each other. The following day they met in Garland's dressing room and made love for the first time.

Garland certainly must have had a huge admiration for his talent. For her part, Garland had much to offer any man, but it seems that she and Mercer shared a particularly intense level of sexual compatibility. After his death, extremely sensual poetry about their sex life was discovered.

Everyone, including Ginger, was aware of what was happening. She was distraught as they had just adopted a child. The day that Mercer asked Ginger for a divorce, mutual friends told Garland that she had to stop it. It was then announced that Garland had eloped with David Rose. Johnny was devastated. Four years later, Garland would get divorced and go on with affairs or marriages to Tyrone Power, Yul Brynner, Vincente Minnelli, and Joseph Mankiewicz. The Mercer-Garland affair would recur over and over, but Mercer would remain married and even adopt another child in 1947. Over the years he would get drunk and lash out cruelly against Ginger until finally in desperation she would get drunk as well.

In 1941, Mercer began writing with Harold Arlen. His lyrics took on a new sadness. Both men had extremely unhappy home lives. One of their first collaborations was a song from a film originally called HOT NOCTURNE sung by an African-American man in prison,"Blues in the Night." The song was so potent that the film adopted BLUES IN THE NIGHT as its title; also heard in the picture was "This Time the Dream's on Me."

Immediately after that they wrote a song that everyone agreed was written for Garland about their love affair for the film STAR SPANGLED RHYTHM. It was said to be the closest thing that any lyricist had ever written about sexual intercourse, "That Old Black Magic."

The early 1940s would be the peak period for Arlen and Mercer. Mercer said their collaboration was wonderful, with no disagreements. However, Arlen expressed disgust for Mercer's drunken behavior. Once in a restaurant Mercer became violent and cast racial slurs upon an African-American waiter. On another occasion at a party Mercer physically attacked Arlen. Over the same period, Mercer was also writing with Hoagy Carmichael and created one of his greatest hits, "Skylark." It was also believed that Mercer was frequently describing his relationship with Garland in his lyrics. He openly wrote of that with his song "I Remember You."

In 1982, after Mercer's death, when Ginger edited his work for a compilation, she left out the song completely. The staff at California State University who received his papers were specifically directed not to mention Garland in her presence. But when Ginger died, an individual who was unaware accidentally and ironically titled the program for her funeral "I Remember You."

When World War II began Mercer joined with a number of other performers entertaining the troops on California bases and at hospitals. He also wanted to write patriotic songs, but had only one hit about the war, "G.I. Jive."

Around that time Mercer met a record store owner who believed he could start a recording company, but needed financial backing. Buddy DeSylva and Mercer each put up twenty-five thousand dollars. In April 1942, Capitol Records was born and Mercer was able to sign Peggy Lee, Jo Stafford, Paul Whiteman, and Stan Kenton to recording contracts. Mercer was named the president of the company. He brought in Miles Davis and George Shearing, followed by Ernie Ford and Tex Ritter. He got their biggest star of all when he discovered Nat King Cole. He was their key performer until 1953 when they added Frank Sinatra. In 1943, Capitol Records earned two million dollars. In 1944 it was three and a half million dollars. By 1945, it had reached six million four hundred thousand dollars.

All this time Mercer never stopped writing. In 1944, he had another big hit, "Ac-cen-tchu-ate the Positive." Following that, he and Arlen wrote "My Shining Hour" for Fred Astaire in the film, THE SKY'S THE LIMIT, and the classic song of unrequited love, "One for My Baby (And One More for the Road)."

Though Mercer loved Gershwin's work, he considered Harold Arlen the finer of the two when it came to jazz. They both had the grasp of Jewish and black rhythms in their jazz. But Mercer said that Arlen's music "comes from the bottom of his feet." Of all the composers, Mercer's favorite was Jerome Kern. In 1942, he had the opportunity to write "I'm Old Fashioned" with him.

In the same year he wrote two songs with Victor Schertzinger, "Tangerine" and "Arthur Murray Taught Me Dancing in a Hurry."

Mercer was named as a replacement for Bob Hope on the PEPSODENT RADIO SHOW and then wrote the theme for the CHESTERFIELD SUPPER CLUB, "Dream."

In 1944, he finally got his own show, JOHNNY MERCER'S MUSIC SHOP, but it didn't last. His style was so much like that of southern African Americans that he was named "the most popular colored singer" on the radio even though he was white. Sponsors found him "too black" and cancelled the show.

That same year, David Raksin wrote a haunting melody for a murder mystery called LAURA and Oscar Hammerstein, now Broadway's biggest lyricist, was asked to write the lyrics. He insisted that if he wrote them he wanted his company to be the publisher. The request was denied and the song was given to Irving Caesar, who had written "Swanee" and "Tea For Two." But the result was so bad they went to Mercer. Johnny then wrote the lyrics for the beautiful song, "Laura."

Mercer was asked to write tlyrics for a movie THE HARVEY GIRLS with music by Harry Warren (which starred Judy Garland). He wrote "On the Atchison, Topeka and the Santa Fe," but was infuriated that the studio had added words that weren't his to fit the story. Warren was equally enraged when he discovered the ads touting the song referred to "Johnny Mercer's 'On the Atchison, Topeka and the Santa Fe.'" As a result neither attended when the song won the Academy Award.

Mercer agreed reluctantly to write a Broadway show with Harold Arlen. It was ST. LOUIS WOMAN. He was assured that Lena Horne would play the lead. At the last minute she quit, persuaded by African-American organizations that the show was demeaning to black women. Constant battles and ads against the show caused it to close after 113 performances. But it did have one of Mercer's greatest hits, "Come Rain or Come Shine."

By 1947, Capitol Records had become quite successful and Mercer was asked to step down as president. Though he had always wanted it to be just a small company, he felt hurt by the request. He remained a significant stockholder, but he never again was involved in its management.

Mercer desperately wanted a successful Broadway show of his own. In 1949, TEXAS, LI'L DARLIN' opened and though it ran for 221 performance it was completely outshined by his friend Frank Loesser's GUYS AND DOLLS.

In 1951, he wrote TOP BANANA for Phil Silvers. Silvers was a big hit and it ran for 350 performances. But the score and lyrics, both written by Mercer, were considered very mediocre. At the same time Garland was coming out of hibernation. She had been a huge smash at the London Palladium and was to open at the Palace in New York. A party was held by friends who knew nothing of the Mercer-Garland connection. Though he came with Ginger, Johnny and Garland disappeared into a bedroom and out to a cot on the terrace where they slept all night in fifty-degree weather. Immediately following that incident, Garland married Sid Luft and they had a daughter, Lorna, in November 1952.

By this time Garland had a complete separation from her mother, whom she actually condemned to the media. Her mother, who worked as a riveter, was found dead in her car. Garland expressed no regrets. Mercer had such strong family feelings, that when he subsequently met her at a party, in a drunken stupor he chastised her by saying, "How could you let your mother die in a parking lot?" Garland sped into the bathroom, slashed her wrists, and was rushed to the hospital.

Contemporary music, with its rock 'n' roll inflections, was leaving Mercer and other composers behind. The new environment was depressing to him. While he was writing very little, he was willing to do what other lyricists were not. He would write for any composer, even some who were not very good. On a positive note he took several foreign songs and wrote English lyrics for them, which accounted for his beautiful "Autumn Leaves" and "When the World Was Young."

He wrote his finest integrated movie musical in 1954. Though none of the songs became hits, the movie is considered a classic, SEVEN BRIDES FOR SEVEN BROTHERS. In 1956, he finally achieved success on Broadway with LI'L ABNER. It ran for two years and 693 performances. He had been able to capture the southern hillbilly idiom, much as

Loesser had captured Damon Runyon's urban idiom for the characters in GUYS AND DOLLS.

Mercer was seen by everyone as constantly unhappy. He resided in a very modest house as opposed to his contemporaries who lived in the glorious part of Hollywood. Though he could afford a more luxurious home, he always felt that he could not. Ginger constantly threw up to him that she could have married Crosby and been wealthy.

His children found him loving and overly generous, caring little for money and giving it away freely. But their parents were constantly drunk and fighting. In later interviews, the children tended not to want to discuss their mother at all. Johnny made constant trips back to Savannah, quietly, in order to avoid celebrity status, as if he were looking for something he never found.

In 1955, he was asked to write both music and lyrics for another movie musical, DADDY LONG LEGS with Fred Astaire and Leslie Caron. Astaire was aging and they needed a song to cross the age barrier, for which Mercer wrote, "Something's Gotta Give."

He followed that with "Midnight Sun," a great jazz hit with music by Lionel Hampton.

That year, Capitol Records was sold. Mercer sold reluctantly and received one million seven hundred fifty thousand dollars. He asked Ginger if he could use the money in a way that was very important to him. When George Mercer died in 1940 only 34 percent of his debts had been paid. By 1955, 72 percent had been paid but no more was forthcoming from his estate. Mercer contacted the bank to tell them he was sending them three hundred thousand dollars in his father's memory to pay off every creditor.

By 1958, he was totally out of the music scene except for writing the lyrics for Duke Ellington's "Satin Doll." At age forty-nine, he had not one new hit.

Edna Ferber of SHOW BOAT fame had offered her novel *Saratoga Trunk* to Rodgers and Hammerstein and then to Lerner and Loewe, but was turned down by both. Arlen accepted and wanted Mercer to do the lyrics. Johnny was not eager to do it, but couldn't say no to a friend, or almost anyone for that matter. Morton Da Costa wanted to direct and Ferber insisted they keep closely to the story. But Da Costa was sick and hospitalized and Mercer and Arlen were left to do everything, for which they were truly not prepared. The show, SARATOGA, was a complete failure and Mercer was more depressed than ever. He was drinking heavily with multiple episodes of cruelty to both friends and family when under the influence of alcohol. He was fifty and felt that no one wanted him any longer. Not knowing where to turn he approached Henry Mancini asking him if he could write with him for the movies. After some unsuccessful efforts, they collaborated on BREAKFAST AT TIFFANY'S and the song "Moon River."

When "Moon River" was first seen in the rushes, the producers wanted to remove it from the film. Mercer had written the lyrics by reaching back into the memories of his childhood in Savannah. After the song won the Academy Award, Mercer came to hate it, because it was played whenever he entered a room where music was being performed.

In 1961, Mercer won his fourth Academy Award for a picture starring Jack Lemmon. As Lemmon told the story he had just completed a very emotional scene. He was overwrought and did not even want to eat lunch. But the producer, Blake Edwards, prevailed on Lemmon to accompany him to a sound studio. There, on a dark empty stage, sat Henry Mancini at a piano and Mercer began to sing. Lemmon said he began crying and could not stop. He claimed it was the most thrilling experience of his career when he heard Mercer sing "Days of Wine and Roses."

Once again all those who knew him believed he was writing about Garland. But it seemed to finally lift him out of his depression.

He was approached again to go to Broadway. This time it was to write a slapstick musical comedy for Bert Lahr titled FOXY. Things did not go well and it ended up more like a one-man show than a Broadway production. Although Mercer worked on the show for two years, FOXY opened and quickly closed.

Sadie Vimmerstedt, a grandmother from Youngstown, Ohio, outraged by Sinatra leaving Nancy to marry Ava Gardner, wrote a letter to Mercer in 1957 suggesting that he write a song based on the title, "I Wanna Be Around to Pick Up the Pieces When Somebody Breaks Your Heart." He did not respond until around 1962. At that time he used her title and wrote the song, which was ultimately recorded by Tony Bennett. Depending on which source is true, Mercer gave Sadie either one-third or one-half of the royalties. The song, "I Wanna Be Around" became such a hit that it changed her life forever.

Mercer was doing well and so was Garland, and once again Johnny asked Ginger for a divorce in order to marry Judy who had just gotten divorced from Sid Luft. Mercer had written a song especially for Garland to sing to her daughter, called "Lorna's Song." Ginger asked if she could take a trip first with her sister to the Far East. She returned with a severe case of hepatitis. Her doctor told Mercer that she might die and Ginger begged him to stay with her for the remainder of her life. Mercer dropped his request and said he would stay. She lived another thirty years.

With Mancini he wrote the title song for CHARADE and with Johnny Mandel the title song for THE AMERICANIZATION OF EMILY. By this time Mancini had stopped writing with him because he could not tolerate the temper tantrums and the delays in completing work.

In 1965, Mercer had a big hit for Frank Sinatra when he combined an old German melody with thoughts of his pastoral south, resulting in the song, "Summer Wind." But the 1960s found him depressed again by among other things, the civil rights movement, which offended him. He thought of himself as a southern gentleman. He was extremely kind to blacks throughout his life, but looked at them through a paternalistic eye. He wanted them "to remain in a different social place than his own."

Jule Styne asked him to write the lyrics for a musical based on Tennessee Williams's THE ROSE TATTOO. He rejected it, infuriated by the fact that it depicted the South as decadent, where Mercer saw it as romantic.

By then Garland's career once again was rapidly going downhill. In a state of constant depression she called Johnny every day, with Ginger frequently answering the phone. As might be expected, Ginger was extremely rude to her. Garland finally died of a drug overdose in a London hotel in 1969.

By 1970, Mercer was back in a deep depression, considering himself a failure. But in 1970 he did help to establish the Songwriters Hall of Fame, with Irving Berlin as its first president.

He bought a home in Savannah and spent most of his time there devoted to three grandchildren. The grandchildren remembered Johnny and Ginger as having separate bedrooms and separate cars going to separate places. Ginger was fine and classy in her Jaguar, Johnny was down-home in his Pinto.

He asked Andre Previn to write a show with him based on a beloved British novel of the 1920s, THE GOOD COMPANIONS. Mercer and Previn traveled to London to write the show for the West End. It got good reviews but misfortune struck again with a series of IRA bombings. The public was frightened out of going to London. So it closed after a short run and was never brought to the United States. But while there he began getting dizzy spells. He returned and was operated on in Pasadena in October 1975. The brain tumor they found was malignant, but the surgeon was overly aggressive. He left Mercer alive but in a vegetative state. Johnny remained that way until he died more than eight months later on Ginger's birthday, June 25, 1976. Three months before his death, when his health insurance had run out, he was taken from the hospital and cared for by two men at home.

His career was remarkable. No one, with the exception of Irving Berlin, produced the number of highly successful songs that Johnny Mercer did. With all of his success his life was fraught with terrible disappointments and a constant cloud of depression hanging over him from the time of his childhood. His own lifelong unhappiness was centered in his marriage and his lost love. Regardless of his successes, there was the constant feeling that he was a failure. He never quite lived up to what he felt he could have accomplished. Finally, there was Ginger's constant, badgering complaints of having missed out on what she "could have had."

He lived a life of sweetness and loving kindness when sober, and the most vicious, and violent cruelty, even to those he loved, when drunk. Johnny Mercer, an American genius, was dead at the age of sixty-six.

MAJOR WORKS

SHOWS:

WALK WITH MUSIC **(CARMICHAEL, 1940)**
ST. LOUIS WOMAN **(ARLEN, 1946)**
TEXAS LI'L DARLIN' **(DOLAN, 1949)**
TOP BANANA **(WORDS AND MUSIC, 1951)**
LI'L ABNER **(DEPAUL, 1956)**
SARATOGA **(ARLEN, 1959)**
FOXY **(DOLAN, 1964)**
THE GOOD COMPANIONS **(PREVIN, 1974)**

COMPOSITION:

MERCER WROTE MAINLY LYRICS, BUT SOME MUSIC, FOR 674 SONGS.

Composer Cole Porter in his Waldolf Towers home, 1964. Reported as the last photo taken of him. (Photofest.)

COLE PORTER

THERE CERTAINLY WAS NO ONE IN THE ANNALS OF American musical theatre like Cole Porter. Most of his contemporaries had their origins in New York City. Cole was born in 1891 in Peru, Indiana. Most grew up in modest means, if not abject poverty.

Porter's maternal grandfather, J. O. Cole, was a multimillionaire. His adored daughter, Kate, married Sam Porter. They had three children, the first two of whom died in early childhood, and the third was Cole. Kate, a slight woman, was strong-willed like her father. Her husband, Sam, was a mild mannered, soft spoken pharmacist who played several instruments, loved literature, and adored his children. But throughout his lifetime, Cole attached himself to his mother rather than his father.

J. O. had one other male descendant, Kate's brother. He was a ne'er do-well and an alcoholic. Since J. O. had no expectations for his son, he expected Cole to stay in Peru, get a good education, and take over the family business. Kate had other ideas. She wanted Cole to go east to be educated. This caused a major battle between Kate and J. O., which Kate won. But they didn't speak to each other for two years.

Kate had complete control of the young Porter. Early on, as were many babies during the period, he was dressed like Little Lord Fauntleroy.

The only sport he was allowed to participate in was horseback riding. Like his mother, Cole was small and thin. At age six he learned to play the piano, and by age ten he was writing music.

In 1905, at age fourteen, he was sent to Worcester Academy in New England. Over the next two years there were very few trips back to Peru and very few visitors from home.

At first he felt out of place, but his piano playing and songs soon made him the center of attention. He was a good student, but music and acting became his forte, and he received constant invitations to play at faculty homes. By his senior year he starred in every production and was accepted to Yale, where he matriculated after spending the entire summer in France, a graduation gift from his grandfather.

He became an immediate hit at Yale. His first successful songs were school cheers, many composed in 1911, when he wrote "Bull Dog" and "Bingo Eli Yale." To this very day "Bull Dog" is the Yale University fight song. Cole became a member of the Yale Dramatic Association, commonly known as "The Dramat", the Whiffenpoofs, and the Yale Glee Club. He mingled with his new friends, the Vanderbilts, Dodges, Achesons and Ferrari-Coopers. Cole wrote the annual college show, and began his lifelong friendship with Monty Woolley. The Yale Glee Club held a national tour each year at Christmas time in major cities across the country. It would end with Porter coming forward to play and sing his own songs as the star of the show. Newspapers across the country called him a future superstar of vaudeville. There would usually be eight to ten encores for him at every performance.

J. O. Cole insisted that Cole attend Harvard Law School. Cole reluctantly agreed, and Dean Acheson became his roommate. There are many stories about what happened to Porter then, but two are most likely to be true. After several months Porter and his roommates had a wild rowdy party one night in the dorm. The dean called them in and said he was considering throwing them all out. Acheson claimed that Porter told the dean it was all his fault, and that he would leave quietly if the others were allowed to stay.

Another story was that Porter came ill-prepared to a law school class with a famous professor and was unable to answer any questions. The professor in anger said, "Mr. Porter, why don't you learn to play the fiddle?" after which Porter rose, left the classroom, and never returned again. Take you choice: Porter was out of law school in the first semester.

At the same time his musical reputation was growing, and Elizabeth Marbury, famous for presenting the Princess Theatre productions, signed Porter up to write his first show, SEE AMERICA FIRST, for which he collaborated with T. Lawrason Riggs. It opened on March 28, 1916. One review said it was the worst musical in town. It closed in fifteen days and Porter was devastated.

America entered World War I in 1917 and Porter enlisted. But to this day no one knows exactly how he served. Some said he was in an ambulance corps. Some say he was in the French Foreign Legion. One observer said he saw him strolling the streets of Paris in different uniforms, sometimes as a cadet and sometimes as a colonel. Whatever he was doing, he was likable, captivating, and in the terms of one writer, "like a leprechaun." After the war he decided to remain in Paris. He was a bon vivant. It was at this point that Porter met a woman who would become a very important person in his life.

Linda Lee Thomas was tall, charming, and beautifully spoken, with deep blue eyes and blond hair. She was called by some the most beautiful woman in America. But she was very poor. In 1901, at the age of seventeen, Linda Lee married Edward Thomas, the owner of the *New York Morning Telegraph*. Thomas was a millionaire. They had servants, yachts, and homes around the world, and Linda Lee possessed a great deal of jewelry. It was said of Linda that her favorite department store was Van Cleef & Arpels. She always sported a pair of long white gloves and disposed of them after one wearing. Thomas was "cruel, aggressive, and sexually unfaithful." In 1912, they divorced and Linda was awarded a gigantic settlement.

Another well-known person played a role in the changing life of Cole Porter. Elsie de Wolfe was a wild character, who was famous for standing on her head at the age of seventy. She was a lesbian, and the leading decorator of the international set. Elsie traveled often with several other well-known lesbians, Anne Vanderbilt, Anne Morgan (of J. P.), and Bessie Marbury. The group of them befriended Linda Lee and Cole Porter. Linda and Cole then met at a wedding in 1918 when Porter sat down at the piano afterward and played. She thought he was a hired musician and asked a friend to arrange for him to play at a party of hers. As a joke he came dressed as a hired musician. They both thought it hysterical and in less than two years they were married. He was seven years her junior. While she was very, very wealthy, Cole had nothing but great expectations. Porter went back to Peru in 1918 asking his grandfather for his trust, telling him what he was doing. The marriage plan and Cole's general lifestyle did not please J. O., and Cole was turned down.

Porter then wrote the show HITCHY-KOO. It closed in two months. As Cole was still unsuccessful financially, it was Linda Lee who was supplying most of the wherewithal for their glamorous lifestyle. Kate subsidized her son to whatever extent she could.

Porter was entering a terrible period of his life. He doubted his ability to write anything successfully. Living off these two women, he became a boulevardier socialite in Paris. He wrote songs that he would play for friends, while continuing to study piano and orchestration. But he

Composer Cole Porter with singer Dinah Shore, 1952. (Photofest.)

Composer Cole Porter (right), with newspaper columnist/TV host Ed Sullivan, 1952. (Photofest.)

always felt inferior. Linda bought a beautiful home near the Eiffel Tower and encouraged him to write, especially classical music. Howard Sturges became a close friend of theirs and moved in with the Porters. Porter was gay. His marriage to Linda was sexless and they had separate bedrooms. But they did love each other. Sturges may well have been Cole's early partner. But Sturges had a severe drinking problem and would disappear for days at a time, sometimes turning up in a hospital.

At the same time the Porters became close friends with the millionaires Gerald and Sara Murphy, as well as Pablo Picasso. Gerald was quite a painter in his own right. But while Picasso was teaching him, he was also having an affair with his wife, Sara.

They were all part of the flamboyant, wild set which included, among others, Noel Coward and Elsa Maxwell. The group established the Lido in Venice as their summer retreat. Linda was constantly trying to divert Cole to concentrate on his music. She even tried unsuccessfully to get Stravinsky to agree to teach him. But Cole protected himself emotionally by claiming "to be a playboy who incidentally wrote songs."

In 1923, J. O. died and left an estate of two million dollars to Kate, but nothing to Cole. Kate gave Cole half of her inheritance. A few years later Kate received another two million and gave half to Cole again. Later when someone asked him if receiving that two million while never working had ruined his life, he responded to the contrary, "It simply made it wonderful."

In 1924, John Murray Anderson persuaded him to write some songs for the GREENWICH VILLAGE FOLLIES. To prove he had no intention of being a professional, Porter made himself unavailable to Anderson whenever there were attempts to reach him about changes. Nevertheless, one of his first hits was in that show. It was "I'm in Love Again."

Around that time Cole fell in love with Boris Kochno, a dancer and the ex-lover of Diaghilev. They exchanged passionate love letters. Linda understood Cole was gay from the beginning. She had made only one request: that he remain discreet. But this relationship became so blatant that it upset her deeply.

There is no clear understanding of Linda Lee's sexual orientation. Various biographers have viewed her differently. Some have even "suggested that she was a lesbian."

Cole and Linda were always very kind to each other. Cole would rise every time Linda entered or left a room, always opening a door for her. It was said that Linda didn't even know how to open a door and would stand interminably waiting for a door to be opened for her.

In Venice, Noel Coward met Rodgers and Hart on the street and invited them to meet Porter. When they arrived at his home Coward played some of his music, as did Rodgers and Hart. When Porter began to play, Rodgers was astounded. He had never heard of him. He questioned why he wasn't writing for Broadway. Porter's response was that he had done that, and would rather just write for friends.

Porter was a heavy smoker, which was the fashion of the time. He had drawers of cigarette lighters, which he lost constantly. So he began engraving them with, "Stolen from Cole Porter." Whether cigarette-related or not, Linda was always ill with constant severe upper respiratory infections, especially in 1927, when Cole's father died. As a result he returned to America alone for the funeral. During that trip he met Louis Schurr, a theatrical producer, and was asked to write LA REVUE DES AMBASSADEURS. It was to open in Paris. Shortly before it opened, Cole met the Gershwins with their sister Frankie at a party in Paris. All evening George played the piano while Frankie sang. Porter was so taken that he asked her to be a part of his show, singing her brother's music. She agreed and the show was a big hit.

In 1926, Irving Berlin married Ellin Mackay, daughter of a multimillionaire mining magnate. They ran off to Europe on their honeymoon, where they became great friends of the Porters. Berlin had been married before. His first wife died of malaria just months after the marriage. His first wife's brother, E.Ray Goetz, a writer and a producer, had remained Berlin's friend. Knowing of Berlin's connection to Porter, he asked Berlin to persuade Porter to write a score for him. Porter agreed and the show was called PARIS, a Broadway hit in 1928.

As good as his music is, Porter's genius is in his lyrics. They are spectacular. They were always cutting edge, suggestive and sensuous, with plenty of sophisticated innuendo. His songs are written with multiple reprises for more and more refrains. It is obvious that he wrote his lyrics first and then fit the music to the words. Such a song was "Let's Do It (Let's Fall in Love)," the hit of PARIS.

He followed that with a hit show in London and Broadway titled WAKE UP AND DREAM. Its most popular song was "What Is This Thing Called Love?"

The year 1929 was a huge one as Berlin was planning to write for his Music Box Theatre a new show titled FIFTY MILLION FRENCHMEN, and decided that Porter's background made him more suitable to be the composer. The lyrics created a stir, with some critics sensitive to racist undertones. His friend Monty Woolley privately came to his defense saying that was crazy as the two of them frequently went with Cary Grant to Harlem for sex, and that Lena Horne, and Ella Fitzgerald were his close friends. It was not a very satisfactory rebuttal. The big song in the show was "You Do Something to Me."

Porter's life was changing. The 1920s had, for Porter, been purely sybaritic. He lived as a dilettante, occupied primarily with travel, play, no work, sex, and parties.

During that period he had stayed away from New York, spending all his time in Europe. The 1930s would bring him back into the theatrical world with a bang. He would accomplish much of his greatest work in that decade. By good fortune he had not invested in the stock market and was not hurt by the Crash.

For the third time, Irving Berlin's former brother-in-law, Ray Goetz, came into his life. The show he was producing was THE NEW YORKERS. In it Porter caused a big stir with his song "Love for Sale," which originally cast a sympathetic light on a prostitute's profession. For years, the lyrics were informally banned from broadcast on American radio. The show opened in December 1930 and by January Cole and Linda were off on a year-long yacht trip.

Around this time an article in *Vanity Fair* provided a wonderful profile of him. It described him as 5' 7 1/2 inches tall, weighing 140 pounds, going almost without sleep while working, taking two baths daily, owning sixteen dressing gowns and nine cigarette lighters, hating baseball, and loving movies, dirty limericks, and all kinds of scandalous news.

He was constantly involved in practical jokes and hoaxes. Together with Elsa Maxwell he created a fictitious family of nouveau riche, Mr. and Mrs. Fitch, about which he always made fun. He wrote them into multiple songs and people began to believe they actually existed as individuals who suddenly found oil in Oklahoma, but loved New York. They even got invited to fashionable parties. Tired of the hoax, Porter killed them off in a car crash in another song.

Once, on a ship, a passenger called his room in error looking for a porter and asking for a pitcher of water. Cole put on a French accent and began asking what size ice cubes he wanted. The completely frustrated passenger later said Porter kept questioning him with at least twenty-five different queries about how he wanted the water and the ice.

The end of 1932 brought GAY DIVORCE with Fred Astaire. The show was not particularly good but it had a very special song. It was one of the rare times in his career that Cole wrote the music for a song before the lyrics. He was working on it in a hotel in Manhattan on a Saturday night when Monty Woolley popped in and said, "I don't know what it is, but whatever it is, throw it away. It's terrible."

The show opened on November 29, 1932, and Astaire, like Woolley, wasn't certain that he liked the song either. It ultimately became one of ASCAP's top ten moneymakers of all time, "Night and Day."

After Porter had a failed show called NYMPH ERRANT in 1933, seen only in London, Elsa Maxwell threw one of the greatest parties ever. It was held in the Astor Gallery of the Waldorf-Astoria, in honor of Porter and Gershwin, and had grand pianos there for the two of them to play.

Up until then Porter had had many lovers, including Sturges. But in the early 1930s he met the love of his life, Eddie Tauch, a young architect. In the summer of 1934, Porter and Tauch were boating on the Rhine when Vincent Freedley persuaded Porter to write a show with Howard Lindsay and Russel Crouse for Ethel Merman. She became his favorite star. Of the fourteen Broadway musicals eventually starring Merman, five were written by Porter. ANYTHING GOES opened on November 21, 1934, and was one of his biggest hits. For the show he had composed two of his finest songs, the title song and "I Get a Kick Out of You."

It was a spectacular Broadway season. Gershwin had OF THEE I SING and Berlin was reaching new heights with AS THOUSANDS CHEER.

As an interesting bit of theatrical history, in Brian Friel's 1990 award-winning drama, DANCING AT LUGHNASA, five brave Irish women leading deprived drab lives allow their spirits to soar when they turn on the radio and begin dancing with each other. The song they dance to on the radio is "Anything Goes."

Another song from the show was not only a huge hit, it created an amazing phenomenon. The song was so catchy that all sorts of people, even other composers like Irving Berlin, began writing parodies for the lyrics. At one point Porter was receiving more than three hundred parodies a month. His original lyrics were extremely sophisticated and sexually suggestive, but some of the parodies were outright raunchy, including the one written by Irving Berlin. In 1943, when Linda was very sick in the hospital, she turned on the radio to hear the Ethel Merman show and her spirits soared as she heard Merman say she was dedicating that very same song to Linda Porter. And that phenomenal song was "You're the Top."

Immediately after the show opened, Cole, Linda, and Monty, and this time Moss Hart as well, were off on another world cruise. Porter and Hart had discussed doing a show together and Hart suggested they go to Morocco to write it. But Cole insisted they do it on a cruise. So every day when there was no port of call, they wrote. But Porter insisted when in port they go sightseeing. They were gone for five months and wrote JUBILEE, which opened in New York in October 1935. It was a great success and featured the song "Just One of Those Things." Some said the show was jinxed. Performers received death threats and a musician actually died in the pit. One of its great songs, "Begin the Beguine," was recorded in a swing version by Artie Shaw four years later and became the largest selling record at that time, at six and a half million copies.

Like the other important composers Porter was ultimately drawn to Hollywood. Linda was unhappy there, because the lifestyle led to much more blatant homosexual behavior on Cole's part. For the remainder of his life he spent half of each year in California. In 1936, his first successful movie was produced, BORN TO DANCE, starring

Cole Porter, 1953. (Photofest.)

Jimmy Stewart. During the filming Stewart asked Porter to lower the higher notes of a song for him. Incredulous, Porter "didn't go for that" and Stewart sang "Easy to Love" in the original key.

It has been suggested that, in another song from that film, "I've Got You Under My Skin," Porter, who was always playing with words and hidden meanings, was not referring to love, but to drugs, which were taken by some people in his social circle.

He began working on the Broadway show RED, HOT AND BLUE starring Ethel Merman, Bob Hope, and Jimmy Durante. In it Merman and Hope sang "It's De-Lovely." The show was a hit, but life at home was getting progressively worse. Linda was insisting he was not fulfilling his promise to keep his sexual behavior subdued. Unable to tolerate Porter's indiscreet behavior, Linda left and went back to Paris. Porter did not rejoin her for months. Meanwhile Louis B. Mayer decided to make George Gershwin's show ROSALIE into a movie and asked Porter to add one song. It was "In the Still of the Night."

While Porter was there political activity in Europe became scary, including increased discrimination toward homosexuals.

So in October 1937, Cole left and came to Mill Neck, near Oyster Bay, Long Island, to stay with an old friend, Tookie. There he went horseback riding, trying a horse he had been told was skittish and difficult to control. The horse fell and threw Porter, landing on his legs. He received multiple fractures, and ultimately developed osteomyelitis at the site of the fractures. It was the beginning of a period of numerous operations and a horrendous change in his life. Much later he would say that while he remained in agony, waiting to be rescued, he worked on the lyrics for "At Long Last Love."

Linda rushed back from Europe when she heard the news. She and Katie forbade the doctors to amputate his legs. He was frequently delirious or unconscious for days. It has been said that Linda was planning on divorcing him while she was in Europe, but felt after the accident that she couldn't desert a sinking ship. Once Cole was heard to mutter, "Fifty million Frenchmen can't be wrong. They eat horses instead of riding them."

Once out of the hospital, he was taken care of by Ray Kelly and Paul Sylvain. Bedridden, they managed his every need. Despite his bedridden state, he wrote another show, YOU NEVER KNOW. The reviews were terrible, and it closed quickly.

In the summer of 1938, he went to Lido Beach on Long Island, where Ray Kelly was his principal lover, but he was in no way monogamous as he had orgiastic parties with sailors and soldiers from nearby bases. While there he wrote a show for Mary Martin, LEAVE IT TO ME! in which she began achieving fame with her rendition of "My Heart Belongs to Daddy."

Even in his disabled condition he wanted to travel. As a result he persuaded Kelly and Sylvain to drag him up and down the difficult terrain of Machu Pichu. On his return he got right back to work on a movie to be called BROADWAY MELODY OF 1939. But it was delayed so much because of his trip that the name was changed to BROADWAY MELODY OF 1940. Its hit song was "I Concentrate on You."

A new project was planned for Bert Lahr, who had just finished THE WIZARD OF OZ. The costars would be Ethel Merman and newcomer Betty Grable. Lahr first thought the music was bad, but later changed his mind when he heard it fully orchestrated. He said his initial opinion resulted from the fact that Porter had become such a poor piano player.

Lahr's opinion of Porter's lyrics was that they were dirty without being subtle. He said, "Nothing I sang in burlesque was as risqué." There were problems with all the leads in the show. Both Lahr and Grable disliked Merman immensely, saying she stepped on their laugh lines and stole one of Grable's songs. But Lahr and Merman brought the house down when they sang "Friendship."

The show was DU BARRY WAS A LADY. "Well, Did You Evah?," another great song from the show, was appropriated years later for the movie HIGH SOCIETY, and sung by Bing Crosby and Frank Sinatra.

Linda, a smoker, was getting progressively sicker with respiratory problems. She persuaded Cole to move with her into a home, Buxton Hill, in Williamstown, Massachusetts. He would go to Manhattan midweek and return there on weekends where he had his separate quarters, in a cottage named "No Trespassing."

While there, he wrote the song "Miss Otis Regrets," for a show that was never produced. Many jazz and cabaret artists still perform it today.

From 1939–44, he had five smash hits on Broadway and five movies. In 1940, he wrote PANAMA HATTIE for Merman, and, in 1941, LET'S FACE IT for Danny Kaye. During the war Porter had frequent assignations with soldiers. But his primary lover was Nelson Barclift, a dancer. Multiple love letters between them have been recovered and he wrote a love song to him which became a huge hit with soldiers during the war, "You'd Be So Nice to Come Home To."

In the 1930s, he wrote a song as a joke for Linda. It was not typical of the things he composed. When completed, it was just thrown into a discard pile. In the 1940s, it was revived, and recorded by Kate Smith, Crosby, the Andrews Sisters, and was one of FDR's favorites. It was "Don't Fence Me In."

Porter was becoming progressively more eccentric during the 1940s. He developed a penchant for having his whole body shaved except for his head. He said hair made him feel dirty.

In 1944, he had legal problems that were common to composers of that era. He was accused of plagiarizing "Don't Fence Me In," "Night and Day," and "My Heart Belongs to Daddy." A long court fight, which Porter eventually won, took a physical toll on him.

At the end of 1944, he wrote a show about which one critic wrote, "The tunes are definitely not Cole Porter's best." It was a Billy Rose extravaganza called SEVEN LIVELY ARTS. But it had a song in it which has been cherished for decades by unrequited lovers, "Ev'ry Time We Say Goodbye."

Two more failures followed. The movie about his life, NIGHT AND DAY, with Cary Grant, and Alexis Smith, and AROUND THE WORLD IN 80 DAYS, a massive Orson Welles project, were both terrible. With that background it was no wonder that funding for KISS ME, KATE was extremely difficult to procure. His private life was also disintegrating. At his peak Porter was surrounded by the greatest writers, painters, musicians, thinkers, and

Left to right: actors Hildegard Knef, Don Ameche, and composer Cole Porter rehearsing for SILK STOCKINGS, 1955. (Springer/Photofest.)

royalty. Now his life was based on wild gay parties and private trysts. In 1947, his longtime secretary suddenly died. Fortunately that role was taken up by Madeleine Smith, a woman with impeccable credentials, who served him admirably for the rest of his life. Sadly she was treated shabbily in his will.

In 1948, he also wrote a movie for Judy Garland and Gene Kelly, THE PIRATE. Kelly asked him one day during the shooting if he could write a fast up-tempo song. The very next day Porter presented him with "Be a Clown."

The writer Bella Spewack initiated what was to become the pinnacle of Cole Porter's career. She first contacted Burton Lane about doing a musical based on THE TAMING OF THE SHREW. He rejected it. Her idea of a play within a play arose, but the project was not progressing well. Part of Spewack's problem was that her co-writer was her husband, Sam, and their marriage was falling apart. Porter agreed to do the score for KISS ME, KATE and all through the problems he kept working and creating the sexiest lyrics he had ever written. Among them was one he supposedly wrote for Linda trying to explain his own promiscuity. The song was "Always True to You in My Fashion."

But no song in the entire Broadway literary library has more sexual overtones than "Brush Up Your Shakespeare."

Porter worked feverishly on the show. He knew he was having a bad run of failures and needed to turn it around. He came to auditions and rehearsals, involved himself in staging, and even solicited backers. It was so difficult to obtain backers that they ended up with seventy-two separate ones. Each one of them made a fortune.

One night he woke Bella Spewack at two a.m. to sing to her his newest song, "Why Can't You Behave?" On another occasion he played a song for her that he said he was placing into an upcoming movie. After hearing it she said, "No way—that's going into the show." It was "So in Love."

Meanwhile, his health was deteriorating. Cole developed abscesses in both legs and a stomach ulcer, but still kept working diligently on KATE, coming up with songs like "We Open in Venice."

Tryouts began in December 1948. Although Moss Hart and Agnes de Mille saw it in rehearsal and had very negative responses, the reviews for KISS ME, KATE were spectacular.

Linda Lee, getting progressively sicker, was in Arizona. Cole visited her occasionally, but was ill-tempered, unable to sleep and in poor spirits. The success of KISS ME, KATE brought on the opportunity for a new show, OUT OF THIS WORLD, but lacking the high quality of the previous production, it did not do well.

Massive celebrations were scheduled to celebrate his sixtieth birthday, the largest at the Yale Bowl, but Porter did not show up, pleading illness. He was losing weight, looked terribly ill. Obviously psychological problems existed as well. Though he was economically secure, friends found him unrealistically cheap. In September 1951, he was admitted to Doctors Hospital in Manhattan. A diagnosis of depression was made, and as a result Porter received a series of shock treatments.

He repeatedly turned down offers to do shows. Finally, he agreed to write one about Paris in the 1890s. It was called CAN-CAN and starred Lilo. With the exception of Lilo, all the rest of the cast found Porter difficult and rude. In mid-1952, while he was writing the score to the show, his mother died suddenly. It was another blow he was unable to handle.

The first song written for CAN-CAN was "I Love Paris." Porter loved Lilo's deep throaty voice but a young new dancer, Gwen Verdon, stole the show from her. Porter did write a song specifically to match Lilo's style, "C'est Magnifique," which was a great hit. The show received poor reviews from the critics, but amazingly still had a long run. CAN-CAN's other big hit was "It's All Right with Me."

Porter was soon offered a show based on the movie NINOTCHKA. The new show was SILK STOCKINGS, which, like OUT OF THIS WORLD, was beset by problems like cast changes and multiple firings. Don Ameche and Hildegarde Neff were the leading performers, but the ingénue collapsed shortly before the opening. She was replaced by an unknown, Gretchen Wyler, who stole the show, incurring hostility from both of the leads. Rehearsals went on for fourteen weeks instead of the scheduled four. Though the show was a hit, the only memorable song was "All of You."

In May, Linda died in her apartment at the Waldorf-Astoria. Porter was at her bedside, but at the funeral could not leave the car to go to the gravesite.

Cole left immediately on a world tour while he arranged for Linda's Waldorf apartment to be completely redecorated for him. It was so spectacular when completed that it was featured in the *New York Times* and *Vogue*. Though Sturges still remained an intimate after all these years, Cole started up two new torrid relationships, one with Robert Raison and the other with Robert Bray.

From July to November 1955, Porter worked on music for the movie HIGH SOCIETY, which Saul Chaplin was producing. His piano playing had become extremely poor. He never practiced and stopped playing any classics. Revived for the movie was the hit from DU BARRY WAS A LADY, "Well, Did You Evah?" Chaplin finally asked him to try to just write something simpler than he had been attempting and the result was the beautiful "True Love."

In 1956, while writing the score for the movie LES GIRLS, his dear friend Sturges died suddenly, and apparently it was even more of a blow to him than the death of his mother or Linda.

In an interview that year, Porter said were it not for two women, Kate and Linda, he would have had no career, because they stuck by him during his nine fallow years from 1919 to 1928.

In January 1957, Porter underwent a gastrectomy, but kept on writing. He tried writing a television special called *Aladdin*, but it was a flop. Just before it was shown in 1958 Cole was back in the hospital with osteomyelitis of the right leg. This time it had to be amputated. He avoided contact with old friends and never wrote another note.

Porter's schedule became very regimented. He woke at 11 a.m., showered, and had a massage, which his staff said by now had become extremely sexual. He lunched. Following that his barber arrived. That was followed by a nap from 3–4:30. He went to rehab, rested, and dressed for his 8 p.m. dinner with guests. At the meal he would consume large quantities of wine and guests were asked to leave the table while he urinated into a container. The only exception to that would be when he became completely incontinent. Guests left at midnight and he would stay awake watching TV until three or four in the morning. When no guests were available, which was common, because no one wanted to participate in this extremely unpleasant dinner arrangement, his butler would alternate as butler and guest. He constantly complained about the food, eating practically nothing. His weight dropped to eighty pounds and he repeatedly said he wished he would die. When challenged by friends who asked, "Wouldn't you miss anyone if you died?" his response was, "Yes! My Queen Anne chairs."

From November 1960 to July 1961, he was hospitalized with pneumonia, emaciation, alcoholism, exhaustion, and malnutrition, but amazingly recovered. In early 1963, he met John Cronin and fell in love again. They were inseparable. Porter changed his will, giving Cronin many of his belongings and two hundred fifty dollars a month for life. But Cronin, thirty-seven years Cole's junior, became an alcoholic, had a heart attack at age fifty, developed throat cancer and a stroke and died at age fifty-four in 1987.

Toward the end of his life, Porter and Woolley also had a permanent falling out when Woolley took an African-American servant as a lover. Porter had significant disdain for anyone of a lower class and probably for African Americans as well. He went back to Hollywood and by June 1964 he was regressing again. Wracked with constant hiccups he fell and injured himself badly. He was flown back to Harkness Pavilion in New York with the diagnosis of a hip fracture, malnutrition, and incontinence. When he returned to California he was back in the hospital with kidney stones. Fearing death from the surgery he asked Robert Raison to quickly return to his home to dispose of all the pornographic photos he had accumulated. The absence of alcohol following the surgery caused him to go into d.t.'s. Two days later on October 15, 1964, with no one with him but servants, Cole Porter died. He was buried with no eulogy in Peru, Indiana, and at his request no service was ever held for him in Hollywood or New York. His last known statement just before his surgery was to Robert Raison. He said, "Bobbie, I don't know how I did it!"

MAJOR WORKS

SHOWS:

SEE AMERICA FIRST **(1916)**
HITCHY-KOO OF 1919 **(1919)**
THE GREENWICH VILLAGE FOLLIES **(1924)**
LA REVUE DES AMBASSADEURS **(PARIS, 1928)**
PARIS **(1928)**
WAKE UP AND DREAM **(1929)**
FIFTY MILLION FRENCHMEN **(1929)**
THE NEW YORKERS **(1930)**
GAY DIVORCE **(1932)**
NYMPH ERRANT **(1933)**
ANYTHING GOES **(1934)**
JUBILEE **(1935)**
RED, HOT AND BLUE **(1936)**
YOU NEVER KNOW **(1938)**
LEAVE IT TO ME **(1938)**
DU BARRY WAS A LADY **(1939)**
PANAMA HATTIE **(1940)**
LET'S FACE IT **(1941)**
SOMETHING FOR THE BOYS **(1943)**
MEXICAN HAYRIDE **(1944)**
SEVEN LIVELY ARTS **(1944)**
KISS ME, KATE **(1948)**
OUT OF THIS WORLD **(1950)**
CAN-CAN **(1953)**
SILK STOCKINGS **(1955)**

COMPOSITIONS:

PORTER WROTE ALMOST 1,000 SONGS OVER HIS LIFETIME.

Richard Rodgers and Oscar Hammerstein working on SOUTH PACIFIC, 1949. (Photo courtesy of The Rodgers and Hammerstein Organization. All rights reserved.)

RICHARD RODGERS & OSCAR HAMMERSTEIN II

AT THE TURN OF THE CENTURY, OSCAR HAMMERSTEIN was the most important of all Broadway theatre owners and producers. A devotee of opera, he went head to head in competition with the Metropolitan Opera and the rest of musical theatre.

Oscar Hammerstein grew up in Europe and ran away from home at the age of eighteen. He came to the United States without any money. At first he earned a living creating and selling inventions. By nineteen, he married Rose Blau and had four sons before Rose died in childbirth.

Hammerstein remarried and had more children, but it was his first four sons who were involved in his theatrical enterprises.

His youngest son, Willie, married Alice Nimmo, the youngest of five children. Just before the marriage, Alice's mother found out her husband was having an affair. She vowed to leave him, but was persuaded to stay married and move in with Willie and Alice. For the remainder of their lives Alice's mother and father lived with them, in separate rooms. Alice's father never worked again and Willie supported all of them. During those early years Willie and Alice had two sons, Oscar II (the grandson of the famous producer), born on July 12, 1895, and Reggie, who was born nineteen months later.

In 1910, when Oscar was fifteen, Alice got pregnant again. She decided to have an abortion and died in the process.

The Hammerstein family was emotionally very cold. Oscar grew up with a father and a grandfather who were nonverbal and unresponsive.

In the summer of 1910, Willie, now widowed, married Alice's sister, Moussie, who had also been living with them long before Alice died.

Willie's primary job was running the Victoria Theatre for his father. He hated it. Oscar II, on the other hand, loved the theatre, but made a sworn promise to his father he would not make it his career. Four years later, while Ockie (Oscar II's lifelong nickname) was a student at Columbia, Willie got scarlet fever, developed Bright's disease, and died of kidney failure. It was 1914, and in that same year two of Willie's brothers died as well. It left Arthur as the only living son of Oscar, the family patriarch . At the time Ockie was writing varsity shows at Columbia. He soon met a bright fifteen year old, the younger brother of a fellow student, who was writing music for their shows, Richard Rodgers.

Oscar continued writing and acting in varsity shows, but was persuaded to go on to law school. His writing was not impressive. In fact, he was more successful as an actor.

In 1917, he and two friends tried to enlist in the army. His two friends were accepted but he was rejected for being underweight. He was unhappy with everything that was going on in his life, until he met a distant cousin of Richard Rodgers, Myra Finn, fell in love, and planned to marry her against both families' wishes. When finally faced with the inevitable marriage, Myra's father asked Oscar if he was a virgin. When he told him that he was, her father's response was, "You mean you're going to practice on my daughter?"

Oscar, desperately wanting to be in the theatre, went to see his only living uncle, Arthur, and asked him to give him a job. Arthur had great misgivings. He had promised Willie never to allow Oscar to make the theatre his career. He finally agreed to hire him as an assistant stage manager, if he would promise not to write for one year. Oscar did so well that Arthur gave him a permanent position.

In 1919, Arthur gave Oscar the chance to write his first play, THE LIGHT. It closed after seven performances, but Oscar took it well.

That year, the first Oscar Hammerstein died. The size of the crowd at the service at Temple Emanuel was immense.

Oscar was busier than ever, working for his uncle Arthur, when, in 1919, Actors' Equity went out on strike. With the theatres closed, it gave him the chance just to write and he began working on a musical. But he had no music. He joined with his uncle's music director, Herbert Stothart, and they wrote their first show together, JOAN OF ARKANSAW (sic). The name of the show was changed to ALWAYS YOU when it reached Broadway. It got good reviews and was a mild success.

His uncle felt that he needed to work with experienced lyricists and put him together with Otto Harbach, twenty-two years his senior, and Frank Mandel, eleven years older than Oscar. They began writing lyrics for musicals together. They worked with two composers, Vincent Youmans and Herb Stothart. One evening of a dress rehearsal, Guy Bolton, an English playwright who collaborated with Oscar, agreed to stay with Myra and their children Billy and Alice, because she was nervous about being alone. It was the beginning of an affair for Myra with Bolton, one of many she would have.

The Hammersteins moved to Great Neck in 1924, when Billy and Alice were five and three. Oscar was busier than ever. Arthur had arranged for Otto and Oscar to write the book and lyrics for a new show, ROSE-MARIE, with Rudolph Friml and Stothart doing the music. One night, during rehearsals, Oscar was having dinner with Arthur when they got an urgent call to go to the hotel where everyone was staying. Stothart's wife decided to surprise him and come visit. When she arrived she found her husband in bed with her sister and she jumped out the window to her death.

It was the beginning of a time when the book of a show was considered important instead of just a way to combine the musical numbers. Throughout his career Oscar had a running battle with critics, feeling they never understood the importance of the book.

Hammerstein's brother Reggie was managing many of the shows while Oscar was spending more and more time on his career with little time for the family. After going to London and Paris to supervise the opening of ROSE-MARIE, Harbach wanted Ockie to collaborate with him and Jerome Kern on SUNNY. It began a long-term partnership. Kern had already composed the score for ten shows by 1925 and would write ten more in the next five years.

Kern met the Hammersteins for the first time in 1902. He sat on a train next to Willie and told him he wanted to be a songwriter, though he was still working in his father's store. Willie asked him to come home with him and play. It lead to a job in a publishing house as an accompanist.

Kern's relationship with Hammerstein was a very special one. Though Kern was considered a difficult man, always insisting on perfection, he and Hammerstein got along beautifully. It was a time when the music was written first and the lyrics followed. Kern challenged Hammerstein to write lyrics for a melody with a B-natural starting every line and lasting for nine beats. Finally he came up with the lyrics for "Who?" which led Kern to decide that Hammerstein was a brilliant lyricist.

In 1925, Oscar wrote his only show with George Gershwin, SONG OF THE FLAME. It was a mixed critical and financial success.

By now Oscar was becoming very affluent. He sold his house to build a new home in Kenilworth, Long Island. It cost one hundred forty-five thousand dollars, a princely sum at that time.

Richard Rodgers and Oscar Hammerstein c. 1949. (Photo courtesy of The Rodgers and Hammerstein Organization. All rights reserved.)

In 1926, he wrote his first show with Sigmund Romberg, THE DESERT SONG. It was a huge hit and the first of five shows and four movies they wrote together. Included among their songs together were "When I Grow Too Old to Dream," "Stouthearted Men," and "Lover Come Back to Me."

Romberg was a funny, romantic, and flamboyant Hungarian. A violin prodigy, his parents wanted him to study engineering and go to the United States. Finding no work, he became a pianist at a Gypsy bar for free food. After five years he was discovered by the Shubert brothers. He went on to write MAYTIME, BLOSSOM TIME, and THE STUDENT PRINCE. Many anecdotes were told about Romberg, who was a larger-than-life character. One was about his first return trip to see his parents in Budapest after becoming famous. For days they had asked him to play his music, but he begged off. Then he took them to a concert hall and seated them alone in the orchestra. When the curtain opened there was a sixty-piece orchestra, which he conducted through two hours of his music. He left the stage in tears, so proud of what he had shown to his parents.

In 1927, Kern and Hammerstein persuaded Edna Ferber to allow them to write a musical based on her book *Show Boat*. The opening of the show was delayed due to shifting scheduling priorities by Flo Ziegfeld, the producer. Oscar was furious and left for London to supervise the European production of THE DESERT SONG. On the ship, he met Harry and Dorothy Jacobson, whose marriage was bad. Oscar's marriage was also in a state of disaster. He and Myra slept in separate bedrooms, and Myra was openly having affairs. Oscar and Dorothy shared their common misfortune with each other, and fell in love.

SHOW BOAT opened on December 27, 1927, starring Helen Morgan and Charles Winninger. It became the biggest hit Broadway had ever seen. It included the songs "Ol' Man River," "Can't Help Lovin' Dat Man," and "Make Believe."

After SHOW BOAT opened, Dorothy had another child with Harry Jacobson and decided she needed to end the relationship with Oscar. In response, he worked feverishly. He was angered by Myra's behavior and asked for a divorce, which was denied. Finally, it all became too much for him and he was hospitalized with a nervous breakdown. Shortly after that Myra agreed to a divorce. In 1929, Oscar and Dorothy were married.

That same year, Kern and Hammerstein had another success with SWEET ADELINE, once again starring Helen Morgan. In that show she sang the blockbuster hit "Why Was I Born?"

The Depression had arrived and Broadway was doing poorly. Hammerstein followed others like Rodgers and Hart and Gershwin and Kern to Hollywood. But his movies were all failures. Oscar had a long-term contract. But the films were so bad that Jack Warner paid Hammerstein one hundred thousand dollars to release him from the contract and stop writing.

It was back to Broadway. During 1930 and 1931, he had three straight failures. The economy was in such a disastrous state that his uncle, Arthur, went into bankruptcy. In 1932, things went slightly better as Hammerstein wrote the successful MUSIC IN THE AIR, which featured "The Song Is You" and "I've Told Ev'ry Little Star."

It was Oscar's last successful show for eleven years. He was only thirty-seven years old, and people were saying he was through. All through the 1930s he was dogged by the Depression. He also made the mistake of going back to Hollywood where he made a lot of money, but never had success. In 1935, he had another failed show. In all fairness, during this period Porter's JUBILEE, Rodgers and Hart's JUMBO, and Gershwin's PORGY AND BESS all lost a great deal of money, but at least they had high artistic aspirations; Hammerstein was in a creative rut.

It was a period of Ockie's life in which he began demonstrating his personal social conscience. He joined intellectuals like Dorothy Parker and Donald Ogden Stewart in the Hollywood League Against Nazism. Frederic March and Florence Eldridge were also on the board. The organization fell apart when it leaned toward Communism. Hammerstein resigned in 1938. As a result, in the 1950s, the State Department questioned him about his affiliation, because of the organization's Communist connection.

The year 1937 was a very traumatic one. While vacationing in Europe, Hammerstein got an urgent call to return, as his dearest friend, Jerome Kern, had had a massive heart attack. Shortly after, the entire world was shocked by the sudden death of George Gershwin. The eulogy for Gershwin, read by Edward G. Robinson at Temple Emanuel, was written by Ockie.

In 1937, he made his only artistically worthwhile original film, HIGH, WIDE AND HANDSOME. It was a financial failure, and Paramount terminated his contract. Columbia picked him up, but he had another failed movie, I'LL TAKE ROMANCE. It did have one great song hit, the title number.

Also that year, Hammerstein produced and/or staged three failed shows in a row, KNIGHTS OF SONG, WHERE DO WE GO FROM HERE, and GLORIOUS MORNING, the last of which grossed only three hundred fifty-five dollars and sold one orchestra seat. Still Ockie would not give up, and in 1939 wrote, with Jerome Kern, VERY WARM FOR MAY. In it was a song some critics believe is the most perfect ballad ever composed, "All the Things You Are."

The producer of VERY WARM FOR MAY, Max Gordon, remained in Hollywood all during production and rehearsal of the show. It received rave reviews in Philadelphia, Boston, and Washington, and it was predicted to be a huge success on Broadway. Gordon decided he didn't like it, and demanded it all had to be changed. Oscar, insecure from his repeated failures, did not resist and rewrote the show. The new production failed on Broadway. Although Hammerstein was not considered to have the sophistication of Porter or Hart in his lyrics, for this show he wrote one of the most sophisticated of all his songs, "All in Fun." The only thing sustaining his income was his ASCAP royalties. "All the Things You Are" reached number one on the Hit Parade.

In 1940, shortly before flying from California to New York, Hammerstein learned that Paris had fallen to the Germans. Saddened because of all the time he had spent as a young man in that city, he wrote lyrics and dropped them off with Jerome Kern before leaving. By the time Hammerstein had arrived in New York, Kern had finished the music to "The Last Time I Saw Paris." It was inserted into the movie LADY, BE GOOD and won the Academy Award for Best Song. It was Hammerstein's first song to achieve that acclaim.

Partially because of his discouragement with Broadway, he and Dorothy moved from Great Neck to a farm in Doylestown, Pennsylvania. Oscar wrote one more show with Sigmund Romberg, SUNNY RIVER. It was a complete flop and Oscar was wondering at age forty-six if he was through.

In 1941, Hammerstein had lunch with Dick Rodgers,

who complained of his difficulty in dealing with the personal problems of Larry Hart. Rodgers asked Hammerstein if he would consider a collaboration. Hammerstein, like Ira Gershwin before him, declined while Hart was still working, but agreed to do the book for SARATOGA TRUNK, which never came to pass. On his own, Hammerstein began working on a show based on the music of CARMEN, which he could do without a collaborator.

In 1942, the Theatre Guild asked Rodgers if he and Hart would make a musical from the book *Green Grow the Lilacs*. Hart refused. So Rodgers again approached Hammerstein, who this time agreed. From the beginning of their collaboration they changed the standard rule of creating a musical. Instead of the music being written first, they began with the lyrics and the music was built around them. At first they sought out Mary Martin for Laurie, and Charlotte Greenwood for Aunt Eller. Both were tied up in other projects. Greenwood ultimately played the role in the movie. Alfred Drake took the role of Curly and Celeste Holm was Ado Annie. They were able to get Rouben Mamoulian to direct and took a chance on a newcomer, Agnes de Mille, to do the choreography. Her choreography ushered in a whole new type of Broadway musical.

The initial out-of-town tryouts were not encouraging. Lots of rewriting was done and opening night was not sold out. Hart was there with his mother, which must have been very painful for him. Rodgers and Hart had written many great shows, with one, or two, or three great songs in them. But OKLAHOMA! was a show in which almost every song would become a standard.

It was a massive hit. It was said of opening night that the first scene, featuring Aunt Eller, sitting by herself downstage at a butter churn, with Alfred Drake in the background singing "Oh, What a Beautiful Mornin'" yielded an audible sigh heard throughout the theatre. Everyone was saying this was the greatest composing team ever.

Alec Wilder later wrote that Rodgers's greatest work was with Hart. Wilder felt that his musicals with Hammerstein were missing "the spark and daring flare" he had with Hart. Even Stephen Sondheim, though he was deeply devoted to Oscar Hammerstein, wrote that Hart's work had more depth and complexity. He believed that Rodgers and Hammerstein's success derived from uncomplicated optimism, such as in "The Surrey with the Fringe on Top."

At 2212 regular performances it became the longest-running musical of its time. It broke the record at London's Drury Lane Theatre, as well, with 1548 performances. After so many years of failure, Oscar came into a period of unbelievable success. Billy Rose decided to produce CARMEN JONES, which Hammerstein adapted on his own from Bizet's immortal opera. Rodgers and Hammerstein then made a hit movie, STATE FAIR, with the great songs "It's a Grand Night for Singing" and "It Might As Well Be Spring (another Academy Award winner for Best Song.)

Rodgers and Hammerstein were a good working team. Both were very well disciplined and loyal, but they were both also aloof. They functioned at arms length emotionally, with no personal relationship. Yet neither ever said anything negative about the other publicly.

It was the middle of World War II, and the country was committed to issues much larger than the theatre. Hammerstein's decision to be involved manifested itself through his position on the Writers' War Board.

Around that time, Foxy Sondheim, who was divorced, moved to Doylestown. Hammerstein's son, Jimmy, was one year younger than her son, Stephen. They became fast friends, and thus began the longtime bond of Stephen Sondheim to Oscar Hammerstein II.

Success now seemed to be around every door. Hammerstein wanted to branch out and began discussing producing a straight play based on the story "Mama's Bank Account." At the same time, Rodgers and Hammerstein were being approached about the idea of doing a musical based on Molnar's LILIOM, which became CAROUSEL. Irving Berlin said that the most beautiful show tune ever written was in that show, the very moving "You'll Never Walk Alone." CAROUSEL also contained the powerful "If I Loved You."

CAROUSEL opened in April 1945 and ran for two years. Many compared it to OKLAHOMA! It was Richard Rodgers favorite of all the shows he had written. John Raitt was the male lead and became famous for his rendition of the memorable "Soliloquy." The big up-tempo song of CAROUSEL was "June Is Bustin' Out All Over."

Four years earlier, Oscar looked like he was at the end of his career. Now he was called "The Man Who Owns Broadway." CAROUSEL, OKLAHOMA! I REMEMBER MAMA, CARMEN JONES, and a revival of ROSE-MARIE were all running at the same time. Oscar was now fifty and moving ahead with plans with Jerome Kern to do a revival of SHOW BOAT, including some new songs. A second movie version was also planned. Kern was also to write a new show based on Annie Oakley with Dorothy Fields, which Oscar Hammerstein and Richard Rodgers would produce.

While the Kerns spent time with the Hammersteins at the farm in Doylestown, Jerome and Oscar planned to meet at the rehearsal hall in Manhattan at 2 p.m. one Monday. While walking there Kern suddenly collapsed with a massive stroke. It devastated Oscar. He spent those last days at the hospital, until Kern died on November 11, 1945.

Dorothy Fields had come to Rodgers and Hammerstein with the idea of doing a musical based on Annie Oakley. Now they needed a new composer and she suggested Irving Berlin. Berlin read the script and came back with "They Say It's Wonderful" and "Doin' What Comes Natur'lly." They loved it and gave him the go ahead. Berlin added "You Can't Get a Man with a Gun," "My Defenses Are Down," "The Girl That I Marry" and the unofficial anthem of the

Composer Richard Rodgers and lyricist Oscar Hammerstein. (Photo courtesy of The Rodgers and Hammerstein Organization.

American theatre, "There's No Business Like Show Business." Two days before rehearsal, Joshua Logan, the director, said, "I need another song with some sort of competition between the lead characters." So Berlin immediately composed "Anything You Can Do." ANNIE GET YOUR GUN became second only to OKLAHOMA! as the longest-running musical on Broadway in the 1940s.

In 1947, Rodgers and Hammerstein produced a comedy, JOHN LOVES MARY, which ran for 421 performances. That was followed by their first unsuccessful show, ALLEGRO. It created a new musical art form, borrowing the theatrical simplicity of OUR TOWN, and utilizing a Greek chorus. Though neither a financial nor critical success, it was always dear to Oscar's heart.

Joshua Logan and Leland Hayward, friends of Rodgers and Hammerstein, presented them with an idea. Logan and Hayward had been impressed by James Michener's short stories. Michener had compiled them during his experiences in the Pacific Theater during World War II. The stories were titled *Tales of the South Pacific*. Logan and Hayward asked Rodgers and Hammerstein to write a show that Logan and Hayward would produce. Rodgers and Hammerstein agreed to do it only if they could co-produce and received 51 percent of the royalties. Logan and Hayward had no choice but to accept the demand. This incident provides insight into the somewhat ruthless businessmen Rodgers and Hammerstein were.

There was a great deal of excitement about the possibilities for the show. Rodgers and Hammerstein worked on it for a year. Ezio Pinza was signed first, when a show he was in got cancelled. Finally, a contract was signed with Mary Martin to play Nellie Forbush. The great opera star Pinza and his rendition of the song, "Some Enchanted Evening," became a highlight of the show.

One day, Rodgers and Hammerstein called Martin to come to Josh Logan's apartment to "give her a present." When she got there they played "A Wonderful Guy." She was so excited when she sang it that she actually fell off the piano bench.

When Mary heard they needed a song about her breaking off the romance and were going to call it "I'm Gonna Wash That Man Right Outa My Hair," she made the suggestion that she actually sing it washing her hair. They agreed, and she washed her hair 1,886 times on the stage.

Of the thirteen songs in the show, eleven became standards. Among them were the famous choral number "There Is Nothin' Like a Dame," "Younger Than Springtime" and "This Nearly Was Mine." which was known to be Pinza's favorite ballad in the show.

It opened on April 7, 1949, and ran for five years, 1,925 performances. SOUTH PACIFIC won eight Tonys and the Pulitzer Prize, and made millions of dollars in profits for its investors.

Some problems did arise with the music they had written. A major struggle came about with the song, "You've Got to Be Carefully Taught," the most serious Broadway tune about prejudice and bigotry yet written. There were many protests, even one from a state legislature. But Rodgers and Hammerstein's position was firm: "Even if it meant the fail ure of the production, it was going to stay in."

There was a dark side to the history of SOUTH PACIFIC. Logan had written at least half the book. It was his first, and he believed the show might win the Pulitzer Prize. At his wife's insistence, Logan sought co-credit for the book. He asked Oscar and got an immediate "Yes." The next day, Oscar called Logan and asked for a meeting. Hammerstein had met with Rodgers and their tough lawyer, Howard Reinheimer. Logan was offered credit in smaller print, no extra royalties, and no copyright rights. Within hours a contract appeared at Logan's attorney's office stating that if Logan did not sign it in two hours, he shouldn't come to the theatre the next day in his role as director. The three of them had been friends for years and Logan could hardly believe it. Logan accepted, but their friendship would never be the same. The reputations of those involved were well known. Most people knew Rodgers was ruthless in the business of music. Reinheimer was known as a "son of a bitch." And it was generally believed that their general manager, Morrie Jacobs, couldn't be trusted. But Hammerstein was not weak and cannot be left off the hook in assuming some responsibility for the decision.

In 1951, Hammerstein earned over three hundred forty thousand dollars just from ASCAP for the use of his songs. And in 1952, his total income was over one million dollars.

After SOUTH PACIFIC, their next show would be in 1951, THE KING AND I. Josh Logan had been offered the opportunity to write the book and direct, but turned it down because of his dispute with Rodgers and Hammerstein over the contract for SOUTH PACIFIC. It was written specifically for Gertrude Lawrence. A relative unknown, Yul Brynner, stole the show as the King. Once again the music was highly praised, including, "Hello, Young Lovers" and "I Whistle a Happy Tune."

Dorothy Sarnoff, as the King's number one wife, actually got a standing ovation in the middle of the show when she sang "Something Wonderful."

Lawrence was ill, dying of cancer, and her performances became poorer and poorer. At times near the end there was even booing.

The show was a huge success with choreography by Jerome Robbins, who created the wonderful scene and music of "Shall We Dance." The score also included "Getting to Know You."

In the midst of all these professional successes a significant event happened in the life of Hammerstein's daughter, Susan. Shortly after Henry Fonda's wife committed suicide, Fonda married Susan Hammerstein. The new couple moved into a townhouse with Fonda's children, thirteen-year-old Jane and ten-year-old Peter.

In 1953, Rodgers and Hammerstein wrote a show that did not receive good reviews, ME AND JULIET. Because of their reputation, it still was a modest financial success. Like so many other great artists, after creating a great many successful projects, the team found the quality of their work was gradually diminishing. John Steinbeck once wrote that he believed that phenomenon occurred due to the inability, after a great deal of success, to take the risk of being unconventional as they had earlier in their collaboration.

Another wonderful story associated with Rodgers and Hammerstein is about a young woman who, in 1952, came from Smithtown, Pennsylvania, to Broadway with only two hundred dollars to her name. Replacements were being sought for SOUTH PACIFIC, so an agent encouraged her to go to the open audition. An assistant was holding the audition. After waiting several hours she sang and he asked her, "Miss Jones, what have you done?"

"Nothing really," she responded.

He asked her to wait to while he called Richard Rodgers from across the street. Rodgers heard her and said he wanted her to wait while he called Oscar to come from home. She sang five or six songs from OKLAHOMA! and she was immediately hired as a replacement in SOUTH PACIFIC just ten days after she arrived in New York. In a few months, when SOUTH PACIFIC closed, she auditioned for the road company of THE KING AND I, but Rodgers and Hammerstein rejected her saying they wanted her to stay in New York as Juliet in ME AND JULIET. A few weeks later,

Richard Rodgers and Oscar Hammerstein. (Photo courtesy of The Rodgers and Hammerstein Organization. All rights reserved.)

Rodgers and Hammerstein wanted her to audition for the lead in the movie OKLAHOMA! She had a screen test and got the role in the film. She became the only performer ever under an exclusive contract to Rodgers and Hammerstein. This all happened in less than one year to Shirley Jones.

Shortly before she was to leave for Hollywood, she was called to Rodgers's office where he kissed her when she arrived. After asking her many personal questions about her marital status he began getting closer and closer to her. She knew his reputation and cleverly said, "You're just like a father to me."

In 1953, Rodgers and Hammerstein started on a musical version of Steinbeck's *Cannery Row*. The title was changed to PIPE DREAM. It was scheduled to open in 1955, but there were terrible problems. On the day rehearsals began Rodgers felt a pain in his jaw. It was diagnosed as cancer and major surgery was performed. Subsequently, Rodgers developed depression and alcohol abuse. The show had a huge advance sale, but the reviews were mixed and it ended as the greatest financial loss of their career.

They turned their attention to a television version of CINDERELLA with Julie Andrews as the lead. Reviewers said it was not of the same caliber as their Broadway shows.

In 1958, during the writing and rehearsals of FLOWER DRUM SONG, problems again arose. Oscar was hospitalized twice for surgery and his brother died of a heart attack. Meanwhile Rodgers was out for three months with depression and alcoholism. The show, however, turned out to be a financial success. Nevertheless, once again, reviews indicated it was not of the quality of their earlier great shows. The three biggest hits in the show were "Love, Look Away," "You Are Too Beautiful," and "I Enjoy Being a Girl."

The following March, they began working on THE SOUND OF MUSIC. By June the writing was completed and production began. Rehearsals started in the last week of August. On September 16, Oscar went for his annual checkup stating he got very hungry in the middle of the night. Tests showed he had cancer of the stomach. At surgery it was grade four, extremely aggressive, and the doctors removed three fourths of his stomach. The doctors told Dorothy he had only about six months to a year to live, but decided not to tell Hammerstein of the severity. He continued working on the show, writing at that time the beautiful "Edelweiss."

The show opened on November 16, 1959. It was, of course, a huge success. Besides the beautiful title song performed by Mary Martin (and Julie Andrews in the film version), the show had "My Favorite Things," "Do-Re-Mi" and "Sixteen Going on Seventeen" The initial reviews were not great, but it became a massive hit.

Oscar said he was feeling very well and began planning to write a new version of STATE FAIR. He also wanted to completely rewrite one of his favorites, ALLEGRO. The two of them went for five weeks, in March 1960, to supervise production of the London opening of FLOWER DRUM SONG. But Oscar began feeling tired and weak. In July a recurrence was found and chemotherapy was started.

Hammerstein knew that he was dying. One by one he said farewell to his friends at luncheons and meetings. By August he was so thin his daughter Susan said he reminded her of the El Greco paintings with the long spindly fingers. On Monday night August 22, 1960, Oscar Hammerstein passed away quietly at home.

Richard Rodgers was only fifty-eight years old. At first he had a difficult time facing up to Hammerstein's illness and death, but was determined to continue to work. Overtures were made to Alan Jay Lerner who had just split from Fritz Loewe, but Lerner said he wouldn't be available for a year. So Rodgers decided he would try to write both the music and lyrics by himself. Collaborating with book writer Samuel Taylor, they came up with the idea for NO STRINGS. He specifically wanted to write a show for Diahann Carroll. He fell madly in love with her, begging her to go out with him with tears in his eyes. But Carroll had her own problems. She was married to Monty Kay and they had a child. Besides that she was in love with Sidney Poitier who was also married and had children. She kept Rodgers at arms length.

Carroll had developed a strong dislike for Richard Rodgers ever since an incident when they were dining together. She never quite got over the shock of hearing him discuss Larry Hart and saying about NO STRINGS, "how wonderful it feels to have written this score and not have to search all over the globe for that drunken little fag." Everyone in the business had great affection for Hart, even with all his foibles. She was offended by how Rodgers had demeaned him. At first there was negative reaction to NO STRINGS because of the interracial love affair at its core, but it turned out to be a hit.

By 1963, Rodgers and Lerner were considering once again the possibility of collaborating on a new show. But Rodgers didn't know about Lerner's terribly neurotic writer's block. Lerner would lie, saying the lyrics were done, and never show up for meetings. One time he actually disappeared for weeks. Very quickly that relationship was officially ended.

Arthur Laurents brought Rodgers together with the young Stephen Sondheim, because he was Hammerstein's protégé. The match did not go well. Rodgers was drinking a lot again. He would fall asleep and snore during rehearsals and there were many arguments between them. The show they wrote together was DO I HEAR A WALTZ? and it had only a mediocre run.

In 1969, Rodgers had a heart attack. When he got better, he wrote TWO BY TWO for Danny Kaye, but the show was not successful.

After several projects fell through, Rodgers began working with the lyricist Sheldon Harnick on a show to be called REX. During the project Rodgers developed hoarseness. He was found to have throat cancer and had a laryngectomy. The show ran for just over a month and the entire investment was lost. Although he was gradually getting weaker, Rodgers wanted to write another show and began working with Martin Charnin on a musical version of I REMEMBER MAMA.

His personal life was going very badly as well. Rodgers and his wife, Dorothy, were fighting constantly. Subsequently, one of their children wrote that she finally realized her parents hated each other. (A full discussion of Rodgers's personal life appears in the next chapter, "Richard Rodgers and Lorenz Hart.") I REMEMBER MAMA opened in May 1979 for a short run before closing.

Rodgers became increasingly ill, at times having seizures and hallucinating. He suffered terrible headaches and probably had brain metastases from his malignancies. Richard Rodgers died on December 30, 1979, three months after I REMEMBER MAMA closed. A private funeral was held at Temple Emanuel and he was cremated. No one knows what was done with the ashes. At his eulogy it was noted he wrote thirty-nine musicals, numerous film and television scores, and nine hundred songs.

MAJOR WORKS

SHOWS:

ALWAYS YOU **(HAMMERSTEIN AND STOTHART, 1920)**
WILDFLOWER **(HAMMERSTEIN, HARBACH, YOUMANS, AND STOTHART, 1923)**
ROSE-MARIE **(HAMMERSTEIN, HARBACH, FRIML, AND STOTHART, 1924)**
SONG OF THE FLAME **(HAMMERSTEIN, GERSHWIN, AND STOTHART, 1925)**
WILD ROSE **(HAMMERSTEIN, HARBACH, AND FRIML, 1926)**
THE DESERT SONG **(HAMMERSTEIN AND ROMBERG, 1926)**
GOLDEN DAWN **(HAMMERSTEIN AND STOTHART, 1927)**
SHOW BOAT **(HAMMERSTEIN AND KERN, 1927)**
THE NEW MOON **(HAMMERSTEIN AND ROMBERG, 1928)**
RAINBOW **(HAMMERSTEIN AND YOUMANS, 1928)**
SWEET ADELINE **(HAMMERSTEIN AND KERN, 1929)**
FREE FOR ALL **(HAMMERSTEIN AND WHITING, 1931)**
EAST WIND **(HAMMERSTEIN AND ROMBERG, 1931)**
MUSIC IN THE AIR **(HAMMERSTEIN AND KERN, 1932)**
BALL AT THE SAVOY **(HAMMERSTEIN AND ABRAHAM, 1933)**
THREE SISTERS **(HAMMERSTEIN AND KERN, 1934)**
MAY WINE **(HAMMERSTEIN AND ROMBERG, 1935)**
VERY WARM FOR MAY **(HAMMERSTEIN AND KERN, 1939)**
SUNNY RIVER **(HAMMERSTEIN AND ROMBERG, 1941)**
CARMEN JONES **(HAMMERSTEIN AND BIZET, 1943)**
OKLAHOMA! **(1943)**
CAROUSEL **(1945)**
ALLEGRO **(1947)**
SOUTH PACIFIC **(1949)**
THE KING AND I **(1951)**
ME AND JULIET **(1953)**
PIPE DREAM **(1955)**
FLOWER DRUM SONG **(1958)**
THE SOUND OF MUSIC **(1959)**
NO STRINGS (RODGERS, **1962)**
DO I HEAR A WALTZ? **(RODGERS AND SONDHEIM, 1965)**
TWO BY TWO **(RODGERS AND CHARNIN, 1970)**
REX **(RODGERS AND HARNICK, 1976)**
I REMEMBER MAMA **(RODGERS AND CHARNIN/JESSEL, 1979)**

COMPOSITIONS:

RICHARD RODGERS WROTE OVER 900 SONGS WITH SEVERAL DIFFERENT LYRICISTS. OSCAR HAMMERSTEIN WROTE MORE THAN 400 WITH MULTIPLE COMPOSERS.

Composer Richard Rodgers and lyricist Lorenz Hart, 1941. (Photo courtesy of The Rodgers and Hammerstein Organization.)

RICHARD RODGERS & LORENZ HART

THE COURSE OF THE LIVES OF THESE TWO SHINING geniuses of the theatre is truly fascinating.

Max Myers Hertz, twenty years old and one of nine children, and Frieda Eisenberg, age eighteen and one of ten, married in 1886. They lived on the tough and dirty Lower East Side, in the Tammany-controlled Fourth Ward. There Max became a promoter, politician, fixer and wheeler-dealer. He changed his name from Hertz to Hart.

Their first child died. Two boys were soon born: Lorenz in 1895 and then Teddy. Max made a great deal of money in his ventures and the boys were well educated. Through Max's contacts, the boys became widely exposed to theatre and the personalities of that day. At age six Lorenz was writing poetry, and by the time they were in their teens he and Teddy were putting on shows for the family.

Lorenz, who was soon being called Larry, lovingly called his father "the crook." Max was bigger than life in his public dealings. He was only five feet tall and a dynamo. A story he loved to tell about himself was that he had been appointed assistant coroner for New York City through political connections. As he described it, the coroner was always drunk, so Max was frequently called in the case of suspicious deaths. The story, probably apocryphal, was that he had received a call one Sunday morning to go to the Vanderbilt estate in Manhattan. There he was greeted by Cornelius, the entire family in the drawing room, and Cornelius's son, lying dead on the floor. There was a bandanna around the head of the deceased.

Cornelius said, "He unexpectedly had a stroke . . . please sign the death certificate as natural causes."

Max removed the bandanna and found a bullet hole right in the middle of his forehead.

Cornelius said, "There must be some way we can keep this quiet."

Max supposedly replied, "Ten thousand dollars."

Vanderbilt agreed, and said he would write a check.

Max rejected that with, "Cash."

Vanderbilt protested that it was Sunday and there was no way he could get the money.

When Max insisted, "No cash, no deal," Vanderbilt came up with the money and the certificate was signed off as natural causes. No one will ever know if it was true because it was the kind of story Max would make up to promote himself.

Larry and Teddy were spending their summers at a camp called the Weingart Institute in the Catskills, with the likes of the Bonwits, the Selznicks, Oscar Hammerstein II, and Herbert Sondheim (Stephen's father). There they wrote and acted in shows.

Larry went on to Columbia Journalism School, but his only interest was in writing the school variety shows. He quit in the middle of his studies and took a job translating German shows into English.

A group, the Akron Club, put on a charity show every year at the Plaza Hotel. In 1917 they had brought in an extremely impressive fifteen-year-old to write the music, Richard Rodgers. Although he was too young to be a member of the club, Rodgers's brother Mortimer belonged to the club. The Club soon decided that there was no one good enough to write lyrics for his music. One member knew about Larry Hart, and suggested that they introduce the two of them and see if it might work.

Dick Rodgers was of average height for fifteen, athletic, and neatly groomed. When he arrived at Hart's home and the door opened, there stood Larry Hart, unshaven, a twenty-two-year-old, barely five feet tall, in slippers and a robe, with a cigar in his mouth. They talked. That is, mostly Larry talked, to this young boy who sat at the piano, played, and shared music and lyrics. They made an immediate connection.

The two of them had come from completely different backgrounds. Hart had education, wealth, and sophistication. Rodgers came from a modest family. His father was a family doctor. Richard Rodgers was born in 1902. At thirteen, he saw a show by Jerome Kern, a composer he would idealize, and determined that composing would be his profession.

In those early years, Rodgers was just developing as a melodist. Hart was by far the dominant partner for the first ten years of their partnership. Rodgers realized that Hart had know-how, contacts, and sophistication far beyond his own. He also came to learn that Hart drank too much, smoked too much, stayed up until dawn and slept until noon.

A third individual soon became a part of their team: Herbert Fields. Fields's father, Joe Fields, comprised one-half of the most successful comedy pair in vaudeville, Weber and Fields. Besides performing, Weber and Fields were producers and theatre owners. Ultimately, they broke up, but Fields continued as a Broadway owner and producer. His son, Herbert , became a close associate of Dick and Larry's and wrote the books for a number of shows with them. His sister, Dorothy Fields, also became a friend and a very successful Broadway lyricist.

In 1919, Herb persuaded his father to put a Rodgers and Hart song into one of his shows. It was "Any Old Place with You," and was performed by Alan Hale. This was Rodgers and Hart's first song on Broadway. Unfortunately, the show, A LONELY ROMEO, was a complete flop and closed in a few weeks, and the song vanished.

Broadway musicals at that time were completely different from today. They were variety shows. There was no story line. Frequently the music of more than one composer would be in the same show. Writers might prepare ten or fifteen songs and find when the show opened that only one or none remained. The producer did whatever he wished with the music he received. Not infrequently a song would be recycled from a previous show because it had been well received. Broadway itself was booming. Gershwin and Irving Caesar wrote "Swanee" which, apocryphally, was said to have been completed in ten minutes. It made them into millionaires. But Dick and Larry were still essentially amateurs, writing for college and charity shows without pay.

Around this time Larry developed a relationship with "Doc" Bender, a dentist and overt homosexual. Bender was extremely disliked in the theatrical community except by Larry Hart. Everyone felt he was a hanger-on, who would take everything he could get from Larry. Though Hart was not yet successful in the theatre, he was financially very secure.

Rodgers and Hart wrote their first Akron Club charity show, YOU'D BE SURPRISED, and followed with a Columbia Varsity Show eighteen days later titled FLY WITH ME.

In 1920, Lew Fields opened POOR LITTLE RITZ GIRL in Boston and asked Larry and Dick to write the entire score, seventeen songs, which they accomplished in just several weeks. Once the work was completed, they went off on their annual summer season at the Weingart camp in the Catskills. When they returned they sadly found almost all of their songs had been replaced by Fields with others from Sigmund Romberg.

In 1921, Dick, now nineteen, fell in love with Helen Ford, a married performer who was becoming successful. It would be the first of many such encounters for him.

Composer Richard Rodgers and lyricist Lorenz Hart. (Photo courtesy of The Rodgers and Hammerstein Organization. All rights reserved.)

The 1922–23 Broadway season was very weak. Larry was growing tired of their amateur productions. Dick quit Columbia and enrolled in what would subsequently become Juilliard. Their partnership was in the doldrums. Rodgers took a job as a conductor in a Lew Fields musical and Larry went back to the Catskills, and for one hundred dollars a song wrote lyrics for the extremely disliked and disreputable Billy Rose. Rose took those songs and used them under his name. Among songs credited to Billy Rose it has been suggested that "Barney Google," "That Old Gang of Mine," "A Cup of Coffee a Sandwich and You," and "Me and My Shadow" were all written by others, possibly Hart.

In 1924, Rodgers and Hart had the opportunity to present a score called WINKLE TOWN to Max Dreyfus, a powerhouse publisher on Broadway. He characterized it as "nothing of value." They were completely discouraged. We think of Rodgers and Hart as being so successful, but seven full years had passed for them with no success whatsoever. They were so down on their careers they decided to try writing a straight play under the pseudonym of Herbert Richard Lorenz. (Fields, Rodgers, Hart) starring Fred Bickel. Bickel later changed his name to Frederic March. The play was a total flop.

The following year, Hart was ready to throw in the towel. He was thirty years old without a single financial success. At the same time, Kern and Hammerstein had big hits on Broadway.

Finally, in early 1925, Dick Rodgers got an offer to work for an underwear wholesaler for fifty dollars a week with an opportunity for advancement. To the surprise of the owner, Dick asked if he could have a few days to think it over. And then their lives changed.

During those few days, the Theatre Guild asked Rodgers to write another musical for a benefit. Hart refused, saying he was tired of writing amateur shows. But

Composer Richard Rodgers and lyricist Lorenz Hart, c. 1930s. (Photo courtesy of The Rodgers and Hammerstein Organization. All rights reserved.)

Rodgers persuaded him to do just one more. They decided to use a song that had been rejected every time it had been presented in the past, "Manhattan."

The officers of the Guild loved it. They wrote fourteen more songs for the revue, called THE GARRICK GAIETIES. It was scheduled for two performances in May 1925. The show was a tremendous success and the audience demanded ten encores to "Manhattan." For the second performance Hart wrote additional verses they could do for encore after encore. There was so much demand that the show was performed at other theatres on off days. Finally, it was opened on its own and ran for 211 performances. Rodgers and Hart each received fifty dollars a week and had seven songs published. Hart was ecstatic. He rented limousines after performances to drive the cast for parties on the beach on Long Island, where they would lie out in the sand singing all night. Everyone was gloriously happy and they adored Larry Hart.

Their new success was immediately followed by DEAREST ENEMY, a show they had written earlier about the

Revolutionary War. Initially it had been completely rejected by producers. It ran for 286 performances and Rodgers was smitten again with one of the leads. Life was good. Hart could be found usually drunk in speakeasies. *Variety* reported they were earning five thousand dollars weekly. They were now in a class with George and Ira Gershwin and Vincent Youmans.

Their 1926 show, THE GIRL FRIEND, was a mediocre show but had a big hit, "The Blue Room." It ran for 301 performances on Broadway and then went on an eight-city tour. Working feverishly, Rodgers and Hart contributed a new score to the 1926 edition of THE GARRICK GAIETIES. One of their new songs was one of their best: "Mountain Greenery."

Their next venture was to create a show in London. They went there and wrote LIDO LADY, but hated the experience. Many of their songs were dropped, and once it opened, they returned by ship. During that trip, Rodgers met his future wife, Dorothy, a privileged daughter of a very famous attorney.

Dick and Larry had returned with a commitment to write another 1926 show, PEGGY-ANN, with Herb Fields, but they had forgotten that they also agreed to do a show, BETSY, for Ziegfeld. The two shows opened a week apart. PEGGY-ANN was a hit and ran for a year, while BETSY was a dismal failure. BETSY was so bad that its star, Belle Baker, begged Irving Berlin the night before the opening to write a song for her. He said he had only parts of songs written. Berlin worked all night with her and her husband and came up with a song she performed the very next evening. "Blue Skies" became the only bright point in the show and had twenty-eight encores. Rodgers and Hart were terribly embarrassed by the entire episode.

After a great year in 1926, in 1927 they wrote ONE DAM THING AFTER ANOTHER. While writing it they were in a near-miss auto accident, and when one of the young women in the car with them said immediately afterward, "My heart stood still," Rodgers supposedly noted it on a pad, went back to the apartment, and wrote a song with that very title.

The show opened at the Palladium to terrible reviews. The Prince of Wales was in the audience opening night. Later at a Yacht Club party in London he asked the bandleader if he knew the song, "My Heart Stood Still." He didn't, but the prince had written it down and sang it for him. The story hit the newspaper. Ticket sales soared and it ran for 237 performances.

That was followed by the tremendously successful Broadway production of A CONNECTICUT YANKEE with its smash hit, "Thou Swell."

All the while Hart's personal life was in a shambles. His father had personal setbacks and went into bankruptcy. Their house, where Hart still lived, was sold. But Larry went on spending wildly with grand and wild parties. Rodgers and Fields found Hart impossible to work with, as he rarely showed up for meetings, and disappeared for days at a time.

The end of 1928 brought Rodgers and Hart's worst failure, a show titled CHEE-CHEE. Besides the show being so bad, there were difficult times approaching. Many of the legitimate theaters on Broadway were being turned into talking picture houses. Prohibition was in its heyday and the effects of the Depression were just starting to hit home. Gangland activity was rampant even on Broadway. The star Ruth Etting had a boyfriend called Moe "The Gimp" Snyder. He liked to come backstage and tease people by sticking a loaded gun into their ribs and saying, "Stick 'em up."

In 1929, Rodgers and Hart wrote the show SPRING IS HERE, which flopped, but had in it the beautiful "With a Song in My Heart."

Rodgers and Hart promised to do a show for Ziegfeld called SIMPLE SIMON. Ziegfeld was a terror and a tyrant. As the story goes, a friend of his jumped out of a window due to the Wall Street crash. Immediately afterward, Ziegfeld had the nerve to contact the widow and tell her that her husband had promised to back the show with twenty thousand dollars. She immediately sent him the money and the plan went ahead. The show had a very short run but featured one great standard, "Ten Cents a Dance" (introduced by Ruth Etting).

During that time Dick became engaged to Dorothy Feiner, whom he had met as a teenager on the return trip from Europe five years earlier. They got married six days after the opening and went to the south of France on their honeymoon.

Who was Dorothy Feiner?

Her grandmother married a wealthy importer who had demanded that his four spinster sisters live with them. In the family they were known as the "evil sisters." Sometime in the 1880s she did a most radical thing. She took her two young daughters, left her husband, and moved to California. One of those daughters, May Adelson, was gorgeous and became known as the Belle of San Francisco. May returned to New York and met Ben Feiner, an immigrant's son. He was a brilliant student and then a lawyer, and eventually became one of the leading attorneys in New York. They were married in 1903, when he was twenty-seven and she was twenty-five. Their second child, Dorothy, was born in 1909. Terribly spoiled, she became known as the "princess."

When she met Dick Rodgers in 1925 she fell madly in love, but she was very young. Over the next few years they saw each other on occasion, and she went off to school at Wellesley. She would have gladly quit school and married him, but he seemed ever elusive, with so many showgirls at his feet. In 1927 and 1928 he was writing to her about once a month. In 1928, Dorothy left with her parents for Europe after she and Dick came to an understanding that they would see each other less often. He found that the separation depressed him. Possibly he was tiring of his well-known escapades with showgirls. But Dorothy remained in Europe until mid-1929. When she returned they decided to marry in 1930. She became pregnant quite quickly and Dick was off to Hollywood to work on a movie. Two days after his return, in early August, he was off to London to work on another new show, EVER GREEN, and remained there until late October. On the way over he wrote an unbelievable letter, subsequently known as the "boat letter," in which he said that he missed her terribly, and that he had a tremendous urge to make love with her. And, if he ever, somehow, ended up sleeping with someone else on the boat, he would tell her and know that she would understand. She was, of course, devastated by the letter. Her father had warned her before they were married not to take the vows if she couldn't cope with the fact that Rodgers would be constantly surrounded by other women. She didn't listen, and throughout his life Rodgers remained an unrepentant womanizer.

EVER GREEN opened in London in December 1930 and was a huge hit. Dorothy wrote constantly in a panic, begging Rodgers to come home, but he was enjoying himself in a social circle with the likes of Noel Coward, Prince George, and the King of Greece. When he finally did return reluctantly in October, he was miffed at having missed all the grand opening night parties.

Mary Rodgers was born in the beginning of 1931, a year that saw two Rodgers and Hart failures: a movie, THE HOT HEIRESS, and a stage musical, AMERICA'S SWEETHEART (their last original show with Herbert Fields). Then, it was off to Hollywood for the next four years. In 1932, they wrote their only really successful movie, LOVE ME TONIGHT. It had three hit songs: "Lover," "Isn't It Romantic?," and a song to be associated forever with the picture's star, Maurice Chevalier, "Mimi."

But it was a terrible year personally, as Dorothy's father developed diabetes that was not well controlled. He stopped working completely and became depressed. One evening, after Dorothy and he had an argument, he committed suicide. She never got over it.

The state of Broadway was such that, although Rodgers and Hart despised most of their film assignments, it was preferable for them to stay in Hollywood. Dick spent most of his time on the tennis court, and Larry just kept disappearing, almost certainly for his secret homosexual encounters. Dorothy went back to New York and Dick was drinking heavily and melancholic when he read a column saying, "Whatever happened to Rodgers and Hart?" For Rodgers, it was a sure sign that their careers were moving in the wrong direction.

Another terrible movie made with Al Jolson, HALLELUAH, I'M A BUM, was a disaster except for one song, "You Are Too Beautiful."

By December 1933, they were thoroughly disenchanted with Hollywood. Hart was thirty-eight and Rodgers was thirty-one. Hart was living wildly, asking several different women to marry him, but always being turned down. Many really liked, and even loved him, but wouldn't consider marrying him because of his alcoholism and homosexuality. He was thought of as a kind and gentle man. But he was seen more and more in the company of the "beautiful boys" who were apparently arranged for by "Doc" Bender, who had essentially become Hart's pimp.

They wrote two more movies—one in1934, one the next year–and they were both disappointments. But the big news on Broadway was Billy Rose's planned extravaganza JUMBO. Billy asked them to do it and they wrote the best score they had created in years. As a horde of gorgeous women paraded across the stage, the chorus sang, "The Most Beautiful Girl in the World." JUMBO also featured "Little Girl Blue," and the show's biggest hit of all, "My Romance." Another song written for JUMBO was "There's a Small Hotel." It has been said that Hart hated the music from that song so much that for months he refused to write lyrics for it. When he finally did it was dropped from JUMBO. Later the song would be placed into ON YOUR TOES. It became one of that show's biggest hits.

JUMBO was followed immediately by ON YOUR TOES, which featured the great ballet "Slaughter on Tenth Avenue" and a song which captured Hart's melancholy philosophy of romance: "Glad to Be Unhappy." With JUMBO and ON YOUR TOES, Rodgers and Hart had the two longest running shows of the 1935–36 season.

After another poor movie in 1936, they wrote the finest score they had created up to that time, BABES IN ARMS. It included, "Where or When," the big up-tempo number "Johnny-One-Note," as well as another great song demonstrating Hart's pained outlook on love. "I Wish I Were in Love Again." They worked to find the perfect song for the star of BABES IN ARMS, Mitzi Green. They came up with the hit, "The Lady Is a Tramp." This spectacular score also included "My Funny Valentine."

They were reaching the pinnacle of success. Rodgers was becoming more dominant, while Hart was more of a problem. Though he always wore expensive clothes, now Hart looked rumpled and disheveled when seen in public. Rodgers believed that Hart would be an impediment to him in his future endeavors. Hart seemed to be under tremendous tension, incessantly rubbing his hands together as he spoke to people. The famous jazz singer Mabel Mercer said of Hart, "He was the loneliest man I ever knew. Even lonely in the crowds he created."

In 1937, Rodgers and Hart agreed to write a political satire about Franklin D. Roosevelt called I'D RATHER BE RIGHT starring George M. Cohan. They had unpleasant experiences with Cohan in the past, but it was difficult to say "no" to such a big star and their collaborators, George S. Kaufman and Moss Hart (no relation). It was a hit, and Rodgers and Hart were more than ever the kings of Broadway.

From 1936 to 1940, they had seven hugely successful shows. They earned more than one hundred thousand dollars annually each during the Depression. They were in a class

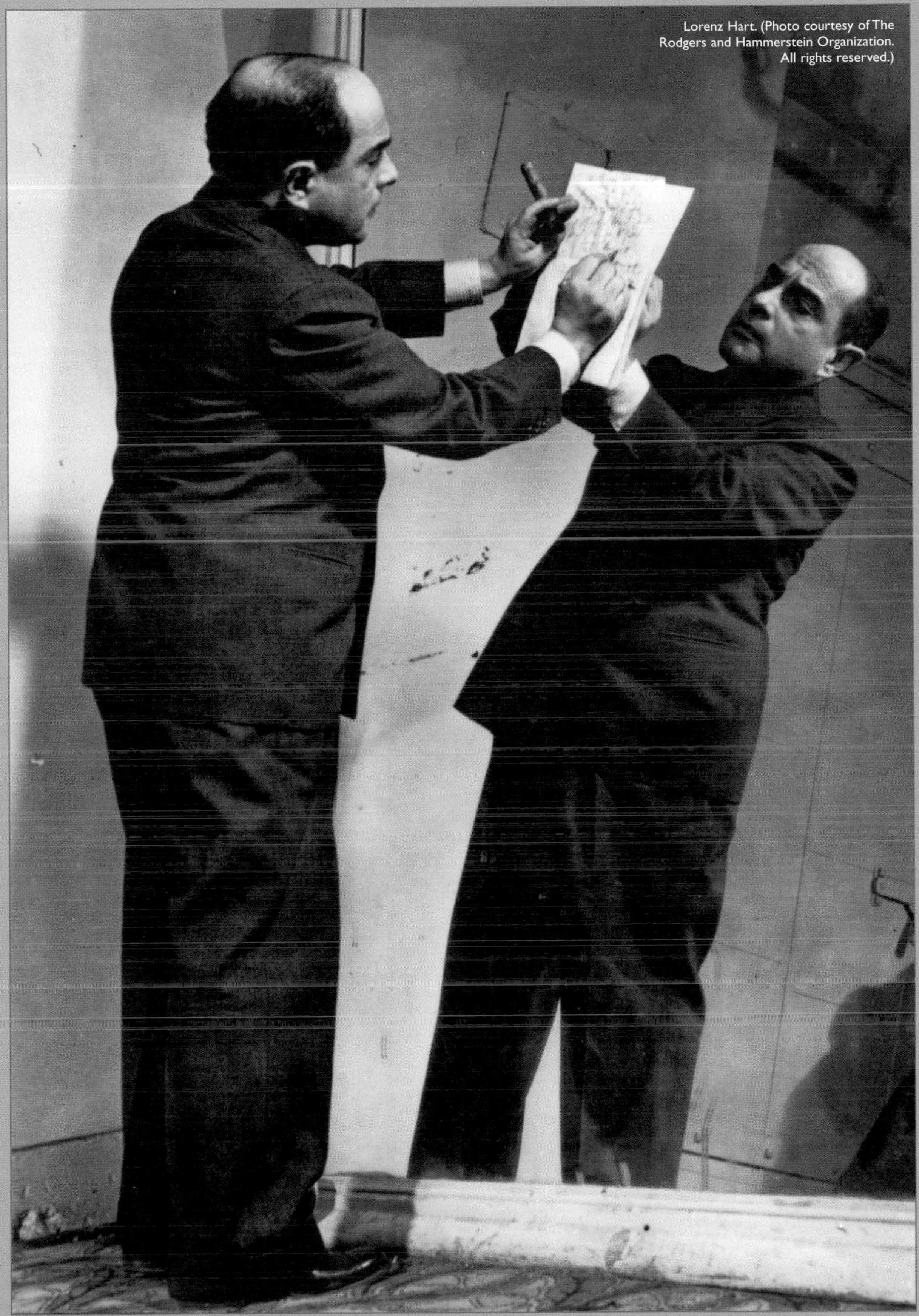

Lorenz Hart. (Photo courtesy of The Rodgers and Hammerstein Organization.)

with Kern and Porter. However, things were not going well in either household. Mary Rodgers said of her father that he was cold, and her mother was hypercritical and mean. Stephen Sondheim referred to Dorothy as being homophobic and treating Hart awfully. As the years went, Rodgers's two daughters thought their mother controlled their father, causing him to drink more and more. And by the spring of 1937, Dorothy actively began questioning his peccadilloes.

Larry Hart's true downfall began in 1938. He spent constant time with Doc Bender, flamboyantly pursuing men together, much the way that Cole Porter did with Monty Woolley. His writing was still brilliant, but sporadic, and Dick was constantly trying to get him to work. At times Hart couldn't be found and corrections of lyrics had to be made by Rodgers. Hart's mother was still living with him. Once his sister-in-law, visiting, came into his mother's bedroom during one of his wild parties and asked if the noise didn't bother her. She responded, "Not really. Except maybe that night when the whole Paul Whiteman band came in." On another occasion his mother walked into the living room only to find a totally naked girl dancing on the piano. She placed her fur coat over the girl saying, "Poor child! You must be freezing."

In 1938, they were starting on I MARRIED AN ANGEL, but they had no book or story. So Rodgers persuaded Joshua Logan to meet with Larry Hart in Atlantic City. Hart only wanted to play cards. Finally, Rodgers locked them in Hart's apartment until the story was written. It was a constant struggle. Vivienne Segal was the star of the show. As he had so many times in the past, Hart asked her to marry him and was again turned down.

I MARRIED AN ANGEL was a smash hit and soon joined BABES IN ARMS and ON YOUR TOES, which still were running on Broadway. All three shows were made into movies (although they were pale imitations of the originals). A *Time* magazine cover, a profile in the *New Yorker*, and a new musical—the first one ever to be based on Shakespeare—made it clear that they were at their peak. The new show, THE BOYS FROM SYRACUSE, was another hit. It had in it "This Can't Be Love" and "Falling In Love with Love." Hart was seriously ill during rehearsals and missed everything including opening night.

Although the partnership was struggling due to Hart's alcoholism, probable drug addiction, wild sexual behavior, illnesses, and long disappearances, in 1939 they wrote another hit, TOO MANY GIRLS, starring Desi Arnaz. The standout song was "I Didn't Know What Time It Was."

George Gershwin had died suddenly in 1937, and as a result, Richard Rodgers, in 1938 or 1939, secretly asked Ira Gershwin to collaborate, but was turned down. No one wanted to break up Rodgers and Hart.

In 1940, they had a flop, HIGHER AND HIGHER. Hart missed much of the writing time and almost all of the rehearsal. Not being able to find Hart, Rodgers did all of the rewriting. Still, Hart wrote one of his greatest and most poignant lyrics, for "It Never Entered My Mind."

With all their problems, 1940 brought them to their absolute pinnacle. The writer John O'Hara was a friend of Hart's (and also an alcoholic) who was writing a series of vignettes for the *New Yorker*. He suggested to Rodgers and Hart that they write a musical based on the stories. The concept was unheard of at the time. The lead would be a lowlife antihero. PAL JOEY would be a serious show about the seedy side of life. It would star a dynamic newcomer, Gene Kelly. During the production O'Hara, Hart, and Kelly were drinking buddies every night. The music and lyrics were sophisticated and spectacular. "Zip," sung by a character mocking the style of Gypsy Rose Lee got such accolades in the tryouts that every day Hart would write additional verses on scraps of paper for the constantly demanded reprises. Vivienne Segal starred with Kelly. Hart knew this was his greatest work. He worked diligently and incessantly with all of his behavioral problems put aside.

Brooks Atkinson of the *New York Times*, who had the power to make or break a show, wrote that though brilliant he wondered if you could make a musical out of an odious story, and asked, "Can you draw sweet water from a foul well?" Hart read it and locked himself in a room sobbing, crying like a baby. Besides "Zip," the score included "I Could Write a Book," "In Our Little Den (Of Iniquity)" and "Do It the Hard Way," all with great double entendres. Its biggest hit was the classic, "Bewitched, Bothered And Bewildered."

Though very controversial, PAL JOEY ran for a year. Ten years later, in a different social climate, it was the most successful revival in the history of Broadway, and Atkinson apologized, completely reversing his opinion . . . but by this time, Lorenz Hart was already dead.

By 1941, Hart was drunk every day by noon. His sexual promiscuity was getting the better of his common sense and at times being badly beaten. He was hospitalized repeatedly at Doctors Hospital, signing himself out before discharge. Rodgers tried to get Hart's family to commit him to an institution, but they refused.

Through all that, in 1942, Hart was able to write another show with Rodgers, BY JUPITER, starring Ray Bolger. It became their longest running show. It was in that year that the Theatre Guild decided to do a musical based on the play GREEN GROW THE LILACS. Kern was approached, and turned it down. Rodgers accepted and presented it to Hart, who complained he was too tired to work and was going with Doc Bender to Mexico. Rodgers said he would join Hart if he admitted himself to a sanatorium and stay there until the show was completed. Hart refused, saying he and Doc Bender were leaving. Rodgers threatened that if Hart left he would ask Hammerstein. Hart calmly said that was a great idea, and that he didn't think the play was very good anyway. When Hart walked out

Rodgers claims to have broken down and cried.

Early reports from tryouts on OKLAHOMA!—the new name of the show—were not good. Hart returned sick from Mexico and was taken directly to Doctors Hospital. Rodgers was now working with Hammerstein. So when Hart got out he started working on a new musical with a Viennese composer, Emmerich Kalman, which never got off the ground. Kalman's daughter said the reason was that every time Hart and Kalman met, Hart was falling down drunk. Hart attended the opening night of OKLAHOMA! with his mother. The reviews were phenomenal, which must have been very painful to him. Three weeks later his mother was hospitalized, operated on, and died. Hart, devastated, went straight from the funeral into a drunken stupor.

In the summer of 1943, Rodgers persuaded Hart to join him in a revival of A CONNECTICUT YANKEE. Hart actually sobered up and worked hard. Once again the star was Vivienne Segal, and once again she turned down Hart's proposal of marriage. He reverted back into his drunken stupor. He planned to go to the opening with Dorothy Hart, his sister-in-law. By show time he was completely drunk. Rodgers, trying to avoid problems, left word with security guards that if Hart caused any commotion, they should take him out. Hart somehow found his way backstage and the first act went without a problem. But during the second act he sang the lyrics so loudly from the wings they could be heard in the audience. Guards escorted him out to the foyer. The weather was nasty that night and Dorothy took him home and let him sleep fully clothed on the sofa. In the morning, in continuing bad weather, Hart was gone and without a coat. Not heard from by that evening, friends began looking for him. Fritz Loewe, of Lerner and Loewe, found him sitting drunk and soaked on a curb in the pouring rain.

They took him to Doctors Hospital where he was diagnosed with pneumonia. He was critically ill. Eleanor Roosevelt interceded in his behalf to get him penicillin, available at that time only for military personnel. But it was not sufficient. At 9:30 p.m., Monday, November 22, 1943, Larry Hart died. He was buried at Mount Zion Cemetery, with no music at his memorial service. Many of the theatre's luminaries attended the funeral. Larry Hart lies in an inauspicious site with an incineration plant on one side and the Long Island Expressway on the other. After his death, his family and Richard Rodgers engaged in ugly battles over his will.

Over twenty-six years, Rodgers and Hart wrote eleven amateur shows, thirty-four Broadway shows, twenty-seven movies, and 650 songs. They were an amazing pair. Rodgers was the ultimate melodist and Hart was without peer when it came to words. Most agree he was the poet laureate of the American musical theatre. As for the personal side of Larry Hart, one biographer said Hart was lovable, generous, brilliant, tragic, infuriating, and irrepressible. Probably no song better typifies Larry Hart's short, sad life than one he wrote for Vivienne Segal, whom he always loved. "Spring Is Here" describing his constant search for love, which was unrequited, was sung by her in I MARRIED AN ANGEL.

MAJOR WORKS

SHOWS:

YOU'D BE SURPRISED **(1920)**
FLY WITH ME **(1920)**
POOR LITTLE RITZ GIRL **(1920)**
SAY MAMA **(1921)**
YOU'LL NEVER KNOW **(1921)**
THE GARRICK GAIETIES **(1925)**
DEAREST ENEMY **(1925)**
THE FIFTH AVENUE FOLLIES **(1926)**
THE GIRL FRIEND **(1926)**
THE GARRICK GAIETIES **(1926)**
LIDO LADY **(1926)**
PEGGY-ANN **(1926)**
BETSY **(1926)**
ONE DAM THING AFTER ANOTHER **(1927)**
A CONNECTICUT YANKEE **(1927)**
SHE'S MY BABY **(1928)**
PRESENT ARMS **(1928)**
CHEE-CHEE **(1928)**
SPRING IS HERE **(1929)**
HEADS UP! **(1929)**
SIMPLE SIMON **(1930)**
EVER GREEN **(1930)**
AMERICA'S SWEETHEART **(1931)**
JUMBO **(1935)**
ON YOUR TOES **(1936)**
BABES IN ARMS **(1936)**
I'D RATHER BE RIGHT **(1937)**
I MARRIED AN ANGEL **(1938)**
THE BOYS FROM SYRACUSE **(1938)**
TOO MANY GIRLS **(1939)**
HIGHER AND HIGHER **(1940)**
PAL JOEY **(1940)**
BY JUPITER **(1942)**
A CONNECTICUT YANKEE **(REVIVAL, 1943)**

COMPOSITIONS:

TOGETHER, RODGERS AND HART WROTE OVER 650 SONGS.

Stephen Sondheim, 1963. (Photofest.)

STEPHEN SONDHEIM

ISAAC AND ROSA SONDHEIM EMIGRATED TO THE UNITED States in 1848. Isaac, a peddler, was hit by a trolley and killed at sixty-five. Of their four sons, only one, Samuel, survived to adult life. He became a successful shirt manufacturer and married Bertha Guttenstein. They had three children. The eldest, Herbert, was born in 1895. A 1908 bank panic led Samuel to lose his business. As a result Herbert's education ended and he became a salesman.

By 1928, Herbert was so successful he bought out his partner in a firm that specialized in women's dresses of high style. He was an aggressive businessman, but gentle and melancholy in his private life. He married Janet Fox, the fifth child of Joseph and Bessie Fox. They were a very religious family. She was artistic and aggressive and described as self-centered, pretentious, and narcissistic.

In later years, her son, Stephen Sondheim, speculated that she had truly married his father out of love, while his father had married her only because he wanted a dress designer.

Foxy, as she would come to be known, was extremely outgoing, blurting out whatever came into her head. But, she was also capable of persuading Van Cleef & Arpels to lend her jewelry for fashion shows. She could be funny and charming.

Foxy decided they should lead a better lifestyle to promote themselves. So they moved into the exclusive San Remo apartments on Central Park West, but not on the very expensive side facing the park itself.

Stephen said she was so ashamed of being Jewish that she claimed she was raised in a convent. It was well known that Foxy was a habitual liar. Stephen was raised non-religiously and his home environment was very strange. He spent almost no time with his parents. They were busy building their business, and his mother was climbing the social ladder. On Saturdays he went to something called "Group", where parents sent their kids to play organized games in the park. Stephen usually spent only a few hours with his parents on Sundays. For five years he spent the entire summer at Camp Androscoggin in Maine, which he loved.

Herbert Sondheim befriended Lloyd Weill, another dress manufacturer who lived at the San Remo. Herbert was a self-taught pianist. Weill sang and wrote lyrics. Together they wrote parodies and performed for charity events. They were called the Rodgers and Hart of Seventh Avenue. Herbert got to know Dorothy Fields and introduced her to the man she would ultimately marry. Dorothy became a frequent houseguest at the many musical parties the Sondheims gave at home.

Stephen was born in 1930 and began studying piano at age seven, but stopped after two years. He would frequently join in the entertaining at home. He has no recollection of his mother as a child. He remembers no attention, no affection, and no love. At age ten he found his mother sobbing. She held him and cried all night. Herbert had walked out and left a note. He had run off with Alicia Babe, who was married to a publisher. Alicia was in charge of fashion for Macy's. Foxy moved out of the San Remo and Stephen was sent to military school in upstate NewYork, where he did rather well in sports, music, and drama. Some weekends he would visit his father and Alicia in their apartment on Fifth Avenue. Herbert and Alicia also had a home in Connecticut and went back and forth to their Manhattan apartment. The hostility between his parents was ferocious. Foxy would have Stephen followed and threatened to have Herbert arrested under the Mann Act (which did not allow a man to take an unmarried female across a state line) every time he and Alicia crossed from New York to Connecticut. Finally there was a legal separation and a Mexican divorce. Herbert and Alicia had a son, Herbert Jr., in 1943 and another, Walter, in 1946. Foxy was vindictive and made Stephen feel that he was responsible for what had happened to his parents. His mother became overtly sexually seductive toward him. As a result, Stephen became very frightened of any aggressive behavior on the part of women. All of this was terribly destructive to his psyche.

Foxy had become friendly with Dorothy Hammerstein, an interior decorator, and her husband, Oscar Hammerstein II. They had a son, Jimmy, who became Stephen's friend. In 1942, when Oscar was in a significant downturn in his career, he bought a home in Doylestown, Pennsylvania. Shortly after that, when Foxy got her legal settlement, she bought a home there as well, just four miles away. The Hammerstein house was filled with children and Stephen loved being there. Stephen's home, on the other hand, was a scene of constant parties with drunken guests and casual sex. He and his mother developed a pattern of meanness toward each other and constant bitchy conversation. Jimmy Hammerstein said all Foxy was concerned about was "getting laid." Oscar disliked Foxy immensely and when she showed up at the Hammerstein house, Oscar would disappear. Foxy maintained the relationship because she liked his celebrity.

Jimmy said the relationship between him and Stephen was like sibling rivalry. Stephen was competitive, much wittier, and sarcastic. Apparently, Stephen could be ruthless and Oscar showed him much more attention than he showed to Jimmy. Even Stephen thought Oscar was not a good parent. Though Oscar had a reputation for benevolence, those who knew him well said he could be a tough businessman. Stephen taught Oscar chess and Oscar taught him bridge. When Mary Rodgers, Richard Rodgers's daughter, was fourteen years old she met Stephen for the first time. Stephen was fifteen. She fell in love with him because of his brilliance.

After graduating from the military academy, Stephen took piano lessons again and considered a concert career, but disliked the idea of performing. He went on to a fine prep school, the George School, and became quite successful in dramatics.

Oscar was reaching new heights of success with OKLAHOMA! and because Stephen loved and admired Oscar so much, he was determined to be just like him. Sondheim said if Oscar had chosen any other profession, Stephen would have followed in the same field. As a senior, he wrote his first musical for the George School.

When Rodgers and Hammerstein wrote ALLEGRO, Oscar gave Stephen a job as a gofer. He was able to see how a show could fail. Agnes de Mille was the director. He felt that she was very hard on the cast. He learned what effect bad behavior by a director could have in the theatre.

At age sixteen, he was enrolled at Williams College. He moved in with his father and stepmother in New York City and Stamford, Connecticut. Quarters were tight, with Alicia's mother and two young step-brothers also living with them in the same apartment.

Sondheim had a girlfriend at Williams, but they only kissed. His first homosexual experiences were after college and he was having a very difficult time trying to understand and cope with his own sexuality.

At Williams, he was greatly influenced by a professor, Bob Barrow, who encouraged him to change his major from

Left to right: Harold Prince and Stephen Sondheim, c. 1980. (Photofest.)

history to music. Another professor, Irwin Shainman, specifically wanted him to write classically, but Sondheim began writing musicals. Williams was not physically set up for a show, but Sondheim persuaded them to try it. He wrote twenty songs for a parody called PHINNEY'S RAINBOW. In 1948, four performances were done. He then wrote a show, ALL THAT GLITTERS, from which five songs were published. In 1949, he was voted Most Versatile, Most Brilliant, Most Original, and Most Likely to Succeed. He did a great deal of acting but although his life seemed quite busy, Sondheim got bored with his life at Williams.

Left to right: Arthur Laurents, Richard Rodgers, and Stephen Sondheim, c. 1965. (Photofest.)

Sondheim graduated magna cum laude and was offered a teaching fellowship at thirty-five hundred dollars per year. He had also won the Hubbard Hutchinson Prize to study music for two years at three thousand dollars per year and took that. He decided to study with Milton Babbitt. He was to study serious music, composition, theory, and harmony, among other topics. Sondheim wanted to learn serious music as a basis for his career. Babbitt was the perfect choice. Besides his own sphere of knowledge, Babbitt had a love of musical theatre. It was around that time that Sondheim met Harold Prince. They were introduced by Mary Rodgers, who said someday they would become the future Rodgers and Hammerstein.

In 1952, he spent the summer at Westport, inseparable

from the eighteen-year-old Mary Rodgers, and wrote a show called CLIMB HIGH, which never got off the ground. An offer came to move to Italy and work as an assistant to John Huston, who was writing a movie for Humphrey Bogart. Bogart and Sondheim became friendly playing chess together. Sondheim soon ran out of money and returned home. Through Hammerstein's contact he got a job writing television scripts for the new show TOPPER in the summer of 1953. Once again he got bored and rented an apartment in New York City, where he lived for the next seven years. He kept trying different projects but nothing was working out.

Two young producers, Lemuel Ayers and John Barry Ryan, decided to produce a show based on the comedy CHICKEN EVERY SUNDAY by Julius J. Epstein, to be called SATURDAY NIGHT. They asked Frank Loesser to write it, but he was too busy, so they tried Sondheim. He agreed. Once written, they hired Jack Cassidy, Alice Ghostley, and Joel Grey to do the backers' audition. It was to open in the spring of 1955. There were some delays and then, suddenly, at age forty, Ayers died of leukemia and the project was scrapped.

At that same time Sondheim met Arthur Laurents at a party and heard that Leonard Bernstein and Robbins were working on a musical based on ROMEO AND JULIET. Bernstein, originally, wanted Comden and Green to write the lyrics. He had written ON THE TOWN and WONDERFUL TOWN with them, but they were busy. Laurents had heard Sondheim's work at an audition and didn't care for his music, but loved his lyrics. So he made Sondheim an offer to cowrite the lyrics with Bernstein, who had already completed quite a bit of the songs on his own. It was to be titled WEST SIDE STORY. Bernstein's lyrics were not great and little by little were replaced by Sondheim's. Jerome Robbins, who had developed a reputation for being brilliant and extremely difficult to work with, was set to direct and choreograph. The 1957 premiere got great critical reviews but was not a great success financially. People who came wanting to see a lighthearted musical walked out in the middle of the experimental show. Sondheim believed his career was in trouble. In London, however, the show was a huge success. It was only because the movie of WEST SIDE STORY in 1961 was such a hit that the music survived.

After Bernstein's lyrics were all replaced by Sondheim's, Bernstein met with Sondheim and said, "The credit is yours. Take the full credit." Bernstein was willing to change the royalties percentage to half and half. But Sondheim was so thrilled to get the billing that he said it was satisfactory to leave the split the same, with Bernstein getting three-fourths and one-fourth for Sondheim. Later Sondheim realized how much money he lost from that youthful judgment. Sondheim wanted to write another show with Bernstein. But more than that he knew that he really wanted to write both music and lyrics.

At that time, Frank Loesser was developing his own publishing house, Frank Music. He invited Sondheim to become part of his stable of composers. He even got an attorney for Sondheim to represent his interests. The attorney advised Sondheim not to sign. He said Loesser was moving too fast and Sondheim had to slow down his career.

David Merrick decided to do a musical about Gypsy Rose Lee, starring Ethel Merman. Jerome Robbins would direct. They tried for Irving Berlin, and then Cole Porter. Neither worked out. The next choice was Cy Coleman and Carolyn Leigh, but Merrick did not like their music. Comden and Green declined to write the book. Robbins wanted Arthur Laurents, though they had fought during WEST SIDE STORY.

Laurents proposed Sondheim for music and lyrics. But Merman took an immediate dislike to Sondheim and refused. Jule Styne was selected to write the music. Sondheim didn't want to write just lyrics, so he went to Hammerstein for advice and Hammerstein persuaded Sondheim to take the assignment for the experience of working with a star. He worked on GYPSY during the summer of 1958 and Merman came to appreciate him after he presented her with her wonderful number "Everything's Coming Up Roses."

Laurents said of Merman, "She was not very bright," and Sondheim called her the "talking dog." There were constant battles among Sondheim, Merman, and Robbins.

Not everything in the early days of the show was hostile. Jack Klugman said when Styne and Sondheim walked in during rehearsals and played and sang "Rose's Turn" he cried like a baby.

Following "Rose's Turn," in the flow of GYPSY, Sondheim insisted they go immediately to the next scene and there be no applause, for how can one applaud someone just gone mad. There were arguments and Sondheim brought in Hammerstein for an opinion. Hammerstein believed that the next scene was too intense and that the audience had to be allowed to applaud to release some of that tension. Sondheim relented. GYPSY would turn out to be the last Sondheim show that Hammerstein would ever see.

Fourteen years later, played by Angela Lansbury, the character took bow after bow at the conclusion of "Rose's Turn", which Sondheim thought was in poor taste until he realized it was a brilliant maneuver by Lansbury to demonstrate her madness.

Sondheim met and befriended Burt Shevelove and they began working on A FUNNY THING HAPPENED ON THE WAY TO THE FORUM. In 1962, Hal Prince turned it down, but Merrick decided to do it. After a disagreement between Merrick and Robbins, who was directing, Merrick withdrew and Prince came back on. Robbins dropped out and they got the seventy-five-year-old George Abbott to direct.

The show was so long it was cut mercilessly. The writers, Shevelove and Larry Gelbart, wanted Milton Berle for the lead, but he wasn't interested and Prince pushed for Zero Mostel, who gave a stellar performance. It would be Sondheim's first full Broadway score. The show was not

Left to right: Stephen Sondheim, Arthur Laurents, Harold Prince, Robert E. Griffith, Leonard Bernstein, and Jerome Robbins on the set of WEST SIDE STORY. (Photofest.)

coming together well and they decided to bring back Robbins to help. That was a problem because Robbins had testified against the wife of Jack Gilford, a leading member of the cast, as a Communist at the House Un-American Activities Committee (HUAC) hearings. Mostel had also been blacklisted, so Robbins was terribly disliked. But the cast agreed to let him work to improve the show. "Comedy Tonight" became the opening song.

In the 1958 Tony Awards, Sondheim was passed over for his work in WEST SIDE STORY. Two years later, there were eight nominations for GYPSY, but he did not win. In 1963, for A FUNNY THING HAPPENED ON THE WAY TO THE FORUM, Mostel won, Abbott won, David Burns won Best Featured Actor, Prince won, and Shevelove and Gelbart won for the book. No one even mentioned Sondheim. He was devastated. He was only thirty-two and all three of his Broadway shows had been critical successes; but, despite the accolades, Sondheim was ignored when it came time for the Tony Awards.

He next wrote ANYONE CAN WHISTLE with Arthur Laurents. Its cynical spirit was before its time, and it closed after nine performances.

Lee Remick was in the show and they fell in love, although Sondheim was gay. Remick was married and her husband was left an invalid after an auto accident. She and Sondheim would meet secretly.

The relationship with Remick was not his only heterosexual one. He had many famous girlfriends, but they all had a sisterly warmth toward him. Mary Rodgers said her heart was broken when he told her that he was gay.

Rodgers subsequently got married and had three children. After she got divorced, her husband said she was still in love with Sondheim. Later she spent a year with Sondheim until it was broken off, and she subsequently married Henry Guettel.

Sondheim began psychotherapy in 1958 in an effort to help him with the difficulty he was having in dealing with his homosexuality.

THE TIME OF THE CUCKOO had been a successful play on Broadway starring Shirley Booth, but a failure as the movie SUMMERTIME with Katharine Hepburn. Rodgers and Hammerstein were approached to do it as a musical, but Hammerstein wanted a little time to pass after the movie. When he found himself dying of cancer, Hammerstein suggested to Rodgers that he take on a younger partner in the future. Rodgers only eventually accepted Sondheim because he was encouraged to do so by Mary Rodgers and Arthur Laurents. It was 1965, and Sondheim did not realize that by that time Rodgers had become an alcoholic. They fought constantly. Rodgers was frequently drunk and they assaulted each other verbally in public. The show, DO I HEAR A WALTZ?, was a disaster in rehearsals and tryouts.

Amazingly, the show ran for 220 performances. It resulted in Sondheim's first Tony Award nomination and had the beautiful title song to its credit.

Difficulties came to Sondheim from 1965 to 1970. There were many false starts and failed projects, a television special, and a Broadway show with Bernstein and

Left to right: James Lapine and Stephen Sondheim working on the score for INTO THE WOODS. (Photofest.)

Robbins, which collapsed. Sondheim started working on a show called THE GIRLS UPSTAIRS, and rejected Prince as its director, which caused some friction.

At that time George Furth, an actor who was a friend of Sondheim's, wrote a series of short plays about marriage to be performed informally at the Actors' Studio. Sondheim thought they had the makings of a larger project and arranged a meeting between Furth and Harold Prince. Prince saw a way to centralize the disparate stories and asked Sondheim to write the score At the same time THE GIRLS UPSTAIRS was floundering. Sondheim changed his mind and asked Prince to come in as director. So the two shows were being created at the same time. They were to become COMPANY and FOLLIES.

COMPANY opened in the spring of 1970 and was a huge hit with great reviews from almost everyone. There were fifteen Tony Award nominations and it won Best Musical, Best Original Score, Best Book, Best Scenic Design, Best Direction. It had so many great songs, including "Being Alive."

Meanwhile FOLLIES was still having some difficulty. The artistic forces—Prince, Sondheim, and codirector and choreographer Michael Bennett—faced many problems. Due to the nature of the show the budget became extremely large. The *New York Times* review was not good, but fortunately most others were. Years later, about a revival, Frank Rich would write that the show was way ahead of its time. It ran for fourteen months, but was so costly it lost its original investment. It won seven Tonys, but FOLLIES had a story the public did not want to hear about, especially as it took the dream world of the 1920s and 30s—and its music—and turned it upside down. On closing night the male lead, John McMartin, and Sondheim sat in the dressing room and cried together for ten minutes.

Sondheim's relationship with his mother was terrible. She was in California claiming to be decorating homes for Jane Wyman and Barbara Stanwyck, but Sondheim knew her to be a pathological liar. She attempted on one occasion to commit suicide to make a lover feel guilty, but used placebos. Neither the suicide nor the attempt to induce guilt in Stephen worked out.

Sondheim's problem with his mother was not his only difficult relationship. Others had trouble relating to him, describing him as cold or impatient and distancing. All, however, thought him to be a genius. His agent said he was shy and extremely wary of anyone of either sex who wanted a close relationship. He could be painfully blunt and insisted on holding a grudge when wronged. Sondheim continued in psychotherapy with Dr. Milton Horowitz for twenty-five years. He was frequently depressed and insecure about his work. Sondheim was capable of great joy and excitement when he felt he had found a word or melody that was just right. Most everyone agreed that over the years Sondheim has mellowed.

In the early 1970s, he became friendly with actor Tony Perkins. The two began writing mystery movies together, which Sondheim found was great fun. One was called THE LAST OF SHEILA. Though it received only modest reviews, it became a sort of cult film. They subsequently wrote two others, neither of which was produced.

Sondheim also became known for his love of games and puzzles of all types. He would have house parties based on puzzles, doublecrostics, chess, jigsaw puzzles, and city-wide searches for clues in a game. He invented new games called Stardom and Analysis. He created a variation of Monopoly based on producing plays for Hal Prince, and, for Bernstein on his fiftieth birthday, a game called The Great Conductor. He even had rooms in his Turtle Bay home redecorated to accommodate his love for that hobby.

Having lost money on FOLLIES, Prince wanted to do something that was small and would make a profit. He wanted to base his new musical on the play RING AROUND THE MOON but was continuously turned down for the rights. So Prince and Sondheim decided to try SMILES OF A SUMMER NIGHT, a film by Ingmar Bergman. It would become A LITTLE NIGHT MUSIC, with a book by Hugh Wheeler. They sought Tammy Grimes for the lead, but agreed on Glynis Johns. Hermione Gingold wanted her part so badly she actually forced her way into an audition. Auditions began in 1972 and rehearsals in 1973. It opened in February and was a big hit, running for 601 performances. A LITTLE NIGHT MUSIC contained the song which would ultimately be Sondheim's biggest commercial hit, "Send in the Clowns." It won six Tonys, including Best Musical over PIPPIN, but was unsuccessful when made into a movie.

Sondheim had reached a pinnacle of stature and the American Musical & Dramatic Academy asked if they could honor him to raise funds for charity. It was the beginning of SONDHEIM: A MUSICAL TRIBUTE, a one-time concert to be held at the Shubert Theatre on March 11, 1973. Almost every major performer from Broadway wanted to be in it. Tickets priced at up to one hundred dollars were sold out for weeks. At the award ceremony during his acceptance speech, Sondheim broke down while expressing his gratitude. He had written, in succession, WEST SIDE STORY, GYPSY, A FUNNY THING HAPPENED ON THE WAY TO THE FORUM, COMPANY, FOLLIES and A LITTLE NIGHT MUSIC. He became more outgoing, drinking a lot, smoking, using pot and occasionally cocaine. He found his first real sexual partner, an actor John David Wilder. But Wilder was promiscuous and a liar, and died later of AIDS.

Sondheim's mother was still hassling him, and after an argument she wrote him a letter stating that the only regret she had in life was giving birth to him. He responded with a letter saying he never wanted to see her again, but would support her to the tune of eighty thousand dollars annually. They never resumed a relationship, and she died in 1992 at the age of ninety-five. For the last ten years of her life he kept her in a nursing home and visited her only once under duress. When she died he did not attend the funeral. Once afterward when an acquaintance asked how his mother was doing, he responded, "She's the same. Oh, I forgot she died."

By then, having learned from other successful composers, he created a publishing and holding company to obtain larger financial success from his work. That became a boon when people like Frank Sinatra, Judy Collins, and Barbra Streisand began recording more and more of his songs.

He then wrote an unique and challenging show, PACIFIC OVERTURES, a highly theatrical look at Japan and its complicated relationship with the western world, told in traditional Kabuki fashion, but it was commercially unsuccessful. It garnered poor reviews, and unfortunately had to compete against A CHORUS LINE. He was chastised for some unpleasant comments he made during an interview and subsequently said he would never do anymore interviews, creating the impression he had become eccentric and reclusive.

In the United States there were complaints saying his music was not tuneful and not commercial outside of the shows. In London, it was just the opposite. There his work was adored and considered witty and intellectual. He was so loved there that he once considered moving to England. A British producer, Ned Sherrin, decided to create a show based on his music. Cleo Laine, the great jazz vocalist, and her musician husband John Dankworth called it A SONDHEIM SONGBOOK and tried it out in a stable at the back of their grounds. It went through several transformations until it was retitled by Burt Shevelove into SIDE BY SIDE BY SONDHEIM. Producer Cameron Mackintosh was asked to put it on. But he was on his way to the United States. Two friends were sent to see it and told Mackintosh it was great, so he decided to go ahead. It consisted of just three singers and a narrator sitting on stools on a stage. The show opened in May 1976 on the West End and ran for three years in London. Hal Prince brought it to Broadway in 1977 where it ran for 384 performances. The show proved Sondheim's work could stand on its own and he became known as one of the great lyric poets of contemporary theatre.

Sondheim began working on an idea for a new show, which would be based on an unprecedented plot for a Broadway musical production, based on the Victorian legend of Sweeney Todd, a demented barber who turns to serial killing and cannibalism to exact a terrible revenge on his enemies. There was a time when people actually believed that Sweeney Todd was an historical figure. In fact he was a fictional character. While Sondheim himself devised the idea for a show, it was still difficult getting backing. Prince thought it was a bad idea.

The writing was extremely intricate and powerful. It also combined a variety of theatrical styles: melodrama, thriller, comedy, revenge tragedy. Thirteen backers' auditions yielded no financing. The producers finally advertised for them in the *New York Times* and got 271 to come onboard.

SWEENEY TODD, THE DEMON BARBER OF FLEET STREET opened in March 1979. During the previews many people walked out. Things were going badly and Sondheim became angry, hostile, and extremely difficult. It was his baby. He could not tolerate its rejection. Fortunately. The reviewers called it one of the greatest musicals ever produced. It ran 558 for performances, and was revived in New York in 1989 and in London in 1993. Another Broadway revival met with great success in 2005. The cast album won the Grammy Award. It contained the beautiful "Not While I'm Around."

Three weeks after the show premiered, Stephen Sondheim had a heart attack at forty-nine.

When he recovered, he changed his life completely. He stopped smoking, began exercising, and changed his diet. He began a new project with Prince based on the George S. Kaufman-Moss Hart play MERRILY WE ROLL ALONG, the story of a playwright who sells his soul for financial success. Prince and Sondheim had considerable disagreements about how it should be created. Sondheim wrote a great score including "Not a Day Goes By." The book by George Furth was considered weak. There were no out-of-town tryouts, just previews in New York, and word got out that it wasn't great. It opened in late 1981 and lasted for only sixteen performances, and its failure resulted in a breach of the long relationship between Sondheim and Prince. It was a blow to Sondheim. Hal Prince went through six years of one failure after another, almost causing him to forego the theatre. Sondheim considered giving it up as well and became quite depressed. Sondheim had never been able to deal with poor reviews. He was not like Noel Coward, who when asked about the critics replied, "It's perfectly simple. They're wrong."

Sondheim soon met James Lapine, who was writing and directing. He was twenty years Sondheim's junior. Together they began looking at photographs to see if anything appealed to them as an idea for a show. Sondheim recalled Seurat's *A Sunday Afternoon on the Isle of La Grande Jatte*. In 1984, it became SUNDAY IN THE PARK WITH GEORGE, starring Mandy Patinkin and Bernadette Peters. Once again the musical was a completely new type of Broadway experience and got mixed reviews. The show struggled for a while, losing out on most of the Tonys to LA CAGE AUX FOLLES, but it won the Pulitzer Prize for drama in early 1985, and wound up running for almost a year.

WEST SIDE STORY, PACIFIC OVERTURES and SWEENEY TODD were revived, and Sondheim was at the top again receiving heavy praise and named to the American Academy of Arts and Letters. There was a retrospective of his work at the Whitney, and a concert version of FOLLIES for a single performance recorded at Avery Fisher Hall. It ran three hours and raised two hundred sixteen thousand dollars for charity.

Sondheim and Lapine started a new project, a fairy tale musical called INTO THE WOODS. It opened in December 1986. The deeper meanings were meant to reflect the lives of Sondheim and Lapine. It was immensely successful, running for 800 performances. It won three Tonys, had success on the road and television and was Sondheim's second longest-running show after FORUM. The most important song was "No One Is Alone."

By 1987, he was earning over a million dollars a year from all his shows and revivals and was named to a chair at Oxford University.

Stretching his imagination he moved on to ASSASSINS, which dealt with the history of assassination attempts on American presidents. The public had difficulty understanding whether he was glorifying assassination or explaining it. It received very mixed reviews in the United States, but was a great success in London. In, the end, the subject may have hit too close to home with American audiences, just as LES MISERABLES faced rejection in France. Sondheim concluded he was happier in England where the praise for his work was unbounded. He believed the 1993 London revival of SWEENEY TODD was the greatest production he had ever seen of his work.

Sondheim and Andrew Lloyd Webber were at their peak. However, the difference between them was stark. Both were living in country homes. Lloyd Webber's home was phenomenally opulent. At Sondheim's house the guests ate in the kitchen.

Once in London, Princess Alexandria met him at a retrospective and asked others if he was married. When told he was gay she commented, "He does look rather a sad man." Over the years Sondheim had suffered much heartache. In 1982, he incurred a deep loss when one of his dearest friends, Burt Shevelove, died. Five years later, Michael Bennett, a collaborator with Sondheim on two major shows, died of AIDS.

Those were not his only losses. He loved Lee Remick and was a constant friend even after she married. He had cast her in the 1985 concert of FOLLIES, even though she was an actress, rather than a singer, because she meant so much to him. She presented the Tony for Best Score for INTO THE WOODS to him in 1988. In 1987, she was found to have lung cancer and in 1991 she died. And, as well, in 1987, Dorothy Hammerstein, Oscar's wife, who had meant so much to him as he was growing up, died. He was inconsolable at the funeral. In 1993, his long-time houseman, chef, butler, and friend, Louis Vargas, died of AIDS, as well as his half-brother, Herbie, who was always in trouble and only forty-nine years old. It was a traumatic decade for Sondheim.

Someone new, however, would come into Stephen's life. In 1991, Peter Jones, a Catholic working in children's theatre, decided to try his luck in New York City. A small, thin young man, he finally got an interview with Sondheim. They met and talked and Sondheim invited him to his country house the following day. While there, Sondheim fell and fractured his ankle, causing him to stay in a cast for two months. He asked Jones if he would stay and help. Jones agreed, and Sondheim said he fell in love for the first time. Jones was feeling overwhelmed by Sondheim's fame and central role in all the things they did. He also felt that Sondheim was withdrawn. He decided to leave in the summer of 1992 while Sondheim was working on PASSION.

Sondheim was distraught. They talked constantly on the phone, usually in tears, Sondheim wanting him to return. He finally agreed and they exchanged wedding rings in January 1994.

PASSION was another very difficult play, complicated and so different from other musicals. There was considerable concern that it would not be accepted. But it ran until January 1995, winning four Tonys, for Best Musical, Best Score, Best Book, and Best Actress.

In the early 1990s a number of special events celebrated his music, including ones at Carnegie Hall in 1994, the Kennedy Center Honors in 1993, the tenth anniversary celebration of SUNDAY IN THE PARK WITH GEORGE in 1994, and in 1997 the National Medal of the Arts at the White House.

In 1995, he decided to write a murder mystery with his old collaborator from COMPANY, George Furth, called GETTING AWAY WITH MURDER. It opened in 1996 and was completely panned. Jones decided to leave again and a short reconciliation in 1997 did not work out. Meanwhile a terrible house fire at his Manhattan home destroyed a large amount of Sondheim's most precious memorabilia.

He worked hard on a new show that went through multiple incarnations and title changes, from WISE GUYS, to GOLD, and finally to BOUNCE. In 2003, after nine years of work, the show opened at the Goodman Theatre in Chicago and the Kennedy Center. It received such poor reviews that it never made it to Broadway. Set in the 1920s and 30s, the story of two brothers—and their respective scams in the businesses of real estate and show business—contains a beautiful score, but has had a problematic time finding its proper style. The piece was remounted in New York in October 2008, under the name ROAD SHOW.

Sondheim composed incidental music for a Public Theatre production of KING LEAR in 2007.

With all of his artistic genius, Sondheim has seemed committed to a life of loneliness. His emotions were mangled as a child and he spent most of his life fighting against any emotional attachments that would hurt him once again.

MAJOR WORKS

SHOWS:

SATURDAY NIGHT **(1955)**
WEST SIDE STORY **(BERNSTEIN, 1957)**
GYPSY **(STYNE, 1959)**
A FUNNY THING HAPPENED ON THE WAY TO THE FORUM **(1962)**
ANYONE CAN WHISTLE **(1964)**
DO I HEAR A WALTZ? **(RODGERS, 1965)**
EVENING PRIMROSE **(TELEVISION, 1966)**
COMPANY **(1970)**
FOLLIES **(1971)**
A LITTLE NIGHT MUSIC **(1973)**
CANDIDE (BERNSTEIN, **1975)**
PACIFIC OVERTURES **(1976)**
SIDE BY SIDE BY SONDHEIM **(1976)**
SWEENEY TODD **(1979)**
MARRY ME A LITTLE **(1980)**
SUNDAY IN THE PARK WITH GEORGE **(1984)**
INTO THE WOODS **(1987)**
ASSASSINS **(1990)**
PASSION **(1994)**
GETTING AWAY WITH MURDER **(PLAY, 1996)**
WISE GUYS/GOLD/BOUNCE/ROAD SHOW **(1999-2008)**

COMPOSITIONS:

SONDHEIM HAS WRITTEN ALMOST 500 SONGS, FOR MOST OF WHICH HE WROTE BOTH THE MUSIC AND LYRICS.

Jung wrote that people of great genius must pay dearly for that privilege, as each of us is born with a limited store of energy. The creative process seizes most of the energy, leaving a deficit in some other aspect of life. An examination of Sondheim's phenomenal career certainly leaves no doubt as to the amount of energy he invested in it.

Charles Strouse, c. 1990s. (Photofest.)

Charles Strouse

CHARLES STROUSE WAS BORN IN 1928 AND RAISED IN New York City. At a very young age he came to realize that his mother suffered from some pyschological disorder that caused her to have massive mood swings. Today she would be diagnosed as being bipolar or manic-depressive.

Charles grew up with the nickname, Buddy. Like his mother he was chubby. And, like her, he was insecure, even though it was well recognized that he was her favorite child. They both loved music and played the piano together.

Charles had an older brother, David, whom everyone knew wanted to be a physician.

When Buddy was five years old he suddenly learned that he also had an older sister who was four years his senior. As he got older, he came to understand that his older "sister" was actually the daughter of his mother's sister, his aunt Marjorie. Lila, as she was called, was really Buddy's cousin. Though it was kept a secret from almost everyone, Marjorie had committed suicide when Lila was four years old. Lila spent the next six years in foster homes before she moved in with Buddy's family.

Buddy's brother David had gone to college as a pre med student before dropping out and joining the Marines as a medical corpsman. Years later Buddy would find out that his brother had flunked out of college and was ashamed to admit it to the family.

Though Charles had made little progress in studying music, he decided after his high school graduation to apply to the Eastman School of Music in Rochester, New York. He was still chubby, and looked very young. He was only fifteen years old at the time, but he was accepted for admission there. In 1944, he began his college life among those who were much older and more sophisticated. To earn some money, Charles took a job in a war plant, working there from 6 p.m. until midnight, while attending school in the daytime.

In 1945, Buddy became aware that another Eastman student had won the Gershwin Memorial Award given for composing a new classical piece of music. Strouse decided he would try to win it in 1946, and wrote "Narrative for Orchestra." His disappointment was palpable when he was notified that no piece of music submitted that year was considered worthy of the prize.

By his senior year at Eastman, Buddy was elected the class president. Even more important to Buddy, he began dating.

Because of his mother's obesity and emotional problems and his father's sickly appearance, Strouse was embarrassed about being in their company and didn't invite them to the graduation. He simply returned home and moved back in with them. His mother, possibly trying to seek attention, constantly threatened to commit suicide. In 1948, his father committed her to a mental institution, claiming she was addicted to her medication. She remained there for two and a half years.

Buddy began studying with David Diamond, the composer and pianist, who knew everyone including Leonard Bernstein, Aaron Copland, and Betty Comden and Adolph Green. Through that connection Buddy decided to apply to spend the summer at Tanglewood. There he studied composition with Copland and got to meet Bernstein. Buddy got turned down by Bernstein in 1952 for the position of rehearsal pianist for WONDERFUL TOWN. Not until BYE BYE BIRDIE was a success in 1960 did Bernstein actually become more friendly.

In 1949, an important thing happened to Buddy. At a Christmas party he made the acquaintance of Lee Adams, who would become his lyricist, and an integral part of his life. Buddy was still trying to find a place for himself in the world of music and through a referral by Copland was able to go to Paris to study with one of the most famous teachers in the world, Nadia Boulanger, who had taught both Gershwin and Copland. He remained there for one year before deciding to return to New York to look for work. He was able to get occasional jobs as a rehearsal pianist, for auditions or at some nightclubs. Sometimes it would be just at a strip joint where no one cared much about the music. He had such extensive training that he frequently got jobs just because of his ability to do arranging and transposing into any key. It also didn't hurt that hiring Buddy was inexpensive.

Finally, he got a permanent job as the accompanist for Butterfly McQueen. She had become famous for the role she played in GONE WITH THE WIND. McQueen had parlayed that into an act she did traveling through the South, for black audiences. In it, she sang in her high-pitched voice, danced rather poorly, recited Rudyard Kipling's "If," and told GONE WITH THE WIND anecdotes. As he traveled by car with her, Strouse faced continuous racial bigotry and slurs. On one occasion he was spat upon. The entire experience would be one of the factors that later caused him in 1965 to join with Sammy Davis Jr. in the march to Selma, Alabama.

Once that job came to a conclusion, Buddy did something unusual for him: he took his father's advice. His dad suggested that he take a course, which had been advertised, in how to compose music for films. It was being taught by the head of the 20th Century Fox music department. Buddy had so much more training than the others in the class that the teacher took an immediate liking to him. He offered Buddy a job at Fox, writing background music for their Movietone News films.

By the time summer came, he was given an opportunity to write dance arrangements for the Green Mansions resort in the Catskills. At Green Mansions, they were doing a weekly revue. In the process, Strouse wrote a few songs with Lee Adams. Fay Dewitt, a singer there, requested that Strouse accompany her for an audition at a club in New York. They liked her and asked who wrote her material. She identified Buddy Strouse as her composer.

The three producers at the audition asked Strouse if he would like to write for their new show, NICE TO SEE YOU. These three elderly producers had been quite successful in the past. One was Irving Caesar, who had written "Swanee" with George Gershwin. Another was Jack Yellen, who wrote "Ain't She Sweet" and "Happy Days Are Here Again." The third was George White of the SCANDALS.

Strouse was thrilled to be working with such eminent individuals. He soon found out, however, that the project was extremely disorganized. It got so bad that Strouse asked that his name be removed from the project. The producers refused. Strouse was totally demoralized. That all changed, however, when the reviews came out, and were excellent. Suddenly Buddy Strouse was "somebody."

The summer of 1956 brought Strouse back to Green Mansions writing a weekly revue with Lee Adams. But his insecurities made him wonder whether he had any talent at all. On top of that he fell in love with a girl who dropped him for Andre Previn. At his mother's insistence he went into therapy, but soon stopped that as well.

His career was not progressing very well when he got a position as the accompanist for a television special starring Ginger Rogers. Otto Preminger was the director. The job was quite terrible as Preminger's reputation for being a wild man on the set turned out to be true.

In 1956, Strouse did nothing more than occasional special material for performers Kaye Ballard and Dick Shawn. Strouse's father passed away at fifty-nine, leaving him with the feeling that he never knew his father, the traveling salesman, very well.

Dejected, Strouse fell back to old friendships from Eastman. One of those was a dear gay friend, Bill Flanagan, who was dating a very pushy young man named Ed. Knowing that Strouse had some friends in the world of show business, Ed kept after Strouse to get people to read the plays he was writing. Strouse brought them to David Diamond, the pianist, who in turn passed them on to a producer, who liked the work enough to have it translated into German and presented in Berlin. The play was THE ZOO STORY and it became a great success. Ed turned out to be Edward Albee.

In 1958, while Strouse was still only an accompanist, a stage manager, Edward Padula, who had heard some of his earlier compositions written with Lee Adams for a show called SHOESTRING REVUE, told Strouse that he liked their work and had an idea for a new show for them. Strouse and Adams wrote seven songs together. They went through a number of librettists, including Mike Nichols and Elaine May. They rejected them all until they came upon Michael Stewart. Gower Champion was chosen to be the director. The story line was based on a news item about Elvis Presley being drafted into the army in 1958 and the anguish of his teenage following.

In the musical, Presley was transformed into Conrad Birdie, a rock 'n' roll singer on his way into the Army. The name of the show kept changing from THE DAY THEY TOOK BIRDIE AWAY, to GOING STEADY, to GOODBYE BIRDIE GOODBYE and finally, BYE BYE BIRDIE.

It was a struggle, and frequently very humiliating, trying to get backers. Frank Loesser, now a very successful producer as well as a composer, showed interest in the project. After a while that fell through as well. Loesser liked Strouse's talent, however, and gave him a job as his musical secretary, where Strouse remained for two years. During that time BIRDIE was still struggling to get off the ground.

Padula contacted Strouse and Adams telling them to prepare for another backers' audition. They had had so many rejections that Adams and Strouse had little stomach for it, but reluctantly agreed.

Two people showed up, a rather unsophisticated Texan, L. Slade Brown, and his banker. When it ended, Brown said, "I like these songs. How much do you fellas need?"

"Seventy five thousand," Padula blurted out, completely unprepared for an approval, and the check was written.

With money in hand they set out to find a leading lady. Carol Haney, Eydie Gorme, Shirley MacLaine, Jane Powell, and Helen Gallagher all fell through. In the end they settled on Chita Rivera.

For the male lead they became interested in a tall young man who was playing a role in a Bert Lahr revue Dick Van Dyke. The problem was that Van Dyke was practically unknown. But a great audition made them decide he could overcome his anonymity.

By the end of the rehearsal time they were running out of money, so they persuaded Goddard Lieberson, the head of Columbia Records, to come up with another seventy-five thousand dollars in return for the cast album rights.

When the show opened, the first review that Strouse saw was by Brooks Atkinson of the *New York Times*. He panned the show and Strouse went into complete seclusion, depressed, and unable to be found. Not until later did he realize that the reviews in every other paper were great and ticket sales exploded.

Suddenly, Buddy Strouse was affluent, with no idea about how to handle his money. He put it all into a simple savings account. Strouse moved into a large apartment, got a maid, and sent his mother on a worldwide cruise. There she met Stephen Sondheim's aunt and they argued the entire time about who was the finer composer, Strouse or Sondheim.

Lee Adams got married, but Strouse, who was already thirty, barely ever went out on dates. He worked constantly. He even attempted to write some chamber music. When he received his invitation to attend the Antoinette Perry awards for 1961, he invited Barbara Siman, a dancer from MY FAIR LADY, to go with him. Dick Van Dyke won, Michael Stewart won, and Gower Champion won Tonys for both direction and choreography. By the time they announced the award for Best Musical, Strouse was so drunk that he was very slow getting up and the presenter said that since Mr. Strouse wasn't there, Mr. Padula would accept for him.

BYE BYE BIRDIE ran for 607 performances. That was followed by touring companies and a London production. In 1962, the rights were sold to Columbia for a motion picture. Van Dyke got the lead, but Chita Rivera was replaced by Janet Leigh.

Strouse and Adams followed that immediately with another show, ALL AMERICAN, adapted from the novel, *Professor Fodorski*. Strouse was certain it would be a hit. Once again, Ed Padula hired Strouse and Adams, but this time, there was the addition of Mel Brooks writing the book and Joshua Logan directing. Problems arose with the casting, which they never felt they got right. All six weeks of the tryouts were characterized by much rewriting and arguing. Strouse developed hives all over his body. His back went out and once again he was overeating and depressed. On top of all that his mother had surgery, which revealed stomach cancer. Barbara Siman was trying desperately to keep Buddy together, when his mother died of her illness. Strouse felt that he was following in the footsteps of his parents, down a path of obesity, insecurity, and depression. Eventually, under pressure from Barbara Siman, Strouse agreed to marry her. He was so filled with anxiety about what he was doing with his life that he fainted as the ceremony was about to begin in September 1962.

It was toward the end of 1963 that the famous story about Strouse and HELLO, DOLLY! emerged. Jerry Herman was having some problems with the score, so producer David Merrick, independently, contacted Strouse and Adams. He told them that Herman wanted Strouse to help out by writing some music for the show. Strouse believed Merrick, but, in fact, Herman knew nothing about the request. Strouse had seen the preview and felt that the show needed some structural changes and suggested a song, which they wrote, titled "Before the Parade Passes By." When Herman discovered what had happened, he was horrified and embarrassed that Strouse had been called in behind his back. Herman wrote a new song using that title. Though Merrick gave away half of the royalties of that song to Strouse, Strouse publicly acknowledged that the song had been written exclusively by Herman. All of the parties involved agreed that the problem resulted from David Merrick's penchant for lying.

Strouse and Adams began a new project in the early sixties, converting Clifford Odets's dramatic 1937 play GOLDEN BOY into a musical. The idea was to use Sammy Davis Jr. as the lead. Davis was already very successful in Las Vegas earning sixty thousand dollars per week. His life there was quite special. He was surrounded by an entourage, but was willing to forego much of that for the opportunity to perform a dramatic role on Broadway.

Strouse and Adams made an agreement with Davis they would later regret. Davis was permitted to reject anything they wrote, if it didn't please him. Working on the show became a major hassle as Strouse and Adams had to shuttle back and forth to Las Vegas. Even when they were there, Davis would consistently be late for their meetings.

Once Strouse was asked to meet Davis at a sauna. There, lying around naked, were Frank Sinatra, Dean Martin, Peter Lawford, and Sammy Cahn. No work was done. It appeared that all Davis wanted to do was to show off "Charles, my composer."

To make matters even worse, Odets, who was doing the book, died before the writing was completed and his work was taken on by playwright William B. Gibson. Nevertheless, the show was important to Davis and he worked very hard during the project. It opened in 1964, and though it ran for 569 performances, it lost all the Tonys to FIDDLER ON THE ROOF.

In 1966, Strouse's first son, Ben, was born. Strouse felt that the pull of his work was stronger than that of paternity. Strouse and Adams received an offer to convert the comic strip character Superman into a musical. Hal Prince agreed to produce and direct it. In the tryouts songs that they thought would be great were not working well, so much of the show was rewritten. The reviews for "IT'S A BIRD . . . IT'S A PLANE . . . IT'S SUPERMAN" were good, but it never took off with the audience. It opened in March and closed in July.

Hollywood beckoned them. Warren Beatty asked Strouse to write a score for BONNIE AND CLYDE. That was followed by a score for Norman Lear's film THE NIGHT THEY RAIDED MINSKY'S. It appeared the film might never be completed when halfway through its star, Bert Lahr, passed away. Lear cleverly shot the remainder of the film with all shots from the rear of a stand-in for Lahr. The film was a success.

In his private life Strouse would have another setback. His dear friend Bill Flanagan from Eastman had become an alcoholic. Flanagan's longtime relationship with Albee had ended. By then Strouse was married, he had a child, and he was spending little time with Bill. When he heard that Flanagan had died at the age of forty-six, serious guilt "ate at him" as Flanagan had always been there for Strouse during difficult times. Strouse wondered to himself whether Flanagan could have been salvaged had he made any effort. In 1968, Strouse brought up the idea to producer Lawrence Kasha of making a musical based on Joe Mankiewicz's brilliant ALL ABOUT EVE. Sidney Michaels, the playwright, was to be the librettist. After Lauren Bacall got the lead, however, she wanted Michaels replaced by Comden and Green, and they were hired instead. The title was changed to APPLAUSE. It opened in 1970 to rave reviews. The show ran for two years and won four Tony awards. After Bacall left the show, she was followed in the lead by Anne Baxter and Arlene Dahl. One eventual choice to replace Bacall was Rita Hayworth, but she was unable to remember any lines as she was in the beginning stages of what was to become later known as Alzheimer's disease.

By the time APPLAUSE made it to London, Strouse and Adams had decided they wanted to write a show with a British theme. It was to be about the lives of Victoria and Albert with the title I AND ALBERT. In London APPLAUSE continued to be a hit, but I AND ALBERT closed after 120 performances. Like the experiences of so many other composers and lyricists, Strouse and Adams believed that I AND ALBERT was one of their finest pieces of writing. The failure hurt Strouse deeply.

By that time Strouse's family had grown. Their second child, Nick, was born in 1968, and it was right about the

Backstage on the set of BYE BYE BIRDIE, *left to right:* lyricist Lee Adams, director Gower Champion, book writer Michael Stewart, producer Edward Padula, and composer Charles Strouse. (Photofest.)

time of the failure of I AND ALBERT that Barbara gave birth to their third child, Victoria, in London. Later, Strouse admitted feeling guilty that he was much more concerned about the demise of I AND ALBERT than the birth of his third child. He was ashamed that he lacked appreciation for the true value of his life's many different aspects.

Later, when his children were grown, his eldest, Ben, started out in the theatre, before deciding he would be much happier as a therapist. Nick, on the other hand, became a lawyer. After a while, however, he discovered that his real love would be musical theatre.

By 1972, for the first time in ages, Strouse had no show running in New York. Because some of his songs had been used in commercial advertising he was offered the job of heading up the music division of a large advertising agency. He took it, not because he needed the money, but because he just desperately needed to keep buoy. While there, he was approached by Martin Charnin with an idea for a show. Charnin wanted to get Tom Meehan to write the book, Strouse to compose the music, and Charnin, himself, to write the lyrics and direct a musical based on the 1930s comic strip character Little Orphan Annie. Strouse was frankly not crazy about the idea of Charnin directing the show and Meehan thought even less of it.

All the while that Strouse was working on the project the ad agency had Strouse creating a commercial for Pabst Blue Ribbon Beer. Strouse ran up his budget to twenty-five thousand dollars, including the use of Gene Kelly. When the commercial was completed, the agency discarded it.

As the work on the show, now called ANNIE, progressed, both Strouse and Meehan became more unhappy with Charnin as director as well as lyricist, but Charnin was absolutely insistent. In fact he threatened that if the position of director was taken from him, he would find another composer. So Strouse reluctantly quit the project and went back to work for the ad agency.

Charnin found no success working alone on the show, and after a year passed he made a counteroffer to Strouse. If Strouse could get a quality director, specifically Jerome Robbins, Gower Champion, or Michael Kidd, then Charnin would step down. Strouse realized how unrealistic it was to even consider that any of one of these three titans would work on their show.

Another year passed and Charnin was, by default, once again the director. Michael Price, who ran the Goodspeed Opera House, signed on to be the producer. The tryouts for ANNIE would begin at Goodspeed. Charnin, Strouse, and Meehan worked well and diligently while the tryouts were progressing, changing things every day. Once again Strouse was feeling guilty. Barbara had suffered a miscarriage and Strouse paid much less attention to her than to the show.

One problem that the team had was some concern about the little girl playing the leading role of Annie. Her voice was fine, but she didn't have the toughness they wanted for the character, struggling through the difficult life in the orphanage. They decided to drop her and replace her with Andrea McArdle.

Word came that Walter Kerr, the *New York Times* theatre critic, had decided not to wait until it came to Broadway. He was going to the Goodspeed to review the show. After seeing it, he wrote that the show was not "Broadway bound." The team went back to the drawing board. But there were no more funds in the Goodspeed budget left for new rehearsals. So Strouse and Charnin funded the rehearsals themselves.

Out of the blue, Jay Presson Allen, an investor in I AND ALBERT, came to see the show and immediately called Mike Nichols. She insisted that he come see it. Nichols liked it and said he would like to join the team as a producer. The project got a second wind.

Strouse made a decision that infuriated everyone except Mike Nichols. He decided that ANNIE was in danger of being perceived as a children's show rather than one for adults. He demanded that none of the advertising would profile anyone in the creative team—not Strouse, not Charnin, not the performers—except the show's producer. It would say just the following: "Mike Nichols Presents ANNIE"—which might persuade audiences that there was some sophisticated entertainment to be had. Strouse threatened that if the team did not agree to his demand, he would withdraw his music. Reluctantly, and angrily, everyone acceded.

Mike Nichols, meanwhile, arranged to get Dorothy Loudon to play the role of Miss Hannigan. ANNIE opened in Washington to great reviews. Strouse added a new song for the opening, "Maybe," which made the show flow even better. The melody for the song came from a commercial he had written for the ad agency, which had been rejected. When it opened in April 1977 on Broadway, even Walter Kerr "apologized in a column" for his previous review. Even the small, fat, insecure boy from Manhattan who lived inside Buddy Strouse's head now believed that he had found success. The lines to purchase tickets extended around the corner. Strouse would stand on the corner of Fifty-Second Street and Eighth Avenue just to stare at them. He even noticed that he was "standing near the Musicians' Union Hall" where he used to list his name for jobs as a piano player thirty years before.

ANNIE won six Tonys, including one for Strouse and one for Best Musical. The show ran for 2377 performances and another 1485 in London, in addition to being performed by a number of touring companies.

The original creative team was contractually kept from participating much in the film, which turned out to be a financial failure. A much finer production was eventually presented on television in 1999, directed by Rob Marshall.

A stroke of good luck occurred in the sale of the original show. While ANNIE was still in the creative stages, ABC had offered to buy the rights for sixty-five thousand dollars. The producers felt that was inadequate and asked for eighty-five thousand. ABC declined. Four years later—now with a spectacular success behind them—they sold it to Columbia for nine million dollars.

Barbara had become pregnant again and decided if she had a girl they would name her Annie. Instead, William was born.

The success of ANNIE, as is so often the case, turned out to be fleeting. Strouse wrote two more shows, A BROADWAY MUSICAL, a spoof on racial double-standards; and FLOWERS FOR ALGERNON, about a brain-damaged man who has special surgery that allows him to become a genius. By coincidence, both shows opened the same night in 1978, one in New York and the other in Canada. A BROADWAY MUSICAL closed in one night. ALGERNON lasted twenty-eight days before moving to London. When ALGERNON came to the United States (under the new title CHARLIE AND ALGERNON), it lasted only seventeen days.

Under some pressure Strouse and Adams wrote a sequel to BYE BYE BIRDIE in 1981 called BRING BACK BIRDIE. It closed after four performances.

Strouse got involved with Alan Jay Lerner, who had a reputation for being a difficult collaborator due to his procrastination and an inability to tell the truth. Strouse later

Charles Strouse, c. 1960s. (Photofest.)

Charles Strouse, c. 1990s. (Photofest.)

said that he should have expected trouble when Lerner told him he would not only write the lyrics and the book, but direct as well. He also told Strouse that his new and eighth wife would be the star. The show, DANCE A LITTLE CLOSER, closed on opening night in 1983. Strouse said the show was later called by insiders "Close a Little Faster."

Over the years Strouse had tried a few times to write both the music and lyrics. Once it was for a small production at the Village Gate based on New York Mayor Koch's book Mayor. Koch had previously requested and received permission to use the song "N.Y.C." from ANNIE as his campaign song. When Koch asked him to make a musical of his book, Strouse thought it was not a great idea. However, when Koch gave him a "no approval necessary" contract, the idea sounded better. As it turned out the show, MAYOR, received good reviews during its Off-Broadway run.

In 1986, Strouse had less good fortune when he wrote a show with Stephen Schwartz based on the screenplay RAGS. The music got good reviews, but the show did not and it closed in four days.

Three years later, Strouse was asked to do a sequel to ANNIE. As was the case with BYE BYE BIRDIE, the sequel did not live up to its predecessor. In the previews the public did not like the negative aspects of the book for ANNIE 2: MISS HANNIGAN'S REVENGE. Three years later, the show was rewritten again, this time for Off-Broadway. After that the show was used predominantly for community theatre and high school productions.

Another theatrical disaster followed soon after. Arthur Laurents was planning a musical based on THE THIN MAN, and approached Strouse with the idea in 1988. They started off on the project with a close personal relationship, but it slowly began to disintegrate. Strouse finally came to the conclusion that Laurents truly did not like him. The situation reached its crescendo at the first full orchestra rehearsal.

The famous orchestrator Jonathan Tunick was part of the creative team. Someone in the cast complimented Strouse on his score. Laurents loudly said, "Charles's songs are not good. Jonathan's orchestrations make them sound that way."

Strouse was furious and rushed toward Laurents. Strouse's son, who was working on the production, grabbed his father, preventing an all-out physical confrontation. Later in the rehearsal, Laurents uncharacteristically apologized.

The title of the show was NICK & NORA and it closed after nine performances.

In 1994, Strouse felt that he had found a much more promising opportunity. The show was THE NIGHT THEY RAIDED MINSKY'S. The project was complicated by repeated changes in lyricists. Sometime after 1996, the creative team was finalized. It was being directed by Mike Ockrent and choreographed by his wife, Susan Stroman. At an early stage of production in 1999 Ockrent was diagnosed with leukemia and died in less than three weeks. The entire project was dropped.

Television star Jason Alexander wanted Strouse to compose the music for a show based on the movie MARTY. But one problem after another made it impossible for the show ever to come to Broadway.

Strouse kept hoping for something to come his way, but his time had passed. Like so many of his idols in the field, as they aged, they were unable to achieve the greatness they had experienced earlier in their lives. Strouse realized that he was emotionally prepared to die. However, he wasn't prepared to grow old.

He went on to write his memoir. But already to his credit he had three very big hits—BYE BYE BIRDIE, APPLAUSE, and ANNIE—and had overcome the insecurities that plagued him during the early years of his career. Even more important than establishing himself in this crowd of musical geniuses was the knowledge that he, Charles Strouse, had found his way out of the chubby little boy, Buddy, whose insecurities had dominated the first half of his life.

MAJOR WORKS

SHOWS:

(LYRICS BY LEE ADAMS, UNLESS OTHERWISE NOTED)
BYE BYE BIRDIE **(1960)**
ALL AMERICAN **(1962)**
GOLDEN BOY **(1964)**
"IT'S A BIRD ...IT'S A PLANE ...IT'S SUPERMAN" **(1966)**
APPLAUSE **(1970)**
I AND ALBERT **(1972)**
ANNIE **(CHARNIN, 1977)**
A BROADWAY MUSICAL **(1978)**
CHARLIE AND ALGERNON **(ROGERS, 1980)**
BRING BACK BIRDIE **(1981)**
DANCE A LITTLE CLOSER **(LERNER, 1983)**
MAYOR **(1985)**
RAGS **(SCHWARTZ, 1986)**
NICK & NORA **(MALTBY, 1991)**

COMPOSITIONS:

STROUSE COMPOSED PRIMARILY THE MUSIC, AND ON RARE OCCASION WROTE THE LYRICS, FOR MORE THAN 200 SONGS.

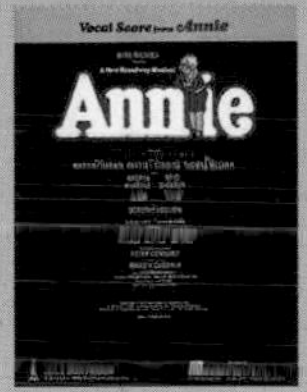

Jule Styne, c. 1960s.
(Photofest.)

JULE STYNE

ISADORE STEIN, BORN IN THE UKRAINE, WAS THE SON OF A butter and egg salesman. Anna Kertman lived nearby. They met in London as orphaned immigrants around 1900 and married. Like his father, Isadore went into the butter and egg business. But he was a poor businessman and the family lived in an apartment upstairs from the store in a crowded immigrant slum. He was, however, very strong and wrestled as an amateur since his childhood. Anna was pretty and sweet, and completely unlike her husband. The few luxuries they had came from her brother, who was a successful businessman.

Jule, their first child, was born on New Year's Eve, 1905. Claire followed in 1907, and Maurice was born in 1912, just a few weeks after they arrived in Chicago from London. Young Jule had studied piano in London from the time he was six years old.

Anna and Isadore spoke a mixture of Yiddish and cockney English. While Anna was in the hospital giving birth to Maurice, their apartment burned down and the family lost everything they had brought from London.

Isadore got a job as an egg inspector, earning nineteen dollars and fifty cents per week. With the family in dire distress, Isadore's brother-in-law provided the financial assistance for them to move into a better neighborhood, much to Isadore's displeasure. Isadore disliked him because of the shame this aid made him feel.

Chicago had already become the center of African-American music and jazz in the United States, with black musicians moving there from New Orleans. Julius, as he was known then, had already shown a significant interest in music. He had seen and actually met Harry Lauder as a young child in London. Lauder had told the family to get Julius a piano, which of course, was financially impossible.

In Chicago they met a violinist with the Chicago Symphony. That man's son would become the comedian Morey Amsterdam. He, like Lauder, encouraged the family to get Julius a piano. At Anna's insistence, Isadore bought him an upright. It took ten years to pay for it. There is no record of it, but Anna's brother most likely paid for all the lessons.

After just seven months of lessons Julius competed in a contest organized by the Chicago Symphony and won the silver medal. Before another year had passed Julius performed as a child prodigy with the St. Louis and Detroit Symphonies. He was practicing four hours daily. The family catered to him in every way. That created a great deal of sibling rivalry.

Isadore was not fond of classical music, so at home he would encourage Julius to play Jewish, Scottish, and Irish music. Though he was not very supportive of a piano career for Julius, Isadore believed him to have a very good voice and encouraged Julius to be a member of the synagogue choir. Julius's ear for music was so perfect that he repeatedly corrected the cantor, saying he was not singing the correct note, which, of course, greatly offended him. But that was to be the pattern for the rest of Julius's life. He was outspoken, challenging, and, later on as an adult, constantly correcting orchestras in the pits during rehearsals. Even though he was always correct in his complaints, at times he would be barred from rehearsals for causing too much of a disturbance.

Anna did everything she could to raise more money for Julius's education, determined that he would be another Paderewski at Carnegie Hall. But as time progressed, and Julius was exposed to more difficult music than the Beethoven and Mozart he had mastered, he encountered difficulty, especially with the compositions of Rachmaninoff and Scriabin. Teachers told him that his hands were neither big enough nor strong enough to allow him to become a great pianist. Anna was determined, but Julius knew it would never happen.

Julius was short, pudgy, and arrogant. Classmates in high school made fun of him, giving him the nickname "Fat." Even when he played, it was classical music, which bored his classmates. So he went to a music store and learned to play "Alexander's Ragtime Band." He was offered a job and took his pay in pop sheet music. At lunchtime he would sit at the piano and play. His classmates's attitude changed and the nickname was dropped.

When visiting in his Uncle Hyman's apartment Julius had become interested in gambling, as he watched what were relatively high-stakes card games. He had gotten a job playing piano in a band for five dollars a night. He gave some of the money to his mother. But some went to bookies for gambling on horse races. He placed his first bet at the age of thirteen.

At fourteen, claiming he was two years older, he joined the musicians' union and became the relief pianist at a burlesque house. His parents had no idea where he was spending his nights. By sixteen, he was sitting in with the greatest jazz musicians in Chicago.

Julius met Mike Todd who asked him if he could write music. He responded that he could. Todd, an up and coming entrepreneur, told Jule, as he was now known, that he had an act with a girl in a cocoon. She would ultimately jump out half-naked and Todd needed a song for it. In just two hours, Todd wrote the lyrics and Jule the music for "The Moth and the Flame."

In a highly successful career, Todd would go on to produce, among other projects, the movie AROUND THE WORLD IN 80 DAYS.

As Jule progressed in his efforts to find success with music, another individual with a similar name became part of his life. Jules Stein, a medical student, played music as a sideline to his studies. Stein would ultimately become the founder of MCA, the Music Corporation of America, the most successful booking agency west of New York City. He heard Jule play and offered him a job at a summer resort. Through that job Jule met great musicians like Benny Goodman, Bix Beiderbecke, Eddie Condon, and Gene Krupa.

When Jule graduated from high school he received no honors, but was known as the best lunchtime pianist at the school. He would spend hours listening to Louis Armstrong, Fats Waller, King Oliver, Earl "Fatha" Hines, Bessie Smith, and Ma Rainey, copying their styles.

Jule got hired to play with the famous Arnold Johnson band in Florida for the winter season. He found that the entertainment business was being run by gangsters, but if he kept to himself no one would bother him, and he would always get paid on time. Unfortunately, he met a horse trainer and began going with him every day to Hialeah. When the season ended he returned to Chicago to play in various orchestra pits, just waiting to return to Florida.

He spent the days of the winter of 1926 at the racetrack, and after playing with the Johnson band in the evening he was at the blackjack tables at night. With some of the money he earned he bought property in Florida with Adolph Deutsch, the band's orchestrator. He soon lost all the property at the blackjack table. Those properties, in the center of Fort Lauderdale, were valued at four million dollars by the mid 1970s.

While in Florida, Jule wrote a song that was given to a lyricist, Ned Miller. It was published and sold five thousand copies. The title was "Sunday." Years later Frank Sinatra recorded it, but so many people took a cut of the receipts that

Left to right: Adolph Green, Betty Comden, Judy Holliday, and Jule Styne in rehearsal for BELLS ARE RINGING, c. 1950s (Photofest.)

Jule received less than a penny a copy. Because of that song, Ben Pollack offered him a job as an arranger and pianist for his band at Chez Paree. In the orchestra were Benny Goodman, Glenn Miller, and Charley Spivack. They taught him a great deal about playing jazz piano.

After awhile, Pollack's regular pianist returned and Jule found a new job at a club called Granada. Once he got into a minor dispute with a secretary there, calling her inefficient. Part of the problem was that Jule had a strange rapid fire way of speaking, which at times was difficult to understand and became known as Steinese. Ethel Rubenstein was a twenty-year old blue-eyed blonde whose family was very important in the catering business. She was a real homebody, not like the tall showgirls that Jule was dating. He described her as neither clever, witty, nor sexy. But her father was a major horse player and he and Jule began going to the track together. Jule dated her in the spring and summer of 1927 and they were married in September. Her family catered the affair.

The two families really did not like each other. The Rubensteins felt that the Steins were of a lower class. The Steins felt that the Rubensteins were too uppity.

Immediately after the wedding Jule was told that the band was going to play for a weeklong party to celebrate the Dempsey-Tunney fight. Jule said he couldn't leave the Granada. He was told that arrangements had already been made and he was to meet Mr. Brown, who had booked fifty rooms at the Metropole Hotel. Mr. Brown was the pseudonym for Al Capone. The hotel was filled with gangsters. Jule was frisked as he entered the room where there were eight men with guns in chest holsters. He was told what was planned and asked only if he could play Gershwin.

At Capone's party there were forty senators and congressmen, and a dozen judges and local politicians. At the height of the big fight night, Capone came to the bandstand and asked for the baton. He then conducted *Rhapsody in Blue*. When done, the orchestra joined the audience in applauding for Capone, primarily out of fear. Capone gave out envelopes containing five hundred dollars for each musician. There was twenty-five hundred dollars for Jule; it covered a lost bet he placed on Jack Dempsey.

The Rubensteins then bought a huge hotel for catering and created apartments in it for all their children to live. Jule would wander into his relatives' apartments to place his bets, because unlike the rest of the family, Ethel did not approve. In 1929, their first son, Stanley, was born.

Jule was not very happy. He hated the entire family's very close-knit relationship. He really didn't like Ethel at all. In 1930, Ethel left to spend the summer with her family and returned home to find Jule in bed with a young woman. Jule admitted his guilt and said that Ethel would have to divorce him. To his dismay, she decided instead to forgive him. But Jule didn't want to be forgiven. He wanted out of the marriage.

Music was beginning to change. Small jazz combos were falling out of favor and the big band sound was coming in.

Jule got a break in 1932. Through his connection with Al Capone, aka Mr. Brown, he was chosen to lead the band in the new 225 Club. It was being managed by an elegant gangster by the name of Eddie Leibensberger. Jule had carte blanche to spend what he needed to get a class orchestra. Present at opening night were Capone, Frank Nitti, and a large number of politicians and millionaires. The maitre d' was Joe Spagot, a well-known mobster.

The wife of the other Jules Stein, who had become the head of MCA, was offended by the fact that people were confusing her very successful husband with this young "piano player." As a result, Jule, the bandleader, was asked to come to MCA's executive offices. He was told that MCA was impressed with his success at the 225 Club and wanted to make plans for him and the band to be featured across the country. But first he had to change his name because it sounded too Jewish. When Jule said he couldn't understand because their boss had the same name, he was told his new name would be Dick Ford. He responded that he would think it over. He anguished and thought his mother couldn't talk to people and say, "My son Dick Ford." So he said he'd change his name, but only to Jule Styne, spelled with a "y" instead of "ei." MCA agreed.

Things went sour at the 225 Club. One day a known bank robber, Gus Winkler, came in and took a table by himself, and returned every evening. Jule was told that it was now Winkler's club. Winkler told Jule that he wanted him to play golf with him every day. Jule, understanding that his job would be on the line, agreed. Liebensberger, Spagot, and Styne were all frightened by Winkler because he seemed a little crazy.

One day a bank was robbed in Minneapolis. Bonds that were stolen were showing up in Chicago. A person who was selling them admitted to the authorities that he was getting them at the 225 Club. That day Spagot went to the liquor storage area of the club and found a bunch of the bonds from the bank. Spagot and the Capone gang never were involved in robberies and this was going to mean trouble.

Spagot, in a panic, provided Leibensberger with a ridiculous excuse for why he would be quitting his job immediately. As Spagot left, he stopped by the bandstand and whispered to Jule Styne, forcefully, "Gei!," which meant "go."

Styne finished the song and said to the band, "Pack up and get out of here!" The next morning Leibensberger's body was found, a supposed suicide. Later information came forth that Leibensberger was told by Frank Nitti to either kill himself or he would be killed. Styne first heard about the suicide at his regular golf game with Winkler. After the game Jule locked himself in his apartment, fearing for his life. Two days later he heard that Winkler had been discovered with 148 bullet holes in his body. Styne got an anonymous phone call to show up at an apartment. To his surprise he was given an envelope with money to pay off the members of the orchestra. So Jule left and took the job that had been promised by MCA. He was paid extremely well, but he lost most of the money to gambling. Meanwhile, Ethel's father provided a great deal of financial assistance to Jule's family.

By this time Jule's brother Maury was quite successful, having now joined the Guy Lombardo Orchestra. And his sister Claire was wealthy. She had married the steel magnate Robert Bregman. Once she went to see Jule's band play and found him to be quite dejected. She persuaded her husband to finance a move for Jule to New York City to find greater opportunities.

In New York, Styne became a pianist for the Meyer Davis society band. Soon thereafter, a leading vocal coach became ill and because of what Styne had learned from singers like Sophie Tucker in Chicago he got the job. He was so impressive that a businessman decided to sponsor him in opening a private vocal coaching school. It was so successful that he soon had twenty students each paying him fifty dollars per lesson. It continued for two years until the Broadway star Harry Richman heard about Jule. Richman had lost his pianist-conductor and hired Styne for the job.

Things were moving rapidly for Jule as 20th Century Fox got wind of him and, with Richman's consent, hired Styne to be the vocal coach for Tony Martin, Alice Faye. and Shirley Temple at three hundred fifty dollars per week. Shirley Temple was particularly difficult. She bossed her parents around, had temper tantrums, and worked only when she wanted.

Styne's salary rose rapidly to seven hundred fifty dollars per week. He worked a few hours in the morning, then spent the remainder of the day playing poker or going to the track. Gambling was rampant on the lot and lots of writers left at lunchtime to go out to Santa Anita. They would return after the sixth race.

The back lot was also overrun with starlets. In 1937, Jule started a relationship with a singer. They became serious and Ethel knew about it. The singer ended it, determining that Jule wouldn't get divorced. Ethel and Jule stayed together and even had another child, Norton, in 1939, even though they were both unhappy about their marriage.

In 1939, it was Alice Faye who insisted that the studio raise Styne's salary to fifteen hundred dollars per week to prepare her for her weekly radio show. Still most of his money was lost at the track. Once he had to borrow ten thousand dollars to pay off a bookie. Actually nine thousand went to the bookie and the other thousand was lost trying to make it back at the track. Styne was severely addicted to gambling.

In 1940, an upheaval occurred at Fox and many artists

on studio contracts were laid off. Jule was offered the opportunity to go on an eight-week trip with Constance Bennett. She was traveling by train on a tour to promote a line of cosmetics. It would end in New York, where she would star in a Broadway show. But she had never sung professionally before and Styne was to train her throughout the multi-city tour.

After a few days they were sharing a bedroom. By the end of the trip she was trying to persuade him to divorce Ethel and marry her. He did not want to marry her. So, as an excuse, he insisted that because of the children there was no way he could leave his wife. He returned to Hollywood and got a job with Republic. It was not the classiest of studios, but it was a job. They prided themselves on being able to shoot a full-length film in six days. They made lots of westerns. Besides the continuous B movies, they would make one or two high-quality films a year.

Styne's salary dropped to a meager one hundred and forty-five dollars per week. For that he was doing vocal coaching, acting as a rehearsal pianist, a choral director, and an orchestra conductor, and occasionally composing songs.

At that time Frank Loesser was coming into his own as a lyricist at Paramount. Cy Feuer, who was running Republic, made a deal with Paramount to borrow Loesser for one picture. Loesser was furious, and said, "I'm writing with Hoagy Carmichael now. I'm not coming here to work with some half-assed piano player who is really a vocal coach." After arguing for two hours with Feuer, he agreed just to talk with Styne.

Loesser had a notoriously foul mouth and ferocious temper. He went into a tirade in Styne's bungalow, chastising him for having the nerve to request Loesser as a collaborator. Loesser complained that Johnny Mercer was getting the best composers to work with even though he himself was writing the best lyrics. Styne persuaded him to calm down and listen to some music. Shortly after he started playing, Loesser told him to stop and said, "Don't you ever play that for anyone else." When Styne agreed, Loesser told him to save it for Paramount.

Loesser stayed, fighting with the management at Republic and finishing up a cowboy movie. He requested that Paramount get Styne for a movie. For the 1942 picture, SWEATER GIRL, they wrote a song based on the melody that Styne had began playing for him when they first met. It ended up spending twenty weeks on the Hit Parade. The song was "I Don't Want to Walk Without You."

Meanwhile Styne was still writing for Republic. Their biggest star, who sold huge numbers of copies of every song he ever recorded, was Gene Autry. Styne longed to write a song for him. But the Sons of the Pioneers, one of the most popular groups singing and composing Western music, had total control of Autry's movies and no one could write any of his songs except them. One day Styne was able to get Autry alone and presented him with "Purple Sage in the Twilight." Autry showed him how it needed to be changed to fit his style. It became a great hit. But the Sons of the Pioneers never let Jule write another song for Autry.

In 1943, the lyricist Sammy Cahn lost his writing partner. A producer put Cahn and Styne together and they wrote their first song, "I've Heard That Song Before."

Cahn and Styne soon became the most successful songwriting team ever in Hollywood. They had hit after hit. Harry Cohn, the dictatorial head of Columbia Pictures, contracted them to write for seven movies in 1943. For the first four they would be paid fifteen thousand dollars each, twenty thousand dollars for the fifth, twenty-five thousand dollars for the sixth, and thirty thousand dollars for the seventh. Styne had no personal relationship with Cohn, but Cahn did.

Harry Cohn would regularly bring Cahn to his home to play gin rummy. Sammy Cahn would always win. Styne asked Cahn to lose once in a while, saying that he thought it wasn't good for them for Cahn to win every time. One day Cahn came to Cohn's office to collect on three hundred twenty dollars of IOU's. Cohn was angry that he had been embarrassed in front of his secretary and was extremely offended. So Styne had an idea to get back into Cohn's good graces.

Harry Cohn was having his fiftieth birthday. Styne and Cahn wrote an entire two-hour show to be performed at his home with a number of movie stars. It was quite spectacular. The following week Styne and Cahn got a message from a very pleased Harry Cohn that he wanted to extend their contract at the same salary scale. Cahn responded by saying they deserved and wanted a doubling of their salary or they would go elsewhere. Cohn was furious and demanded they come to his home. When they arrived he was at his poolside and shouted at them that they were ungrateful. He was extending their contract. After shouting back and forth, Cohn told them to leave and that they were fired. Up to that point Styne had said nothing. He called back to Cohn as he was leaving the grounds that he was terribly disappointed because he was planning such a great party for Cohn's fifty-first birthday.

In 1944, they wrote the hit song "I'll Walk Alone" for FOLLOW THE BOYS; it was Dinah Shore's first big break in movies.

Cahn and Styne believed that they could write a show for Broadway, rather than just writing for the movies. It was to be called GLAD TO SEE YOU, starring Danny Thomas and Lupe Velez. There were many problems with the production and as a result they kept losing one lead performer after another. By the time of the tryouts, no one was left for the lead. They actually decided to use Sammy Cahn himself to play the lead. He was so bad that the entire show was an embarrassment and Styne lost forty thousand dollars of his own money.

MGM was making the movie ANCHORS AWEIGH with Frank Sinatra and Gene Kelly. Sinatra was told he could have anyone write the score, even Kern or Porter. Sinatra responded that he wouldn't make the movie unless it was Cahn and Styne. The movie was a huge hit and the

In rehearsal for SAY, DARLING, *left to right:* David Wayne, Vivian Blaine, and composer Jule Styne. (Photofest.)

big song was, "I Fall in Love Too Easily."

For the Hollywood crowd in the mid 1940s, Monday night was very special. The most exclusive club in the world met at the home of the dean of popular music, Jerome Kern. There, Kern was joined by Ira Gershwin, Harry Warren, Harold Arlen, Johnny Mercer, and Hoagy Carmichael. They would play the newest songs they were writing. A music publisher, Buddy Morris, who knew both Kern and Styne, called and asked if he could bring Styne to meet the group. Kern said he would like to meet Jule. Once there Jule was introduced and asked to play. It was wartime and many of the newest songs related to that subject. So Jule played one of his newest songs, "It's Been a Long, Long Time."

He played several other of his songs and by the end of the evening was asked to be a permanent member. Jule was overwhelmed. The following evening at a dinner party, the hostess answered the phone and said it was Jerome Kern calling for Jule. He asked if Jule could come to his house for breakfast the next day. The remainder of the evening was filled with expectation. Did Kern want Jule to collaborate on a show? Was he going to request some special material?

The next morning, after Jule sat nervously through breakfast, Kern went to a drawer and pulled out a racing form and said, "I hear you're the greatest handicapper in town."

By the end of the 1940s, Cahn and Styne had written so many hits that Cahn was a millionaire. Styne, on the other hand, was on the edge of bankruptcy having lost all of his money to gambling. The team, however, was beginning to fall apart. They used separate agents. At a party at Sinatra's home, unaware that Styne was within hearing distance, Cahn's agent asked Sinatra how he would feel about Cahn writing Sinatra's music in the future with Harry Warren rather than Styne. But Sinatra was very fond of Jule and responded that as a matter of fact he was considering having Styne write with Ira Gershwin rather than Cahn. Cahn's agent got word back to Cahn immediately, after which Cahn called Styne to find out why he was dropping him and switching to Gershwin. Styne responded angrily that he had been privy to the conversation and that Sinatra had just made up that story because he was offended by the disloyalty. He told Cahn there was no such plan. But things were never the same between the two of them.

More than anything, Styne wanted to reverse the terrible failure of his first effort for Broadway. He found a story that he thought would work. In 1947, after wheeling and dealing he got Jerome Robbins to be the choreographer and George Abbott to direct. They ended up with the hit show HIGH BUTTON SHOES, which ran for 727 performances and had two hit songs, "Papa Won't You Dance with Me" and "I Still Get Jealous."

It was now just a matter of time before Styne would abandon Hollywood and Sammy Cahn. Jule's longtime relationship with Frank Sinatra, who was beginning a downhill period before his later resurgence, was becoming less important. However, Sinatra did not take Styne's departure very well. Even Jule's relationship with his family had become unimportant to him.

Warner Brothers did sign up Cahn and Styne for one more picture, 1948's ROMANCE ON THE HIGH SEAS. It was from a script that had been tossed around for years. Doris Day had never done anything more than sing with the Les Brown Orchestra until that time. She got the role over several other name stars but received only fourth billing in the ads. But Day became a star overnight singing Styne's song, "It's Magic."

At home things were bad. Jule and Ethel were living together but hardly speaking. They were as good as divorced. In 1948, he went to New York alone, staying for six weeks. By that point, Anita Loos had been working on a story for several years. An entire crew had been selected before a composer was sought and Styne was suggested. Leo Robin, who lived near Styne in Los Angeles and had already had two failed shows on Broadway, was suggested for the lyrics. Robin was doing well in Hollywood but agreed because they said he could remain in California and write the show with Styne. Initial backer auditions went poorly but when Rodgers, Hammerstein, Leland Hayward, and Joshua Logan each committed five thousand dollars, money poured in. Several stars auditioned, but when Styne heard Carol Channing in the show LEND AN EAR, with her big eyes and strange voice, he knew she was it. He insisted they hire her. GENTLEMEN PREFER BLONDES accumulated a record advance, fabulous reviews, and became a smash that ran for 740 performances. Its hit song was "Diamonds Are a Girl's Best Friend."

During the production Anita Loos introduced Styne to Ruth Dubonnet, who had grown up in New York high society. She was a beauty who had family ties back to Revolutionary days. Her husbands had been the painter Goldbeck, Comte de Vallombrosa, and Andre Dubonnet from the aperitif family. Much of her life was spent in Parisian society. She started dating Jule, who was from quite a different background. She taught him how to dress and how to act with the likes of the Baruchs, the Sloans, and the Sarnoffs. Eventually they accepted him because of his talent. Ruth wanted to marry him, but Jule could never make up his mind to go that far.

Immediately after GENTLEMAN PREFER BLONDES Styne was told that the eccentric millionaire, Howard Hughes, wanted him and Robin to make a movie starring Tony Martin and Janet Leigh, with Gower Champion as the director. After one month they were told that Hughes wanted to see one scene. Hughes immediately fired Champion and most of the others. Styne and Robin quit and the project ended.

Through all of this Styne's addiction to gambling had only gotten worse, even though Ethel and Ruth Dubonnet had both tried to get him to stop. In 1951, a bookie threatened to have him killed if he didn't immediately come up with ten thousand dollars. That same year Styne decided he wanted to produce a revival of Rodgers and Hart's PAL JOEY, which had been unsuccessful in its first run, primarily due to a poor review by Brooks Atkinson in the *New York Times*. It had broken Larry Hart's heart. Styne struggled to get backers. Even Rodgers was not very interested. Styne cast Harold Lang in the original Gene Kelly role and persuaded Vivienne Segal to return to her original role. It got great reviews this time, even from Atkinson. Running for 542 performances it became one of Broadway's greatest revivals.

In 1952, he wrote the music for the Broadway revue TWO ON THE AISLE, which ran for 279 performances. The following year, he wrote HAZEL FLAGG, which lasted for 190 performances. He was working constantly to produce money for his gambling addiction.

Ethel was granted a divorce in 1952 on the grounds of desertion. It cost Jule a great deal financially as the IRS claimed that all the years of New York expenses listed as business were really as a result of the desertion, and disallowed them as business expenses. They claimed six hundred fifty thousand dollars from him.

Styne and Robin got another opportunity. David Selznick, whose light had now faded in Hollywood, had a script that they wanted. Selznick demanded and received a ten thousand dollar advance. When Styne got the cancelled check back it was stamped by the grocery chain, Gristede's. Styne was concerned that the check had gotten into the wrong hands and contacted the store management. He was told not to reveal the information, but that Selznick owed the store sixteen thousand dollars and that's why they had gotten the check. Styne felt sorry for Selznick and even embarrassed about finding out the information. The show, however, closed immediately. Styne said the only source that profited from the show was Gristede's.

The friendship with Sinatra blossomed again. Sinatra had made a comeback with FROM HERE TO ETERNITY. Styne was to do a new movie for him and Marilyn Monroe. But under terrible stress she quit and eloped with Joe DiMaggio. At that time, while in Los Angeles, Styne was living at the Beverly Hills Hotel. One day, returning to his room, he was told he no longer lived there and asked why. He was told that Sinatra had come there, checked him out, and moved all his clothes to Sinatra's apartment at Wilshire and Beverly Glen. Sinatra's marriage to Ava Gardner had fallen apart and he was lonely and unhappy. When he arrived, Sinatra told him to get dressed in formal wear. They were going to a party. Styne did as he was told. Once at the party, Sinatra told him not to come back to his apartment that night. Styne, baffled, exclaimed, "You've just moved me in!' Sinatra told him that he had date with a woman Styne knew. Sinatra was obviously bringing her back to the apartment. He told Styne to go back to the Beverly Hills Hotel and return the next day.

Jule began working with Comden and Green. He was brought in during the previews to add five songs to Mary Martin's PETER PAN.

In 1955, Cahn and Styne won their first Oscar, for the song "Three Coins in the Fountain." Styne had previously been nominated but lost with "I Don't Want to Walk Without You," "I'll Walk Alone," "It's Magic," and "I've Heard That Song Before."

Styne next wrote and produced a show with George Axelrod that starred Jayne Mansfield called WILL SUCCESS SPOIL ROCK HUNTER. It ran for 452 performances.

Styne was working constantly, and produced a show for Sammy Davis, Jr., with music by the young Jerry Bock and Sheldon Harnick, MR. WONDERFUL. It ran for one year but was not very well reviewed.

By November 1956, Styne had another show of his own, BELLS ARE RINGING starring Judy Holliday. The show remained on Broadway for 924 performances. Written with Comden and Green, the hit songs were "Just in Time" and "The Party's Over."

Around the end of that year, David Merrick bought the rights to GYPSY and wanted Styne and Comden and Green. But Comden and Green were having difficulty trying to write a book for the musical, so the project languished.

Styne was now confronted with the problems of aging parents. His mother had died and now his father was dying as well. While Jule was at his father's bedside with Ruth and his sister Claire, the two women once again asked Jule to swear off gambling, but he refused to make such a commitment. After his father's death Ruth Dubonnet took Jule to Europe to introduce him to high society. Following that they moved in together and again seriously considered marriage.

With Comden and Green deserting the idea of GYPSY, Styne went on to write SAY, DARLING, which ran for a year and only closed because of a newspaper strike that disrupted the entire life of the city. Then GYPSY found new life. Ethel Merman was chosen to play Mama Rose. Arthur Laurents would write the book and Jerome Robbins would direct. It looked exciting because Merrick was the busiest producer on Broadway. But no one had selected a composer and no one was talking to Styne, which upset him immensely. Through the grapevine he had heard that Porter had turned it down because of ill health and Berlin was unhappy with the plotline. Laurents was pushing for Stephen Sondheim to do the music and lyrics, as they had worked together on WEST SIDE STORY. But Merrick, Merman, Robbins, and Hayward all wanted Styne to compose the music. Laurents felt that Styne wasn't capable of producing a truly dramatic score. Robbins suggested Laurents audition him. Laurents didn't believe that Styne would agree to such a thing and was shocked to discover how willing the composer was. In that setting Styne won him over. When Sondheim had found he was rejected as composer he no longer wanted to write the lyrics. But on the advice of his dear friend and mentor, Oscar Hammerstein II, he undertook the job.

When Styne and Sondheim did get together they immediately hit it off wonderfully. They discussed each song in depth. Styne was tremendously impressed by Sondheim. It took them five weeks to complete the show. But Merrick kept insisting on a big special number, which they finally achieved with "Rose's Turn."

The score was considered by some to be one of the finest ever created for Broadway. It included "Everything's Coming up Roses," "Together, Wherever We Go," "You'll Never Get Away from Me." and "Some People."

Jule fell in love again. This time it was with Sandra Church, who had been chosen to play the role of Gypsy Rose Lee. She was thirty years younger than Styne. Jule wanted to get married. This time it was Church who was uncertain.

The opening of the show was spectacular. GYPSY is generally considered Styne's greatest work. Unfortunately, at the cast party Ruth Dubonnet and Sandra Church had a confrontation. Ruth walked out, asked Jule to vacate the apartment, and left for Europe alone. Sandra said their ages were too far apart and rejected him as well.

The show was subsequently made into a film in 1962 and had revivals on Broadway in 1974 with Angela Lansbury, Tyne Daly in 1989, Bernadette Peters in 2003, and Patti LuPone in 2008. Even a television version appeared in 1993, starring Bette Midler.

From his earliest days in New York, Jule had hired Sylvia Herscher to manage his life. She ultimately hired Dorothy Dicker, a bright twenty-year-old, to assist her. Over the years Dicker came to manage everything and understand Jule very well, even his strange, rapid manner of speech. She also understood his gambling addiction and did everything she could to control it. When GYPSY began to bring in large sums of money, Dorothy understood how deeply in debt he was to Ethel and the IRS, who were demanding four hundred thousand dollars. She called Vegas to try to stop all his credit lines. The struggle with him became so difficult that she quit. His response to her was, "If you leave, I'm leaving too." She stayed on.

In 1960, he wrote the show DO RE MI with Comden and Green. They got Perry Como to record the song, "Make Someone Happy," three months before the opening, which guaranteed that the show would be a success.

DO RE MI was playing to packed houses when Styne got a call from Pierre Salinger letting him know that President Kennedy was coming to New York and wanted tickets for that night. Everything was sold out. But Styne found out that a Jewish agency had bought a block of tickets and the person organizing it was a Mrs. Jacobson. He contacted her and explained his problem. If she would give up her two seats, he would put up two chairs elsewhere for that performance and give her eight more tickets with no charge to later performanc-

Jule Styne, Barbra Streisand, and Bob Merrill. (Photofest.)

es. Mrs. Jacobson responded, "If the President of the United States wants my ticket, let him ask me."

Styne told Salinger his problem and was assured that was no problem. That evening in the lobby the President was brought up to her and said, "Thank you very much. You're most kind." At which point Mrs. Jacobson fainted dead away.

The show ran for 400 performances.

Styne wanted to make a musical of A TREE GROWS IN BROOKLYN and told Richard Zanuck he wanted the leads to be Frank Sinatra and Marilyn Monroe. Zanuck said if Styne could pull that off he would give him a quarter of a million dollars. Styne told Sinatra that Monroe was dying to do it with him. He did the exact same thing with Monroe. With both leads enthusiastic, a meeting was arranged for the two of them for the following Monday. On Sunday, Styne heard the news that Marilyn Monroe had been found dead of an overdose.

By 1961, with Comden and Green, Styne was back on Broadway with SUBWAYS ARE FOR SLEEPING, which lasted for 205 performances.

The word was out on the street that Fanny Brice's daughter wanted her mother's story to be told. Her husband was the powerful agent and producer Ray Stark, who presented the idea to David Merrick. Mary Martin would be the star. When the idea was presented to Styne and Sondheim, they felt Martin was wrong because Brice was an ethnic Jewish comedienne. Sondheim lost interest and was replaced by Bob Merrill. Styne was impressed when he gave Merrill a score and only three days later Merrill came up with the lyrics for "Don't Rain on My Parade."

Anne Bancroft was the next suggested lead, but Merrill thought that she was wrong for the part as well. Styne encouraged Merrill to keep on writing even without anyone selected to play the lead. Merrill then wrote the lyrics for "People."

Merrill had not known Styne personally before this and was shocked by the characters who came to talk to Jule while they were working. They were gangster-type bookies. When Styne and Merrill completed their work they played it for Stark, Merrick, and Bancroft. They loved it, but Bancroft backed out because she knew it was beyond her musical talent.

While working on the show, Styne got invited to a dinner party at Stark's home and was seated next to a young actress who whispered into his ear that he was the rudest person she had ever known. Baffled, he asked "Why?" Two years previously he had arranged a date with her and inadvertently forgot about it. Jule never showed up or contacted her. He asked if he could make it up by taking her to lunch the next day. After all the years of indecision with so many women, he asked her to marry him and in two more weeks they were wed. His bride, Margaret Brown, was thirty years his junior, tall, beautiful and had red hair. At Jule's insistence, Dorothy Dicker, his guardian and watchdog, told Maggie nothing of his gambling addiction. Later Maggie said she married him strictly on the basis of the life he was promising. It sounded exciting.

Styne told Maggie to go shopping for the wedding and she spent five thousand dollars. When Dorothy saw the bills she advised her not to shop anymore, but would not tell her the reason why. In short order Jule borrowed fifty thousand dollars from Maggie, a major portion of her life savings. Maggie said their first year was difficult. She had always realized that she was beautiful and felt insecure in the belief that it was her only strength. But during a conversation with him, Jule once said that when he married her he hadn't noticed any particular physical beauty; it was the rest that attracted him. She was completely won over.

Styne was certain that a performer he had seen in another show would be perfect for the lead in what was now known as FUNNY GIRL. When he presented the idea to Jerome Robbins he agreed. The show would star Barbra Streisand. But Robbins got into a fight with Stark and quit.

Styne knew he had to keep working, and earn money fast. He signed a contract to write three Broadway shows for ABC, and another for Merrick. In fact he had six separate projects working. Dorothy Dicker understood the problem. Styne had just borrowed twenty thousand dollars from her father. Bob Fosse was hired to replace Robbins and then he quit. Streisand, unknown when they had hired her, had now become a big star in Las Vegas.

Of the multiple projects Styne was working on, the first to get into a theatre was a Brecht play called ARTURO UI starring Christopher Plummer. Styne wrote incidental music. It closed immediately in November 1963. The show FUNNY GIRL had now been in the works for three years.

By now Maggie knew of his gambling, but was unsuccessful in trying to get him to stop. She became pregnant and had a miscarriage.

FUNNY GIRL was in constant trouble. Fosse quit and was replaced by Garson Kanin, who also quit. Even Merrick was no longer involved in the show. Finally, in full circle, Kanin was replaced as Robbins was brought back to doctor the show. It opened in March 1964 and ran for 1348 performances. At a party Sinatra told Styne that the reason he had refused to record the huge hit "People" was that the song wasn't very good. They didn't speak to each other for another three years.

By that time the IRS was taking all of Jule's income from FUNNY GIRL and from ASCAP. He had no source of money at all. Dorothy Dicker was keeping him afloat. She took no salary for nine months, constantly protecting him from creditors. One friend told him that the best thing Styne could do would be to commit suicide. But it was Comden and Green's attorney, William Fitelson, who came to his rescue. He persuaded Louis Dreyfuss, the head of the Chappell Music Corporation, to give Styne a three hundred fifty thousand dollar interest-free loan to pay off the IRS and everyone else. The IRS liens were lifted.

In 1964, he also wrote FADE OUT—FADE IN with Comden and Green. It was on Broadway for 271 performances.

On Christmas Day, 1964, Nicholas Styne was born. For the first time Jule began acting like a father, doing everything a devoted father would do for a newborn.

Even though MR. WONDERFUL had not been what he wanted, Styne still believed a African-American show could be a success. He wrote HALLELUJAH, BABY! for Leslie Uggams, which ran for ten months. The reviews were mediocre. Styne couldn't believe it when the show won the Tony for Best Musical when BELLS ARE RINGING, GYPSY, and FUNNY GIRL had all lost.

In 1968, Maggie delivered a baby girl, which brought Styne joy. But otherwise things were going poorly. In 1970, he had two failed shows, one with Bob Merrill and another with Sammy Cahn. He had not had a really big hit since 1964 with FUNNY GIRL. Jule began a new project with Merrick, Merrill, and Gower Champion. There were constant battles and firings. The show, SUGAR, finally opened. It was based on the film SOME LIKE IT HOT. Though it ran for eighteen months, the reviews were terrible, so Styne had not really gotten out of the slump.

But 1971, brought a new opportunity, a revival of GYPSY. Merman wouldn't repeat her role. Arthur Laurents thought the one to play Mama Rose was Angela Lansbury. But she rejected the part as well. The project got put on the shelf for more than a year before Lansbury changed her mind and spent a month working with Styne. It opened in London in 1973 to rave reviews with Lansbury getting eleven curtain calls on opening night.

Another revival started in Oklahoma City. It was a modification of GENTLEMEN PREFER BLONDES titled LORELEI and starred Carol Channing. It reached New York by January 1974 and ran there for a year.

In May 1974, Jule was honored by the New York community in a celebration called JULE'S FRIENDS AT THE PALACE. Styne even played the piano and stood crying during the standing ovation. That year also brought another success, as the Lansbury production of GYPSY opened in New York to reviews even greater than those garnered by the original opening.

The gambling was now under control so Styne did not have the need to get multiple projects off at the same time. But another opportunity arose. His children Nicky and Katherine, who knew their neighbor Neil Sedaka was always performing, asked their father to do that as well. An offer came to perform at the Rainbow Grill for one night. It was so well received he returned for a six-week engagement, which was a huge success and a wonderful culmination to a spectacular career. He ended by singing what he said was his favorite song of all he had written, "The Party's Over" from BELLS ARE RINGING.

But Styne was not finished writing shows. In 1978 when he was seventy-three he wrote BAR MITZVAH BOY. It ran in London for seventy-eight performances but never made it to Broadway. In 1980, his show ONE NIGHT STAND opened and closed after eight previews.

In 1985, when Styne was eighty, his show PIECES OF EIGHT opened and closed in Canada.

Eight years later, he wrote THE RED SHOES. The lyrics were written by Bob Merrill, with whom he had written FUNNY GIRL. However, Merrill used a pseudonym, possibly because he did not want to be identified with the show. It lasted only five performances though a subsequent article about it said it was "a work of the most spirited content."

Over a seven-decade career, Styne wrote 1,500 songs, a vast number becoming major hits. His career was among the most remarkable of the great composers of Broadway.

In 1994, at the age of eighty-nine, Styne underwent open heart surgery and died six weeks later. In a 1976 interview he said, "Any composer who could write for both a Sinatra and a Streisand in one lifetime is lucky and if I think about GYPSY, what a privilege it was to work with Jerry Robbins, Arthur Laurents, Steve Sondheim and Ethel Merman. That's a lot of talent for one show."

MAJOR WORKS

SHOWS:

HIGH BUTTON SHOES **(CAHN, 1947)**
GENTLEMEN PREFER BLONDES **(ROBIN, 1949)**
TWO ON THE AISLE **(COMDEN AND GREEN, 1951)**
HAZEL FLAGG **(HILLIARD, 1953)**
PETER PAN **(COMDEN AND GREEN, 1954)**
BELLS ARE RINGING **(COMDEN AND GREEN, 1956)**
SAY, DARLING **(COMDEN AND GREEN, 1958)**
GYPSY **(SONDHEIM, 1959)**
DO RE MI **(COMDEN AND GREEN, 1960)**
SUBWAYS ARE FOR SLEEPING **(COMDEN AND GREEN, 1961)**
FADE OUT—FADE IN **(COMDEN AND GREEN, 1964)**
FUNNY GIRL **(MERRILL, 1964)**
HALLELUJAH, BABY! **(COMDEN AND GREEN, 1967)**
DARLING OF THE DAY **(HARBURG, 1968)**
LOOK TO THE LILIES **(CAHN, 1970)**
SUGAR **(MERRILL, 1972)**
LORELEI **(ROBIN/COMDEN AND GREEN, 1974)**
THE RED SHOES **(MERRILL, 1993)**

COMPOSITIONS:

HE COMPOSED OVER 1,500 SONGS.

Fats Waller in his favorite place, at the piano. (Evening Standard/Hulton Archive/Getty Images.)

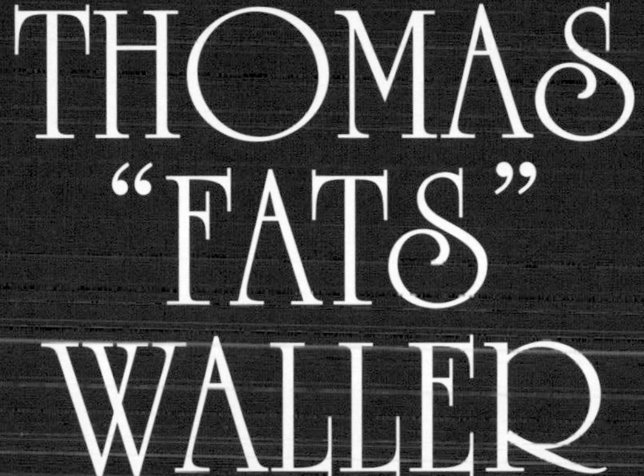

THOMAS "FATS" WALLER

THE DATES ARE NOT WELL RECORDED, BUT SOMEWHERE around 1870 Edward Martin Waller was born in Virginia. In his late teens he married Adeline Lockett. She played the piano, the organ, and sang. Edward wanted to leave the South and find work in New York City.

The African-American community that Waller found in New York was in a state of flux. One tends to think of Harlem as a nexus of African-American life, but at that time it was not so. The first black community in New York City established itself in the South Fifth Avenue area, in what is now called Greenwich Village. In time Irish and Italian families displaced them and African-American Manhattanites moved to the West 60s. That area's nickname was San Juan Hill, commemorating the significant assistance provided by African Americans to Teddy Roosevelt's Rough Riders. Middle-class African Americans were not happy there, as considerable gang warfare was erupting.

At that time, in the area we now know as Harlem, real estate speculators commissioned the famous architect Sanford White (who was fatally involved in a love triangle with performer Evelyn Nesbit and her husband) to design luxury houses and apartments. They were lavish, but a total failure, as affluent New Yorkers did not want to live so far from the centers of cultural life in Manhattan. They remained empty until the idea came to develop them into housing for affluent blacks. It became a very elite African-American community right after the turn of the century.

Everything changed with World War I. A huge influx of southern and West Indian blacks came to New York City to work in war industries. They moved into Harlem, which experienced a renaissance in the 1920s. Black artists, writers, and musicians flocked there to live and work, and white audiences followed to soak up the cultural scene.

When the Wallers first came to New York City, the family moved in to the South Fifth Avenue area. They had a child around 1900, one of the seven children of theirs who would die at birth or infancy. Thomas Wright Waller was born in May 1904. By then the family was living in Harlem, on 134th Street. Two surviving brothers were born before him and two surviving sisters after him. The family was deeply religious and Edward became a firebrand preacher. But he also had a moving business and was a good provider for the family.

Thomas learned to play the piano before he was ten. He would skip school and go anyplace where he could hear music, including Harlem nightclubs, as a teenager. His parents grew frantic about his behavior. Once he created such a stir at home that he received a severe beating from his father, resulting in a major rift between them.

His mother was an extremely obese diabetic. His father believed that Thomas's disruptive behavior aggravated her condition. There was always more than ample food available and like his mother, Thomas consumed it, resulting in the nickname of "Fats."

He was only a fair student except in music. His classmates included Edgar Sampson, who later wrote "Stompin' at the Savoy," and the future great actor, Canada Lee.

In 1910, the family purchased a piano. Thomas was the obvious prodigy in the family, listening and replicating without any instruction. To the displeasure of his parents, he played the popular music of the times. When Thomas was eleven, his father accepted the fact that his son would opt for music, and not the ministry, for his life's course. He took Thomas to Carnegie Hall to hear Paderewski. Thomas was enthralled, but his love was still ragtime, the popular music of the times.

When Thomas was fourteen, he left school and took a job in a factory. Meanwhile he made friends with the sexton of the nearby Trinity Church so he could practice on their piano. Eventually, Fats quit the job and persuaded the pianist at the local movie house to allow him to sit in for her on her breaks. When she left the job, he took it full time for twenty-three dollars per week.

Every Saturday the theatre had a vaudeville show for which he played, and there he met the leading entertainers like Bert Williams. He made friends with all of them, and also began drinking for the first time.

When he was only sixteen, he met a girl named Edith Hatchett and embarked upon a serious relationship with her. She began bringing him home to her family.

Fats was also learning a new style of music that developed following ragtime. It was called "stride." James Johnson was its stalwart and Fats found a way to meet him.

In 1920, he had a terribly traumatic experience. Waller's extremely obese mother suddenly died. The horror of her death was compounded by the fact that she was so obese, her body could not be brought through the door, so it was lifted out through a window with block and tackle. Fats was so devastated that he moved out and in with the family of a friend, Russell Brooks. They had a player piano and Fats would play piano rolls made by Johnson and attempt to duplicate them.

Johnson, who was a busy performer, agreed to go hear Waller, and was extremely impressed. He decided he would teach Fats. A great teacher-student relationship developed between them. This time would come to be known as "the golden age of Harlem keyboardery." Pianos were so important, because there was no radio yet and phonographs were still in their infancy. Everyone who could find a way to afford it owned a piano.

The standard piano method involves the left hand playing supportive chords. The new development, stride, had the left hand playing both chords and a melody line, while bouncing from octave to octave. It was the new jazz piano. Johnson was untrained, but brilliant and imaginative. He studied by playing in the dark, in order to know the keyboard by feel, much as if he were blind. He even put a sheet over the keys to soften his touch.

Waller considered Johnson a surrogate father, and studied constantly with him. Through Johnson, seventeen-yearold Fats was introduced to the other most prominent stride performer of the time, Willie "The Lion" Smith. Smith was not nearly as warm and friendly as Johnson. He really had no interest in this new upstart, but Johnson prevailed on him to listen to Waller. Smith changed his mind completely and they became the three most important performers in the world of jazz piano as it was being played in Harlem.

In 1922, Waller made his first recording. Johnson had just started recording in 1921 and Smith was not recording at all. Clarence Williams, who wrote "Baby Won't You Please Come Home," got into the business of making recordings and fostered Waller's career in that direction. Waller hated touring and relished the idea of concentrating on recording.

Shortly after his mother died, Fats married Edith Hatchett and they soon had a son. That early commitment had a devastating effect on the rest of his professional life. Waller was always in financial distress. The result was that he spent years hiding from process servers for nonpayment of alimony and child support.

In the 1920s, in Harlem, many African Americans were just scraping by economically. By the end of each month it

American jazz pianist, singer, and songwriter Fats Waller in London. (Evening Standard/Hulton Archive/Getty Images.)

was time to come up with money for the landlord. "Rent parties" grew out of this monthly struggle. People would scrape together some food and liquor. The elite white society would come, for an entrance fee of up to fifty cents, and purchase the food and liquor. The focus of the party would be the upright piano, where the local greats would play for hours on end, like a battle of the pianists. George Gershwin was known to play there. Waller was finally invited to play in 1922. Toward the end of his career he wrote a song characterizing the rent party environment, "The Joint Is Jumpin'."

Johnson, Smith, and Waller were the big attractions in that world. But, by comparison, Gershwin was also playing in big concert halls, to which they did not have access. Independently, in different venues, black and white musicians were developing the same music. Once in a while the black musicians got invited to play at swank uptown parties for food, liquor and, occasionally, a fee.

All during that time Waller continued composing. He was carefree and light- hearted, unprofessional, disorganized, and frequently just forgot what he had composed. He could write a new composition in a few minutes, play it for a publisher, get twenty-five to fifty dollars and forget it completely. Sometimes, when requested, he could not play songs that had been published under his name, because he didn't remember them. He was always in desperate need of quick money to pay what he owed. At times he would make the rounds of publishers telling them he had worked for some time on a new song and make it up, right on the spot. Then he might play the same song for another publisher and sell it to him as well, very likely unintentionally, as he was not dishonest. The quick advance would go straight to the process server, as he had gotten divorced just a few years after his childhood marriage. But publishers soon caught on to that. He foolishly signed many terrible contracts, with no legal advice, committing him to produce a lot and receive very little.

Fats's consumption of food and liquor was unbelievable. Once after he ordered a dozen hamburgers to his dressing room, friends stopped by and began to help themselves. He told them to keep their hands off. They were for him and they could order what they wanted for themselves.

On another occasion, in a restaurant, he ordered three large porterhouse steak dinners and the waitress refused to serve him until his other two guests arrived. His voracious appetite resulted in obesity, which surely affected his health. Also, the volume of liquor he consumed certainly influenced the length of this life. A friend once said of him that "he was drunk for eighteen years and never had a hangover." He consumed about two fifths of alcohol a day. He was never a sad drunk, always smiling and happy. His amazing personality was a part of his performance. It is not possible to know what Fats was like as a performer without having the opportunity to see him. Fats was always outgoing, fun-loving, and jovial. When he entered a room it seemed to explode with humor and joy.

Thomas Waller was constantly in court on charges of non-payment of alimony and child support, charges for which he was jailed at least twice. One of those times he was placed in a cell with a millionaire who was there on the same charges. Though having no difficulty in paying, it was against the affluent prisoner's principles. He was so wealthy he was able to arrange for guards to bring into his cell gourmet food, liquor, and even a piano. When friends came to bail out Waller, he was having so much fun that he told them to "come back later, much later."

His fellow musicians were always on the lookout for the process servers. At the slightest indication they would warn him so that he could dash off the stage and vanish. Once, before anyone realized it, a process server got to him. He said, "You must be Thomas Waller." To which Fats replied, "Oh no sir! He's bigger . . . much bigger than me."

But in the late 1920s, he tried to reform. He had fallen in love again and married Anita Rutherford. He lowered his price to publishers for compositions in order to have a constant flow of money and was known to sell some pieces for as little as two dollars and fifty cents.

He completely lacked an understanding of how to manage his career financially. At one time he sold all the rights to thirty of his songs for three hundred dollars. Included in that group was one of his great favorites, "Honeysuckle Rose."

At the same time, others like Louis Armstrong, Duke Ellington, and Bix Beiderbecke made fortunes recording Waller's songs.

At times he didn't even show up for recording sessions. Victor Records was so upset with him that on one occasion they arranged for Eddie Condon, a famous musician, to be responsible for getting Fats to the session. Waller got Condon drunk. After a three-day binge, Condon finally realized the session was hours away and nothing had been prepared. He awakened the sleeping Waller, who quickly called a group of sidemen, telling them to meet him on a corner, where he picked them up and went completely unprepared to the studio. They performed wonderfully. The producers said they were thrilled with the results that Waller could achieve when he did serious preparation.

In 1928, Louis Armstrong, with Earl Hines on the piano, recorded Waller's song "Squeeze Me." It became a huge hit but it yielded almost no money for Fats.

By this time, Andy Razaf had become the major lyricist for Fats Waller's songs. In July 1929, the two were given an assignment in a Harlem show for a scene depicting an African-American girl in a bed bemoaning the trials of being black. The instructions were very specific. It was to be a comedy number. After all, it was prepared for a white audience, and all the media at that time portrayed blacks as foolish, dumb, and weak. But Waller and Razaf did not find it funny. So they created a very sad song that Duke Ellington turned into a smash hit, "Black and Blue."

Music historians believe that Waller wrote a number of songs that were published by great musicians under their own names because Waller had sold all the rights and never claimed his authorship. Thus, he never received credit for many of his compositions.

For example, Waller would frequently go to the apartment of Fletcher Henderson, the most important African-American musician/orchestra leader before Duke Ellington achieved that status. Henderson's wife was a wonderful cook who would prepare delicious food for Fats. Waller would trade songs to Henderson for the meals.

Bill Challis, a great arranger at that time, was given the assignment of arranging D Major Blues for Fletcher Henderson with a promise of receiving royalties. In a conversation with one of Henderson's musicians twenty years later Challis complained of not having received any royalties from Henderson's song. The musician said that it wasn't actually Henderson's song anyway—it just had his name on it. "That was Fats Waller's," he explained.

As fine a pianist as Waller was, his skill on the organ was renowned. No one before him had ever used the organ as a jazz instrument. Others tried it subsequently, but no one ever came close to matching his talent. He made a number of recordings on the organ in 1927 when he was twenty-three, which are still astonishing. They have a gospel flair to them.

He was so tied to the instrument that he not only had one in his home, he also owned a portable organ with which he traveled. Aside from jazz, he played religious and spiritual music on the organ. One of his last organ recordings was of "Sometimes I Feel Like a Motherless Child" with both gospel and jazz intonations. Immediately after that he recorded his version of Ellington's "Solitude." He was known to sit and play the organ for hours on end.

On tour he once had a Christmas party for his musicians in his room, where he played Christmas carols on his organ until everyone, homesick, was in tears.

Waller recorded a number of sessions that have never been found, including jazz versions of classical music on the organ, discarded because of the producers' mundane tastes. One such session was held with Bix Beiderbecke on the clarinet. Those who had heard it live said it was an absolute masterpiece. It was never found.

Waller developed his love for the organ very early. As a teenager he had been a delivery boy in Harlem for the

Immerman family's delicatessen. Once Prohibition started it became an outlet for liquor, which Fats delivered.

Just before he turned twenty, Fats was hired to play the organ at the Lafayette Theatre. But after spending more time talking to his girlfriend, Anita Rutherford, than playing, he got fired. Fortunately, the Immermans had purchased a club called Connie's Inn. In between the regular orchestra sets Fats was welcomed to play the organ for tips, which helped him tremendously.

Nightspots filled all of Harlem, which was the center of New York nightlife. Waller began writing shows with Razaf and Johnson in the late 1920s. During the intermission of these shows, he and Johnson would play piano duets. But his career took a sudden downturn when he was jailed for non-payment of alimony and didn't get out until 1929.

When Fats was released, Razaf immediately told him they were to write a new show. The show, LOAD OF COAL, was a big success and led to the opportunity to write another show, HOT CHOCOLATES in 1929. They completed two songs at Razaf's house and were working on a third when Waller suddenly insisted he had to leave for a heavy date. After Fats departed, Razaf could not remember the bridge and began making phone calls to find him. Once reached, Fats said he couldn't even remember the beginning. It is believed that hundreds of songs were lost because he was so disorganized that he didn't write them down and after a short while couldn't remember them. Razaf's hummed version of the original melody reminded Fats of the bridge, which he hummed back. Razaf told Fats to wait a minute as he rushed to the piano to see if it fit it in with the lyrics he had already constructed. He raced back to the phone to tell Fats that it worked. But Fats had already hung up. The song they hummed back and forth to each other became "Ain't Misbehavin'."

At the rehearsals for HOT CHOCOLATES, Fats would frequently compose a new song on the spot. While there, most of the time he kept the crew and performers in a constant state of laughter.

While performing at Carnegie Hall in 1927, he met a white songwriter who asked to buy a song. Fats sold it for five hundred dollars. It ultimately yielded seventeen thousand five hundred dollars to the buyer. Waller wasn't stupid. He knew he was being taken advantage of and resented it. His constant impoverished state forced him to allow himself to be victimized.

Recording was his primary source of income. In 1929, he had twenty records. By the year after the Depression struck, he had only one.

By then radios were inexpensive and had become very important. Waller had first done a radio performance in 1923. He got a contract for a radio show called *Paramount on Parade* for twenty-six weeks and followed that with *Radio Roundup*. He would sing, play the piano, and talk constantly. By 1932, his radio showhad run its course.

He was at a loss concerning what he should do when he bumped into an old friend, Spencer Williams, with whom he had written "Squeeze Me." Spencer had moved to France, having long since given up on the United States, discontented with its racism. Williams told Waller of his grand lifestyle abroad, and Waller subsequently persuaded Anita to let him go to France with his buddy. To pay for the trip, he and Williams composed twenty-seven songs in three days and sold them. They left on the *Ile de France* in July. For five days on the cruise Fats entertained the passengers and crew and consumed a great deal of alcohol.

France and England had not yet been hit by the Depression and the dollar was strong and went far. They lived wildly from one bistro to another until the money ran out. As a result he was forced to return to the United States. Fortunately, he got two new recording dates.

By the end of 1932, Waller got a radio job in Cincinnati. The show was called *Fats Waller's Rhythm Club*. He developed a Midwestern following and remained with the show for an entire year. The station also had him doing a late-night show called *Moon River*, featuring Fats playing classical music on the organ.

He wanted to return to New York although the economic conditions were terrible there. Paul Whiteman lined him up to play piano at a private birthday party for George Gershwin in a Park Avenue apartment. Waller was doing his usual routine, singing, playing, mugging, and joking. A teenage girl could not tear herself away from the piano. Finally, she went to get her father, Bill Paley, the president of CBS, to hear Waller. The next day Paley arranged for Waller to have a show on CBS. Waller's life would change immensely as a result of that fortuitous meeting.

Waller began doing his *Rhythm Club* two nights a week and played classical music on the organ every other Saturday. On Sunday nights he was on the *Columbia Variety Hour*. Recording contracts began to come again. He had the third largest radio audience behind Amos 'n Andy and FDR. It ran on CBS from 1934 to 1942.

Now he was financially successful. It was no longer necessary for him to compose and sell at a furious rate. As a result he was writing better music in the 1930s than he did in the 1920s.

By 1935, he was the highest selling African-American recording artist, attracting both white and black consumers, which was very unusual for the time. He was now being heard across the nation, instead of just in Harlem. Promoters wanted him out on the road. Waller, however, hated the road and didn't like performing with big bands. He would at times disappear in the middle of a tour and return to New York. He despised the bad food, substandard accommodations, and lack of sleep that accompanied the one-night stands. Out of boredom he would drink more than ever. By breaking contracts he developed a bad reputation with promoters.

Around 1935, he got involved in a dispute that made national news, reaching all the way to the United States Congress. The estate of John Philip Sousa, through ASCAP, complained that Sousa received the same amount of royalty for his songs as Waller did for his song "Flat Tire Papa." Waller, who thought the entire episode was funny, couldn't even remember when he had written it. ASCAP really should never have been involved because they actually represented both of them. Waller began to get angry and went to the press claiming that jazz was just as good as Sousa's music. He added that Sousa's music "sent men to war," while Waller's music made them dance. Congress asked Waller to testify. He emphasized how eager he was to comply by saying, "I'd rather testify than eat." But nothing came of the whole matter.

Waller's career did suffer to some extent because of his bad behavior on the road. He wanted to be in Harlem where the great musicians were, including the new young sensation Art Tatum. He and Tatum became friends and once they went to a party together both dressed as women.

Waller loved and admired the great pianists Earl Hines, Thelonius Monk, and Billy Kyle. The respect they developed for Waller was mostly the result of hearing him play and improvise for hours on end in Harlem clubs. Those who only heard him on recordings and the radio did not experience the same Waller. What he played at the clubs was never recorded or written down. To the people who knew him well, he was an overgrown kid, filled with talent, humor, flamboyance, and a total lack of structure or organization.

Fats had a very short attention span and very little attachment to anything he composed. He frequently thought about his mother's death and the manner in which her body was removed from their dwelling. As a result, when he was alone, playing for himself, the music was mostly sad and emotional.

In 1938, his career took a downward turn. His agent was in failing health and not representing him well. Waller once again found himself deep in debt. Luckily, Ed Kirkeby, who worked for Victor while Waller recorded there, took him under his wing. Waller was in trouble with the IRS, his wife, the musicians' union and promoters. And above all, no work was available to him. Kirkeby, who had great personal affection for Fats, steered him in a new direction.

Kirkeby quietly arranged for Mr. and Mrs. Waller and himself to sail on the SS *Transylvania*. The guest list included the wealthy and titled. But by the end of the trip the best-liked passenger was Fats. He taught the ship's orchestra jazz and played with them the remainder of the cruise. Kirkeby's first booking was in Scotland. He had a world of experience, and had worked with Red Nichols and the Dorsey Brothers. Fats got ten curtain calls at the first engagement. Kirkeby was committed to helping him.

The tour through England and Scandinavia was extremely successful. But there was a problem, namely the rise of the Nazi party. They were, however, able to make a swift retreat to the United States on the *Ile de France*.

The trip to Europe was so successful that, on his return, Fats was able to buy a house in Queens, New York, near his mentor, James Johnson. He would wander into Johnson's home at four or five in the morning to play on the piano and compose, either not to disturb his own children or more likely to protect himself from being disturbed. Johnson, though in semi-retirement, was still composing symphonies, ballets, and operas. He and Fats were very close.

One of Fats's sons recalled that he would frequently play songs at home until four in the morning that were never recorded.

Kirkeby soon got a three-month run at the Yacht Club for Waller's group, Fats Waller and His Rhythm. It was the longest gig Waller had ever had in New York City.

When asked about his European tour he described how the audiences were different. He said they were much more knowledgeable and appreciative of music. When they played there it was not uncommon for the audiences to stop dancing and just listen. He said Americans only wanted loud and boisterous music, not allowing him to play things that were more sensitive.

When the Yacht Club engagement ended, Kirkeby planned another European trip. Fats composed a suite characterizing different areas of London, with Kirkeby doing a narration. Kirkeby thought it was so great he had it recorded, but just before its release war broke out in Europe. It was lost until Kirkeby found it again in 1948 and released it two years later. It presents an emotional and romantic side to Waller rarely heard in public. The music sounds like Mozart, Chopin, and Brahms.

After a while problems again developed with the road tours. There were cancelled engagements due to promoters' ineptitude. Occasionally, discrimination led to violence. The war was on and Waller gave a great many free concerts for servicemen, which disrupted his schedule. He pushed himself unmercifully to entertain the troops. But soon an exciting opportunity appeared.

Waller was booked to be the first jazz musician to do a solo concert at Carnegie Hall in 1942. For whatever reason, he went ahead with very poor preparation. The result was an extremely disappointing performance. He had invited friends to play with him there in a jam session. But by all accounts Waller was drunk. Soon after, his doctor had told him that he was drinking himself to death. It was news that led Waller to go on the wagon, drinking only soda pop.

But that did not last long.

The last recording session with his group, The Rhythm, was in 1942. The government was actually restricting recordings because of the raw materials needed for the war effort. The government enlisted Waller to write a song promoting conservation. He penned "Get Some Cash for Your Trash."

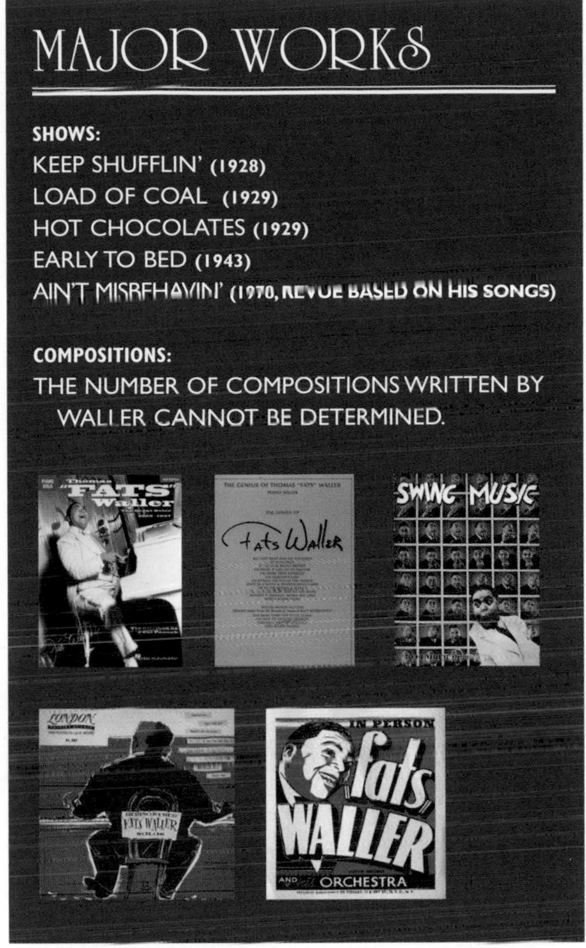

But it was quickly withdrawn when it was realized that trash was a euphemism for sex in prostitution slang.

In 1943, Waller got a role in the Lena Horne film STORMY WEATHER. Waller got great reviews for his performance and Kirkeby wanted to get him into more movies. By then he was composing very little. Kirkeby heard about a new show opening on Broadway called EARLY TO BED and thought there might be a performing part for Fats in it. But when he spoke to the producer, Dick Kollmar, Kirkeby found that they had not yet even selected a composer. So he persuaded Kollmar to sign Waller to write the score. Fats was exhilarated. The possibility of getting to Broadway was thrilling.

The show opened in Boston. A grand cocktail party was held at one of the luxury hotels there just before the opening, right after the interviews with the media. The city's most prominent people were there and he was the guest of honor. After the party he went to the front desk to get the key for his room. He was told that there was no room for him and he was turned away. He sadly recalled how well he had been treated in Europe, as opposed to the United States.

The show got mixed reviews, while Waller's music was highly praised. It ended up being a financial success.

In 1943, Victor finally arranged another recording session for him, during which he played and sang Vincent Youmans "Hallelujah," Ellington's "Solitude," and "Sometimes I Feel Like a Motherless Child," among other numbers.

Immediately after, Waller got an engagement at the Zanzibar Room in Los Angeles. It was warm and there was an air conditioner hovered immediately above his piano. Fats, at 285 pounds, was always in a profuse sweat while playing. He had cold air blowing down on him. At the end of the two weeks, he came down with a serious case of the flu and went to bed for ten days.

Waller was thoroughly exhausted. On the last night he went to a party in his honor, which Kirkeby wanted him to skip. He was so fatigued that he ultimately fell under the piano and went to sleep.

Kirkeby insisted on no more partying, and put him on the transcontinental train to back to New York City. But he was soon recognized in the club car and caroused all night. He spent the entire next day sleeping in his compartment. Kirkeby, concerned, went to check in on Waller and found it freezing in there. He stayed with him and fell asleep, only to be awakened by a choking sound coming from Fats's bed. Kirkeby jumped up and saw Fats trembling, but he couldn't awaken him. He rushed out of the room and, with a porter, searched for a physician. When the three men returned to the compartment, the doctor looked at Fats and said, "This man is dead!"

Thomas Wright "Fats" Waller died at thirty-nine, succumbing to influenzal bronchial pneumonia. The shaking and trembling that Kirkeby observed was probably Waller essentially drowning in his own secretions.

Newspapers throughout the country presented long obituaries about his life. The length of them was very unusual for an African American at that time.

Fats Waller had lived his life with great enthusiasm. To fully appreciate Waller it was necessary to see him perform with his constant smile and fun-loving patter that never let up during a performance.

He had a great passion for the food table, the bottle, and the bed. If it was said that the piano was his mistress, then certainly the organ was his wife.

He must have understood what he was doing to himself physically, but he made no effort to prolong his life. He was a great American composer and sadly, an untapped source of genius. Waller might have remained a cherished but fading memory if it had not been for a stage revue, highlighting his songs and his career, AIN'T MISBEHAVIN'. The show was developed Off-Broadway and made a triumphant Broadway debut in 1978, winning the Tony Award for Best Musical. It ran for more than 1,600 performances, has been frequently performed and revived around the world, and has introduced the ebullient, jaunty, infectious music of Fats Waller to new generations of listeners.

Harry Warren.
(Photofest.)

HARRY WARREN

HARRY WARREN'S LIFE COULD BE CONSIDERED SOMETHING of a mystery. He frequently complained about not being recognized for the talent he possessed. He is probably unknown to many, except those well versed in the history of American music. Thirty-three of Irving Berlin's songs made it to *Your Hit Parade* during its 1935–50 run, making him the radio show's second most popular composer. Forty-two of Harry Warren's songs were so honored. Warren was an integral part of the crowd of great composers of Broadway and Hollywood during the first half of the twentieth century, including Berlin, Gershwin, Porter, Kern, and Rodgers. But Warren's name is rarely heard.

He was born on Christmas Eve, 1893, in Brooklyn to Antonio and Rachel Guaragna, and was christened Salvatore. He was the last of eleven children. Until he started school, his nickname was Tuti. But by that time, even the family name had been changed.

Harry s father left Italy in 1871. He was an expert boot maker, and there was a large demand for that skill in Argentina, where he first moved. Warren disliked living there, so he left with his family for New York City. He started out in Brooklyn Heights, where he practiced his trade. The Warren household was always lively with music, but there was no piano.

Harry dropped out of school at age sixteen to become a drummer in his godfather's band. He had never had any formal musical training. However, he taught himself to play his father's accordion and then the drums.

A barber named Frank De Rosa worked as a part-time musical instrument salesman and part-time agent. Frank allowed Harry to use his instruments to teach himself. In return, Harry entertained at parties that De Rosa had booked. Warren learned how to play the piano and six other instruments while spending his days at the shop.

Harry's early life was deeply tied to his church. He couldn't wait to participate in choir activities. The church organist liked him a lot and spent time with him, teaching Harry about scales and chords. Through singing, Harry became familiar with the concepts of harmony. Though he played in his godfather's band, he was shy and not aggressive. As a result, jobs did not come easily to him in the early years of his career in music.

For a while Harry worked in a factory and as a clerk in an insurance office. Although one of his siblings was a song-and-dance man and another joined a professional singing group, the furthest Warren got was performing at private parties.

In 1915, when he was twenty-two, three singers who worked at the Vitagraph movie studio in Brooklyn needed a fourth for a quartet. He joined them. That led to jobs there first as a property man, then an assistant director, and even occasionally as an actor.

He sometimes accepted jobs playing the piano in movie houses. He was so good at it that an actress asked him to play the piano as background music during a film she was shooting.

In 1917, he married Josephine Wensler, whose father was of German descent. But their courtship wasn't easy. Her father didn't like Italians, and he didn't like Harry Warren. After awhile, Harry was finally allowed to make formal visits to her home. Her father came to like Harry because he would play operatic selections on the piano. However, at 11:30 p.m., Harry was made to understand it was time for him to leave.

The year after he was married, when he was about to be drafted into the Army, Harry enlisted in the Navy. He was stationed at Montauk Point on Long Island. Because he played the piano he became an entertainer on the base. It was there that he first developed the desire to write songs.

When he got out of the service he found it extremely difficult to get any songs published, and work at Vitagraph was very slow. Soon he and Josephine had a son and he felt an even greater need to find work. Harry got a job as an investigator for an insurance company. At the same time, he was hired to play piano at a saloon. One evening several song pluggers were having drinks there. They liked the way he played and as a result got him a job as a song plugger with the company that employed them. Warren was an exceptionally fine piano player.

In his new role Warren began meeting other composers and lyricists, and had several of his songs published. He wrote more than a dozen songs in 1926 including "I Love My Baby, My Baby Loves Me."

The following year, he wrote "Clementine from New Orleans," which became one of the tunes that the famous trumpeter Bix Beiderbecke featured. Beiderbecke died a few years later in 1931 at the age of twenty-eight.

In 1928, Warren went to work for the very important Remick Music Corporation. While there he published another twenty songs and became a little more financially successful. The Warrens now had two small children and bought a home in Forest Hills.

Though 1929 brought the Depression, it also established a new era for music. The era of silent films had come to a conclusive end and now there were new opportunities that came with the advent of the new movie musicals. The movie industry began buying up the music publishing firms in New York as well as the rights to Broadway shows. It also asked composers to write new songs to be added to Broadway shows as they were being converted into movies. Harry Warren was sent to California to write six new songs to be woven into the score written by Rodgers and Hart for the original Broadway production of SPRING IS HERE.

Warren didn't like working in California very much. He felt the producers, unlike those in New York, didn't particularly care how the music or lyrics were presented, or whether they honored the songwriters' intentions.

In 1929, he was named a director at ASCAP and retained that position until 1932.

Warren had established a relationship with Billy Rose. He found Rose to be bright, but mainly interested in accumulating wealth, sometimes with his own ideas and sometimes with those belonging to others. When Harry returned to New York, Rose asked him to write a new show with Ira Gershwin called SWEET AND LOW. But Rose insisted that all the songs have his name added as the co-lyricist.

In much the same way, in 1931, Warren wrote a song for Al Jolson, who also insisted that his own name be listed as the co-lyricist. One of the reasons for that demand was to increase Jolson's fame. Also,when the sheet music was sold, Jolson would share in the royalties.

Around this time, Warren had his first big hit when he wrote "I Found a Million Dollar Baby (In a Five-and-Ten-Cent Store)" for Bing Crosby. As a result of that success, the important lyricists now became available to him, such as Al Dubin, Gus Kahn, and Ted Koehler.

THE LAUGH PARADE, starring Ed Wynn, contained Warren's first full Broadway score. Produced in 1931, the show had a very poor book and was mostly like

Harry Warren, Al Dubin.
(Photofest.)

Harry Warren, Al Dubin.
(Photofest.)

a variety act, featuring Wynn doing a lot of ad-lib humor. The show did have one very good song of Warren's, "You're My Everything."

Once again, Warren was sent back out to Hollywood. There he was paired up with Al Dubin. They hit it off very quickly. Dubin was a huge man with unbelievable appetites for food and alcohol. Unlike Warren, Dubin really liked California. In Hollywood, songwriting teams were expected to have no other involvement once they presented their songs to the studio. As nobody even wanted them around, they had loads of leisure time. That appealed to Dubin.

Warren, on the other hand, hated that compartmentalization. He liked being a part of the entire production, which was the experience in New York.

Dubin had been born in Zurich and came to the United States as an infant. He did most of his early writing for vaudeville and for a long time wondered if there was any future in it for him. It wasn't until 1925, when he was thirty-four years old, that he began to achieve some real success.

The specific purpose of bringing Warren back out to California was to write the music for 42ND STREET. But Warner Brothers had run into financial difficulties and was rethinking whether they should go on with the project. In 1929, they had made fifty musicals. By 1931, they were down to twenty. The following year, the number dropped to an even dozen. The films were quite poor and the public had tired of them. But, head of production Darryl F. Zanuck believed that he had the stars, the composers, and lyricists to make a success out of 42ND STREET. He was right. 42ND STREET turned the direction of movie musicals around and Harry Warren was at the heart of it.

42ND STREET was a big-budget movie for those days. Part of the cost was the extravaganza that Busby Berkeley created for it. The stars they had selected were Dick Powell and Ruby Keeler, who was Al Jolson's new young bride. Several unforgettable hits came out of the film, including the title number, "Shuffle Off to Buffalo" and "You're Getting to Be a Habit with Me."

Keeler and Powell would ultimately do seven pictures together. Powell was certainly the studio's big star. By the end of his career he had had the leading role in thirty films for Warner Brothers. Of those films, in eighteen all the music was written by Harry Warren. However, Warren perpetually complained about his life and lack of recognition in Hollywood. He would say that during the production of those movies a great deal of attention was paid to director Busby Berkeley, and that everyone, including the actors, ignored and gave little credit to him. He said the studio had no respect for the work of Warren and Dubin.

42ND STREET was so successful that there was a call for a sequel to be started immediately. Warren had hoped to return to New York, but the studio had different plans. He was to become a fixture in Hollywood as Warner signed the team to a longterm contract.

The sequel, GOLD DIGGERS OF 1933, was even more of a Berkeley spectacle. Its smash hit was "We're in the Money (The Gold Diggers Song)." Capitalizing on their good fortune, Warner Brothers cashed in with Warren and Dubin's FOOTLIGHT PARADE.

Warren recalled that, even with all the success he had brought to Warner Brothers, a producer of theirs once listened to a song they had just finished and commented, "It couldn't have taken you very long to write that." Warren also said that, even though they never received respect for their work, it was actually Al Dubin—and not Berkeley—who put together the ideas for all those Warner Brothers hits. The team's nickname for Berkeley was "the madman." Warren said that Berkeley constantly conned the producers and didn't have the slightest idea of what he was going to do, just making it up as he went along.

Warren and Dubin finally made it back to New York and there did a film for Sam Goldwyn, starring Eddie Cantor, called ROMAN SCANDALS. Once again it was Dubin who conceived the story. It was Cantor's biggest hit. Warren felt that Cantor was one of the nicest people he had worked with.

They were writing the scores for multiple films every year. Warren said that while some composers had trunkloads of rejected songs that they would pull out for new projects, everything that he and Dubin wrote was accepted. So they were required to write new songs constantly, not having any reserve supply waiting in the wings.

Of all the producers, they liked working with Zanuck best of all because they said he treated them with the most respect. When Zanuck left Warners for 20th Century Fox, Warner loaned Warren and Dubin to him for one picture.

The star of so many of their pictures was Dick Powell, and they got to know him quite well. Warren and Dubin felt the same way about Powell as they did about Cantor. He was easy to work for. But Warner Brothers was equally unfair with Powell. Even when he was starring in 42ND STREET, Powell was only receiving one hundred seventy-five dollars per week.

Warren and Dubin wrote four movies in 1934. The picture DAMES had in it "I Only Have Eyes for You." In that same year they wrote "I'll String Along with You."

In 1935, there would be eight more movies. When they wrote "Lullaby of Broadway" for GOLD DIGGERS OF 1935, Jack Warner told Warren to throw out the lyrics. Warren was furious because he felt that Dubin's lyrics were great. He told Warner that he would write a new song, but he would never throw out the lyrics to "Lullaby of Broadway."

One of their pictures in 1935, GO INTO YOUR DANCE, starred Helen Morgan near the end of her career.

Harry Warren and Nat "King" Cole on the set of *The Nat King Cole Show*, 1956–57 season. (Photofest.)

It was one of her last appearances. She had lived a sad life of unhappy love affairs and alcoholism.

Jolson was in several of their movies. But they hated working with him. When asked who wrote most of the songs he sang (they had been written by Warren and Dubin), he would refuse to answer. He wanted them to be considered his songs. Within the industry, although he was a remarkable performer, Jolson was extremely disliked.

Movies starring Marion Davies became a part of Warren's life. Davies was the mistress of millionaire William Randolph Hearst, and he wanted her to be a star. Hearst made a deal with Warner Brothers to star her in four films to be written by Warren and Dubin. Hearst came to every rehearsal to watch the love scenes between Davies and Dick Powell, which made Powell extremely nervous. Powell had just recently married Joan Blondell. Marion Davies was well liked and considered to be an extremely nice woman. But her career was very short-lived.

Five more pictures came along in 1936, as well a very unpleasant episode. Harold Arlen and Yip Harburg had signed a contract with Warner Brothers for one year. They were assigned GOLD DIGGERS OF 1937. When their work was all done, Busby Berkeley decided that he didn't like their music and persuaded Warner Brothers to throw it out and replace it with a score by Warren and Dubin. Warren, Dubin, Arlen, and Harburg were all friends and very respectful of each others' work. The development created unpleasant friction, even though Warren and Dubin tried to explain that it was none of their doing.

In 1937, Warren and Dubin wrote all the music for six more films, but Dubin was becoming a problem. He disappeared frequently and couldn't be found. The problem was his addiction to alcohol. For one of the pictures, due to Dubin's constant absence, Johnny Mercer was asked to complete the lyrics. Hal Wallis was in charge of production at that time at Warners and asked Warren if he would recommend someone to write permanently with Mercer. Warren suggested Richard Whiting. Mercer and Whiting wrote together for about one year before Whiting's sudden and untimely death at the age of forty-seven.

Warren and Dubin also wrote their greatest hit in 1937, the standard "September in the Rain."

All during 1938, Warren insisted that Dubin co-write his lyrics with Johnny Mercer because of Dubin's problem drinking. Dubin was hurt and angered and demanded a release from his contract. It was granted and he went back to New York. There he began writing with Jimmy McHugh. They did one show together and then Dubin died in 1945. Mercer became Warren's permanent collaborator until he left Warner Brothers.

The greatest tragedy of Harry Warren's life happened in the spring of 1938, when his nineteen-year-old son contracted pneumonia and died. The experience was so traumatic that the Warrens sold their home to relieve themselves of the memories. For years it had a terrible effect on Warren's wife.

With Mercer, Warren had a number of hits in 1938 including "Jeepers, Creepers," "Love Is Where You Find It," and "You Must Have Been a Beautiful Baby."

By 1939, the movie musical at Warner Brothers had temporarily run its course. Warren was loaned to MGM for a picture and it seemed obvious that his agreement with Warner Brothers was about to end. Most of the Warner musicals during the thirties had been orchestrated by Ray Heindorf, who really liked Warren. Heindorf felt when Warren was leaving Warners, they were losing a genius. He said of Warren, "He was a bit too humble . . . and easily hurt," and was uncomfortable dealing with the tough executives out in Hollywood.

In 1940, 20th Century Fox hired Warren for just one picture, but that was about to change with the advent of the new wartime musicals. Warren would eventually write fourteen musicals for Fox. Alice Faye or Betty Grable would star in ten of them. While at Fox he would write everything with Mack Gordon. He continued to maintain the pattern that he had with Al Dubin. He would first write the music and turn it over to the lyricist, which was just the opposite of the way in which Richard Rodgers and Oscar Hammerstein composed their music.

In 1941, Warren and Gordon wrote the score for the picture SUN VALLEY SERENADE for John Payne and Sonja Henie. The film is still shown on a continuous basis, without interruption, at the Sun Valley Lodge. The hit song of that film was "Chattanooga Choo Choo."

The next picture was WEEKEND IN HAVANA. It was an unpleasant time because Warren contracted pneumonia and was out for three months time. Part of that time he was in critical condition. The memory of the loss of his son from that illness created some anxiety. Fox amazingly withheld his salary while he was out and he complained bitterly. But his attorney said that Warren had no recourse in the matter. From that point on Warren was constantly attempting to terminate his contract and the relationship was never the same.

In 1942, he wrote music for another film, ORCHESTRA WIVES, which was not good. But it had three classic songs: "I Got a Gal in Kalamazoo," "At Last," and "Serenade in Blue." Warren credited Glenn Miller, whose orchestra was in the film, with being the inspiration for a lot of that music. He considered Miller to be quite a great musician.

Another flop that year, ICELAND, had one of his most beautiful songs, "There Will Never Be Another You."

For the picture SPRINGTIME IN THE ROCKIES, they composed the biggest hit of the entire year, "I Had the Craziest Dream Last Night."

In 1943, they wrote a song for one of the last pictures

that starred Alice Faye, who was marrying bandleader Phil Harris and giving up her career. The picture was HELLO FRISCO, HELLO, and the song was undoubtedly Warren's biggest hit of the entire period, "You'll Never Know."

Harry Warren left 20th Century Fox for MGM. Billy Rose was doing a film titled BILLY ROSE'S DIAMOND HORSESHOE, and asked for Warren to be loaned back for one picture. Rose had originally signed a contract with Fox stating that his name would be in the title. Fox changed their mind about the title. So Rose went to court and won his case. Harry Warren was thrilled to be writing the picture, because he was so angry with Fox. He was happy to be participating in it, because Fox lost the court fight. The hit song of the movie was "The More I See You."

Dick Haymes was the star of the picture, which pleased Warren, who believed that Haymes was the second finest pop singer around, even better than Sinatra. His absolute favorite was Bing Crosby.

While he was at Fox, Herbert Spencer was the arranger and orchestrator of all Warren's music. He had tremendous praise for Warren, saying he was absolutely the easiest composer to worth with, certainly much more so than Berlin or Porter.

Warren seemed happiest when he joined MGM. He liked Louis B. Mayer and especially Arthur Freed, who was in charge of all their musicals. His first project with Freed was an extravaganza, ZIEGFELD FOLLIES, which was nothing more than a giant variety show starring Lucille Ball, Fred Astaire, Lena Horne, Fanny Brice, Red Skelton, Esther Williams, Gene Kelly, and Kathryn Grayson. Its best song was "This Heart of Mine."

In 1946, he wrote the music for THE HARVEY GIRLS with Johnny Mercer. In it was the song that would win the Academy Award, "On the Atchison, Topeka and the Santa Fe." But neither he nor Mercer showed up at the award ceremony because they were both angry with the studio.

Harry Warren's absolute favorite of any of the movies he ever wrote for was SUMMER HOLIDAY, based on Eugene O'Neill's AH! WILDERNESS. The critical praise was superb, but it never caught on with the public and was not a financial success. Critic Rex Reed claimed that it was his second all-time favorite of all movie musicals, only behind SINGIN' IN THE RAIN. The lyricist for the songs he contributed was Ralph Blane. The greatness of the film was obviously due to the quality of the original play, and the quality of the screenplay. No big hit songs emerged.

Warren's next venture was THE BARKLEYS OF BROADWAY, set to star Judy Garland. Garland ran into continuous problems with illness and drugs and was dropped. She was replaced by Ginger Rogers, who reunited with Fred Astaire. It had been ten years since their last picture. Warren absolutely loved working with Astaire.

Over the next few years Harry Warren wrote music for

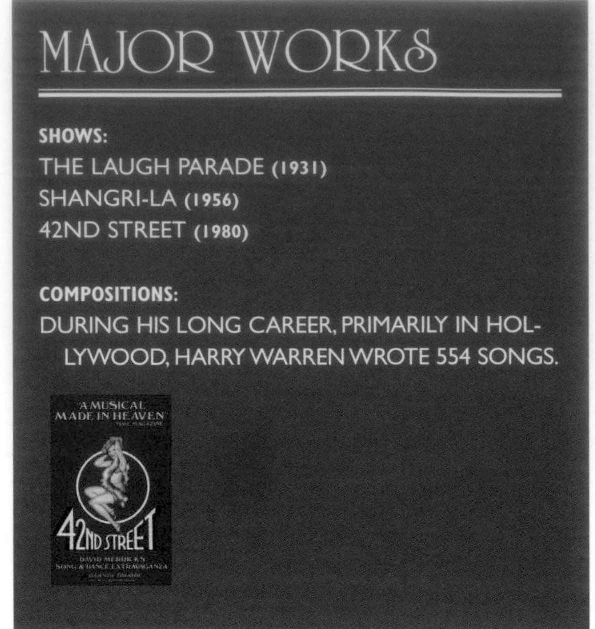

MAJOR WORKS

SHOWS:
THE LAUGH PARADE (1931)
SHANGRI-LA (1956)
42ND STREET (1980)

COMPOSITIONS:
DURING HIS LONG CAREER, PRIMARILY IN HOLLYWOOD, HARRY WARREN WROTE 554 SONGS.

a series of films for MGM that were only mediocre. With the explosion of television in 1949, the movie musical was dying, with the exception of a few great films in the fifties.

In 1952, Warren got a call from Crosby asking if he would like to make a film at Paramount. It was the beginning of a run of pictures he would do with Dean Martin and Jerry Lewis. From all those pictures only one song would ever have any lasting power. It was "That's Amore," featured in THE CADDY.

His greatest success in the mid-fifties was writing the theme song for the television series WYATT EARP and the title song for the motion picture MARTY.

In 1957, Paramount decided to do a remake of the 1939 film LOVE AFFAIR. They renamed it AN AFFAIR TO REMEMBER and Warren wrote the beautiful title song.

In 1961, at the age of sixty-eight, he wrote the music for one last Jerry Lewis film, thus ending his career in the movies. He found no more opportunities in Hollywood. He had no financial problems due to his huge royalties, but like the other great composers, his ego was shattered by the lack of interest in anything new he would write.

The American Guild of Authors and Composers gave Warren a giant birthday celebration when he was eighty years old in 1973.

In 1980, David Merrick decided to produce 42ND STREET for Broadway. The score had previously only been heard in the 1933 film. It opened at the Kennedy Center in Washington, D.C., in July and on Broadway on August 25, 1980. After the show received rave reviews in Washington and eleven curtain calls on opening night in New York, David Merrick appeared on the stage to announce that its director, Gower Champion, had died that afternoon. Merrick had kept it a secret from everyone, including the cast, to guarantee that the news would hit the headlines the following day and achieve enormous publicity. It was not atypical of the behavior that David Merrick exhibited. 42ND STREET was the last hit show that Merrick would ever have.

Fortunately, Harry Warren, who lived until 1981, was able to see his great show become a success on Broadway, where it would win the Tony Award for Best Musical. Warren would not live to see its tremendous success in London in 1984, nor the revival on Broadway in 2001 which won the Tony for Best Revival of a Musical.

Over his career Harry Warren wrote more than 400 songs for almost ninety movies. His songs were written in every conceivable musical style. His success on Broadway was primarily with 42ND STREET. But throughout his life the one thing that was missing, as far as Warren was concerned, was any proper recognition for the contribution that he made. An unbiased examination of his career would seem to validate that claim.

Andrew Lloyd Webber. (Retna.)

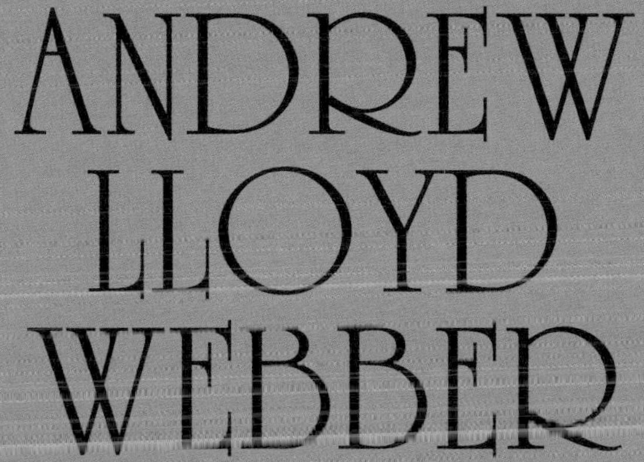

ANDREW LLOYD WEBBER

IN 1913, WILLIAM CHARLES HENRY WEBBER, A JOURNEYMAN plumber, married Mary Winifred Gittins. Just before the war broke out the following year, she gave birth to a son whom they named William Southcombe Lloyd Webber. When he grew up, William studied organ at the Royal College of Music. Another Webber was studying there as well. So William began calling himself Lloyd Webber. Though it would never be hyphenated it remained permanently attached as the family surname.

William became a soldier in the Royal Army and, in 1942 at the age of twenty-eight, he married twenty-year-old Jean Hermione Johnstone. By this time William was known as Billy. His ambition had been predominantly to be a composer. Billy achieved great stature as an organist and teacher in the academic community, but never as a composer.

Jean had come from a broken family, and her father left home by the time she was two years old. She had a much older sister, who would become quite a successful stage actress, and a significant influence on Andrew Lloyd Webber. She also had a brother who was five years her senior. In a fatherless home, with a sister much too old for her to relate to, Jean formed a very close bond with her brother, Alastair.

When Alastair was eighteen years old, he went out on a small sailboat with a friend. It capsized and he was washed away to sea, his body never to be found. It had a profound and devastating effect on Jean, from which she never fully recovered.

William and Jean set up their household near Westminster Hospital where Jean gave birth to Andrew in 1948, and, three years later, to Julian. Andrew grew up as a very difficult child, quite different from his brother Julian, who had a relaxed and even personality. Julian liked sports, which Andrew hated. Andrew's interest was in music, which he learned from his mother very early. He was also extremely opinionated. That trait would remain with him throughout his life, as his lyricist-collaborators would later discover. Regardless of how talented his collaborators might be, Andrew Lloyd Webber would retain control of the creative process.

But in the early years of Andrew's life no one could have suspected that he would find his career in music. Though he had learned to play at the age of four, his interest was in the field of ancient architecture. Even as a ten-year-old he was writing monographs on the subject. Around that age, his attention turned seriously to music. But even as a child he was more interested in playing his own compositions than those of accepted classical composers.

His mother, Jean, was quite an interesting person. She was always searching for emerging talent, especially in underprivileged communities. She would visit those communities with her mother, Andrew's grandmother. Among others they would discover a young man, John Lill, who became a well-known concert pianist. For a while he actually moved in with the family. Lill's mother, who was extremely poor, resented the Lloyd Webbers. She believed Jean forcefully removed John from his poverty-stricken life at home, to live in their greater affluence. She was offended and felt she had lost a son to this dominating woman, Jean Lloyd Webber.

Andrew's mother and grandmother could be considered politically to the left of center. His grandmother was one of the founders of a rather unusual group called the Christian Communist Party.

Jean was absolutely committed to the idea that Andrew and Julian would be successful adults, using her own strength to direct them. Julian would become a performer, but Andrew was uncomfortable in that role. Julian had started with the piano and moved to the cello, where he would remain as a very successful musician throughout his life. Andrew was studying the viola and the French horn and was writing significant music by the age of nine.

He had formed a close attachment to his mother's sister, Viola Johnstone, who had retired from her career in the theatre when she married a physician. She retained a tremendous interest in the theatre, however, which stimulated Andrew's thoughts.

Andrew attended a rather exclusive prep school in London, the Westminster Underschool. He had previously been a student at a school where all the teachers were women and the atmosphere was very low-key. Now he found himself among much physically larger male students and dominating male teachers, with an emphasis on sports. The environment was not comfortable for him, and he remained mostly a loner, though a very good student. He had no interest in the required sports. By the time he had arrived there his passion had turned mostly to music.

While very attracted to the pop music of the time, Andrew was learning the concepts of harmony and orchestration from his very talented father. Andrew was already taking the position that rather than just writing pop music, he wanted to be writing music for the theatre. He believed that England was far behind the United States when it came to musicals, and his idol was Richard Rodgers.

The music director at the school was primarily interested in the classics. Fortunately for Andrew, he was replaced in 1963 by a new young master, David Byrt, whose interests were much more diverse. He recognized immediately that Andrew had promise.

When he reached the age of fourteen, Andrew competed for a type of scholarship. A small group would become live-in students, with tuition paid. His father was teaching music, and not extremely wealthy. Such a reward would certainly help the family's finances. The scholarships were awarded through competitive examinations. Although Andrew was extremely advanced in history and architecture, he left a lot to be desired in the field of mathematics. Amazingly, and probably due to the erudition in his writing about architecture, Andrew won one of the scholarships at Westminster. It meant that Andrew, at the age of fourteen, would move into the school, while John Lill would move into his home. Though John would always remain a close friend, both Andrew and Julian, in some ways, thought of him as an interloper, not deserving of their parents' attention, and diminishing their own positions in the family dynamic.

In one specific area Jean was always supportive of Andrew. While he lived at the school, and was required to participate in multiple sporting activities, Jean constantly argued with the administration that Andrew should be excused from them, due to his lack of interest and ability. Her complaints yielded no success. In fact, during his stay there, the school showed very little concern that his main interest was music.

It has been suggested by some biographers that Jean's overbearing insistence on controlling all these boys' lives may well have contributed to Andrew Lloyd Webber's strained relationships later in life. Lloyd Webber's insecurity and the impression of being aloof to others, very well may be the result of her influence.

When Andrew graduated from prep school he was accepted to Oxford. Much like the scholarship he had won at Westminster, the acceptance was once again surprising,

Left to right: Valerie Eliot (widow of T. S. Eliot), Andrew Lloyd Webber, and Sarah Lloyd Webber at the Premiere of CATS at the New London Theatre, Drury Lane, London, 1981. (Photofest.)

Tim Rice and Andrew Lloyd Webber accepting the Academy Award for Best Song for "Evita" at the 69th Annual Academy Awards. (Retna.)

as Andrew was just an average student in studies other than music and architecture. As he did at Westminster, Andrew felt that Oxford did not provide much in the way of developing his musical talent.

Andrew and his father developed a closer relationship, based on their common love of theatre music, which included opera. Both felt that no one could compare with Puccini, but they also loved the crowd of new American theatrical composers. Billy's favorite of all Broadway show tunes was "Some Enchanted Evening" from SOUTH PACIFIC. He once informed Andrew that if he ever wrote anything that beautiful, that he would tell Andrew so.

In April 1965, a young man, lyricist Tim Rice, wrote Lloyd Webber asking if he would be interested in writing with him. Andrew was only seventeen years old and thrilled. Tim was three and a half years older. Their first meeting went well.

Rice came from a typical middle-class family. After prep school he spent a semester at the Sorbonne. He tried multiple jobs including working in a law firm. He decided that he wanted to write a book and presented the idea to a literary agent who didn't particularly like what he read. However, the agent knew Andrew Lloyd Webber and suggested Tim contact Andrew to see if they could collaborate.

Andrew had already realized that Oxford was not going to help him develop his interests. As a result he decided, after one semester, to leave and write with Tim Rice. Andrew saw

Tim as a real opportunity he did not want to pass up.

Friends at Oxford remember him as being quite unhappy there and insecure about his decision to attend. However, he was concerned about the risk of leaving so early in his education for a musical career that, at the time, showed no clear sign of bringing him success.

As to the question of whether there had been opportunities in music for Andrew while at the two schools, there is some disagreement. A friend at Westminster, Robin Barrow, remembered their relationship as one in which Robin continually made overtures to Andrew to write more lyrics for Andrew's songs. Lloyd Webber's recollection was quite different. He recalled that, although they had done some writing together, Barrow was never very interested in him.

Andrew's father, Billy, was achieving such importance in the world of academic music that it must have been a shock to the family to find out that Andrew had dropped out of Oxford so suddenly. When Andrew was writing at Westminster with Robin Barrow, there was never the slightest expectation on anyone's part, with the possible exception of Lloyd Webber himself, that anything they wrote would be published or recorded. However, Andrew and Tim Rice never seemed to have the slightest doubt that they would be successful.

Andrew's grandmother Mollie, who lived next door, had an extra room and Andrew invited Tim to rent it from her. Now Billy, Jean, Mollie, John Lill, Tim Rice, Andrew, and Julian were all living there.

For two years, Tim and Andrew worked together with almost no success whatsoever. They actually did better as entrepreneurs than as a writing team. One song was recorded, but only because of a scheme they concocted. They had heard of a newspaper contest for the "Girl of the Year." They decided to rig the contest by stuffing the ballot boxes with the name of a young woman they knew. When she won, they arranged to have a song recorded by the "Girl of the Year." It was the only thing she had ever recorded, and it wasn't very good.

Their next idea was to get word passed around by former friends and classmates at Westminster that they were an up-and-coming writing team. Alan Doggett, a teacher at a school called Colet Court, had heard about them. He called to ask if they would be willing to write a cantata for his school choir to perform at their annual concert. His one proviso was that it was to be a Bible story for young children. Neither Rice nor Lloyd Webber were religious, but they knew enough of the Bible to believe they could find a good story. Later on they considered it quite amusing when it was suggested that they studied the Bible deeply to write the cantata. Andrew said that actually it took "about four minutes of reading *The Children's Wonder Book of Bible Stories*. And so began the first step in the journey of JOSEPH AND THE AMAZING TECHNICOLOR DREAMCOAT. It was approximately twenty minutes in length.

Andrew's father encouraged them to enlarge the piece. By accident, at the second performance organized by Andrew's father, Derek Jewell, the jazz and pop critic of the *Sunday Times*, was present because his young son was in the choir. Also in attendance was Marion Brown of the *Times Educational Supplement* and some staff of the British Broadcasting Company (BBC).

Jewell was completely surprised by the quality of what he heard and reported about it in the *Times*. Andrew and Tim were surprised as well. They had been attempting to write successful pop songs, but that had alluded them for several years. They had no expectation that a cantata would be a pathway toward success for them. Though the review in the paper was marvelous, nothing of any consequence resulted from it until Norrie Paramor, for whom Tim Rice worked, persuaded Decca to record it after reading the great reviews.

They agreed to record an album of JOSEPH. It was released in January 1969 with a very fine publicity campaign and the reviews were exceptional. Up until that time Andrew was still struggling to stay afloat financially.

As the years have passed, JOSEPH has been revised and revived from a cantata to a full-fledged theatrical production. The largest was on Broadway in 1982.

As far as earnings were concerned from JOSEPH, Andrew and Tim received very little. They had signed away so much of it during the piece's development. They still had relatively modest expectations for their future.

Through a friend, Sefton Myers, they met an agent, David Land, and told him that what they would like to do is establish a theatrical museum, never raising the issue of writing together. They made a rather bizarre presentation of their plan to him. But, nevertheless, on a personal basis, he liked them. He asked, "Are you working?" They responded, "No, and we really need bread." He offered them a job at thirty dollars per week, while agreeing to be their agent as well. He had seen the performance of JOSEPH, and believed they had great potential as a writing team, rather than as creators of a museum.

Tim and Andrew had been considering an idea for a show about Richard the Lionhearted. But Land encouraged them to stick to a religious theme and write about anything "except Jesus Christ." He told them he was a nonreligious Jew, but felt the subject of Jesus for a musical was disrespectful.

They decided, however, they wanted to write about Christ and went ahead with JESUS CHRIST SUPERSTAR. They were a little concerned about the title. Just three years previously John Lennon had faced the condemnation of the clergy when he jokingly said the Beatles were "more popular than Jesus." But Tim and Andrew felt somewhat more secure when the Reverend Father Martin Sullivan, the Dean of St. Paul's Cathedral, gave his okay for the subject.

Once again they were writing just a series of songs they hoped to record with no theatrical production involved.

When it came time to record JESUS CHRIST SUPERSTAR, they felt they needed one more song. Lloyd Webber and Rice had a few songs published by Southern Music before they met Land. Land heard a song that they had written and was owned by Southern, and he liked it. Southern Music considered Andrew and Tim a pair of insignificant young men with no future. So when Land offered them fifty pounds for the song, they gladly agreed. It ultimately became "I Don't Know How to Love Him." The song earned a quarter of a million pounds in the first five years.

Some of those who had helped Tim and Andrew get started would not live to appreciate what would become of them. Alan Doggett, who provided them with their initial opportunity to write the cantata for Colet Court, died in 1973. Even sadder, Sefton Myers, who originally saw promise in them, died of cancer at the age of forty-three in 1970.

When the idea of JESUS CHRIST SUPERSTAR got started Andrew had a number of conversations with members of the clergy. By May 1969, they had firmly decided that the story of Jesus and his disciples would be their subject. Their only intent was to write music for a recording. It was completed in six weeks. Every record company rejected it based upon their concerns that is was too controversial. The Music Corporation of America decided to chance it. They still were concerned about whether radio stations would allow a rock song about Jesus to be played. They decided to release some single songs to test the reaction. Some of the first songs released had weak sales in the United States and in England. But MCA told them to continue and write an entire score for an album. Tim and Andrew isolated themselves for five and a half days and completed it. The first songs had been released in November 1969. By October of the following year, the entire album was ready for release—with much trepidation.

A media frenzy erupted when a plan was announced for its first presentation at St. Paul's Cathedral. It was a rumor without basis. The story was that John Lennon, the center of the religious controversy three years earlier, would sing the part of Jesus Christ in the Cathedral.

Actually, no performers wanted to record the album. With difficulty they finally found a cast, made the recording, and did a live presentation. But there were plenty of problems, like picket lines outside the theatre, protesting the performance.

In June 1970, Lloyd Webber and Rice, having completed the album for SUPERSTAR, went to the United States, where on Long Island two priests were presenting the JOSEPH cantata. SUPERSTAR was just being released in the United States. Many stations refused to play it. But, where it was played, there was a very positive response. Still Andrew and Tim were without any significant income. When they arrived they moved into a small apartment in Greenwich Village.

Robert Stigwood—an Australian who had produced HAIR and OH! CALCUTTA!—was convinced of the potential of these two young men. He made arrangements to meet them and bought out their contract from Land. Stigwood started out by purchasing 51 percent of them, and subsequently the remaining 49 percent from Land. Besides that he bought 25 percent of all their earnings from Tim and Andrew. He had total control of them for the next nine years.

While the recording of JESUS CHRIST SUPERSTAR was only doing fairly well in England, it took off like wildfire in the United States. By February 1971 it was number one on the charts.

In January 1970, Andrew met sixteen-year-old Sarah Tudor Hugill at a party in Oxford. Her father was a major executive of a sugar company. Her parents had insisted that they not marry until she was eighteen. In July 1971, they were wed. Andrew was twenty-two.

By then Stigwood was pressuring Andrew and Tim to get the score converted to a Broadway show as the music was being pirated and converted into productions in many different locations. Stigwood instituted lawsuits to stop the other productions. Andrew worked day and night like a demon. But Tim was completely the opposite. He was carefree, casual, much more easygoing and likeable. Tim enjoyed working sporadically, but could rapidly produce material when it was needed. Because of their work habits, significant friction developed between them.

Preparations for a Broadway production were not going well. As a result, Stigwood fired the director and hired Tim O'Horgan. Lloyd Webber and O'Horgan saw the show completely differently. Andrew was not happy with what developed. The show opened in September 1971 with mixed reviews. On Broadway, it never achieved any great critical acclaim. But it was also produced in thirty-seven different countries, almost always to rave reviews and great success, yielding a fortune in profits. Nevertheless, Andrew was always upset that the New York production never achieved the spectacular success that the property had worldwide.

JESUS CHRIST SUPERSTAR was eventually sold to the movies under the direction of Norman Jewison. It received an Oscar nomination for Best Music, Scoring, Original Song Score and/or Adaptation.

Before SUPERSTAR opened on Broadway, Rice and Lloyd Webber did something extremely unusual. They contacted Clive Barnes of the *New York Times*, the most important critic in New York, and asked if they could meet him. He agreed and they met in his apartment. At that meeting they told Barnes about their concerns over the negative reaction to the music as being sacrilegious, which they considered to be without basis.

The meeting was very cordial and afterward Barnes said that he found them to be "charming, delightful, and above all, sincere." He had nothing but positive things to say about them personally. One can imagine the surprise they experienced when the review came out. Barnes was unimpressed by Lloyd Webber's music and downright negative about Rice's book and lyrics.

Some other reviews were much better. Derek Jewell, the *London Times* reviewer, who was basically a music critic, not a theatre critic, attacked the United States press. His complaint was that American newspapers assigned drama critics to evaluate musicals. To him that made no sense. He believed that they had insufficient background and understanding of music, and that their reviews were worthless.

Barnes's condemnation of Rice went even further at a later date, when he wrote that Andrew's best work came after he left Rice, as indicated in CATS.

Between 1971–74, Andrew and Tim did relatively little work except that Webber wrote music for the film, THE ODESSA FILE. They also worked on converting JOSEPH into a true theatrical piece, rather than a cantata.

At that time, Andrew and Sarah bought a country estate, Sydmonton Court. After a while they held the Sydmonton Festival, with music, theatre, and lectures there on an annual basis.

Separately, Tim and Andrew each began developing an idea for a new project they wanted to develop. Tim had become entranced by the story of the life of Eva Peron. Andrew had qualms about it, mainly because he was offended by the negative side of her life and felt it would not be accepted well in the theatre.

Andrew was thrilled by the writing of P. G. Wodehouse, and wanted to convert his work into a musical. Rice was very fond of Wodehouse's writing, but he did not see it as adaptable.

The main problem confronting them, however, was not the choice of subject matter. It still was their view of work and life. Andrew was compulsive about his work. He actually detested the idea of vacations. Rice wanted freedom and spare time to do anything but write. They were really incompatible, except that they believed so strongly in each other's talent.

Finally, to Andrew's dismay, Tim completely severed his attachment to the Wodehouse project, now called JEEVES. After considerable searching Andrew decided on the brilliant theatrical writer, Alan Ayckbourn, to write the book and lyrics. Ayckbourn had absolutely no experience with musicals.

Meanwhile Anthony Bowles, a musical director who had done THE ODESSA FILE with Lloyd Webber, requested permission to do a French version of SUPERSTAR. They agreed without even needing to hear his plan. As it turned out his production was far superior to that on Broadway. Andrew and Tim were so pleased they requested that it be used in London, where it was also very successful, running for the next eight years.

JEEVES progressed, opened in London to horrible reviews, and closed in five weeks. It was Andrew Lloyd Webber's worst disaster and a major financial loss. The production of JEEVES was fraught with mistakes. Ayckbourn not only did not know how to write a musical, he didn't even like them. Andrew insisted on doing his own orchestrations even though his background had not prepared him in any way to orchestrate that type of show, which reviewers called overlong and ponderous.

After such a sad turn of events professionally, a happy one occurred for Andrew. In 1976, Andrew and Sarah's first child, Imogen, was born.

Andrew Lloyd Webber still had concerns about EVITA, but had promised he would do it once JEEVES was completed. In the case of EVITA, Lloyd Webber would not make the same mistakes he had made with JEEVES. Like JESUS CHRIST SUPERSTAR, it would start with the music. Then it would become an album. Finally, it would be converted into a theatrical piece.

EVITA opened in London in June 1978 to the most wonderful reviews. "Don't Cry for Me Argentina" had been released as a single in the U.K. almost eighteen months before the show opened. It became one of the largest-selling records of all time. That was a significant help in making the show a success. Producers felt considerably hesitant to put up such a great deal of money for the costly show, especially since they (including Lloyd Webber) had all taken a beating on JEEVES. But the profit that accrued covered the initial costs very quickly.

Anthony Bowles had been a close associate of Lloyd Webber for some time. He had worked all through the disastrous period of JEEVES with Andrew, and was to be the music director of EVITA. Once the album was ready to be converted to a stage performance, Stigwood, who had selected Bowles for the recording, switched his allegiance to Harold Prince. Throughout the 1970s, there was no more important director on Broadway than Prince. However, Prince would not be available to start until shortly before the show was ready. As a result Bowles was to remain in charge until then.

As soon as Prince arrived, he fired Bowles without any explanation. Bowles came to Lloyd Webber and asked him to intercede. But the composer, disregarding Bowles's years of loyalty, declined. He claimed he had no say in the matter. It was a decision he left in the hands of Stigwood and Prince. Bowles was deeply hurt, after all the years he had spent with Andrew.

It was not the only problem with relationships that Andrew would have. Others, including Lloyd Webber's personal secretary and his publicist, quit after several years with him, characterizing him as ruthless. They claimed that whenever he made a decision, wrong or right, he held to it.

When EVITA opened on Broadway in 1979, the reviews were mixed. Some claimed the creators had glamorized this terrible woman and were offended. Andrew said, on his own behalf, that there was no way anyone could leave the show without assuming "she was a fairly grisly piece of work." The reviews notwithstanding, it ran for 1567 performances, more than four years, twice as long as JESUS CHRIST SUPERSTAR.

When EVITA was to receive an award from the Society of West End Theatres, a young successful producer, Cameron Mackintosh, was chosen to produce the event. Mackintosh had already produced SIDE BY SIDE BY SONDHEIM, and revivals of MY FAIR LADY, GODSPELL, OLIVER! and OKLAHOMA!

The event was held in a ballroom rather than a theatre, making the production difficult. Mackintosh wanted the cast to do one number, "Don't Cry for Me Argentina." Andrew, however, wanted a more comprehensive presentation with a medley of songs and large sets, which would present problems. Mackintosh took a considerable amount of abuse as they argued all day during the preparations. Finally, Andrew blurted out, "Hal Prince, directing it. That's exactly what this cabaret needed tonight." Mackintosh was on the verge of coming to blows with Andrew as the evening ended with major hostility.

The following morning Lloyd Webber felt guilty about his behavior and sent a letter of apology and asked if they could meet for lunch. After that, the relationship became so cordial that they began discussing the possibilities for Andrew's idea based on T. S. Eliot's *Old Possum's Book of Practical Cats*. Mackintosh suggested that the perfect person to direct it would be the Royal Shakespeare Company's Trevor Nunn, who had never done a musical. Mackintosh sought him out on Andrew's behalf. After some second thoughts, Nunn agreed to assume the role.

As early as 1975, Andrew was writing music for individual poems from T. S. Eliot's collection. He had already played some at his annual Sydmonton festival. Lloyd Webber had invited Eliot's widow, Valerie, to the festival. She brought with her an outline of the cats' relationships to each other, which Eliot had created. It had never been published. When Andrew saw it, he realized it would serve as the framework for the show.

While all of this was developing, Andrew was working on another idea. He had written his own *Variations on a Theme of Paganini*. He had promised his brother Julian many years before that he would write a piece to be played on the cello by him. Andrew felt his modification to the Paganini would be a perfect choice. He titled it *Variations*, and perceived it as a dance composition that might be combined with the idea for CATS.

He went forward with other compositions. Andrew wanted to write a one-woman show for a singer, Marti Webb. For Webb, he had written "Tell Me on a Sunday" as a one-hour television program (lyrics by Don Black). Finally, everything was falling into place in his mind. CATS would be a separate production. Andrew would do another show in two separate halves. The first was a vocal portion with Miss Webb called "Tell Me On A Sunday," and the second would be just dance, based on "Variations." The title for the show was SONG AND DANCE.

CATS's success transformed Andrew Lloyd Webber's life. He had lost considerable money on JEEVES and had already mortgaged his home once. It was necessary to obtain several hundred separate investors to get CATS started. Even Sydmonton had to be mortgaged once again.

The first issue to be confronted was how to stage CATS, which would obviously be something quite different than any show previously done. Mackintosh and Lloyd Webber needed to find the proper location. There also needed to be some resolution as to Tim Rice's role in the project.

Lloyd Webber had never been certain as to whether Rice wanted to be involved in the production of CATS. The lyrics would obviously be mostly derived from Eliot's writing. As far as a book, Andrew now had a direction to follow from the information that he had been given by Valerie Eliot. After long discussions with Mackintosh and Nunn, it was decided that the emotional spine of the piece would revolve around Grizabella, the glamour cat, and what time and age had done to her.

Andrew had long since written the melody for her big solo song, but no lyrics had been prepared. Trevor Nunn spent an entire weekend reading and re-reading Eliot's *Old Possum's Book of Practical Cats*. After hours of work he constructed a lyric for her song. When Nunn presented it, Mackintosh and Lloyd Webber were quite pleased. They had found what they needed. The song, needless to say, was "Memory."

The British theatrical star, Judi Dench, was to play the role. She was not a great singer, but her acting ability would make this the hit of the show. Only days before the opening, Dench fell on the stage, seriously injuring herself. With only days remaining before the opening, Andrew turned to Elaine Paige, who had starred in EVITA. She agreed to go on. She would sing the song for which Trevor Nunn had written the lyric.

By this time Paige had become Tim Rice's significant other. It is assumed, but not documented, that Paige went to Rice to tell him that he could write better lyrics for her. She wanted Tim to change his mind and tell Andrew he would like to write new lyrics for the song. Tim spoke with Lloyd Webber to ask if that would be acceptable. Andrew, Nunn and Mackintosh agreed to let him try.

When Nunn got the lyrics back his impression was that they were very good, but did not strike the correct tone for either the character of Grizabella or the theme of the show. He pondered what to do. After Lloyd Webber and Mackintosh met with Nunn, they decided to accept the director's advice and reject Rice's lyrics. Obviously there was a conflict of interest, as Nunn had a lot to gain by having his own lyrics remain. It was a terrible blow to Rice, and it put Paige in the difficult position of having to perform the song for which her boyfriend's lyrics had been turned down. It has been said that Rice instructed her not to relinquish the role because of his rejection.

Subsequent interviews revealed a deep hurt felt by Rice and a schism between Rice and Lloyd Webber that now seemed irreparable. A reunion of the pair seemed possible with the plan to make a film from EVITA. But the restoration of their partnership fell through when there was a disagreement about which actress would play the lead. Rice insisted on Elaine Paige, but she was rejected for the movie.

CATS opened in early October 1982 and just three weeks later Andrew's father, Billy, suddenly died. In April of the following year, Andrew announced he was getting divorced. He had fallen in love with a dancer from CATS, Sarah Brightman.

CATS completely changed his life. It began with Arlene Phillips. She was a choreographer whom Andrew had known for several years. She suggested to him that he be watchful of a dancer, Sarah Brightman, she knew as part of a rock dance group. The dancer was planning to audition for CATS. Phillips especially praised her singing ability.

Lloyd Webber was a discreet professional and did not have a reputation for fooling around with the dancers and singers trying to make their way into the theatre. His first wife, Sarah, was a homebody. She raised their children and ran their household and private life very efficiently. Sarah Brightman's personality was completely different.

Brightman, like her mother, exuded sexuality. Her mother, as a young girl, had worked at Murray's Cabaret Club, the equivalent of a Playboy Club. Though it claimed to provide no sexual services, two of its employees, Christine Keeler and Mandy Rice-Davies, brought down Harold Macmillan's government. Pictures of her mother, Paula, show her to be a scantily clothed, striking beauty. Sarah Brightman, like her mother, was beautiful.

At first, Andrew's interest was strictly professional. But after Sarah left CATS in 1983, he went to see her perform in another show. They went away for a weekend in Italy and he asked her to marry him. In July 1983, he obtained a legal separation and gave Brightman an engagement ring. After negotiations, a settlement in excess of one million pounds was reached with his first wife, Sarah.

Lloyd Webber was now in the midst of several new projects. He, Rice, and Nunn began working on ASPECTS OF LOVE, but after several months Rice dropped out. It was obvious the two would no longer work together.

In 1982, SONG AND DANCE, the combination of "Variations" and "Tell Me On A Sunday," opened in London.

In a separate venture, Andrew had tried twice before to purchase a West End theatre. His dream came true in August 1983 when he was able to buy the Palace, which was in rundown condition.

He had also started on STARLIGHT EXPRESS. It became apparent that, even with its complexities, CATS had been a small challenge compared to STARLIGHT with respect to the construction of a set. STARLIGHT was the most expensive musical ever staged on the West End. Richard Stilgoe was hired to write the lyrics. The reviews heaped praise on the sets and presentation, while they trashed the music.

Five days before the show opened, Lloyd Webber and Brightman were married in March 1984.

Lloyd Webber decided to overcome the disaster of STARLIGHT EXPRESS by writing a piece of classical music, his *Requiem*. The reviews were not great. He was as yet unable to attain respect in the United States, something he wanted very badly.

Lloyd Webber was about to embark on the most important project in his career. From its very first days THE PHANTOM OF THE OPERA had a very special attraction for Andrew. He had started working on it with Trevor Nunn before switching to Hal Prince. His indecision about who would be best for this show was apparent, as he switched back to Nunn, and then once again to Prince. It was to be written specifically for Brightman to be the lead. Ultimately, it would be the most successful show he had ever written, even though it received some negative criticism in the United States. The show became such a gigantic hit, that along with everything else now yielding a great deal of money, Lloyd Webber found no extravagance too great, including properties, planes, and the most expensive cars. Andrew was earning twelve million dollars a year. PHANTOM won many awards in Britain and the United States. As of 2008, it has become the longest-running musical in Broadway history.

There was a protracted and intense battle to forbid Brightman from playing the lead when it opened in the United States. There had been a long-standing bad relationship between Lloyd Webber and Actors' Equity. However, Andrew had leverage because of the huge amount of business he brought to Broadway. Brightman had competed in an audition for the role on Broadway even though she was already the lead in England. Prince brought his case to Equity on two grounds, one specified and one implicit. The specified reason was that Brightman was better than any of the American singers who had auditioned. The implied one was that without Brightman Lloyd Webber would not bring the show to Broadway at all. It was agreed she could assume for role for the first six months and in return Lloyd Webber would cast an American in his next show in London. By the time it opened advanced sales had reached sixteen million dollars, breaking the LES MISERABLES record of twelve million.

Of all the American critics, none were more negative about PHANTOM than the *New York Times*'s Frank Rich, who had been Andrew's nemesis from Day One. But Rich's prediction that Lloyd Webber's bubble was about to burst proved wrong. PHANTOM played to packed houses all over the world.

ASPECTS OF LOVE did not fare as well. Starting in

1980, it had been written, rewritten, done in concert, and tried with different casts repeatedly. It finally made its way to Broadway by 1989. Some critics thought it was Lloyd Webber's finest work. Certainly its most important song was "Love Changes Everything."

Lloyd Webber was now forty-one years old. He was the most successful composer in the theatre world. There were, however, rumors in the press that all was not rosy at home. Infidelity had been rumored concerning Brightman. Because of all the stories, Lloyd Webber decided she must go.

Another woman came into Lloyd Webber's life, Madeleine Gurdon, the daughter of a British general. Andrew was introduced to her by a dear friend and immediately fell in love. He asked her to marry him. Brightman "had simply outlived her usefulness" as a partner. Lloyd Webber and Brightman would continue their professional relationship. In fact Brightman toured the United States, singing in concert "The Music of Andrew Lloyd Webber" and immediately afterward assumed the lead in ASPECTS OF LOVE.

They obtained a divorce in November 1990 on the grounds of Andrew's adultery. She received something between six and twenty million pounds depending on which source is to be believed. Andrew and Madeleine married in February 1991. At the wedding, Elaine Paige sang "One Small Glance," the original title of "With One Look," a song from the new show Andrew was working on, SUNSET BOULEVARD. Meanwhile ASPECTS OF LOVE was doing terribly in New York and closed with a loss of eight million dollars.

SUNSET BOULEVARD, which debuted in the West End with Patti LuPone, became a hit in Los Angeles, but closed there once Glenn Close, who starred as Norma Desmond, left the show to open with it in New York. In London, it ran for over four years. In New York, the show had one of the largest advance sales in history and won seven Tony Awards. Amazingly, considering the length of its run, the show lost twenty-five million dollars, due to the huge expense of the production.

Lloyd Webber began looking more toward Hollywood. A film of EVITA starring Madonna soon took shape.

By 1997, his shows had earned more than four billion dollars and had been seen by one hundred million people. During the 1990s, half of all the tickets sold on Broadway were for shows that he had written. His net worth in 1996 was one billion dollars. He owned five homes, and he and Madeleine had three children. His creative career, however, was slowing down. He had reached a financial peak in 1994. SUNSET BOULEVARD had closed in London and New York by 1997. He sold his home in London and then his wine collection.

Lloyd Webber knew that he couldn't retire. The many people who were reaping benefits from his public company had only one asset, Andrew. They needed him to continue working.

He wrote WHISTLE DOWN THE WIND, but it failed. The reviews generally said there was an absence of good music. For goodwill, he decided that his company would assume 75 percent of the losses to take some of the burden off the investors.

THE WOMAN IN WHITE turned out to be another failure for him after a very short run on Broadway. Among other factors, its lead performers suffered constant illnesses.

As far as films and Hollywood were concerned, Andrew Lloyd Webber has been an outsider. Three of his shows did make it to the screen, JESUS CHRIST SUPERSTAR, EVITA, and PHANTOM OF THE OPERA. However, the age of the big movie musicals was temporarily over.

All during 2007, Andrew made multiple appearances on television in the United States and England. In those cases, segments of his previously successful shows have been used for different charitable efforts. There have been rumors, as well, of revivals and searches for new talent to play the established roles.

His career has been more than remarkable. Though there have been failures along the way, his life has been filled with exceptional achievements. Lloyd Webber composed fifteen shows, and almost all of them have been seen on Broadway. He has been the recipient of seven Tony awards, seven Olivier awards, one Oscar, and three Grammys. A 2006 Kennedy Center honoree, he is now known by many as Sir Andrew Lloyd Webber, having been knighted by the Queen of England in 1992.

MAJOR WORKS

SHOWS:

THE LIKES OF US **(1965)**
JOSEPH AND THE AMAZING TECHNICOLOR DREAMCOAT **(1968)**
JESUS CHRIST SUPERSTAR **(1970)**
JEEVES **(1975)**
EVITA **(1976)**
TELL ME ON A SUNDAY **(1979)**
CATS **(1981)**
SONG AND DANCE **(1982)**
STARLIGHT EXPRESS **(1984)**
THE PHANTOM OF THE OPERA **(1986)**
ASPECTS OF LOVE **(1989)**
SUNSET BOULEVARD **(1993)**
WHISTLE DOWN THE WIND **(1996)**
THE BEAUTIFUL GAME **(2000)**
THE WOMAN IN WHITE **(2004)**

COMPOSITIONS:

LLOYD WEBBER HAS BEEN THE COMPOSER OF HUNDREDS OF SONGS.

Kurt Weill, Dessau, 1916. (Courtesy of the Weill-Lenya Research Center, Kurt Weill Foundation for Music, New York.)

KURT WEILL

IN MARCH 1897, THIRTY-YEAR-OLD ALBERT WEILL MARRIED twenty-five-year-old Emma Ackermann. They were the children of two prominent German families in Dessau, Germany, both of which had established strong credentials in Jewish liturgical music. Albert became a cantor in the local synagogue.

The city of Dessau had long held an important place in Germany's history of theatre and music. Its most famous performing venue was the Dessau Ducal Court Theatre. In 1829, Paganini had played a recital for its grand opening. It burned down in 1855. Duke Leopold Frederick, the royal leader of that area, was a strong patron of the arts. He arranged to have it rebuilt and the premier performance of Wagner's TANNHAUSER was seen there in 1857.

The Weill family, especially Emma, was becoming much more bohemian, and involved in non-liturgical music.

Emma gave birth to four children. She had two sons before giving birth to Kurt on March 2, 1900. In October 1901, she had her only daughter, Ruth.

Showing his talent for music early, Kurt began composing at ten. His first pieces were simple songs, much like German folk music. Interestingly, at times this output was quite dissonant. He soon became part of Duke Frederick's musical family when, even during those teen years, he was responsible for giving lessons to the Duke's children, as well as being the rehearsal pianist for the opera at the Dessau Court Theatre.

When Kurt was fifteen years old, Albert Bing was named the musical director of the Court Theatre, the highest position a Jew had ever held there. He became Weill's teacher. Kurt was considered the Duke's piano prodigy. Deeply involved with his music, Kurt had lost all interest in religion. Bing had introduced Weill into an assimilated German Jewish business society, which also had little interest in religion.

It was a time in Germany when there were strong pro-war sentiments. The philosophy was that "peace breeds softness, but war, a race of heroes." Kurt became eligible for the draft just shortly before the Armistice of 1918 but apparently was excused on the basis of being almost the sole economic support of his family. Because of the war, there had been no money at the synagogue to pay his father's salary as the cantor.

In 1918, Kurt entered the Hochschule of Music, due to the influence of Bing. But he remained there for only one semester. Economic pressures forced him to go back to work as a vocal coach. Another reason why he left was possibly his desire to be in the real world rather than remaining a student.

In the short time that Kurt had spent at the school, he became very influential. He was the president of the student council. Germany's loss of the war and the subsequent economic devastation it endured left the country in tremendous political upheaval. Even at the school the director was thrown out. In his role of student council president, Weill had recommended Ferruccio Busoni as the replacement. But Busoni was rejected even though he had lived most of his adult life in Germany, because he was not a pure German.

Kurt, who was only nineteen, had become the opera coach of the local opera company, which had also named a new music director, Hans Knappertsbusch. He was only thirty-one, but had already become an extremely successful conductor. Knappertsbusch and Weill did not get along. Hans was a strict Wagnerian while Kurt was finding his own more modern approach. Another factor may have been that they were competing for the same woman. Their relationship truly soured when Weill accidentally fell through a trap door and was knocked unconscious in the middle of an opera. That incident caused a performer to be delayed in his appearance. Weill quit the position after a few months.

An opportunity arose for Weill to be the conductor of a minor opera company. He felt no need to remain in Dessau as his family was now all dispersed throughout different German communities. Weill kept the position for one year. It was followed by another position in Leipzig, where he learned a great deal about the theatre as well as opera. He was still only twenty. In Leipzig, he was able to live once again with his parents. Kurt decided that his goal was to compose, and he wrote two operas that have since disappeared. He also wrote two pieces of chamber music in the style of Schoenberg.

Weill became aware that his idol Busoni had been given a teaching post in Berlin. Though his life would be much more difficult for him economically there, he applied to be in Busoni's master class and was accepted late in 1920. Busoni was in the center of the new musical movement rising primarily in Germany, centered around the twelve-tone system. But Busoni, though writing atonal music, rejected the new system. His music moved back and forth through tonal and atonal forms.

The master class had five students who met with Busoni twice a week in his apartment. Among them, only Weill was German. The class lasted from January to June of 1921 and was an essential ongoing part of Weill's conservatory training."

Berlin was grim, full of postwar poverty and crime. Weill got odd jobs, such as playing the piano in cafés. As inflation mounted conditions became even worse. As a result the Communist Party developed strength. A young poet and acquaintance of his, Johannes R. Becher, would later become a major official in the East German Communist government. Though Weill was no longer religious in any way, his Jewish cultural background continued to affect his thinking and he was unable to embrace the hard line of Marxism. During that time Weill wrote a sketch for his first symphony, based on a tone poem by Becher. Around this time Weill was approached for incidental music to a drama by the socialist playwright Johannes Becher; though this came to nothing, the play's title, Workers, Peasants and Soldiers: A People's Awakening to God, might almost have been intended for that of the symphony (a quotation from the play was seemingly inscribed on the title-page that Weill later discarded).

Even though the situation in Germany was in complete chaos, Weill received his diploma from the Academy of Arts in 1923 after completing his studies with Busoni.

In January 1924, it took 48,000 marks to purchase one dollar. By October it took 400 million. Everyone lost their life savings. By November the exchange rate was four trillion marks to the dollar.

Adolf Hitler took to the streets to seize power, was arrested, and sent to jail. Meanwhile Weill was composing a string quartet, an opera, and a cycle of seven songs titled *Fraudentanz*, in the style of Schoenberg and Hindemith.

Georg Kaiser, a writer who by now had become quite famous, offered to write a one-act opera with Weill based on his story "The Protagonist." In July 1924, Weill was to meet Kaiser in his summer home. Weill arrived by train to a lake on the opposite side from Kaiser's home. Kaiser had arranged for Weill to be met by a young woman who was staying at the Kaiser house. Her name was Karoline Blamauer. But she was known by her stage name, Lotte Lenya. Lotte was two years older than Kurt.

She had been born in Austria in 1898. Her mother was a laundress and her father a coachman. As a child, Karoline lived in poverty and slept in a coal bin. Her father would have her dance for him, and at age six she began dancing for a circus. By eight she could stand on her head and walk on a tightrope. A fine student, Karoline went to a school for gifted children and finished all the way through secondary school. She subsequently studied ballet and drama at the civic theatre. By the end of the war she was in the ballet company and performing dramatic roles in Zurich. She moved with her drama teacher to Berlin, and joined a Shakespeare company, playing all the female roles.

Late in 1922, Lenya went for an audition to dance in the children's ballet *Zaubernacht*. The composer, Kurt Weill, was playing the piano. But she neither saw nor spoke with him on that occasion.

When Lenya met Georg Kaiser and his wife they were completely taken by this waif. At times she seemed so simple and innocent. But beneath that they saw great strength of character. They also believed she had a wonderful voice.

When postwar inflation put Lenya into great financial difficulty in the summer of 1924, the Kaisers took her in to stay with them. In return she performed household chores. The day came when they asked her to row across the lake to pick up a composer at the train station. She saw a young man with thick heavy glasses and a receding hair line who was only five feet three-and-a-half inches tall. Weill returned many times during the summer and a romance developed.

It was not the first for Weill. Two years earlier he had fallen madly in love with a wealthy woman from Zurich. She was three years older than Weill, married with two children. In the summer of 1923, they went on a trip to Italy. On their return she asked her husband for a divorce. Her husband refused and took her to the United States to end the relationship. A thoroughly dejected Weill dedicated his *Fraudentanz* to her.

Kurt was on the rebound and he had never met anyone with a personality like Lotte's before. The fact that she was not Jewish distressed his family. But, it presented no problem for Weill as he had long before given up religion of any sort. A bohemian from the working class, she was a tough fighter and a perfect match for him. His music was receiving attention through this new promising relationship with Georg Kaiser, who also was promoting Weill's personal relationship with Lenya.

So this young man who looked more like a divinity student than a composer, shy, deliberate, soft-spoken and professorial, moved in with Lotte Lenya at the end of 1924.

By 1925, Weill was becoming more and more successful. With Georg Kaiser he completed THE PROTAGONIST. Weill and a young Frenchman, Yvan Goll, wrote a short opera called THE ROYAL PALACE in which, for the first time, a semblance of jazz is heard in his music. In January 1926, Weill and Lenya married, but his family would not attend.

They moved into two rooms on the third floor of a pension. Lotte soon learned that Kurt would be at the piano by 9 a.m. and that she would not see him, except for meals, for the remainder of the day. When she complained his response would be, "Lenya, you know you come right after my music."

In March 1926, THE PROTAGONIST opened, and Weill, too nervous to attend, sat in his tuxedo drinking with Kaiser in a bar outside the theatre. After thirty-five curtain calls the stage manager was able to find him and lead him to the stage for ten additional ones. He began to develop a new self-confidence. He was getting attracted to the music of Louis Armstrong and was developing a new style. Weill had been affected by Paul Hindemith's incorporation of jazz themes he had heard in America into his music.

Bertolt Brecht now entered his life. One biographer said they met in 1922. But Lenya disagreed, saying it was several years later. Brecht was five years older than Weill and had already established himself, along with his friend Arnolt Bronnen, as one of Germany's foremost postwar playwrights and poets. By 1927, Bronnen would enter the Nazi Party and Brecht would tie himself to Marxism. The relationship between Weill and Brecht began when Kurt wrote a review for a radio presentation of a play by Brecht.

For their first idea they planned to create a short opera about a fictitious city, a fool's paradise called Mahagonny. Brecht wrote five poems about a town in the American West characterized by fighting, gambling, whoring, and drunken behavior. Their ideas came from books, movies, and newspapers. Neither had ever been to the United States. They were both attracted to and repelled by this new capitalistic spirit

Weill's music had the feeling of low comedy. He was trying to capture the idea of a "song" rather than the complicated music that Europeans were writing. He was especially impressed by Gershwin's crossing between serious and light music. Both Brecht and Weill had tried their hand at writing cabaret songs, but Weill had a greater gift for the music.

They considered using Lenya, but she had a nonoperatic voice. She had a cabaret style with what today would be called a Broadway voice rather than a classical one. Brecht wanted her to do her number, "Alabama-Song," in the nude. But neither Weill nor the authorities approved. Instead it was done as a raucous scene in a fighting ring. Lotte was lascivious and it ended with the audience and the performers whistling and jeering at each other. The scaled-down production, known as THE MAHAGONNY SONGSPIEL, was a grand success. But not everyone was thrilled. Aaron Copland, who was in the audience, wrote, it was created by a young composer "trying too hard to be revolutionary."

Because of the massive inflation, and then the Depression, Berlin had changed from a honky-tonk town to a state of total perversion with rampant sex, all barriers being dropped.

In the period of 1927–28, theatre reached its peak there.

In the spring of 1928, Ernst-Josef Aufricht, a little-known actor, had received a substantial amount of cash as a gift from his wealthy father. He wanted to become a producer. Aufricht met with Brecht and told him of a play he wanted to do based on the eighteenth-century THE BEGGAR'S OPERA by John Gay. Aufricht allowed Brecht to bring Weill into the project, but he was uncertain whether Weill was up to using the new modern style of music. Weill, Lenya, Brecht, and his new girlfriend, an actress, went to the French Riviera and worked diligently, night and day. It was to become Weill's first complete score in the popular style. He also worked continuously with Brecht on the book.

The show was scheduled to open in August. At the end of July, Weill told Aufricht that he wanted his wife to play one of the prostitutes. Aufricht agreed and said he could not imagine how "little Weill" had gotten such a beautiful wife. But the show's preparation was fraught with problems. The husband of the female lead was dying in Switzerland. She left temporarily, only to find on her return that the size of her role had been cut. She quit and a replacement had to be found.

One of the male leads was the young Peter Lorre. Lorre got sick and had to be replaced.

It took Weill and Brecht only one night to create the great ballad, "Moritat", better known as "Mack the Knife."

There were rumors that the strange combination of straight theatre, opera, jazz, and cabaret was going badly. Some friends who came to watch rehearsals suggested that it should be discarded and not even open.

On opening night, August 31, 1928, the audience was unresponsive during the first act, until the response suddenly began to swell. It was apparent that they had a hit on their hands with THE THREEPENNY OPERA.

Backstage, things were not going as well. Weill realized that they had inadvertently left Lenya's name off the playbill. He went berserk and refused to let her go on stage. Lenya calmed him down by saying, "They'll know who I am tomorrow."

Weill and Brecht had become rich and famous by combining drama and music to satirically portray the German bourgeoisie class. For Weill he had moved from intellectual music to a new form of art by the end of 1928.

By early 1929, THE THREEPENNY OPERA had transferred to a larger theatre, and Lenya was now in demand for other roles. Weill and Lenya had a new affluence, a luxury apartment, and their first car. Brecht and Weill were back at work, usually in Brecht's apartment, constantly surrounded by visitors. But once work began they would ask the visitors to leave. The two men had great mutual respect and admiration, but not a real friendship. Their political beliefs were in significant opposition.

While the two began work in 1929 on THE RISE AND FALL OF THE CITY OF MAHAGONNY, a full-scale operatic version on their earlier project. Weill continued working on orchestral pieces. They also began working on a new show, HAPPY END, about gangsters and the Salvation Army in Chicago. Halfway into the production Brecht became disenchanted and told Weill and the producers that he had no desire to write for "fun and profit." He wanted only to write for a "higher moral purpose." Brecht fought with everyone, even the cast. At times, with Brecht sitting out front during rehearsals, he and the cast would shout obscenities toward each other. In the end he refused to have his name credited on the playbill. The original story had come from Elisabeth Hauptmann, a collaborator and mistress of Brecht's. Three years later, in 1932, Damon Runyon published a story that closely resembled it called THE IDYLL OF SARAH BROWN, which would become the basis for Frank Loesser's GUYS AND DOLLS. A copyright dispute was eliminated by the decision that both stories were based on Shaw's MAJOR BARBARA. HAPPY END turned out to be a failure, though it contained some great Weill music. Brecht even refused to have it listed in a collection of his works.

The wild world of the 1920s came an end when the stock market collapsed on October 29, 1929. The effect would be felt to the greatest extent in Germany. Brecht and Weill were moving further apart. Brecht's writing reflected his Marxist views, characterized by an extremely negative attitude toward the United States. He wanted Weill merely to supply music for his philosophy. Weill, on the other hand, wanted to be an operatic composer with Brecht functioning merely as a non-philosophical librettist. Weill also had a much more favorable attitude toward the United States.

Brecht wanted MAHAGONNY to be about a fictional town in America characterized by total immoral turpitude. It wasn't that Weill was against the theme of the opera. He wanted MAHAGONNY to take place in a town that could exist anywhere, not specifically the United States.

By chance Weill found himself at a Brownshirt rally and heard the speaker say that Germany was being threat-

Kurt Weill and Lotte Lenya, c. 1930s.
(Photofest.)

ened by the presence of people like Albert Einstein, Thomas Mann, and, to his shock, Kurt Weill. At the premiere of MAHAGONNY in the Leipzig State Theatre , there were demonstrations outside. Brecht did not attend, but Weill and Lenya did, and it was an ugly scene. The opera does have a Marxist theme and is still considered to be a fine piece of work. But Weill would move away from those themes. At the finale a riot, probably preplanned, broke out in the audience and spread to the stage.

Though Weill and Brecht were distancing themselves, they did jointly agree to sign a contract for the filming of THE THREEPENNY OPERA. Several problems arose. Brecht wanted to rewrite it stressing a more Marxist theme, but the producers resisted. Brecht decided to sue them for prohibiting the changes. Weill decided to sue because the producers had wanted to eliminate some of his music. So Brecht and Weill joined forces for separate purposes. In a grand show trial, the judges found for the producers against Brecht, and for Weill against the producers.

The most important result of the film was that for reasons not quite clear the role of Polly Peachum shrank considerably and Lotte Lenya's small role grew in importance. She was given the song "Pirate Jenny," and became the star of the film and the subsequent recording. Lenya had entered her career in a minor role in the beginning of the Brecht-Weill collaboration and had reached a new peak at the end of that partnership.

Weill moved ahead with a new opera with his former collaborator Georg Kaiser. Though it was not Marxist, it was an anathema to the rising Nazis. In 1932, Paul von Hindenburg won the German presidential election over Hitler, but by only a plurality. Weill's work expressed his protest at the gradual restriction of artistic freedom in Germany. By February 1933, Hitler had been appointed chancellor. When the Reichstag fire occurred later that month, Brecht drove his family across the border into Czechoslovakia. Weill remained and continued to compose. He had been commissioned to write a symphony. It took him another month to realize that he was in danger.

At the same time, Weill and Lenya grew estranged. His first love was his work. She on the other hand was much more jovial and began having extramarital relations. He did as well, but not as openly. Weill went back and forth for a while between Paris and Berlin.

On March 21, warned that he was about to be arrested by the Gestapo, he drove close to the French border, abandoned his car, and surreptitiously walked into France. Though he arrived in Paris penniless, he was already well-known, as MAHAGONNY had been a huge success since December.

Through former contacts Weill received a commission to write a ballet for the new phenomenon, George Balanchine. Weill had decided to add vocals and asked Brecht to write it with him. Lenya was added to do the singing. Called THE SEVEN DEADLY SINS, it received only mediocre reviews. It was the catalyst, however, to reuniting Kurt and Lotte.

Weill decided to move out of Paris and rented a chateau outside the city as he began work on a symphony, which was well-received. In 1934, he was asked to write what was termed a "boulevard musical" with a French theme. MARIE GALANTE opened in December 1934 to good reviews.

Weill became involved with a Jewish immigrant by the name of Meyer Weisgal, who grew up in Chicago and went to Columbia University School of Journalism. He was a fervent Zionist. He had written a number of Zionist publications and became a phenomenal fundraiser for the movement. In 1930, he began promoting theatrical productions dealing with Zionism to raise additional funds. Horrified by the rise of Hitler, he began reaching out to Jewish intellectuals fleeing Germany. He started by asking Max Reinhardt to produce a spectacle to be performed in New York. Reinhardt suggested that it be written by the Viennese novelist Franz Werfel, with music by Weill. The theme was to be the ongoing history of Jewish exile.

Weill not only needed the money, he also liked the theme and the chance to come to the United States.

None of these three individuals was particularly committed to Judaism, but the rise of Adolf Hitler inspired them to work diligently and in harmony. Weill began researching Jewish music, and the chosen title for the piece became THE ETERNAL ROAD.

After much work the time had come for them to go to New York and begin the actual production. Things were much better between Kurt and Lotte and he decided he could not travel to the United States without her. So, in September 1935, they sailed with Weisgal. Kurt and Lotte were put up in style at the St. Moritz on Central Park South. They were completely enthused by Manhattan's gigantic skyscrapers and by the brand-new Rockefeller Center.

Weill was becoming much more familiar with the English language, and a funny incident occurred on the boat to New York. Weisgal, a particularly homely man, had gotten very seasick during the crossing. Upon seeing him, Weill said, "You are not good-looking," meaning, of course, "You are not looking very well."

George Gershwin was one of the first people Weill and Lenya would meet in the United States. Gershwin, who did not know Lenya when the three of them met, told them that he loved the recording of THE THREEPENNY OPERA, but not the woman with the squeaky voice. George was embarrassed to discover it was Lenya singing. However, it was all forgotten when Gershwin took them to a rehearsal of his new show PORGY AND BESS. The show and the country overwhelmed Kurt and Lotte. They were enraptured.

Because of the delays in the planning of THE ETERNAL ROAD, all of the leading personnel left for other endeavors. Weill and Lenya, in need of money, left the St. Moritz Hotel for more modest quarters. Weill's reputation brought him contacts but no work as of yet. He was particularly discouraged by the poor reception to PORGY AND BESS as he saw himself in the model of Gershwin, combining classical music with theatre and opera. So he considered returning to France.

While nothing of any great import was happening to Weill, a new organization known as the Group Theatre was developing under the direction of Harold Clurman, Lee Strasberg, and Cheryl Crawford. Most of their actors and writers lived in a ten-room tenement on Fifty-Seventh Street. In 1935, they had great success producing Clifford Odets's WAITING FOR LEFTY and followed that with his AWAKE AND SING! Clurman met with Weill, who was proposing that they perform a musical, something they had never done. It was to be based on a Czech novel called THE GOOD SOLDIER SCHWEIK. The Group thought that the original format wouldn't work, but considered doing an Americanized version.

Clurman discussed it with a former Group member, Paul Green, who was now in North Carolina. Weill was instructed to take the train to Chapel Hill where Green would pick him up. But Weill missed the stop and didn't get off the train. So Green left. Later, Green received a call from Weill, who had gotten off at the wrong stop. Green found Weill in the hot sun, forlorn and in a baggy suit. Due to his terrible financial situation he would be wearing that same suit all summer. They finished a draft and Weill returned to New York with Green sending him material every week. Weill meanwhile was preparing the score. Clurman and Strasberg read it and were displeased enough that they began looking for something else for the Group to produce. But Crawford disagreed and encouraged them to keep working. Soon Clurman and Strasberg were convinced. It now had the working title of JOHNNY JOHNSON.

There was dissension in the Group. Among other problems there was a dispute as to who would direct JOHNNY JOHNSON. Weill wanted Strasberg. Stella Adler and Elia Kazan were considered and rejected. Finally Strasberg took the assignment in an atmosphere of hostility.

The rehearsals went poorly. At previews many people walked out. But Strasberg and Weill worked feverishly and things began to improve by opening night in 1936. The quality of the cast certainly was a great asset. It included John Garfield, Morris Carnofsky, Luther Adler, Elia Kazan, Lee J. Cobb, and Albert Dekker. The reviews were mixed and it ran only into January, closing after sixty-eight performances.

The huge cost overruns of THE ETERNAL ROAD had finally been resolved after ten postponements. It opened at the Manhattan Opera House in January 1937. Weill had now had two New York productions to his credit, but one show, JOHNNY JOHNSON, closed so quickly, and the other, THE ETERNAL ROAD, was so expensive that he had earned little from either. The Weill-Lenya living quarters were still very modest. He was also providing financial assistance to his parents in Palestine. An opportunity to compose soundtracks in Hollywood presented itself. While Weill was-n't too excited by it, he couldn't resist the opportunity to earn money. So he went west. When he arrived there, the chance was already gone.

Weill met a number of people at a party at the Gershwin home, including Harold Arlen, Arthur Schwartz, and Yip Harburg. A project developed with a story to be written by Sam and Bella Spewack, with music by Weill and lyrics by Harburg. It was a story about a Jewish theatrical group fleeing Nazi Germany. As in the past nothing materialized, not the Spewack project, nor the possibility of a film version of JOHNNY JOHNSON, nor another film being considered about the Spanish Civil War.

Weill considered writing a musical version of Ferenc Molnar's LILIOM, but Molnar rejected the idea. Eight years later Molnar would agree and Rodgers and Hammerstein would write CAROUSEL.

Weill returned to New York in the summer of 1937. His life was in a state of flux. He wanted to write THE COMMON GLORY with Paul Green about Revolutionary times in Boston. Another project he considered was DAVY CROCKETT; both projects fell through.

Hollywood beckoned again and he began working on two movies. Though the work dragged on, the difference in Hollywood was that through all the delays you got paid, and very well. Finally, frustrated, he returned to New York in May 1938.

Now Maxwell Anderson was the hit of New York with the screenplay to ALL QUIET ON THE WESTERN FRONT and the play WHAT PRICE GLORY? Weill had contacted him back in 1936 to see if they could collaborate. Though Anderson admired THE THREEPENNY OPERA, he had given only a polite reply.

Out of nowhere, Anderson contacted Weill in 1938 asking if he thought something worthwhile could be done with Washington Irving's *Knickerbocker's History of New York*. The idea enticed Weill for several reasons. He had wanted to do something related to American history. The lead role would be a comic character of Dutch origin, similar to German. This was an opportunity to work with America's most important playwright at the time.

Anderson had decided to use the play as a satire on the power of President Roosevelt. He disliked FDR immensely. Weill felt much differently, which caused him concern about his decision to work together. Weil's concerns vanished quickly because the Playwrights Producing Company was also pro-Roosevelt and persuaded Anderson to eliminate much of the anti-Roosevelt sentiment.

As the project progressed there seemed to be an obvious choice in the selection of a director. Joshua Logan, at twenty-nine, was the hottest director on Broadway. He had just completed a Rodgers and Hart show when he received the offer to direct and accepted it. The next most important decision was selecting the lead to play the role of the peg-legged Peter Stuyvesant. Walter Huston was at his peak. He had just starred in the play and the movie of Sinclair Lewis's DODSWORTH, but he had never done a Broadway musical. At first he thought the role was too small. He didn't want it bigger, just better. Huston said, "Couldn't this old bastard make love to that pretty young girl a bit? Not to win her . . . and she could even consider him . . . when she hears his song." Logan promised if he would take the part, it would be done. As the story goes, in one hour, Anderson and Weill wrote "September Song" for him.

KNICKERBOCKER HOLIDAY did not have the feeling of a standard Broadway show. It borrowed some themes from Gershwin, Gilbert and Sullivan, and from Sigmund Romberg. It was more in the tradition of THE THREEPENNY OPERA. Critics have said that Weill commercialized himself for Broadway for economic reasons when he wrote KNICKERBOCKER HOLIDAY. Actually only "September Song" belonged to a style of music that would have popular appeal—in other words, a more commercial style. Even that is very similar to a song he wrote for HAPPY END called "Surabaya Johnny," which dealt with the passion of love. He had long before rejected Brecht's bitterness and extreme leftist leanings. Actually the "long, long while" of "September Song" "was a pun on his name Kurt Weill, which in translation is "a short while."

The opening was attended by Roosevelt, who was a friend of Walter Huston. He loved the show. It turned out to be only a mild success. But it was quite different for "September Song." Though the song yielded Weill a considerable source of income for the remainder of his life, he had not reached the stature of Porter, Rodgers and Hart, or Kern.

Nevertheless, he and Lenya were now making money. She had a six-week engagement at the New York supper club Le Ruban Bleu. They were living in a Manhattan duplex, but decided they would rather dwell in the compound of artists that was forming around Maxwell Anderson's home in Suffern, New York.

Weill was commissioned to write the score for an extravaganza at the New York World's Fair called RAILROADS ON PARADE. He went on to write the THE BALLAD OF MAGNA CARTA with Anderson.

Critics chastised him for giving up "serious music" for "light music." He responded by saying he saw no difference between them, only the difference between good and bad music.

In November 1939, Weill met Moss Hart. Once again finances had become an issue as Lenya was having difficulty finding jobs. Hassard Short, who had staged a number of Moss Hart productions including Berlin's FACE THE MUSIC and AS THOUSANDS CHEER, as well as Porter's JUBILEE, put the two of them in contact. They thought of creating a show based around the practice of psychoanalysis; this topic had rarely been used on stage, and never in a musical.

They needed to select a lyricist. Weill suggested Ira Gershwin, who had done nothing for the two years since he completed the movie scores for two films that he and his brother had been working on at the time of George's death. Ira, who was only forty-three, was living a life of leisure when the call came and he immediately agreed.

The early title was I AM LISTENING. Hart wanted Katherine Cornell to play the lead, but with all the singing that would be necessary, she declined. One evening, Moss Hart bumped into Gertrude Lawrence at a party and asked if she would be interested. They met for lunch, where he explained the plot to her and she grew excited. She said she couldn't accept it yet because her astrologer had advised her not to make any decisions until April 7. Hart was miffed, cursing out the astrologer to himself, as he waited the necessary two weeks while he and Weill continued to work on the project. When he finally contacted Lawrence, her response was, "It all works out . . . Noel is arriving on the very day." Hart wanted to know what Coward had to do with it. He was told that the astrologer had approved the decision, but she couldn't agree to anything without Noel's advice. Hart would have to read the script to Coward. Fortunately, Coward loved the script. The two of them went to tell Lawrence of their decision. After Coward spoke with Lawrence he told Hart, "Now your troubles are really beginning."

Hart was shocked and asked, "But Gertie said yes, didn't she?"

Coward looked at Hart and said, "That's just the point, my boy! Gertie said yes!" And then he just walked off.

Hart, Weill, and Gershwin worked feverishly. The story was laid out in a series of dream sequences. With extremely complicated stage settings the costs soared out of sight, which forced them to make major changes to bring them to a more realistic cost structure. The show was now being called LADY IN THE DARK.

Danny Kaye, at the time a new young comedian, was selected to play the role of a gay fashion photographer. He sang the spectacular patter song "Tschaikovsky." In it Kaye would rattle off the names of forty-one Russian composers at record speed.

Most of the major roles had been cast, with the one remaining calling for a "beautiful hunk of a man." Victor Mature had come to New York to play a role with Clurman's Group Theatre. When Hart was able to sign him on for the role in LADY IN THE DARK, Clurman threatened to sue until finally an arrangement was worked out.

Gertrude Lawrence's big song was "The Saga of Jenny." Everyone was concerned because it immediately followed Kaye's "Tschaikovsky," which would get huge applause. But Lawrence had star quality and the applause for her was even greater. The show was a great hit, but not all the reviews were great. Virgil Thomson of the *New York Herald Tribune* panned Weill severely, calling the music "monotonous, heavy, ponderously German." Weill was hurt, but the success of the show and the subsequent recording lessened the blow. It was sold to the movies for the highest price ever paid for any property.

Things were so good that Weill bought a home in suburban New York in the enclave established by Maxwell Anderson, whom he immensely admired. He and Lenya bought a new Buick and lots of clothes.

It was necessary for Weill to keep working on the show due to problems with its temperamental star. Lawrence continually demanded changes and then said she was taking three months off for the summer. The show had to close during that time while cast members left for other shows. Danny Kaye got the lead in a new Porter show, LET'S FACE IT. Weill had to train an entire new cast when they re-opened.

Hart was ready to start writing a new show with his two new partners, Weill and Gershwin. But Gershwin wanted to return home to California so the idea was dropped. All sorts of people, like William Saroyan, Philip Barry, and John Latouche, who wanted to make a musical about Billy Sunday, came to Weill with ideas. There was the possibility of a new show with Anderson. Playwright S. N. Behrman proposed a musical based on the Lunt-Fontanne vehicle, THE PIRATE. Even Georg Kaiser wanted to collaborate on a musical version of BILLY BUDD. But nothing worked out. Weill considered writing a new symphony but decided it was not the right time for him, commercially.

Of special interest among these possibilities was Weill's rejection of several offers from Brecht, who had returned to the United States. He knew well Brecht's strident political philosophy, but probably didn't know that the two of them were under FBI surveillance. Weill was very anxious to obtain his U.S. citizenship and didn't want anything to undermine that effort. Though his family could be traced back to 1329 in Germany, he claimed, whether accurately or not, never to have felt the "oneness" with Germany that he came to feel toward his new home. But Weill did seem to have a true love affair with America. During the war he predominantly wrote for patriotic causes, including a project with Moss Hart called LUNCH TIME FOLLIES. It was a non-profit production presented during lunch breaks in war plants. Weill even functioned as the production manager. It traveled all over the country.

Once Weill got his citizenship in 1942, he began working fully on a musical he had become interested in years earlier, based on a play called THE TINTED VENUS. In the play, a young London barber, engaged, goes to a garden party. On a whim he tries out the ring he is about to give his fiancee on a statue of Venus, which brings the statue to life. She will not leave him alone until the end of the play, when he is finally able to get it off her finger.

Weill needed to find a producer. Cheryl Crawford, whom he had met in his first United States opportunity, had now left the Group Theatre. She became interested in the project. After several possible writers were sought unsuccessfully for the book, they agreed upon Sam and Bella Spewack. Marlene Dietrich was chosen for the lead. But Spewack and Weill didn't get along and when she completed the book, he rejected it. They turned to S. J. Perelman, a major humorist who had also written two of the Marx Brothers' movies. His script created a much sexier Venus and Dietrich quit. Although she had appeared practically nude earlier in her career, she claimed that she would be embarrassed to assume such a role as she now had a nineteen-year-old daughter.

Once again they were searching for a leading lady. Since several ballerinas were being considered for the role, they sought Vera Zorina for the part. Agnes de Mille—just off her success with OKLAHOMA!—was named the choreographer. At the advice of her friend and ex-husband, George Balanchine, Zorina also declined the part.

The writers then changed everything, eliminating the ballets and making Venus more British. They offered the part to Gertrude Lawrence, who also rejected the offer. Finally, they selected Mary Martin and made the role "as American as apple pie."

They wanted to persuade American couturier Mainbocher to do the costumes. In an apartment in New York City they brought Weill to play the piano and Martin sat directly in front of Mainbocher and sang the hit song "That's Him." Mainbocher said he would do the show if she would do that song exactly the same way every night. As a result she did sit in a chair right at the footlights in a Mainbocher negligee, singing directly to the audience. ONE TOUCH OF VENUS opened in October 1943 and ran for 566 performances.

Martin's role was somewhat shocking for Broadway at that time. It is clear that the one thing Venus wants from her young barber is sex. By the end of the show his fiancée has left him and Venus has been taken back by the gods. She had dreamt of marrying him and ending up as a housewife in Ozone Heights. When she is gone he returns to the museum to gaze at the statue of Venus, when another museum visitor looking much like Venus (also portrayed by Mary Martin) shows up. She looks to be the country cousin of Venus. He asks her where she lives and she responds, "Ozone Heights and would never live anywhere else." Together they leave the stage to the strains of "Speak Low."

Martin was projected into the front ranks of musical stars, and her star would ascend further when, in 1948, Oscar Hammerstein II, with fond memories of ONE TOUCH OF VENUS, would set his sights on Martin to play the role of Nellie Forbush in SOUTH PACIFIC.

Weill had achieved the true Broadway style with ONE TOUCH OF VENUS. It was light humorous satire that was the equal of Cole Porter. For some a change had come in his writing. They believed when something seemed not to have commercial value he would discard it. Detractors said that his earlier work championed artistic merit above all else.

Weill had an amazing work ethic. As opposed to other Broadway composers, he assumed the responsibility for all his own arrangements and orchestrations. He would work day and night incessantly before an opening. Weill had reached an impressive peak with two consecutive Broadway hits, LADY IN THE DARK and ONE TOUCH OF VENUS. Both of them plus KNICKERBOCKER HOLIDAY had been sold to Hollywood, which kept him commuting between the coasts.

Weill wanted to write another show with Ira Gershwin. THE FIREBRAND OF FLORENCE, a play that had bounced around among other writing teams finally ended up in their hands. The project failed. They would never have the opportunity to work together again.

The war had come to an end, and Weill was feeling a pull to his roots. He had a sense of guilt that he had survived so beautifully while so many fellow Jews had perished in the Holocaust. Ben Hecht, the writer, felt the same pull. Together they wrote a pageant for the theatre with a lot of great American talent willing to work for little or no remuneration including Luther Adler, Paul Muni, and the little-known Marlon Brando. It was called A FLAG IS BORN and dealt with the attempt to establish a Jewish homeland. It was blatantly anti-British because of the restrictions England was placing on Jewish Palestinian immigration. It opened at the Alvin Theatre in September 1946.

Some years before Weill had become interested in Elmer Rice's Pulitzer Prize–winning play of 1929, STREET SCENE. Now seemed the propitious moment to try it. Weill saw it as a true American opera in a class with Gershwin's PORGY AND BESS. But Rice was not a lyricist, so he tried unsuccessfully to get Anderson. The idea arose of getting Langston Hughes, who was willing to join Weill.

Hughes and Weill worked well together, but problems arose with Rice, who was writing the book. It was difficult getting him to believe that much of what had been portrayed by words could be replaced by music. Both Rice and his wife soon became ill. Produced by the Playwrights' Company it ultimately opened in Philadelphia in the fall of 1946. They were having trouble with financing. Weill independently asked Rodgers and Hammerstein, who were producing and writing other projects, if they would be interested in co-producing. That resulted in a major dispute with the Playwrights' Company, which was very concerned about the possibility of failure based on the lack of star power in the cast and whether the public would accept an operatic form on Broadway.

In fact the Philadelphia tryouts were a disaster with empty houses and reviews calling it "a tired and discouraged Puccini." It opened on Broadway in January 1947. Initial ticket sales were good. But FINIAN'S RAINBOW opened the next night and BRIGADOON one month later. Both were big hits, and STREET SCENE ticket sales plummeted.

Less than two months after it opened it was in trouble. Weill's brother Hans suddenly died at forty-eight. Among his entire family, parents and siblings, Hans was the one Kurt loved the most. Kurt, who was one year younger, suffered a nervous breakdown. It was all quite a shock for Weill, as his entire adult life was characterized by good health, with the exception of the psoriasis attacks that plagued him when he was under tension.

It was an extremely difficult time for Weill. He had not seen his parents for fourteen years. They had emigrated to Palestine, while he was ambivalent about his Jewishness and a vehement anti-Zionist. He only half-jokingly had said that all Jews should marry gentiles and end the question of being Jewish. But he developed guilt about his negativism toward his roots when the knowledge of the Holocaust came to be. That is when he joined Ben Hecht in his change of heart about Israel.

All this and the death of his brother brought a new need to see his parents. On May 6, 1947 he began his trip by ship. Stopping in London, Paris and Switzerland, he made his way to Nahariya, Palestine, by May 20. Both his parents and brother Nathan, a radiologist, lived in that city. Nathan gave Kurt his first physical exam in years, and found him to have high blood pressure like his brother Hans. Kurt then went to see his sister Ruth in Haifa. It was a very special time in which he had meetings with most of the most important people involved with music in Palestine.

By the time he returned STREET SCENE had closed and he was looking for a new project. After making tentative arrangements with a number of people, one finally took hold. Alan Jay Lerner and Fritz Loewe had had a falling out. Lerner was eager to find a new partner, so Weill joined Lerner in writing LOVE LIFE. The reviews were mixed. But it ran for 252 performances, which the producer Cheryl Crawford called respectable. However, it was not up to the level of Weill's previous work.

Weill was also disappointed in the film version of ONE TOUCH OF VENUS. It had opened at the same time and not made good use of his music.

Composer Kurt Weill, 1949 (Photofest.)

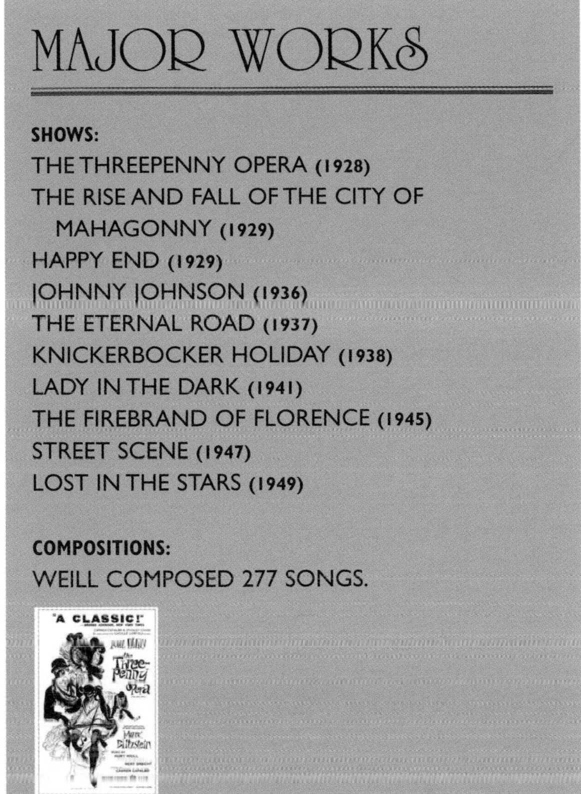

MAJOR WORKS

SHOWS:
THE THREEPENNY OPERA **(1928)**
THE RISE AND FALL OF THE CITY OF MAHAGONNY **(1929)**
HAPPY END **(1929)**
JOHNNY JOHNSON **(1936)**
THE ETERNAL ROAD **(1937)**
KNICKERBOCKER HOLIDAY **(1938)**
LADY IN THE DARK **(1941)**
THE FIREBRAND OF FLORENCE **(1945)**
STREET SCENE **(1947)**
LOST IN THE STARS **(1949)**

COMPOSITIONS:
WEILL COMPOSED 277 SONGS.

By this point most of the Weills's social life centered around Anderson and their other neighbors, Burgess Meredith, Milton Caniff, and Marion Hargrove.

Finally, he found a project with Maxwell Anderson. It was based on Alan Paton's book *Cry the Beloved Country*, which became their "musical tragedy" LOST IN THE STARS. It was a hit on Broadway in 1949.

Projects were now coming rapidly. He had helped construct a small folk opera for colleges based on folk music, DOWN IN THE VALLEY. He and Herman Wouk were planning a musical just as soon as THE CAINE MUTINY was completed. Walter Huston had persuaded Weill and Anderson to write a show based on *Moby Dick* in which he would star and subsequently his son John Huston would make into a film. But to precede all of these projects was a musical with Anderson, to be directed by Rouben Mamoulian, who had directed LOST IN THE STARS. It was to be HUCKLEBERRY FINN.

Suddenly, LOST IN THE STARS got into financial difficulty. There were disagreements and the Playwrights' Company wanted to close it down in New York and move it to Los Angeles and San Francisco. But Weill and Anderson were very concerned about what was happening as they were not only the creators. They were investors.

Weill seemed to be more tense and unnerved than usual. At the end of February 1950 he had the worst psoriasis attack he had ever experienced. He celebrated his fiftieth birthday in early March and on the March 16, he developed chest pain. He was kept at home under observation but took a turn for the worse. Three days later, he was admitted to Flower Fifth Avenue Hospital and placed in oxygen.

By Saturday March 25, he was improving significantly. The oxygen was removed and he told Anderson to get back to work on HUCKLEBERRY FINN. That day he was noted to have read the *New Yorker* and listened to the Metropolitan Opera on the radio. Lenya checked out of her room at a nearby hotel to go home for the night.

The following Tuesday a TV set was brought into his room and he was told that he could resume work the next week.

But on Monday, April 3, Maxwell Anderson got a call to come to the hospital immediately. He arrived at 6:15 p.m. and within forty-five minutes, Kurt Weill was dead. A small, almost non-religious funeral was held on Wednesday. But at the graveside his brother-in-law, Leon Sohn, moved toward the grave and recited the Kaddish, the Jewish prayer for the dead.

As the years have passed the question frequently has been raised about Weill's position in the pantheon of American theatre. It has been the conclusion in the minds of many, even with the great successes of a series of Broadway hits, that his greatest contribution was in his German period with THREEPENNY OPERA and MAHAGONNY.

Musician and composer Meredith Willson during a visit to his hometown in Iowa. (Art Shay/Time Life Pictures/Getty Images.)

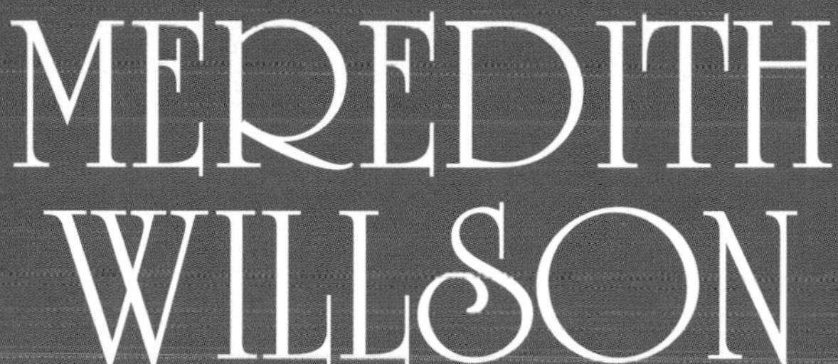

THE LARGEST CHILD EVER BORN IN IOWA WEIGHED fourteen pounds and six ounces. That's quite a frightening thought for an obstetrician. The child was born on May 18, 1902. His name was Robert Meredith Willson.

The young boy had come from strong stock. His grandfather, Alonzo, went to California during the gold rush, leading a group on horseback. He faced the challenge of hostile Native Americans during the course of the trip. After several years he went back east and settled in Mason City, Iowa. By buying land and loaning money, Alonzo became one of the wealthiest men in the county. He constructed their first school, was its first teacher, established the public library, and served as justice of the peace.

His son John was the last of eight children. John took a two-year course in law at Notre Dame, and at eighteen went to Indianapolis to take the bar exam, pretending to be twenty-one to pass the state bar s age requirement.

John practiced law for several years but grew bored and ultimately became interested in real estate.

Rosalie Reiniger, whose father was a judge, wanted to be a teacher. She and John met and were married in 1888 and she soon started the first kindergarten in Mason City, Iowa.

They had six children. The first, Lucille, was born in 1890. She was nicknamed Dixie. A daughter was born in 1894 and died of meningitis five months later. John Cedric, who was called Cedric, was born in 1900. Meredith was born in 1902. Information on the other two is not recorded.

All through their childhood the three living children were encouraged to perform. There was constant music at home. Both Rosalie and Meredith played the piano. Meredith also played the flute, Cedric the bassoon, and Dixie the harp. As they entered adult life all three children achieved success. Whether that was the result of a strange decision by their parents is certainly up for question, but their parents certainly had a plan for them.

From a theory John Willson had read about, they encouraged each child into a career from a time in early childhood. They decided Dixie should be a writer and from the time she was very young, she was instructed to write and write, while being constantly exposed to literature. They also decided that Cedric would be a businessman. And finally, they decided Meredith would be a musician.

When Meredith was very young he showed an interest in acting. But, before he was ten, his passion turned toward music. His piano lessons from his mother began at age six. He progressed beyond her ability to teach him and switched to the flute. Meredith studied with a traveling musician who told his father, John, that Meredith knew more about the flute than he did. So arrangements were made for a teacher to come from Minneapolis once a week. Meredith dreamed of playing first flute for John Philip Sousa.

While Meredith was in high school, the local paper did a story about the propensity of students to be found in pool rooms. Meredith never forgot the story and incorporated it into his score when he created THE MUSIC MAN.

At the end of his freshman year in high school he took a summer job in the orchestra at a resort. They required that he play the piccolo as well as the flute. So he bought one for ninety-six dollars, which he paid off in eight weekly installments of twelve dollars. His salary happened to be twelve dollars a week, which meant he used his entire salary for the purchase. In the last week of the season the bandleader had to leave and Willson was given the opportunity to conduct. At the end of the performance he was so excited that he accidentally sat down on his piccolo and broke it.

Less than a year after he graduated from high school he married Peggy Wilson, (with one "l" as opposed to the two in his name). He fulfilled his dream that he wrote in his high school yearbook, to "consolidate the Wilsons."

When he graduated he went to New York to try to get into the Institute of Musical Art, under Walter Damrosch, which subsequently became Juilliard. During that time he took some courses at the Institute and was able to get a few jobs as a substitute musician.

Still, his goal was to play for the famous Sousa band. John Philip Sousa was born in 1854. In 1880, he became the conductor of the Marine Band and remained there under Presidents Hayes, Garfield, Arthur, and Benjamin Harrison. In 1892, he resigned to start his own band. He was constantly composing and in 1896 he wrote "The Stars and Stripes Forever."

Between 1900 and 1905, Sousa toured Europe three times and at the end of 1905 made a world tour with his band.

In 1920, Frank Simon, the great cornet player who had been the only musician up until that time ever signed by Sousa without an audition, went to Mason City as a guest soloist. He heard Willson play and recommended to Sousa that he hire him because he played "like an angel." Willson became the second one Sousa ever hired without an audition.

Meredith toured with Sousa for three years. Each tour ended at Madison Square Garden in New York. All the concerts would end with "Stars and Stripes Forever." In New York all previous Sousa members were invited to join in with the finale. Willson recalled at his first Madison Square Garden concert there were twenty-two piccolos, forty trumpets, thirty trombones, and twenty-two drummers. It inspired him to write "Seventy-Six Trombones" thirty years later.

After three years Willson joined the New York Philharmonic under Toscanini. He also had the opportunity to work with Lee De Forest to create background music for movies, giving him his first taste of the film industry.

His siblings also achieved success. Dixie married the son of a congressman, but she wanted a career in her own right. That caused friction and the marriage ended quickly in divorce. She became a dancer and joined the *Ziegfeld Follies*. She spent two years working as a critic before joining Ringling Brothers and Barnum & Bailey Circus because she wanted to write a book about the circus from the inside. She wrote a screenplay, which won the equivalent of today's Oscar. By the late 1920s she was a frequent screenwriter earning fifty thousand dollars annually. In 1945, she remarried and in attendance at her wedding was a fourteen-year-old child whom she was raising. She claimed the child had been given to her by an aspiring actor who felt she was unable to care for her. The rumor always existed that the child was actually hers.

Cedric followed Meredith's footsteps and joined the Sousa band as a bassoonist. But, he had no interest in permanently being a musician. He went on to study engineering and became a vice president at Texas Industries and an expert in aggregate concrete production.

However, all was not perfect in the Willson family. John and Rosalie were of completely different personalities and by 1920 the marriage reached a bitter end. After an ugly public divorce, John soon married a woman who was four years younger than his daughter Dixie. They set up their home one block away from Rosalie. From that point on Rosalie referred to herself as a widow.

In 1931, when both Rosalie and John died, Dixie came home and persuaded John's widow, Minnie, to raise the infant child she had just been given. Minnie agreed and kept the child until she died in 1940, when Dixie assumed the role of guardian.

Meredith and Peggy had gotten married right at the height of his parents' debacle, which probably accounted for the fact that their marriage was an elopement. In Willson's three autobiographical books he never mentions his parents' divorce. The first, *And There I Stood with My Piccolo*, tells the story of a king who had an orchestra play for him every evening at supper. He was so pleased he invited the members to come to his treasure room and fill their instruments with gold pieces.

In 1929, Willson was hired to be a guest conductor for the Seattle Symphony. But it was an unsuccessful performance. Still, in 1930 he was hired as the musical director of KFRC radio station in Seattle. It was a golden period for radio. His next assignment on the radio was in San Francisco where he developed a reputation as a very demanding conductor. He constantly sought perfection from his musicians. It was there he wrote *A Symphony of San Francisco in F Minor*. Following this achievement, he wrote *Symphony No. 2 in E Minor*.

The most significant assignments in radio were now being found in Los Angeles and Willson was becoming known as the most important musical director in radio. In 1940, a giant anniversary celebration was held in San Francisco where he conducted a major concert.

Radio now demanded a new side of him. He became the conductor for two consecutive radio shows, SHOW BOAT and GOOD NEWS (neither based on the Broadway musicals). The conductor also played the straight man to the show's comedian. Willson, who was always self-effacing, found it very easy to assume the role of a dope, no matter how brilliant and skilled he was. As part of that new role he became the music director of a new program from Hollywood featuring Robert Young, Fanny Brice, and Frank Morgan, the *Good News Show*, with a constant flow of movie stars as guests on the show. It was on that show that he introduced his new song, "You and I," which was to be the theme song for the program and ended up at number one on the Hit Parade for nine weeks.

Willson himself had created the precursor to the Hit Parade when he started a radio show in 1934 called the BIG TEN.

He became more and more involved with movies. Charlie Chaplin produced his first talking movie, THE GREAT DICTATOR, in 1940. Although Willson was named its music director, Chaplin ruled over every aspect of the production and was overbearing even about the music. Willson received an Academy Award nomination for the score, but he lost. The following year he was nominated again, this time for his work on THE LITTLE FOXES starring Bette Davis. Once again, he lost.

Meredith Willson leading a high school band. (Art Shay/Time Life Pictures/Getty Images.)

World War II had begun and Willson wrote patriotic songs for different military units, but none was successful. He enlisted in the Army and was placed in the Army Radio Service. He helped to provide music for hundreds of programs.

Just as the war ended, Burns and Allen needed a music director for their new show. Harry von Zell was to be the announcer. He had worked with Willson on Armed Forces shows. Willson was given the job and the role of Burns and Allen's next-door neighbor in the show's story line, once again acting as a straight man.

Shortly thereafter, Willson got his own show, called Meredith Willson's Music Room. His was the summer replacement for the Burns and Allen show.

In 1947, a shocking announcement was made. The Willsons were getting divorced. In the divorce papers Peggy claimed infidelity. The perfect marriage had ended. She then married a businessman who was sixteen years older than she. Meredith married an opera singer nine months after the divorce. She was Russian. He had conducted for her in the past. Willson took her back to Mason City for its big annual festival and she was a hit with the crowd. Throughout his career he emphasized his relationship to small-town, Middle America, specifically Mason City, Iowa.

In 1950 Willson had a radio program called THE BIG SHOW with many guest stars. But most important he kept writing and came up with a new hit to play on his show. It was sort of a hymn, "May the Good Lord Bless and Keep You." Advertisers were at first reluctant to have it played on their shows, believing it was too religious, but it became very popular.

Television was now coming into its own in a big way. Willson found it to be a new and difficult medium for him, so he began to turn his attention to Broadway.

In 1951, the producers Feuer and Martin and Frank Loesser, who had just had a phenomenal success with the show GUYS AND DOLLS, approached him with the idea of writing a show about Iowa, which he continually refused to do. With radio dying and television not picking him up, he got an opportunity to be on a television panel show called THE NAME'S THE SAME. Television panel and quiz shows were the big thing.

Willson was called to New York for a new show being planned called THE BIG SURPRISE. The audition was a complete flop. So he returned to California to try working on a new project as a possible Broadway show with the working title of THE SILVER TRIANGLE.

He worked on it obsessively every day for five years, taking a break each day for a long walk. The first completed version lasted three hours and forty-five minutes. He presented it to Feuer and Martin, who were working on two other musicals, THE BOY FRIEND and SILK STOCKINGS. They said they liked it and would get to it when the other two shows were all settled. SILK STOCKINGS opened on Broadway in February 1955. The next day Martin flew out to California to help rewrite THE SILVER TRIANGLE.

They decided to present it to CBS to be used as a television special. But the deal fell through when CBS insisted on control of the casting. By 1956 Feuer and Martin became involved in other projects and told Willson that they thought he needed to look elsewhere for a producer. They terminated their contractual relationship and suggested that he might try to see if Sol Siegel might be interested. And, he was.

Willson, for the umpteenth time, auditioned the musical and Siegel loved it. He suggested Bing Crosby or Ray Bolger for the lead. But when they both were not available, Siegel lost interest.

Trying to earn a living, Willson went to San Diego to conduct concerts. There he discussed his show with another producer, Franklin Lacey. He was interested as well.

In November 1956, Martin again contacted Willson asking if he would consider a new show called INDIAN JOE, but Willson begged off, not wanting to drop his original show, which now had a new working title, THE MUSIC MAN.

On a whim Willson decided to call Kermit Bloomgarden, who had just produced THE MOST HAPPY FELLA, and arranged for another audition n New York. It was scheduled for midnight. They returned to their hotels at 4 a.m.

By nine in the morning Bloomgarden called and asked to meet Willson in his office. Finally, after five years of disappointments, Willson heard Bloomgarden say they wanted to produce his show.

They weren't sure who would be the lead. They considered Danny Kaye, Gene Kelly, Dan Dailey, Ray Bolger, Bert Parks, Art Carney, Jason Robards, Milton Berle, Jackie Gleason, and on and on.

They decided to do an audition for Moss Hart to see if he would direct. He declined. Then Morton Da Costa accepted. The first people to be signed in the cast were the Buffalo Bills. But the question remained, "Who would play the lead?" They still had no one when a theatre was arranged for a December 1957 opening.

Bloomgarden brought in Robert Preston. The song he sang was "Trouble."

They definitely had their professor Harold Hill. Following that casting, they signed Barbara Cook, who had starred in revivals of OKLAHOMA! and CAROUSEL, to be Marian the Librarian. Eddie Hodges got the little brother role after being seen on *Name That Tune* and sang the wonderful "Gary, Indiana."

For six weeks they rehearsed for a November out-of-town opening in Philadelphia. All the kinks were worked out and it opened exactly one year to the day of the midnight audition for Kermit Bloomgarden.

The reviews were, without exception, spectacular. It ran on Broadway for four years and won eight Tonys, including Best Musical and Best Actor for Robert Preston. It also received a Grammy for the original cast album.

Possibly the most beautiful ballad that Willson ever wrote was in that show. It is the lovely "Till There Was You."

Willson was earning five thousand dollars per week. By March 1958 five albums consisting of the music from the show had been produced, but the original cast album stayed at number one. Three movie studios were vying for the film rights.

One sad note was that Meredith's sister, Dixie, wrote a nineteen-page letter to the *Iowa Globe-Gazette* claiming she had written the original story and that she should have been given credit. The editor who knew Meredith, and all the work he had done, sent her an angry reply in response.

Now Willson was in tremendous demand and as a result he and his wife traveled around the country doing concerts, during which he told the story surrounding THE MUSIC MAN, and she would sing some of the songs like "My White Knight."

Willson was offered the opportunity to write a new musical, THE UNSINKABLE MOLLY BROWN, about an illiterate woman whose prospector-husband finds millions of dollars in gold. Ultimately she becomes a survivor of the

Titanic disaster. It starred Tammy Grimes, who won the Tony for Best Actress. The reviews were mixed but it ran for a year and a half.

It was made into a movie starring Debbie Reynolds, which was a big hit as well.

Meanwhile Warner Brothers, 20th Century Fox, and MGM all wanted to make THE MUSIC MAN. Big stars like Crosby and Sinatra wanted the lead. Willson held his ground firmly. Although Sinatra was certain that he would get the part, at Willson's insistence it went to Robert Preston.

Where to have the grand opening of the film became a question. The North Iowa Band Festival is held annually in Mason City. By 1941, fifty-six bands were represented. In 1958, with THE MUSIC MAN a giant hit on Broadway, Meredith and his wife, Rini, were the guests of honor. They rode in the first car of the parade. The band broke into "Seventy-Six Trombones." Willson could not contain himself. He jumped out of the car, took the baton from the drum major, and led the band. It had seventy-six trombones and one hundred and ten cornets. There were ninety-three bands playing.

When the movie was released in 1962, Willson demanded that the premiere be in Mason City. A giant three-day celebration was held, and 75,000 people were in attendance, which was three times the population of Mason City. Arthur Godfrey served as the master of ceremonies and included among the dignitaries were the governor of Iowa and their two United States senators.

In 1963, Willson had his last hit on Broadway, HERE'S LOVE, a musical version of MIRACLE ON 34TH STREET. The reviews were mixed, but it had a successful run of just under one year. The one hit song from the show was "It's Beginning to Look a Lot Like Christmas."

In 1964 he took one more shot at network television. He signed to do three specials with his wife, Rini.

Willson yearned to do another show on Broadway. He decided to tell a story of Christopher Columbus's life and plans in the year before his voyage to the New World called 1491. It was scheduled to open in January 1970, with John Cullum and Chita Rivera in the lead roles. A September 1969 tryout in Los Angeles received very poor reviews. The Broadway plans were scrapped.

Disappointed, Willson toyed with the idea of writing a play or another autobiographical book. It was about that time, while performing at an Easter Seals fundraiser, he announced that Rini was not with him because she was seriously ill. Shortly thereafter she died of cancer at fifty-four and was buried at Forest Lawn Cemetery. Subsequently, in 1979, her body was removed and she was permanently interred in Mason City, Iowa.

But another woman was a part of Willson's life in a professional role. Rosemary Sullivan had first met Willson in 1941. As a teenager, she obtained his autograph in Detroit, Michigan. Such fans were she and a girlfriend that they went to Los Angeles to see him starring in the *Maxwell House Radio Show*. They called NBC and left a message that they had come all the way from Detroit and were dying to get tickets. A return message told them to come to the artists' entrance. From there they were taken to celebrity seating in the sponsor booth. They were overwhelmed.

In 1958, when his secretary quit, Rini suggested that Meredith call "that girl" who is always hanging around to see if she wanted the job. Rosemary had been working at Monogram Studios. She assumed the role of his secretary until 1964 when she was hired by Universal Studios.

In 1968, two years after Rini's death, Meredith and Rosemary were married. The most important thing she said she learned was never to disturb him while he was working.

In a period of less than one year during 1974, his sister Dixie and his brother Cedric both died. And, Cedric's son was killed in Vietnam.

In 1981, at the age of seventy-nine, Willson made the *Guinness Book of World Records* by conducting the largest band in history. There were 2700 members occupying three full blocks in downtown Minneapolis, Minnesota.

In 1984, eighty-two-year-old Meredith had surgery performed for a bowel obstruction and initially did well, but he suddenly went into heart failure and died on June 15 of that year.

Two years later, his first wife, Peggy, died at eighty-five.

President Ronald Reagan awarded Willson the Presidential Medal of Freedom posthumously in 1988. Rosemary, his third wife, accepted the medal at the ceremony.

Dr. Galen Hauser, a sociologist from Minnesota, wrote of Meredith Willson that no one had ever written a finer study of small-town America than Willson had done in THE MUSIC MAN.

Vincent Youmans, 1933.
(Photofest.)

VINCENT YOUMANS

DANIEL DUSINBERRE YOUMANS WAS BORN IN WARWICK, New York, to Samuel and Hannah in 1829. Tuberculosis struck the family and Samuel died in his mid-thirties. All except two of his children died of the disease in their twenties. Daniel contracted it in his youth and was an invalid until he was twenty-five. But being very strong-willed, he overcame the disease and became an athlete and very well self-educated.

He decided to try his luck in New York and moved to Brooklyn in 1858. Daniel studied bookkeeping at night and got a job with a hat manufacturer. In 1862, the business was doing poorly and it was necessary to lay him off. Daniel found a vacant store on Broadway and used all of his money to rent and refurbish it. But, he had no money to buy hats to sell. He persuaded his ex-employer to provide them on credit. Youmans was immediately successful and in four years he moved to a larger store where he remained for thirty years. He married and had two sons, Vincent and Ephraim. Suddenly his wife died of scarlet fever. In 1876, he met the daughter of a fellow churchgoer. Her name was Sarah and they married. Her only child died at sixteen days of age. Meanwhile Daniel's business was prospering. He earned between forty and seventy-five thousand dollars annually, an enormous amount for those days.

In 1896, his mother died at 100 and Sarah suggested that they take a

Vincent Youmans, c. 1920s. (Photofest.)

trip to Europe to take his mind off his loss. Well traveled, this was their ninth trip to Europe. They visited Norway and on July 4, went on a private picnic to a lake. Their carriage accidentally overturned and they were thrown into the lake and drowned. Their sons Ephraim and Vincent had been spoiled children. They were Yale graduates with lots of money. But, primarily, they were playboys. They loved horse racing, theatre, and nightclubbing. They took over the business but ultimately destroyed it. Ephraim remained a bachelor, but Vincent married Lucy Gibson Miller in 1897.

On September 27, 1898, Lucy gave birth to Vincent Youmans II the day after Jacob Gershwine (later to be called George Gershwin) was born in the Jewish tenements. In 1901, a sister to Vincent, Dorothy, was born. Lucy was a more astute businessperson than her husband and bought a house in Larchmont, New York, for two hundred fifty dollars. She managed all their business affairs.

The senior Vincent had been an excessive drinker, once falling down a flight of stairs. In addition to having an alcoholic father, young Vincent found his mother to be strict and dour.

His sister recalled that when his pet cat died after being hit by a trolley it had a terrible effect on him. She claimed he never would allow himself to have a close relationship with anyone after that incident. His mother started him at the piano at an early age but unlike some of the other famous composers, no one could have guessed early on that it was a calling, Vincent was more interested in cars and motorcycles. He wanted to study engineering in college but couldn't sustain the work level and quit. His father insisted he go into the business but that only lasted for a month. He liked the piano and later, with his engineering interest, he was impressed by player pianos and began working with them.

In 1917, he enlisted in the Navy but there are very few records of that time. He did play in one of the Navy bands. When he got out of the Navy, he became a song plugger for the Remick Music Corporation. He also played the piano at speakeasies and then worked as a rehearsal pianist. Youmans had the good fortune to meet Victor Herbert. He got a job as the rehearsal pianist at two of his shows. Youmans sold a few songs that were interpolated into others' shows, including "Who's Who with You," sung by Clifton Webb. It was praised and his name appeared in the program. He was now able to get a job at Harms Publishing, where he had previously been turned down by Max Dreyfus, who had discovered Kern and Gershwin. When Youmans brought his first songs to Dreyfus, he responded as he customarily did, "Go back and write a hit." It was his way to stimulate his writers.

A lyricist who heard his music, however, was more impressed. It was Irving Caesar, who had written "Swanee" with George Gershwin. Through Caesar, Youmans got to meet Gershwin. It is said that George Gershwin was responsible for Youmans getting his first show when Youmans and Ira Gershwin wrote TWO LITTLE GIRLS IN BLUE for Broadway. Being only one day apart in age, Youmans called Gershwin "Old Man" and Gershwin called Youmans "Junior."

TWO LITTLE GIRLS IN BLUE opened in Boston in 1921. The reviews were mixed, but Youmans's songs, including "Who's Who with You?" received praise. Youmans inserted snatches of another melody he would use later, which would develop into one of his biggest hits.

The show ran for 135 performances before going on the road. It was enough to yield a good income for Youmans in 1921–22. It also established a lifetime friendship with Paul Lannin, who wrote some of the songs in that show. They worked together, got drunk together, and even were arrested together.

In his private world Youmans associated primarily with the affluent. They were Ivy Leaguers and members of the Metropolitan Club and the New York Athletic Association. Basically, Youmans was irritable, unhappy, and a terribly excessive drinker, a true alcoholic.

With no work forthcoming, he went back to song plugging and serving as a rehearsal pianist for Victor Herbert. Oscar Hammerstein II and Harbach were starting on a new show with the composers being Rudolph Friml and Herbert Stothart. But Friml got into an argument and quit, which created an opportunity for Youmans. The

Vincent Youmans and Gloria Swanson, 1930. (Photofest.)

show became the smash, WILDFLOWER, with Youmans's hit song "Bambalina." His music had a style all its own. . He used short, efficient themes and livelier rhythms. WILDFLOWER ran for 477 performances and yielded a grand income for Youmans. He purchased an apartment on Central Park South, kept the Larchmont house, and bought a fishing boat and the first of many expensive cars. He had his first affair with the star, Grace Moore. It continued on and off for years, ending so unpleasantly that she never mentioned Youmans in her autobiography.

Now he began receiving many offers. He wrote two rather undistinguished shows, MARY JANE MCKANE and LOLLIPOP. But the two did run for 151 and 152 performances, respectively. Since WILDFLOWER was still running, Youmans had three shows on Broadway at one time.

Youmans soon met a businessman who was interested in producing theatre. His name was Harry Frazee and he was even more famous for being the owner of the Boston Red Sox, the team that sold Babe Ruth to the New York Yankees. But Frazee seemed unwilling to commit to Youmans as composer, until Youmans's mother offered to back the show to the tune of ten thousand dollars. Otto Harbach, with assistance from Irving Caesar, would be the lyricist. One night during their collaboration, Youmans awakened Caesar to tell him he had a great song. Caesar wanted to deal with it in the morning but Youmans insisted they get together immediately and together they wrote "Tea for Two."

However, Youmans and Caesar decided they had written enough good songs for Frazee and would save "Tea for Two" for another show.

Frazee's show was NO, NO, NANETTE and it opened in Detroit to good reviews. But in Cincinnati the show garnered mediocre reviews and poor ticket sales. Frazee was upset and told Youmans and Caesar if they didn't come up with some new songs right away he was going to hire a new composer and lyricist. That persuaded them to give him "Tea for Two" and to write another song that he loved, "I Want to Be Happy."

The show was a hit and another producer asked Youmans and Caesar to write A NIGHT OUT, which closed out of town. It did have one great song, which Youmans would find use for later.

With its road companies, NO, NO, NANETTE was the biggest financial theatrical success of the 1920s. Frazee made over two million dollars and Youmans earned half a million. But Youmans was unhappy because he didn't believe that Frazee should make so much more money on the show than he did. In an interview, Harbach later said that Youmans's problem was that he wanted to do everything— compose, produce, direct, design costumes, and more. Harbach believed if Youmans concentrated just on composing, he would be the greatest.

Youmans was reaching the height of his career. NANETTE and WILDFLOWER were running in Europe. Ravel commented very favorably on Youmans's talent. But Youmans, possibly out of jealousy, wanted to write music that was more serious, like Gershwin was doing.

Frazee wanted Youmans to write a new show for him that he would call YES, YES, YVETTE. But Youmans declined unless he could be co-producer. The show turned out to be a failure. Youmans was waiting for an offer from Ziegfeld that never materialized. But Youmans agreed to do a show for a competitor of Ziegfeld, Charles Dillingham. It was to star Beatrice Lillie. Youmans and Lillie did not get along. The show, OH, PLEASE, opened in December 1926, and got poor reviews except for Lillie. That rankled Youmans, who was becoming more and more paranoid, believing everyone was his enemy. Interestingly, Youmans's two future brides were in the chorus of the show. With his lifestyle of carousing Youmans did not seem like the marrying kind. But in February 1927 he married Anne Varley.

That same year, he began producing and joined with Lew Fields to produce HIT THE DECK. (Lew's son, Herbert, wrote the book; Clifford Grey and Leo Robin wrote the lyrics.) As part of the strange relationship he had with his mother, he wrote a contract saying she would receive half of all his profits. As he had just gotten married, one of the suspicions was that he wanted to keep the money away from his wife, should the marriage not work. He was said to go into harangues about how terrible his mother was when talking to others about her, and then call her and say, "Mother dear!"

The show had two hits, the wonderful "Hallelujah!" and another that would have an interesting story associated with it.

When Frazee had asked Youmans to write YVETTE and he refused, Irving Caesar agreed to do the show. At that time Caesar asked Youmans if he could use a song from their failed show A NIGHT OUT, but Youmans said no. Caesar was in Europe when HIT THE DECK made it to Broadway. When he returned he was congratulated on his great song in the new show. He couldn't understand until he found that Youmans had used their song in HIT THE DECK that Youmans had not allowed Caesar to use in YVETTE. Moreover, he had done it without getting Caesar's permission. Caesar, extremely angered, told Youmans to take it out "or pay a stiff weekly royalty." Youmans paid up. The song was, "Sometimes I'm Happy."

Around that time Kern was changing musical theatre with SHOW BOAT. Youmans wanted to go in that direction. He was offered a show with Hammerstein called RAINBOW. But before they could get started Hammerstein had a nervous breakdown and Howard Dietz was suggested as a replacement. Youmans asked Dietz if he would do it. Dietz said he didn't want to offend Hammerstein and asked if he could first get Hammerstein's approval.

Youmans responded, "You're another one suffering from integrity," and dropped the offer.

Another lyricist, Edward Eliscu, was suggested, but he was under contract to Harms. Harms was angry with Youmans for breaking a contract and denied Eliscu. So he switched to Gus Kahn. Youmans wanted his show to have the historical sweep of SHOW BOAT, but his libretto was not nearly as good. The problem was that it was rushed to New York before it was ready, without sufficient tryout time. It closed in thirty days.

So Youmans decided to do another show on his own and rented the Cosmopolitan Theatre. It was out of the Times Square area and was a white elephant. Unsuccessful in the past with other shows it was converted into a movie theatre. The show was originally called LOUISIANA LOU. It was similar to both SHOW BOAT and RAINBOW. He chose Eliscu as lyricist for this show, and producer Billy Rose made a small contribution to the words. But Eliscu had problems with Youmans's drinking and not showing up for meetings. It opened in June 1929 with a new name, GREAT DAY, in Philadelphia.

The show was fraught with conflicts, and instead of going to the Cosmopolitan, Youmans took the show to a theatre in Jamaica, New York. Youmans was in financial trouble and went to Flo Ziegfeld, promising to do a show for him if he would lend him money to be able to keep GREAT DAY running while changes were made. Ziegfeld accepted the deal and immediately gave Youmans ten thousand dollars. Youmans wrote a warm thank you letter, but in another year there would be a legal battle between them.

Immediately two problems arose. The show he promised to do for Ziegfeld was EAST IS WEST. But Gershwin was already well underway with the show and when Youmans heard the news he was furious. Besides that Ziegfeld had a show of Gershwin's running called SHOW GIRL, which was not doing very well. Ziegfeld got Youmans to promise to write a song that Ziegfeld could interpolate into Gershwin's show. That only made matters worse as Gershwin absolutely refused to allow it.

Meanwhile GREAT DAY finally opened on October 17, 1929. It did not do well. But few failures ever had so many hit songs, including "Without a Song."

The stock market crashed one week after the bad reviews and the show closed after thirty-six performances. During that time, Vincent, although still married, had an affair with the female lead, Mayo Methot. She sang another of the wonderful songs from the show, "More Than You Know."

Youmans had already lost a lot of money, but he was committed to the lease of the Cosmopolitan Theatre. He rushed in a straight play to recoup some of his expenses, but that show was awful and closed in eight days.

Now Ziegfeld was ready to move ahead. The idea for EAST IS WEST was dropped and replaced by an extravaganza starring Marilyn Miller and Fred and Adele Astaire. It was to be called TOM, DICK AND HARRY. Youmans was to write it with William Anthony McGuire who, if it were possible, drank more than Youmans. When it became clear that nothing was being accomplished, the plans for the show were postponed.

Vincent Youmans, 1945. (Photofest.)

Broadway was hurting due to the Depression and composers and lyricists were flocking to Hollywood. But before going, Youmans's bad luck continued when a revue for which he wrote a single song closed in a week.

Once again Vincent found another love, Mildred Boots, who had been in the Ziegfeld Follies and then in the chorus of OH, PLEASE, like his wife, Anne Varley. She was said to be "regally beautiful." But nothing worthwhile was happening for him in Hollywood as he wrote an insignificant portion of one failed movie. He returned to Larchmont to spend the summer on the water with Boots.

Ziegfeld wanted Youmans to get started and allowed him to choose his own lyricist. Youmans selected a student at Harvard, Harold Adamson, who had done nothing other than write for Harvard's student theatrical group, Hasty Pudding. Youmans paid him only twenty-five dollars per week to write lyrics for two years. One reason why he might have entered into this relationship was because he was having trouble finding anyone who would work with him. Another is that perhaps this was the only way to get a lyricist for so little money. When nothing of value was being created, Ziegfeld called in

Ring Lardner to help with the lyrics. The show's title had been changed by then to SMILES.

The show was a disaster but one song ultimately turned out to be a hit, "Time on My Hands."

Marilyn Miller starred in the show, which was conducted by Youmans's friend, Paul Lannin. Miller complained about the music and the conductor, so Ziegfeld promised to replace Lannin with Victor Baravalle. As the story goes, when Baravalle came to Boston where tryouts were going on, Youmans and Lannin took him out on the town, got him drunk, and persuaded him to leave. This served no purpose as Ziegfeld brought in another conductor. The reviews praised the performances and the beautiful extravaganza and totally panned the book and the score. SMILES closed after sixty-three performances but before it was over Youmans left for Europe. The only thing worthwhile that happened there was that the Prince of Wales, who could be quite a tastemaker when it came to popular music, took a liking to "Time on My Hands" and was partially responsible for its success.

In the spring of 1931, another opportunity presented itself. A successful play called SMILIN' THROUGH was suggested for a musical. Once again Youmans worked with a new young lyricist, Edward Heyman. The show seemed to revert back to the old operetta form. Its title was changed to THROUGH THE YEARS. The critics panned it, and the show closed after twenty performances.

Youmans was not in true financial difficulty, but he was having one failure after another. Also, he did not want to give up the lavish lifestyle he had with Boots and, possibly, other women. But his parents had fallen on to hard times and he was supporting them as well.

One project after another didn't work out until he had the opportunity to add a few songs to a show being written by Richard Whiting and Nacio Herb Brown. Youmans contribution was not significant. But the show, TAKE A CHANCE, was a hit. It was the last show on Broadway in which Youmans would participate. The songs were released for sale by Harms and another publishing house, Miller. But not through Youmans. He felt he was being cheated, not receiving the proper amounts from the sale and as a result sued them, but the case was not settled until after his death.

By 1933, Hollywood musicals, which had been in the doldrums due to an excessive number of productions, were now making a comeback. Youmans decided to go with RKO and did the music for a picture titled FLYING DOWN TO RIO.

Youmans was still having affairs and one day several burly men burst into his apartment where a "society woman" was found in her negligee. Multiple pictures were taken. The men had been private detectives hired by Anne Varley, with whom he had had twins, because she wanted to obtain a divorce in order to remarry. Youmans was able to keep the woman's name out of the case. They were divorced in 1933.

He went to Hollywood and kept writing to Boots. He told her that great things were happening and that he was expecting to sign contracts that would make them financially secure for the remainder of their lives. It is somewhat difficult to understand what kept her attached to him, considering the constant broken promises, constant lying, and known infidelity.

Youmans continued working on FLYING DOWN TO RIO, which was very successful and a big hit for Fred Astaire. He returned to Europe, but no work was forthcoming. He had done so well in the early 1920s but his repeated failures in the latter part of that decade and the early 1930s had tarnished his reputation. RKO was negotiating to do a sequel to RIO, but in the recorded notes of the meetings is a statement that Youmans is "one of the world's worst drunks."

Boots had an appendectomy and went to Bermuda to recuperate. He went there with her and during the trip began spitting up blood. Vincent secretly went to the hospital in Hamilton where an X ray showed that he had tuberculosis. He filed for bankruptcy due to his poor financial health.

Youmans now went to Colorado Springs to be under the care of a TB specialist, Dr. Webb, for a prolonged recuperation. The recovery was slow. He wrote to Boots that Dr. Webb said he would be back to work in no time. Negotiations continued with RKO. They wanted a sequel to RIO for Astaire and Rogers. But Youmans decided he would rather write more significant music and wanted to do another operetta. He also kept raising his financial demands.

Boots came to Colorado Springs and in October 1935 they were married. Finally negotiations with RKO broke down. They made a deal instead with Jerome Kern to write the big hit SWING TIME for Astaire and Rogers. Youmans meanwhile went back to Hollywood to persuade others to allow him to write an operetta. He was turned down by everyone.

In 1937, he began drinking heavily again and suffered a relapse of the tuberculosis. It caused him to return to Colorado Springs. When he was ready to leave he decided to go to New Orleans to study more about serious music. At the same time Anne Varley was suing him for child support of their twins. He was no longer able to support his family in Larchmont but told them he would send fifty dollars a week.

What is amazing is that he was still getting repeated offers from Broadway and Hollywood. But regardless of what they would offer he would increase his demands, which now included up to one hundred thousand dollars per deal and complete control of his work. No one was willing to accept those demands and Youmans remained in financial difficulty. It is almost as if he did not want to work and used the demands to foreclose any possibility. But he said he was committed to writing a concerto.

MGM sent out Julian Abeles to negotiate a contract with Youmans. Abeles said that after Youmans had rejected every offer—even those that included all kinds of concessions—he found it very depressing, because as he left Youmans asked if Abeles could lend him five hundred dollars.

Youmans decided to fly out to San Francisco to meet and try to work with Eugene O'Neill. He wanted to persuade O'Neill to allow him to make one of his plays into a musical, much as Kern and Hammerstein had done with Ferber's SHOW BOAT. They could come to no agreement. But Youmans wrote to Boots that they were hoping to reach an accord and that he believed that O'Neill would terminate his contract with the Theatre Guild to produce his plays and give those rights to Youmans. It is difficult to know whether he really believed these bizarre plans or not.

Youmans kept changing music teachers in New Orleans and then suddenly left with another student, Waldo Williamson, to go to Banff and study. They traveled with several young women, while Youmans kept writing to Boots to assure her he was working hard on his concerto. Boots, "feeling blue," stayed in Larchmont with his parents. He finally returned there during Thanksgiving and Christmas of 1940. But in the cold weather he suffered a relapse of tuberculosis. He decided to leave immediately for Mexico to recuperate. He stayed there for a few weeks before sailing to Nassau in the Bahamas.

After one month he returned to Boots for a few days before going back to Colorado Springs.

By the summer of 1941, he returned to Hollywood. He had not made a movie for seven years and there appeared to be no more interest in him. But he kept traveling back there for no good reason.

In 1942, United Artists finally agreed to meet with him. He was on the East Coast and decided to drive across, stopping in Colorado Springs to see Dr Webb. The doctor found no improvement in his condition.

When out in Hollywood Youmans continued with the same unreasonable demands and the negotiations collapsed. He became ill again and returned to Colorado Springs. While there he began writing what was called YOUMANS' CONCERT REVUE. The producers, concerned about the title's appeal to the audience, persuaded him to change the name to YOUMANS' REVUE. It opened in Baltimore in June 1944 and quickly closed, never making it to New York.

In May 1944, Youmans's mother died and left the Larchmont house to Boots rather than her son. She felt that Youmans could not manage it. Boots made arrangements to sell the house and move his father into a nursing home.

By 1945, there was an interest in doing biographical movies about composers and MGM wanted to make one about Youmans. He turned them down. Composer Arthur Schwartz wanted to do one about Youmans as well but was rejected. At last, by November 1945, Boots could no longer tolerate Youmans being away constantly with no sign of anything ever improving and filed for divorce. Youmans met with her lawyer and promised if she would stop the divorce hearings he would offer her twenty-five hundred dollars at his death plus a share of his estate. His will left nothing for his sister or his children but continued the fifty dollars weekly for his father. The remainder was to go to the Vincent Youmans Tuberculosis Memorial Fund. He was giving one last slap to his family. His attorney warned him against such a will written while he was ill, saying it would be thrown out by the courts, but Vincent insisted.

The will was signed on January 7, 1946, and the divorce was finalized on January 21, 1946. By February he was confined to bed and went into a coma in April. Vincent Youmans died on April 5, 1946, at 5:35 a.m. He was fifty-six years old. Both Mildred Boots and Anne Varley brought suit to break the will, but reality set in when it was found that his debts outweighed the value of his estate.

There have been some revivals but in general his work has been forgotten, as has he to a great extent. An interview with his son some fifteen years after his death was titled "The Forgotten Man of Melody." And the principal biography of his life by Gerald Bordman is perceptively titled *Days to be Happy, Years to Be Sad.*

MAJOR WORKS

SHOWS:

TWO LITTLE GIRLS IN BLUE (1921)
WILDFLOWER (1923)
MARY JANE MCKANE (1923)
LOLLIPOP (1924)
NO, NO, NANETTE (1925)
OH, PLEASE (1926)
HIT THE DECK (1927)
RAINBOW (1928)
A NIGHT IN VENICE (1929)
GREAT DAY (1929)
SMILES (1930)
THROUGH THE YEARS (1932)
TAKE A CHANCE (1932)

COMPOSITIONS:

YOUMANS COMPLETED 151 SONGS AND LEFT MANY UNDONE AT THE TIME OF HIS DEATH.

Bibliography

Bergreen, Laurence. *As Thousands Cheer: The Life of Irving Berlin.* New York: Viking, 1990.

Bordman, Gerald. *Jerome Kern: His life and Music.* New York: Oxford University Press, 1980.

Burton, William Westbrook. *Conversations About Bernstein.* New York: Oxford University Press, 1995.

———. *Days to Be Happy, Years to Be Sad.* New York: Oxford University Press, 1982.

Citron, Stephen. *The Wordsmiths.* New York: Oxford University Press, 1995.

———. *Jerry Herman: Poet of the Showtune.* New Haven: Yale University Press, 2004

Comden, Betty. *Off Stage.* New York: Simon and Schuster, 1995.

Dietz, Howard. *Dancing in the Dark.* New York: Quadrangle, 1974.

Fluegal, Jane. *Bernstein Remembered.* New York: Carroll and Graf, 1991.

Fordin, Hugh. *Getting to Know Him.* New York: Unger, 1977.

Furia, Philip. *Skylark: The Life and Times of Johnny Mercer.* New York: St. Martin's Press, 2003.

Gottfried, Martin. *Broadway Musicals.* The Netherlands: Harry N. Abrams, 1979.

———. *More Broadway Musicals.* New York: Harry N. Abrams, 1991.

Harburg, Ernie and Harold Myerson. *Who Put the Rainbow in the Wizard of Oz?* Ann Arbor: University of Michigan Press, 1993.

Hasse, John Edward. *Beyond Category: The Life and Genius of Duke Ellington.* New York: Da Capo Press, 1993

Jablonski, Edward. *Harold Arlen: Rhythm, Rainbow and Blues.* Boston: Northeastern University Press, 1996.

———. *Alan Jay Lerner.* New York: Henry Holt & Company, 1996.

———. *Gerswhin: A Biography.* New York: Doubleday, 1987.

Kander, John, Fred Ebb, and Greg Lawrence. *Colored Lights.* New York: Faber and Faber, 2003.

Kantor, Michael and Laurence Maslon. *Broadway: The American Musical.* New York: Bullfinch, 2004.

Kasha, Al and Joel Hirschhorn. *Notes on Broadway.* Chicago: Contemporary Books, 1985.

Kirkeby, Ed. *Ain't Misbehavin'.* New York: De Capo Press, 1975.

Lawrence, A. H. *Duke Ellington and His World.* New York: Routledge, 2001.

Lees, Gene. *Portrait of Johnny: The Life of John Herndon Mercer.* Milwaukee: Hal Leonard Corporation, 2004.

Loesser, Susan. *A Most Remarkable Fella.* Milwaukee: Hal Leonard Corporation, 1993.

McBrien, William. *Cole Porter.* New York: Vintage Books, 1998.

McKnight, Gerald. *Andrew Lloyd Webber: A Biography.* New York: St. Martin's Press, 1984.

Nolan, Frederick. *Lorenz Hart: A Poet on Broadway.* New York: Oxford University Press, 1994.

Peyser, Joan. *Bernstein: A Biography.* New York: Billboard Books, 1998.

Robinson, Alice M. *Betty Comden and Adolph Green: A Bio-Bibliography.* Westport, Connecticut: Greenwood Press, 1994.

Rodgers, Richard. *Musical Stages.* Cambridge: Da Capo Press, 1975.

Sanders, Ronald. *The Days Grow Short: The Life and Music of Kurt Weill.* New York: Limelight Edition, 1985.

Secrest, Meryle. *Leonard Bernstein: A Life.* London: Bloomsbury, 1995.

———. *Stephen Sondheim: A Life.* New York: Alfred A. Knopf, 1998.

———. *Somewhere for Me.* New York: Alfred A. Knopf, 2001.

Skipper, John C. *Meredith Willson: The Unsinkable Music Man.* El Dorodo Hills, California: Savas Woodbury, 2000.

Strouse, Charles. *Put on a Happy Face.* New York: Union Square Press, 2008.

Sudhalter, Richard M. *Stardust Melody.* New York: Oxford University Press 2002.

Taylor, Theodore. *Jule: The Story of Composer Jule Styne.* New York: Random House, 1979.

Thomas, Tony. *The Hollywood Musical: The Saga of Songwriter Harry Warren.* Secaucus, New Jersey: Citadel Press, 1975.

Vance, Joel. *Ain't Misbehavin'.* New York: Berkeley, 1977.

Walsh, Michael. *Andrew Lloyd Webber: His Life and Works.* New York: Harry N. Abrams, 1989.

White, Mark. 'You Must Remember This . . .' Popular Songwriters 1900–1980. New York, 1985.

Winer, Deborah Grace. *On the Sunny Side of the Street: The Life and Lyrics of Dorothy Fields.* New York: Schirmer Books, 1997.

Wyatt, Robert, and John Andrew Johnson. *The George Gershwin Reader.* New York: Oxford University Press, 2004.

Non-print sources: *www.songwritershalloffame.org; www.ibdb.com.*

Notes

ARLEN

4 "he loved performing": Jablonski, *Harold Arlen*, 14.
4 "fell in love": Jablonski, *Harold Arlen*, 21.
4 "It was a lucky accident": Jablonski, *Harold Arlen*, 25.
4 neurotic: Jablonski, *Harold Arlen*, 113.
7 "'Rainbow' stays or I go": Jablonski, *Harold Arlen*, 135.
8 inebriated : Jablonski, *Harold Arlen*, 166.
8 "Chaim, do something for your younger brother": Jablonski, *Harold Arlen*, 207.
9 "remain there for the next six years": Jablonski, *Harold Arlen*, 235.
10 "depressed people": Jablonski, *Harold Arlen*, 273.
10 "To enjoy it you've got to be on the weed": Jablonski, *Harold Arlen*, 304.

BERLIN

13 "Irving Berlin does not have a place in American music": Laurence Bergreen, *As Thousands Cheer: The Life of Irving Berlin* (New York: Viking, 1990), 223.
13 "There was always bread, butter, and hot tea": Bergreen, *As Thousands Cheer*, 8.
14 "nigger Mike": Bergreen, *As Thousands Cheer*, 21.
14 "country": Bergreen, *As Thousands Cheer*, 86.
15 "However did you escape": Bergreen, *As Thousands Cheer*, 161.
17 "that Tin Pan Alley tunesmith": Bergreen, *As Thousands Cheer*, 227.
17 "those people should marry their own kind": Bergreen, *As Thousands Cheer*, 259.
17 "Please come over here": Bergreen, *As Thousands Cheer*, 276.
19 "It will always be words and music by Irving Berlin": Bergreen, *As Thousands Cheer*, 401.
19 "No, it's our idea, our play": Bergreen, *As Thousands Cheer*, 450.
20 "I'm crazy about it. Put it back": Bergreen, *As Thousands Cheer*, 453.
20 "willing dupe of the Nazis": Bergreen, *As Thousands Cheer*, 384.
20 "She's your mother": Bergreen, *As Thousands Cheer*, 510.
21 "You're right. I married up": Bergreen, *As Thousands Cheer*, 582.

BERNSTEIN

24 "How did I know he was going to become Leonard Bernstein": Secrest, *Leonard Bernstein: A Life* (London: Bloomsbury, 1995), 17.

24 "two dollar whores": Meryle Secrest, *Leonard Bernstein*, 26.
24 "Why aren't you standing": Secrest, *Leonard Bernstein*, 37.
26 "famous": Secrest, *Leonard Bernstein*, 45.
26 "Do not sleep in too soft a bed": Secrest, *Leonard Bernstein*, 51.
26 "smoked like fiends": Secrest, *Leonard Bernstein*, 68.
26 "incredibly vibrant": Secrest, *Leonard Bernstein*, 70.
26 "the thing": Secrest, *Leonard Bernstein*, 72.
27 "Ged out": Secrest, *Leonard Bernstein*, 76.
27 "mood of despair": Secrest, *Leonard Bernstein*, 84.
27 "because when I was a girl": Secrest, *Leonard Bernstein*, 85.
27 "secretive": Secrest, *Leonard Bernstein*, 87.
27 "we've been cuddling for years": Secrest, *Leonard Bernstein*, 90.
27 "What does the shiksa want?": Secrest, *Leonard Bernstein*, 90.
27 "in love with him": Secrest, *Leonard Bernstein*, 95.
29 "desperately disappointed": Secrest, *Leonard Bernstein*, 97.
29 "youthful and enthusiastic . . . boy next door": Secrest, *Leonard Bernstein*, 122.
29 "abandoning high art": Secrest, *Leonard Bernstein*, 128.
30 "I think a lot of Bernstein—but not as much as he does": Secrest, *Leonard Bernstein*, 143.
30 "No, you are wrong. I never was in Rochester": Secrest, *Leonard Bernstein*, 146.
31 "Koussevitsky died in my arms": Secrest, *Leonard Bernstein*, 178.
33 "enormously intelligent child": Secrest, *Leonard Bernstein*, 276.
33 "was so handsome and talented": Secrest, *Leonard Bernstein*, 296.
33 "to have is to be": Secrest, *Leonard Bernstein*, 298.
34 "the love of his life": Secrest, *Leonard Bernstein*, 340.

CARMICHAEL

37 "poor white trash": Richard M. Sudhalter, *Stardust Melody* (New York: Oxford University Press, 2002), 9.
38 "miserable": Sudhalter, *Stardust Melody*, 23.
38 "fleshpots": Sudhalter, *Stardust Melody*, 24.
38 "I wove you": Sudhalter, *Stardust Melody*, 24.
38 "My sister Joanne the victim of poverty": Sudhalter, *Stardust Melody*, 28.
39 "high society . . . rich girls . . . plenty hot looking": Sudhalter, *Stardust Melody*, 48.
39 "perhaps he should consider professional music after all": Sudhalter, *Stardust Melody*, 50.
39 "treatises on nonsensical arcane subjects": Sudhalter, *Stardust Melody*, 58.
40 "Hoagie wanted to call it 'Free Wheeling'": Sudhalter, *Stardust Melody*, 71.
42 "Nobody ever lost money writing songs about the South": Sudhalter, *Stardust Melody*, 136.
46 "trumpets away into the sunset": Sudhalter, *Stardust Melody*, 272.
46 "pathetic": Sudhalter, *Stardust Melody*, 287.
47 "Well if they don't care, I'll be damned": Sudhalter, *Stardust Melody*, 334.

COMDEN AND GREEN

50 Baby Basya Betty: Betty Comden, *Off Stage* (New York: Simon and Schuster, 1995), 21.
50 "recognized": Alice M. Robinson, *Betty Comden and Adolph Green: A Bio-Bibliography* (Westport, Connecticut: Greenwood Press, 1994), 2.
52 "the most original material I have ever seen": Robinson, *Betty Comden and Adolph Green*, 5.
53 "a little bit stuffy . . .We bombed": Robinson, *Betty Comden and Adolph Green*, 8.
56 "it was successful for us": Comden, Off Stage, 115.
57 "when one of them starts a sentence": Robinson, *Betty Comden and Adolph Green*, 43.
57 "Better call first. Miss Comden and I": *New York Times*, December 29, 2002.

DIETZ

59 "The ten years since your father died": Howard Dietz, *Dancing in the Dark* (New York: Quadrangle, 1974), 4.
60 "a strange man came by": Dietz, *Dancing in the Dark*, 45.

60 "Yes, but keep copies": Dietz, *Dancing in the Dark*, 55.

64 "Marry that nice Monsieur Dietz": Dietz, *Dancing in the Dark*, 243.

64 "I guess you don't stand in so good with him": Dietz, *Dancing in the Dark*, 261.

ELLINGTON

69 "jungle music": John Edward Hasse, *Beyond Category: The Life and Genius of Duke Ellington* (New York: Da Capo Press, 1993), 106.

70 "Thanks, kid. Buy yourself a cigar": A. H. Lawrence, *Duke Ellington and His World* (New York: Routledge, 2001), 119.

70 "Respectable negroes": Lawrence, *Duke Ellington and His World*, 156.

75 "I have nothing to live for": Lawrence, *Duke Ellington and His World*, 400.

75 "I'm easy to please": Lawrence, *Duke Ellington and His World*, 401.

FIELDS

79 "ever saw 3000 people sleeping together": Deborah Grace Winer, *On the Sunny Side of the Street: The Life and Lyrics of Dorothy Fields* (New York: Schirmer Books, 1997), 65

80 "vulgar": Winer, *On the Sunny Side of the Street*, 91.

80 "Thank you, Miss Fields": Winer, *On the Sunny Side of the Street*, 109.

GERSHWIN

88 "was too talented to subordinate his talent to that of another songwriter": Edward Jablonski, *Gershwin: A Biography* (New York: Doubleday, 1987), 36.

89 "who really needs the money": Jablonski, *Gershwin: A Biography*, 36.

90 "I don't know. I think they're friends of Arthur's": Jablonski, *Gershwin: A Biography*, 120.

91 "I've got to go to Europe, now": Jablonski, *Gershwin: A Biography*, 121.

92 "I should study with you": Jablonski, *Gershwin: A Biography*, 168.

93 "Did I write that there?": Jablonski, *Gershwin: A Biography*, 238.

95 "Leave him there . . . All he wants is attention": Jablonski, *Gershwin: A Biography*, 319.

HARBURG

98 "it's too sorbid": Ernie Harburg and Harold Myerson: *Who Put the Rainbow in the Wizard of Oz?* (Ann Arbor: University of Michigan Press, 1993), 54.

99 "too esoteric for public consumption": Harburg and Myerson, *Who Put the Rainbow*, 95.

100 "No! That's for Nelson Eddy": Harburg and Myerson, *Who Put the Rainbow*, 131.

100 "You ain't heard nothin' yet": Harburg and Myerson, *Who Put the Rainbow*, 164.

103 "Racists may not sing": Harburg and Myerson, *Who Put the Rainbow*, 230.

103 "Yip, I love you. . . . Will you marry me?": Harburg and Myerson, *Who Put the Rainbow*, 269.

104 "But you did things": Harburg and Myerson, *Who Put the Rainbow*, 291.

105 "That's the rainbow": Harburg and Myerson, *Who Put the Rainbow*, 235.

HERMAN

112 "while there is a legal cloud over the property": Stephen Citron, *Jerry Herman: Poet of the Showtune* (New Haven: Yale University Press, 2004), 109.

112 "bogus suit": Citron, *Jerry Herman*, 109.

112 "Stephen Sondheim could have": Citron, *Jerry Herman*, 129.

KANDER AND EBB

118 "Why don't we treat this new idea of yours seriously": Fred Ebb and John Kander, *Colored Lights* with Greg Lawrence (New York: Faber and Faber, 2003), 21.

118 "It's the Palace": Ebb and Kander, *Colored Lights*, 28.

119 "That's the best thing I've ever heard in my life": Ebb and Kander, *Colored Lights*, 37.

121 "I was horrified": Ebb and Kander, *Colored Lights*, 121.

121 "Because you are vulnerable": Ebb and Kander, *Colored Lights*, 123.

123 "You get over death": Ebb and Kander, *Colored Lights*, 218.

KERN

126 "charming and benign elephant": Gerald Bordman, *Jerome Kern: His Life and Music* (New York: Oxford University Press, 1980), 107.
129 "who knows from lyrics": Bordman, *Jerome Kern*, 364.
130 "they fell on each others' necks": Bordman, *Jerome Kern*, 353.

LERNER

134 "Sign or else": Edward Jablonski, *Alan Jay Lerner* (New York: Henry Holt & Company, 1996), 30.
135 "With apologies to Mr. Bernard Shaw for": Jablonski, *Alan Jay Lerner*, 101.
136 "I may never work again": Jablonski, *Alan Jay Lerner*, 100.
136 "How could it have happened?": Jablonski, *Alan Jay Lerner*, 111.
138 "That's beautiful": Jablonski, *Alan Jay Lerner*, 157.
138 "I'll get this . . . You paid for lunch": Jablonski, *Alan Jay Lerner*, 161.
140 "Alan doesn't want you": Jablonski, *Alan Jay Lerner*, 233.
140 "One doesn't get married to escape boredom": Jablonski, *Alan Jay Lerner*, 249.
141 "He never told the truth in his life": Jablonski, *Alan Jay Lerner*, 286.
141 "a taste for champagne": Jablonski, *Alan Jay Lerner*, 311.

LOESSER

144 "four sleepy people": Susan Loesser, *A Most Remarkable Fella* (Milwaukee: Hal Leonard Corporation, 1993), 30.
146 "Okay, everybody, let's all sing": Loesser, *A Most Remarkable Fella*, 90.
147 "At one party they wrote": Loesser, *A Most Remarkable Fella*, 101.
147 "A couple of weeks": Loesser, *A Most Remarkable Fella*, 105.
148 "Anyway, you don't really care": Loesser, *A Most Remarkable Fella*, 166.

MERCER

152 "Race records": Philip Furia, *Skylark: The Life and Times of Johnny Mercer* (New York: St. Martin's Press, 2003), 5.
152 "rare jewel": Furia, *Skylark*, 27.
152 "I couldn't see living in a menage-a-trois": Philip Furia, *Skylark*, 39.
154 "Johnny and I could have flooded the market with hit songs": Gene Lees, *Portrait of Johnny: The Life of John Herndon Mercer* (Milwaukee: Hal Leonard Corporation, 2004), 99.
155 "Don't worry about it. Today I lost Mercer": Philip Furia, *Skylark*, 91.
156 "hot sex": Philip Furia, *Skylark*, 123.
157 "comes from the bottom of his feet": Philip Furia, *Skylark*, 144.
157 "the most popular colored singer": Philip Furia, *Skylark*, 147.
159 "to remain in a different social place than his own": Philip Furia, *Skylark*, 246.

PORTER

162 "Mr. Porter, why don't you learn to play the fiddle": William McBrien, *Cole Porter* (New York: Vintage Books, 1998), 50.
162 "cruel, aggressive, and sexually unfaithful": McBrien, *Cole Porter*, 65.
165 "a playboy who incidentally wrote songs": McBrien, *Cole Porter*, 96.
165 "It simply made it wonderful": McBrien, *Cole Porter*, 85.
165 "suggested that she was a lesbian": McBrien, *Cole Porter*, 103.
167 "Porter didn't go for that": McBrien, *Cole Porter*, 195.
168 "Nothing I sang in burlesque was as risqué": McBrien, *Cole Porter*, 231.
168 "are definitely not Cole Porter's best": McBrien, *Cole Porter*, 286.
171 "Yes, my Queen Anne chairs": McBrien, *Cole Porter*, 386.
171 "Bobbie, I don't know how I did it": McBrien, *Cole Porter*, 397.

RODGERS AND HAMMERSTEIN

174 "You mean you're going to practice on my daughter": Hugh Fordin, *Getting to Know Him* (New York: Unger, 1977), 32.
177 "Spark and daring flare": Meryle Secrest, *Somewhere for Me* (New York: Alfred A. Knopf, 2001), 303.
178 "Give her a present": Fordin, *Getting to Know Him*, 264.
179 "even if it meant the failure of the production": Fordin, *Getting to Know Him*, 271.

179 "son of a bitch": Fordin, *Getting to Know Him*, 275.
179 "Miss Jones, what have you done?": Fordin, *Getting to Know Him*, 318.
180 "You're just like a father to me": Secrest, *Somewhere*, 333.
180 "how wonderful it feels to have written": Secrest, *Somewhere*, 359.

RODGERS AND HART

183 "the crook": Frederick Nolan, *Lorenz Hart: A Poet on Broadway* (New York: Oxford University Press, 1994), 5.
184 "He unexpectedly had a stroke": Nolan, *Lorenz Hart*, 5.
185 "nothing of value": Secrest, *Somewhere*, 52.
187 "my heart stood still": Secrest, *Somewhere*, 103.
187 "stick 'em up": Nolan, *Lorenz Hart*, 125.
187 "princess": Secrest, *Somewhere*, 88.
188 "boat letter": Secrest, *Somewhere*, 136.
188 "Whatever happened to Rodgers and Hart": Secrest, *Somewhere*, 160.
190 "except maybe that night when the whole": Nolan, *Lorenz Hart*, 237.
190 "can you draw sweet water from a foul well?": Nolan, *Lorenz Hart*, 281.

SONDHEIM

194 "getting laid": Meryle Secrest, *Stephen Sondheim: A Life* (New York: Alfred A. Knopf, 1998), 34.
196 "take the full credit": Secrest, *Stephen Sondheim*, 124.
196 "she was not very bright . . . talking dog": Secrest, *Stephen Sondheim*, 136.
199 "Oh, I forgot she died": Secrest, *Stephen Sondheim*, 272.
200 "It's perfectly simple . . . They're wrong": Secrest, *Stephen Sondheim*, 324.
200 "He does look rather a sad man": Secrest, *Stephen Sondheim*, 368.

STROUSE

204 "somebody": Charles Strouse, *Put On A Happy Face* (New York: Union Square Press), 54.
205 "I like these songs": Strouse, *Put On A Happy Face*, 77.
206 "Charles, my composer": Strouse, *Put On A Happy Face*, 145.
208 "Broadway bound": Strouse, *Put On A Happy Face*, 226.
208 "apologized in a column": Strouse, *Put On A Happy Face*, 239
208 "Standing near the Musicians Union Hall": Strouse, *Put On A Happy Face*, 240.
208 "Close A Little Faster": Strouse, *Put On A Happy Face*, 258.
211 "Charles's songs are not good": Strouse, *Put On A Happy Face*, 279.
211 "I apologize": Strouse, *Put On A Happy Face*, 279.

STYNE

216 "piano player": Theodore Taylor, *Jule: The Story of Composer Jule Styne* (New York: Random House, 1979), 52.
216 "my son Dick Ford": Taylor, *Jule*, 53.
216 "Gei!": Taylor, *Jule*, 55.
217 "I'm writing with Hoagy Carmichael now": Taylor, *Jule*, 82.
217 "Don't you ever play that for anyone else": Taylor, *Jule*, 83.
218 "hear you're the greatest handicapper in town": Taylor, *Jule*, 107.
219 "You've just moved me in": Taylor, *Jule*, 175.
220 "If you leave, I'm leaving too": Taylor, *Jule*, 219.
221 "If the President of the United States wants my ticket": Taylor, *Jule*, 223.
221 "Thank you very much": Taylor, *Jule*, 225.
223 "Any composer who could write": Taylor, *Jule*, and Jule Styne Web biography

WALLER

227 "rent parties": Joel Vance, *Ain't Misbehavin'* (New York: Berkeley, 1977), 44.
228 "come back later, much later": Vance, *Ain't Misbehavin'*, 67.
228 "Oh no sir . . . He's bigger, much bigger than me": Vance, *Ain't Misbehavin'*, 69.

228 "That was Fats Waller's . . .": Vance, *Ain't Misbehavin'*, 74.
230 "sent men to war" Vance, *Ain't Misbehavin'*, 130
230 "I'd rather testify than eat": Vance, *Ain't Misbehavin'*, 131
231 "This man is dead": Vance, *Ain't Misbehavin'*, 191

WARREN

237 "It couldn't have taken you very long to write that": Tony Thomas, *The Hollywood Musical: The Saga of Songwriter Harry Warren* (Secaucus, N.J.: Citadel Press, 1975), 38.
239 "He was a bit too humble": Thomas, *The Hollywood Musical*, 124.

WEBBER

246 "Are you working?": Gerald McKnight, *Andrew Lloyd Webber: A Biography* (New York: St. Martin's Press, 1984), 95.
246 "except Jesus Christ": McKnight, *Andrew Lloyd Webber*, 96.
246 "We're more popular than Jesus": Michael Walsh, *Andrew Lloyd Webber: His Life and Works* (New York: Harry N. Abrams, 1989), 61.
247 "charming, delightful and above all, sincere": McKnight, *Andrew Lloyd Webber*, 134.
248 "she was a fairly grisly piece of work": Walsh, *Andrew Lloyd Webber*, 108.
249 "Hal Prince, directing it": McKnight, *Andrew Lloyd Webber*,185.
251 "had simply outlived her usefulness": Walsh, *Andrew Lloyd Webber*, 237.

WEILL

254 "peace breeds softness, but war, a race of heroes": Ronald Sanders, *The Days Grow Short: The Life and Music of Kurt Weill* (New York: Limelight Editions, 1985), 22.
255 "Lenya, you know you come right after my music": Sanders, *The Days Grow Short*, 73.
255 "trying too hard to be revolutionary": Sanders, *The Days Grow Short*, 92.
256 "little Weill" Sanders, *The Days Grow Short*, 105.
256 "They'll know who I am tomorrow" Sanders, *The Days Grow Short*, 111.
256 "fun and profit" Sanders, *The Days Grow Short*, 137.
258 "You are not good-looking" Sanders, *The Days Grow Short*, 218.
259 "Couldn't this old bastard make love" Sanders, *The Days Grow Short*, 275.
260 "it all works out" Sanders, *The Days Grow Short*, 297.
260 "Now your troubles are really beginning" Sanders, *The Days Grow Short*, 297.
260 "beautiful hunk of a man" Sanders, *The Days Grow Short*, 301.
260 "monotonous, heavy, ponderously German" Sanders, *The Days Grow Short*, 311.
261 "oneness" Sanders, *The Days Grow Short*, 320.
261 "as American as apple pie" Sanders, *The Days Grow Short*, 325.
262 "a tired and discouraged Puccini" Sanders, *The Days Grow Short*, 355.

WILLSON

266 "to consolidate the Wilsons": John C. Skipper, *Meredith Willson: The Unsinkable Music Man* (El Dorado Hills, California: Savas, 2000), 23.
266 "like an angel": Skipper, *Meredith Willson*, 27.
269 "that girl": Skipper, *Meredith Willson*, 161.

YOUMANS

272 "Go back and write a hit": Gerald Bordman, *Days to be Happy, Years to be Sad* (New York: Oxford University Press, 1982), 29.
272 "Old Man": Bordman, *Days to be Happy*, 33
274 "Mother dear": Bordman, *Days to be Happy*, 100.
274 "or pay a stiff weekly royalty": Bordman, *Days to be Happy*, 105.
274 "You're another one suffering from integrity": Bordman, *Days to be Happy*, 108.
275 "regally beautiful": Bordman, *Days to be Happy*, 129.
276 "society woman": Bordman, *Days to be Happy*, 158.

276 "one of the world's worst drunks": Bordman, *Days to be Happy*, 167.
277 "feeling blue": Bordman, *Days to be Happy*, 191.

Index